MiG ALLEY

OSPREY
PUBLISHING

THOMAS
McKELVEY CLEAVER

MiG
ALLEY

THE US AIR FORCE IN KOREA
1950–53

OSPREY PUBLISHING
Bloomsbury Publishing Plc
PO Box 883, Oxford, OX1 9PL, UK
1385 Broadway, 5th Floor, New York, NY 10018, USA
E-mail: info@ospreypublishing.com
www.ospreypublishing.com

OSPREY is a trademark of Osprey Publishing Ltd

First published in Great Britain in 2019

ISBN: HB 978 1 4728 3608 3; PB 978 1 4728 3609 0; eBook 978 1 4728 3606 9; ePDF 978 1 4728 3605 2; XML 978 1 4728 3607 6

19 20 21 22 23   10 9 8 7 6 5 4 3 2 1

Maps by Bounford.com
Index by Sandra Shotter
Typeset by Deanta Global Publishing Services, Chennai, India
Printed and bound in Great Britain by CPI (Group) UK Ltd, Croydon CR0 4YY

Front cover: A flight of F-86 fighters are heading for MiG Alley as back up to intercept a swarm of MiG-15s that have taken off from a base in Manchuria. They still have their wing tanks on so they are not in combat yet. The emblem painted on the side of the aircraft states that they were assigned to the high scoring 335th Fighter Squadron, 4th Fighter Wing. (E. Arriaga collection / Warren Thompson Collection)

Osprey Publishing supports the Woodland Trust, the UK's leading woodland conservation charity.

To find out more about our authors and books visit www.ospreypublishing.com. Here you will find extracts, author interviews, details of forthcoming events and the option to sign up for our newsletter.

CONTENTS

LIST OF ILLUSTRATIONS

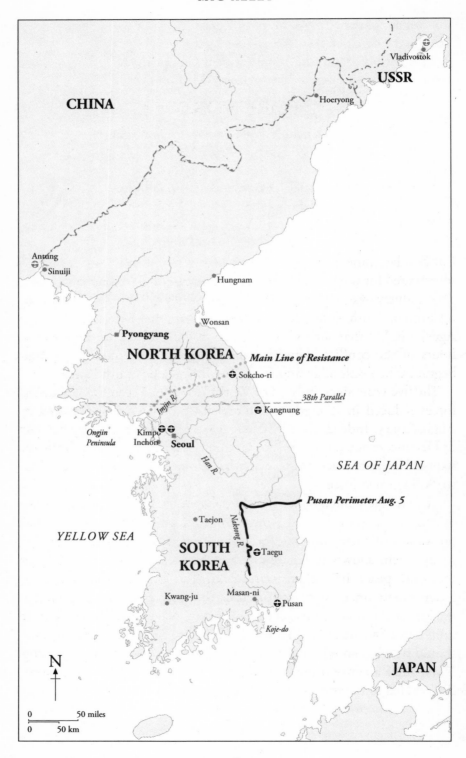

FOREWORD

On Sunday, June 25, 1950, the United States' armed forces were as unprepared for war as had been the case on Sunday, December 7, 1941. The country was taken completely unawares by the North Korean invasion of South Korea, despite warnings from the Central Intelligence Agency (CIA) that such a move was possible. Indeed, in the opening hours of the conflict, American officials were concerned that it had begun as the result of an attack on North Korea by South Korea.

The five years since the end of World War II had seen the US armed forces reduced in strength to a mere shadow of what had existed in August 1945. Indeed, the Fiscal Year 1950 budget for the Department of Defense, enacted the previous October, was the least expenditure on national defense since 1940, when the United States was 13th in the world in armed force.

The fact the United States was the sole possessor of the atomic bomb during this period had led American political leaders to believe that possession of these "ultimate weapons," together with the willingness to use them shown at Hiroshima and Nagasaki, would be sufficient to insure peace in the postwar world. The US Air Force (USAF), independent since 1947, saw itself as the force best able to deliver a nuclear strike if necessary; with the Army, Navy and Air Force now united in a Department of Defense, the service had argued that its force should be augmented if necessary by reductions in both the Army and Navy, since a conventional conflict was now seen as unlikely. Indeed, this had led to the three services attacking each other over the two years before the outbreak of war in Korea, creating far more disunity than unification of purpose in the reorganization of 1947.

Unfortunately for the grand theorists, the previous five years had demonstrated that the possession of nuclear weapons did not lead to world peace with the United States as world policeman. Through first-rate industrial espionage during the war, the Soviet Union had stolen a march on development of its own nuclear weapons, and Soviet dictator Josef Stalin had determined that the best defense during the period of nuclear vulnerability was a short-of-war offense. Between June 1948 and July 1949, the Air Force had been involved in the Berlin Airlift, an effort that required the majority of service resources for successful completion. At the same time, with President Truman and Secretary of Defense Louis Johnson committed to a continuing reduction of military expenditures, Air Force conventional warfare forces were two-thirds of what the service leadership believed was the minimum necessary to meet any unforeseen events.

Secretary of State Dean Acheson stated after the war broke out that Korea was the worst place possible for a war. The US Army in the Far East was an occupation force grown soft in Japan; the US Navy was only able to finally send an aircraft carrier to operate with the Seventh Fleet for the first time since 1947 in January 1950. The Far East Air Force had only the 19th Bomb Group, equipped with B-29s, three fighter groups newly equipped with F-80 Shooting Stars, a single squadron of B-26 light bombers, and three reduced squadrons of F-82 Twin Mustang night- and all-weather fighters. None of these forces was able to provide the kind of air support needed in the face of North Korean aggression. During the opening weeks of combat, a mad scramble in Japan and the Philippines was able to produce an improvised squadron of F-51D Mustangs that could operate from the primitive airfields on the Korean peninsula. The Air Force was forced to recall 145 F-51Ds from stateside Air National Guard units to re-equip two of the three F-80 groups in order to provide battlefield close-air support.

The war was always seen by the United States as a proxy battle with the Soviet Union, the sponsor of North Korea; as a result, American leaders were constantly concerned that some action in Korea would lead to a nuclear war directly with the Soviet Union. Thus, US forces were restricted in how they could operate in Korea. Most particularly, they were not to cross the Yalu River border with Communist China.

The appearance of advanced MiG-15 jet fighters, secretly flown by experienced Red Air Force pilots, made operations by B-29s and F-80s over North Korea extremely dangerous. As a result, the Fourth Fighter Wing, equipped with the new F-86 Sabre, was sent to Korea to counter the Soviet air threat.

Much of what has been recorded as "official history" of the Air Force in the Korean War is little more than recycled wartime propaganda. In the past 65 years, Korea has become the "forgotten war" to most Americans, and as a result few historians have challenged these "facts." One of the main myths is that the pilots who arrived in Korea in December 1950 with their Sabres were combat-experienced veterans of World War II. In fact, it was the Sabre pilots who faced combat-experienced enemies during 1951, a year that US pilots called "The Year of the Honcho," during which the Americans played catch-up with their opponents. Captain Dick Becker, recognized as the second Air Force "MiG Ace" of the war (but the first whose victories are all confirmed by Soviet loss records), said of the fighting in 1951:

> There was no 14-to-1 kill ratio when I was there. The guys we flew against were good, and they were as committed as we were. Every fight that I was in was decided by the guy in the cockpit who was better able to take advantage of the moments presented by luck. The MiG-15 was a dangerous opponent. We were very evenly matched and I am certain that overall in that first year, we fought them to a draw.

In fact, when actual losses are tallied up, 1951 was a draw, with the Sabres and MiGs scoring 1:1.

The MiGs were so good that in October 1951, they succeeded where the pilots of the Luftwaffe had failed in World War II: they inflicted such losses on the B-29s that the Air Force was forced to abandon daylight bombing missions and use the Superfortresses only at night for the rest of the war. Even with the Sabres providing cover over MiG Alley to block the MiG-15s from getting at the fighter-bombers over North Korea, the Russians and later the Chinese became such a threat that, by late 1952, fighter-bomber missions were not flown into MiG Alley until more Sabre-equipped fighter wings arrived as reinforcements in 1953, and even then the fighter-bombers were in seriously dangerous air north of the Chongchon River.

Regardless of the validity or accuracy of Air Force claims of enemy aircraft shot down, or of aircraft lost in combat, one thing stands clear: despite being outnumbered by as much as 10:1 during 1951 and much of 1952, the Air Force was successful in maintaining air superiority over North Korea. No Red Air Force combat aircraft ever flew over the battlefield on the 38th Parallel during three years of war. This is an accomplishment that is even more impressive when based on more realistic facts and figures than were given out at the time. Korea was a hard-fought war from the first day to the last.

My friend Tom Cleaver has found first-person accounts of Sabre pilots, Thunderjet pilots, bomber crews, and pilots from both the Soviet and Chinese air forces to flesh out this balanced account of what really happened over MiG Alley. This account presents the story of what happened in Korea through the eyes of participants on both sides of the battle line and is a significant contribution to understanding a war we as a nation have largely forgotten.

Col Walter J. Boyne, USAF (Ret.)

INTRODUCTION

Historian Andrew J. Bacevich recently wrote: "'The United States of Amnesia.' That's what Gore Vidal once called us. We remember what we find it convenient to remember and forget everything else. That forgetfulness especially applies to the history of others. How could their past, way back when, have any meaning for us today? Well, it just might."

It just might, indeed, and nowhere is this more clear than in the relationship between the United States and the two nations on the Korean peninsula over the past 70 years since the founding of the two states, North and South Korea.

In the United States, the Korean War is largely considered "the forgotten war." The first war the United States did not "win," it became forgotten to the American public even as it went on. Several years ago, a study was made of media coverage of the war. The result was that the coverage of the war in US newspapers at the time declined by nearly 80 percent in the year after July 1, 1951, as compared with the coverage of the previous year following the North Korean invasion of the south and the decision by the Truman Administration to intervene in what was essentially a civil war.

The drop in coverage coincided with the end of the "active phase" of the war, the period of large-scale troop movement as the two sides seesawed militarily in their successive attempts to unify the peninsula under one government or the other by force, which saw Chinese troops inflict a defeat on US forces that then-Secretary of State Dean Acheson said was "the greatest defeat of American arms since the Second Battle of Bull Run." Once the war settled into stalemate as the two sides attempted to negotiate a ceasefire, two subjects were of interest in American newspapers: the prospects for peace at the negotiating table, which was largely frustrated by what reports termed "Communist intransigence" to UN peace proposals, and the successes gained by American fighter pilots in what came to be known as "MiG Alley."

Coverage of these air battles began to resemble that given over to the "knights of the sky" during World War I, and for much the same reasons. It was a story of winners and losers that was easily understood by reporters – at least it was as explained to them by US Air Force public affairs officers whose job it was to get "the Air Force story" into the papers. In these reports, Americans were winning against the Communists, unlike the bloody minor small-unit actions that happened on the Main Line of Resistance, fights that were costly in lives for the few involved, but of little note in the grand scheme of things while the two sides sought momentary political advantage at the conference table from events on the battlefield.

For most Americans, the longer the Korean War went on, the less sense it made. The most popular song to come out of the war was "A Dear John Letter," a song of emotional pain written by Billy Barton, Fuzzy Owen and Lewis Talley and performed as a duet by country music artists Ferlin Husky and Jean Shepard, with Husky speaking his part while Shepard sang hers. It was recorded on May 3, 1953, a little more than 11 weeks before the war would end. The song quickly became Number One on the Billboard magazine country charts and reached Number Four on the Billboard pop charts. It turned the two then-unknown singers into star performers, with the 19-year-old Shepard becoming the youngest female artist up to that point to have a Number One country single. It perfectly encapsulated the feelings of those in Korea that they were abandoned by too many back home, as well as the frustrations of those back home over the loss of a family member gone to the war.

It wasn't a surprise that this song would be Number One in country music. The audience was composed of that group of Americans most likely to be in uniform in Korea in 1953: lesser-educated working class men without the opportunities available to those in the middle class to qualify for a deferment from the Selective Service draft that supplied manpower for the unpopular war. As one veteran put it to me years later, "By then, only the losers were dragooned into going to war."

Fifteen years later, an unpopular draft for an unpopular war would lead to massive protests against further prosecution of that war and would eventually end the government's ability to continue the battle. But in 1953, the nation was under the spell of Senator Joseph McCarthy and his ever-changing list of "Communists" in the government; political dissent was thoroughly suppressed, with any dissenters labeled "Communists," and their lives and livelihoods put at risk. It has been of great personal interest to me as both a historian and a veteran of the war in Vietnam to talk to Korean War veterans and those on the home front 70 years ago, to discover today how much like my generation they were in terms of their private attitudes toward the military and the war at the time.

For Americans of the time, the major opportunity for an act of dissent against the war was provided during the 1952 presidential election campaign, when General Dwight Eisenhower declared, "If elected, I will go to Korea"; it led directly to his landslide victory that November. His promise was taken by an electorate tired of the war to mean he would personally find a way to end the conflict. No one knew at the time that the method he chose was to take advantage of the death of Soviet leader Josef Stalin in March 1953 and make what the new Soviet leadership took as a "credible threat" of escalating the conflict to include the use of atomic bombs, made at a time when the United States had an overwhelming virtual monopoly on the means of delivery of such weapons.

In the summer of 1953, the boys came home at last (only they didn't – American troops have been stationed in South Korea ever since) and Americans got back to the business of creating the peace and prosperity by which the 1950s are nostalgically remembered today. If there was anything to remember about the Korean War, it was quickly forgotten. In the aftermath of the war, motion pictures like *The Bridges At Toko-Ri*, *The Hunters*, and *Pork Chop Hill* would provide elegiac tales of sacrifice; none would be as popular or commercially successful as any "World War II movie" released in the same period, however. As actor George C. Scott would state in the opening scene of the film *Patton*, released at the height of protest against Vietnam:

Men, all this stuff you've heard about America not wanting to fight, wanting to stay out of the war, is a lot of horse dung. Americans, traditionally, love to fight. All real Americans love the sting of battle. When you were kids, you all admired the champion marble shooters, the fastest runners, big league ball players, the toughest boxers. Americans love a winner and will not tolerate a loser. Americans play to win all the time. I wouldn't give a hoot in hell for a man who lost and laughed. That's why Americans have never lost and will never lose a war, because the very thought of losing is hateful to Americans.

That last is as good an explanation as any for why Korea is "the forgotten war" in America. It is not "the forgotten war" in Korea, on either side.

The air war in Korea is not remembered there as a fight between "knights of the sky." It is remembered as a bombing campaign that destroyed everything of value in North Korea, a campaign that became increasingly indiscriminate and ever more destructive to civilians. Initially, the campaign saw leaflets dropped on potential targets, warning civilians to avoid the area. With a lack of defensive opposition, the B-29s bombed from an altitude of 10–15,000 feet, which provided greater accuracy. By the end of the first 90 days of the war, which saw the invaders pushed back to the 38th Parallel in mid-September with the successful invasion of Inchon, the four bomb wings of B-29s that had operated over Korea since the end of July had dropped nearly half as many bombs on North Korea as the B-29s based in the Marianas during World War II had dropped on Japan in their entire campaign. And yet the bombing had no effect on the enemy.

Over the next year, 1951, the B-29s would continue their bombing in North Korea until they were driven from the daylight skies by Soviet-flown MiG-15s, culminating in the battle over Namsi that saw US bombers take such losses that their commanders reverted to night bombing for the remaining 21 months of the war. Night bombing, which was primarily "area bombing" rather than "precision bombing," was even more inaccurate and indiscriminate than had been the case in the daylight campaign. In the meantime, in an effort to deny supplies to the enemy armies on the front lines, a bombing campaign by fighter-bombers of the Air Force and Navy saw every transportation target hit repeatedly. As the campaign continued to fail, the answer by US commanders was to increase it. The North Korean capital of Pyongyang was subjected to a bombing campaign over the course of a week in the summer of 1952 that leveled nearly every building. The city had been bombed before and would be bombed later, an exercise described as "bouncing the rubble" by one participant. Eventually the North Korean electrical supply system would be bombed, and the system of agricultural irrigation destroyed. Within months, however, the enemy was able to make repairs.

The result of this campaign was summed up in a single sentence by Vice Admiral J. J. "Jocko" Clark, commander of the US Seventh Fleet in the final year of war: "The interdiction campaign didn't interdict."

In 1966, the US Army Center for Military History commissioned a study, "The Effectiveness of Air Interdiction During The Korean War." The study compared US Air Force claims for success in Korea with battlefield results. It concluded:

> American logistics officers never ceased to be amazed at the staying power of the Communist armies opposing them in Korea. Here was a force operating on a peninsula without the benefit either of naval or air superiority. United Nations warships ranged its coasts continuously, and American and Allied aircraft attacked its supply lines almost daily. Yet this force was able not only to maintain itself logistically, but actually to build up its strength.
>
> Notwithstanding the heavy damage inflicted by UN air power, the overall air interdiction campaign in Korea had only partial success. The destruction did not succeed in significantly restricting the flow of the enemy's supplies to the front lines, or in achieving interdiction of the battlefield. The attrition caused the enemy to triple and re-triple his efforts to supply the front lines; it laid a costly burden upon his supply organization; it caused him widespread damage and loss. Yet no vital or decisive effect could be observed at the fighting front. Throughout the campaign, the enemy seemed to have ample strength to launch an attack if he wished. His frequent and heavy artillery barrages were evidence that he did not suffer from a shortage of ammunition. Captured prisoners said they had plenty of food, clothing, medical supplies, and ammunition for their small arms.

Ironically, in the final week of the war, USAF fighter-bombers would be able to inflict a defeat on their enemies that did have an immediate effect on the outcome of the conflict, when the 18th Fighter-Bomber Wing spotted trainloads of ammunition supplies for the final Communist battlefield offensive of the war on July 15, 1953. Over the course of several hours, the pilots thoroughly destroyed the ammunition trains, and the planned Communist offensive never happened, with the Armistice finally signed ten days later. Ironically, because the operation managed to violate all the Air Force command and control of air operations policy and procedure, and was not officially approved by Far East Air Force headquarters, no credit could be taken officially for the success. This singular operational success disappeared from the official historical record and was only rediscovered in a 1993 account by then-Major Flamm D. Harper, the junior officer who coordinated the mission, published that year in *Sabre Stories*, the magazine of the Sabre Pilots Association, and ignored by other researchers of the war.

With regard to the "MiG Alley" battles, the fight the Air Force "won," as regards the validity of pilot claims for aerial victories and bombing success, the Army report concluded:

> In 1952, for example, the Fifth Air Force in Korea noted that the experience of World War II had proved the validity of halving pilot claims, and that the need for a similar reduction of claims was being borne out by the Korean experience. The USN, in a study of close air support in Korea, went even farther, concluding that pilot claims were of such questionable reliability as an index of performance that they should be omitted from consideration altogether.

The "MiG kill" number became the measure of success for commanders of the USAF fighter units in Korea, in a manner similar to the "body count" in Vietnam. As a result, the numbers were increased by lowering the standards for measuring success. Over the 65 years since the end of the Korean War, Air Force propaganda has consistently held that the pilots in the Sabres achieved a 10:1 victory ratio over their Communist opponents. In the immediate years after the end of the Cold War, when Western researchers were able to gain access to Soviet records, it was found that the rumors Americans were fighting Russians over the Yalu were true. Comparing American claims with recorded losses again demonstrated the result of such studies regarding claims made in World Wars I and II: pilot claims of victories were approximately 200 percent of actual losses. In the case of both the Red Air Force and the USAF, those admitted losses are inaccurate, since any airplane that returned to base, no matter how badly damaged in combat and no matter that it never flew again, was not recorded as a "combat loss."

The USAF policy of "fudging the figures" regarding combat losses makes it difficult to come to a firm number of actual victories versus losses. In fact, for the entire war, researchers now believe that the "victory total" favors the USAF by something between 1.3 and 1.5 to one.

This is not to denigrate the men who fought in those deep blue skies high over the Yalu. As with pilots in the preceding wars, the combatants on both sides made claims in good faith, based on the limited knowledge they had of hard-fought battles where one could not stick around to see the ultimate fate of an opponent's airplane. The acceptance of those claims was the province of those whose careers depended on the "victory total." Over the course of the war, the requirements to validate a claim became progressively more lax for the USAF.

Indeed, the only way to judge the success or failure of an aerial campaign is to look at the final result: which air force prevented another air force from achieving its goals. Using that standard, the US Air Force was indeed successful in the Korean War, whatever the claims of victory or evasion of losses might have been: throughout the war, no enemy aircraft appeared over the battlefield. That this achievement was not the "cake walk" wartime propaganda would have one believe, but was rather a hard-fought battle between evenly matched opponents, makes the achievement all the more important.

It is also important to recognize what was not achieved. There was no real opportunity for "strategic" bombing in a primitive country with only a very limited industrial base, no single target the destruction of which would be so important to the enemy that it would influence the enemy's peace negotiation strategy. The UN air forces were never able to choke off supplies to the battlefield. However, the effort to achieve this did result in the near-destruction of every structure in North Korea over the three years of war, and a loss of approximately 10 percent of the North Korean civilian population, by the US Air Force's own admission.

More bombs were dropped on North Korea between 1950 and 1953 than were dropped on Germany between 1939 and 1945. This is a fact forgotten in the United States but known by every North Korean through the stories of their parents and grandparents who survived the bombs. It is why North Korea has remained intransigent in its relations with the United States in the years since the war, and why the country has developed its own nuclear deterrent to counter what is perceived as an aggressive United States with a demonstrated willingness to use nuclear weapons. So long as Americans fail to understand the events of the Korean War, the stalemate that exists will continue.

In my research, I was fortunate to find numerous first-person accounts of the air war in Korea from Americans, Russians, and Chinese. With these and the additional records that became available following the end of the Cold War 30 years ago, it is now possible to present a more balanced account of those distant battles in MiG Alley. To me, it is history long overdue for correction. I hope the books I have written on this conflict, of which this is the last, go some distance in changing national ignorance about this war that still affects the US today. Such a loss of ignorance is necessary if the US is to take effective advantage of the opportunity for change in Korea that exists now.

Thomas McKelvey Cleaver
Los Angeles, 2019

CHAPTER I

FIRST BLOOD

Life in postwar Japan for the Americans in the Army of Occupation was good; in fact, it was better than what any member of that army might have achieved anywhere else. An Army private paid $25 per month could afford a Japanese houseboy who would make up his bed, shine his boots, and press his uniform. The perks only got better as one moved up the chain of command. Married personnel could bring their families with them, and a first lieutenant with a wife and children could live in a manner that would have been impossible back in the United States. It would soon become apparent, however, that this method of occupation did not lead to a force able to go to war quickly.

The events of Sunday, June 25, 1950, when North Korean People's Army (NKPA) infantry units attacked out of the darkness in a driving rainstorm and crossed the 38th Parallel separating the two Korean states at several locations at 0400 hours, caught the United States as militarily unprepared as it had been on Sunday, December 7, 1941. The weekend found American military leaders in Japan at home with their families, or away from their commands. General George E. Stratemeyer, commander of the Far East Air Force, was in flight over the Pacific, returning from a conference in Washington. The general had a mild-mannered appearance and was remembered by those who worked for him as being "genial." The apparently soft surface, however, was deceptive. Stratemeyer was a tough bomber general who had commanded the Tenth Air Force in the China-Burma-India Theater during World War II.

Air defense forces had been taken off alert due to a weekend weather forecast of a front with low clouds and heavy rain coming out of

Siberia across the Sea of Japan. While the duty officer of the Office of Special Investigations in Seoul sent a report within an hour of the commencement of the North Korean attack, it was not received by General MacArthur's Tokyo headquarters until 0945 hours. General Earl "Pat" Partridge, commander of the Fifth Air Force within whose sphere of operational responsibility Korea lay, was not notified of the invasion until 1130 hours.

Taken completely by surprise by the massive artillery barrage supporting four attacking infantry divisions spearheaded by T-34 tanks, Republic of Korea (ROK) troops at the border abandoned their positions as they broke and ran. The invaders were headed to Kaesong and Chunchon where they met up with North Korean infantry and marines who came ashore at Kangnung. By 0900 hours, Kaesong was under North Korean control. This was no momentary border crossing, such as the numerous incidents both sides had instigated along the border during the previous six months.

The news of the new war arrived in Washington in the middle of a sunny summer Saturday, June 24. The president was out of town, visiting family in Missouri. Both the State Department and the Pentagon were manned by mid-level duty personnel, with all senior leaders absent. Ambassador to South Korea John Muccio's dispatch reporting the invasion arrived at 2126 hours that evening, and telephones finally began to ring. Secretary of State Dean Acheson notified Secretary General of the United Nations Trygvie Lie and managed to reach President Truman by telephone at midnight.

Throughout the Far East, American forces were at a low ebb. In Japan, there had been no serious military training in any unit for over a year; this was in part due to budgetary restraints, reinforced by the widespread official belief there was no likelihood of the Soviet Union starting a war in Asia at any time in the foreseeable future.

On June 25, 1950, American air power in the Far East was a shadow of what it had been in 1945, yet the Far East Air Force was the military force in the region most able immediately to conduct operations. In numbers, FEAF appeared ready for any possibility. As of May 31, 1950, there were a total of 1,172 aircraft: 504 F-80s, 47 F-51s, 42 F-82s, 73 B-26s, 27 B-29s, 179 transports, 48 reconnaissance aircraft, and 252 miscellaneous types. However, of these, only 657 aircraft were available for use in Korea, and not all were combat ready.

Following the creation of the independent US Air Force, one of the first jobs undertaken by leadership was to discard the old army organizational structure, in which the combat group commander reported to the base commander, who was often a Regular Army officer with no flying experience. Air Force Chief of Staff General Carl A. Spaatz established a new policy: "No tactical commander should be subordinate to the station commander." Thus, the basic organizational unit of the USAF became the base wing, reversing the old command structure and placing the wing commander over the base commander. Base support functions – supply, base operations, transportation, security, and medical – were organized as squadrons, usually commanded by a major or lieutenant colonel. The squadrons were then assigned to a combat support group under the command of a base commander, usually a colonel. The operational fighter or bomber squadrons were assigned to the combat group; this was a retention of the old USAAF group. Both the combat group and the combat support group were assigned to the wing, which was commanded by a wing commander. The wing commander was an experienced air combat leader, usually a colonel or brigadier general, who commanded both the combat operational elements as well as the non-operational support elements. All of the organizations carried the same numerical designation. Thus, the 51st Fighter-Interceptor Wing controlled the 51st Fighter Group with its three operational aircraft squadrons, and the 51st Support Group that supported the 51st Wing. On June 16, 1952, the legacy combat groups would be inactivated and the operational aircraft squadron assigned directly to the wing, the organizational structure that has remained since.

Fifth Air Force, headquartered in Japan with bases spread from Kyushu in the south to Hokkaido in the north, was responsible for the defense of Japan against a Soviet attack. The 35th Fighter-Interceptor Wing at Yokota AFB outside Tokyo, the 8th Fighter-Bomber Wing at Itazuke AFB on Kyushu, and the 49th Fighter-Bomber Wing at Misawa AFB in northern Honshu operated the Lockheed F-80C Shooting Star, which had finally replaced P-51s in 1949. Kadena AFB on Okinawa was the base for the F-80Cs of the 51st Fighter-Interceptor Wing, while the Thirteenth Air Force in the Philippines operated the F-80-equipped 18th Fighter-Bomber Wing at Clark AFB.

The F-80-equipped units were backed by three fighter (all-weather) squadrons equipped with the piston-engine F-82G Twin Mustang: the

68th at Itazuke, the 339th at Yokota, and the 4th at Kadena. The F-82s had both the range and loiter capability to operate over Korea, but there was only a total of 36 aircraft between the three units and the Twin Mustang was unsuited for close air support. The 3rd Bombardment Wing (Light), based at Yokota AFB, operated the Douglas B-26 Invader light bomber, which could be utilized for battlefield interdiction, but the unit only had 26 aircraft.

Twentieth Air Force – the command that had decimated Japan in 1945 – was based on Okinawa and Guam, where the veteran 19th Bombardment Wing (Medium) had 22 B-29s at Anderson AFB; these were the only B-29s in the Air Force not assigned to the Strategic Air Command (SAC) and based outside the continental US. The 19th Group's Superfortresses were veterans of the Pacific War. 1st Lt Michael Curphey remembered, "We had the oldest, grungiest stuff in the air force and were kind of proud of our rowdy, unseemly appearance. In contrast, the SAC boys had creases in their flight suits, spit-shined brogans and airplanes that were as silvery as a new toy." Navigator 1st Lt Ralph Livengood described the aircraft operated by the bomb wing. "They were using the same airplanes that had been used in World War II, with the same colors, the same nose art, the whole works. We were told that one airplane in the group had 200 missions to its credit on the day the war started." The crews had to do more than merely fly the bombers. Then-Private 1st Class Richard E. "Gene" Fisher, a gunner, remembered that "there had been a reduction-in-force a few months earlier. Flight crews had to load, fuel and fly the aircraft. That's how short we were."

The B-29s were the only aircraft capable of hitting Korea, but would have to be moved closer in order to do so. On June 26, 1950, the wing transferred four B-29s – "Double Whammy" (44-87734), "The Outlaw" (44-65306), "Lucky Dog" (44-86370), and "Atomic Tom" (44-69682) – to Kadena AFB on Okinawa, from where they would quickly begin operations over the Korean peninsula. These four would be followed by the rest of the wing over the coming weeks.

Throughout the first day, confusion reigned in Tokyo. According to early reports by American advisors with the ROK forces, several units had held their positions and it seemed there was a chance the line of resistance could be stabilized; later reports claimed the North Korean drive appeared exhausted. The appearance of four North Korean Air Force Yak-9P fighters over Seoul at 1300 hours changed the situation, since the ROK air force had nothing with which to oppose the flight of four, which remained overhead for 20 minutes. Two hours later, two other Yak-9s strafed the control tower at Kimpo airfield outside Seoul, setting a fuel dump on fire and damaging an American C-54 on the tarmac. At 1900 hours, more Yak-9s appeared over Kimpo and set the C-54 on fire. By midnight, reports were received in Tokyo that North Korean tanks were only 17 miles north of the South Korean capital.

Fortunately, the Air Force leadership in Japan was able to move to a wartime footing quickly enough to take action over Korea the day following the invasion.

Among those immediately affected by the North Korean invasion was 1st Lt Robert E. "Bob" Wayne, an F-80 pilot in the 35th Fighter-Bomber Squadron of the 8th Fighter-Bomber Group based at Itazuke, the air base in Japan closest to Korea. He and his wife – who was six months pregnant with the couple's third child – had spent that Saturday night and Sunday morning engaged in an all-out bridge game with another squadron pilot and his wife, a popular domestic entertainment among the 8th Group pilots and their wives. By 1000 hours, everyone was ready to "call it a night" when the telephone rang. Wayne answered, amazed to hear the voice of the squadron intelligence officer on the other end: "Bob, don't go anywhere. The North Koreans have invaded the south." When he hung up and passed the word, all thought of sleep was forgotten. Wayne and his friend piled into his car and headed for squadron ops.

Squadron ops was abuzz when they arrived. 1st Lt Robert "Slick" DeWald, a fellow member of "C" Flight, had been engaged in finishing an inventory of engineering supplies when he got the word. The other members of "C" Flight, 1st Lt Ralph "Smiley" Hall and Captain Ray Schillereff, soon joined them.

Bob Wayne was not one of those pilots who had fallen in love with airplanes as a youth. Born in the Bronx, his childhood obsession was football. He never gave a thought to flying until December 7, 1941. He and his father had gone to see the New York Giants football game that so many other Americans would remember following on the radio when they heard the announcement that Pearl Harbor had been bombed. Shortly after the announcement was made over the stadium loud speakers, a P-40 appeared overhead; the pilot performed stunts to the crowd's approval, and Bob Wayne decided flying was for him. Football, however, would continue to dominate his life. Following his graduation from high school in 1943, he was accepted to the US Military Academy at West Point, where he played varsity ball for the Army until his graduation in 1946.

Following a year in which he completed flight training, Wayne found himself back at West Point, assigned as an assistant football coach; he scouted high schools for the academy for two years as he and his wife began their young family before finally going to Japan as a replacement pilot in the 35th Squadron. Six months after his arrival, the 8th Wing moved on from the F-51 Mustangs he really loved flying to equip with the Lockheed F-80C Shooting Star that introduced Wayne and his fellow pilots to the speed of the jet age.

Unfortunately, the F-80 was not suited for operation in the war Bob Wayne and the other members of "C" Flight would soon find themselves fighting. The jets could not deploy to the peninsula nor use the primitive unpaved airfields in Korea, while their range was too limited, even when flying from Itazuke, to provide effective loiter time over the battlefield; they could only carry a limited ordnance load on such maximum-range missions.

The ROK Air Force (ROKAF) had already requested an emergency supply of F-51 Mustangs to give the force an airplane capable of entering combat against the North Korean People's Air Force, which flew Yak-9P fighters and Ilyushin Il-10 "Shturmovik" ground-attack bombers in support of their invading army. The 47 F-51s in Japan were what was left after the mass modernization of the Fifth Air Force fighter units the year before. Most were used as "hacks" by the squadrons, useful for towing aerial targets and providing pilots with ground assignments the opportunity to get in sufficient monthly flight time to qualify for flight pay. All had been disarmed. Thirty of these Mustangs had been promised to the ROKAF in May, and there was even a group of American fighter pilots already in the country, assigned to train the South Korean pilots to fly the F-51. Now, however, everyone wanted those Mustangs.

The 8th Wing was ordered to rearm its Mustangs and prepare four of them to be flown to Korea where they would be handed over to the South Koreans. Bob Wayne had left squadron ops to find out "the straight scoop" at wing headquarters and walked in just as the order to arm the Mustangs was received. He hurried back to squadron ops where he went to his squadron commander, Major Vince Cardarella, and volunteered to fly one of the Mustangs over to Korea once it was ready.

The next morning, Monday, June 26, Bob Wayne was one of the 8th Wing pilots who flew the four reconditioned Mustangs across the Tsushima Strait to Suwon, 60 miles south of Seoul. The other six Mustangs that arrived shortly thereafter came from the 35th Wing. That afternoon, a C-47 picked up the ten pilots and returned them to Japan.

While Bob Wayne and the other pilots spent the day flying to Korea and waiting for a ride home, events were moving quickly.

Evacuation of American nationals following the outbreak of hostilities was Fifth Air Force's only assigned mission in Korea; this could only take place at the request of the American ambassador. The F-80 and F-82 fighters based at Itazuke had the assignment of covering an evacuation of Seoul when ordered. By the end of the day on June 25, 12 C-54s and three C-47s had arrived at Itazuke. Colonel John M. Price, commander of the 8th Fighter-Bomber Wing, was ordered to take charge of operations. The transports were ordered to be ready to leave for Korea at 0330 hours the next day.

Ambassador Muccio finally ordered the evacuation of American women and children from Seoul and Inchon at 0030 hours on June 26. FEAF commander General Partridge received orders from General MacArthur at 0100 hours to cover the evacuation. The air cover was not to enter Korean air space and was only to engage in combat if the freighters standing by at Inchon were directly threatened. The F-82 Twin Mustangs were the only fighters able to make the 500-mile trip from Japan and stay overhead for any length of time. Since the 68th Squadron only had 12 F-82s available, the 12 F-82s of the 339th Squadron were transferred to Itazuke from Yokota as reinforcement.

The evacuation of Seoul began at first light on June 26, with eight F-82s orbiting overhead as the evacuees went aboard ship in Inchon. At 1330 hours, a North Korean Air Force La-7 dove through the American formation from out of the clouds, cannons blazing; it disappeared back into the clouds as the F-82s broke into evasive action. Following receipt of the fighter leader's message of the attack, orders came clearing US fighters to enter Korean airspace and provide cover for refugee convoys. Relay flights of F-82s remained overhead until the freighter carrying the refugees left Inchon at last light and rendezvoused with the destroyers USS *Mansfield* and *DeHaven*, which escorted it to Japan.

On June 27, the refugee airlift got underway. Six C-47s and two C-54s, escorted by F-82s, departed Itazuke before dawn and arrived at

Kimpo and Suwon airfields shortly after dawn. The F-82s maintained low-altitude cover with flights replaced every hour, while the 8th Fighter-Bomber Wing kept four F-80Cs overhead at 25,000 feet over the city.

Among the 8th Wing pilots providing cover were Bob Wayne and the other members of "C" Flight, who flew a patrol that morning. After returning to Itazuke, they were refueled and prepared for a second patrol, to depart Itazuke at 1200 hours.

Minutes after "C" Flight lifted off at Itazuke and headed across the Sea of Japan toward Seoul, five Yak-9s were spotted over the capital, inbound to Kimpo. Five F-82s of the 68th and 339th squadrons intercepted them and shot down three in a one-sided five-minute dogfight. 1st Lt William G. Hudson of the 68th Squadron shot down a Yak-9 to become the first American pilot to shoot down an enemy fighter in the Korean War.

Bob Wayne and the rest of "C" Flight took station over Seoul about 40 minutes later. Flight leader Wayne directed element lead Schillereff and his wingman "Slick" DeWald to split off to provide better coverage over the city. At 1300 hours, Bob Wayne's wingman "Smiley" Hall called out a bogey to the north. Wayne later recalled, "I looked and looked and couldn't see a thing, so I told Smiley to take lead and I'd follow him." However, as quickly as Hall took lead, he lost sight of the dots he'd spotted in the sky. Wayne scanned the sky for the possible enemy. A moment later, he spotted a formation at 9 o'clock, level with the F-80s at 5,000 feet. He called them out to Hall, who replied he couldn't see them.

Wayne took lead and accelerated. He identified eight Il-10 "Shturmovik" attack aircraft in an echelon-left formation as they passed behind his left wing. He continued north for a minute, till the F-80s were at maximum speed. As he led Hall around in a 180-degree turn that put them on the enemy's tail, Wayne realized that with the enemy formation in an echelon-left, the pilots would be tacked on their leader and open to attack from the right. He called Hall: "Smiley, you get the last one. I'll get the next-to-last. We'll make a 360 and get the rest."

At the last moment, Wayne realized he hadn't positively identified the formation as enemy. Before takeoff, they had been briefed that other allied aircraft might be over the city. Suddenly the eight two-seat airplanes with their pointed noses seemed like they could be Royal Navy Fireflies. "Oh shit, Smiley, these could be Fireflies. Drop back and I'll make a pass and see what they are." As he dove on the formation, searching for any identification, his doubts were settled when a stream of tracers from the rear cockpit of the plane nearest tore past his cockpit. "Smiley! Go ahead and fire!"

Hall broke hard left, overshot the Il-10s and pulled around in a tight 360 behind Wayne as he closed on the lead Shturmovik and opened fire at point-blank range, getting solid hits in the engine. The enemy bomber caught fire and exploded, showering Wayne's F-80 with parts as he flew through the fireball.

Wayne broke hard left into another 360 and came around again to find the Il-10 formation had started to break up as the North Koreans desperately tried to escape the two American jets. He closed quickly on a second plane and again opened fire at minimum range. The Shturmovik belched smoke and fell off on its left wing. Wayne pulled around for another pass, but by now the enemy pilots were running for their lives and had ducked into the broken cloud cover. Looking around the empty sky, he checked his fuel gauges and realized he was just below "bingo" fuel. He called to Hall and the two Shooting Stars set course for Itazuke.

Schillereff and DeWald had been 40 miles northeast when Wayne spotted the enemy bombers. They broke off their patrol and headed at top speed toward the fight, arriving moments after Wayne and Hall had departed for home. Despite being low on fuel, they were hot on the heels of the Il-10s.

DeWald, who had wanted to be a fighter pilot since he was ten and regretted not getting through flight school in time to see combat in World War II, was at 10,000 feet when he spotted one of the surviving Il-10s low over the Han River valley southwest of the capital. When DeWald spotted him through the clouds and called out the bogey, the frequency was overwhelmed with chatter from other pilots. Finally, Schillereff called: "If you see him, go get him. I'll follow you."

The two F-80s were nearly directly overhead of the Il-10. DeWald rolled inverted and pulled the stick into his stomach as he split-essed onto the Shturmovik's tail. As he closed the distance, the rear gunner opened up. DeWald fired a long burst into the cockpit that silenced the gunner. He zoomed past the North Korean and looped his F-80 back onto the enemy's tail. The North Korean pilot put his nose down and hugged the treetops to escape. DeWald closed and opened fire again, damaging the fleeing bomber. Breaking up and away, he came around a third time; his six .50-caliber machine guns tore into the enemy's engine cowling, blasting the oil cooler. The Shturmovik streamed oil. DeWald was so close that the oil nearly covered his windscreen. Barely able to see, he broke off and climbed away as the Il-10 crashed into the trees just below.

While DeWald was chasing his Il-10, Schillereff spotted another one and broke away to chase it. The enemy pilot tried a low-level escape, but Schillereff quickly closed and set the bomber afire when he hit its engine. He pulled up and realized he had lost sight of DeWald.

"Hey, Slick," Schillereff called, "how's your fuel?" DeWald realized he might not have enough fuel to make it home. Rather than join up, the two Shooting Stars set course across the Sea of Japan for home. DeWald's engine came to a stop, out of fuel, just as he turned off the main runway at Itazuke after landing.

Back at 35th Squadron ops, morale was sky-high when the three pilots reported dropping four of the eight Il-10s. These were the first victories ever scored by American jet fighter pilots, which put Bob Wayne, "Slick" DeWald, and Ray Schillereff into the history books.

The next day, June 28, the four B-29s of the 19th Bomb Wing that had deployed to Okinawa flew their first mission against targets in North Korea to attack North Korean troops north of Seoul. They bombed the Seoul railway station and the bridges that crossed the Han River on the southern edge of the city. That same day, the rest of the wing flew from Guam to Kadena.

B-26 Invaders of the 3rd Bomb Wing flying from Ashiya air base attempted unsuccessfully to attack road targets near Seoul in the early evening. On June 29, 20 Invaders bombed the Munsan rail yards near the 38th Parallel and hit rail and road traffic between Seoul and the North Korean border. One B-26 was heavily damaged by antiaircraft fire; all three crewmen were killed when it crashed on return to Ashiya, marking the first USAF casualties of the Korean War.

Bad weather over Japan limited sorties, but 30 F-80s from the 8th Wing escorted C-54s flying between Japan and Suwon throughout the day; the transports brought in 150 tons of ammunition from Tachikawa air base for the ROK forces and returned with refugees, bringing out the last 851 US citizens to be evacuated from South Korea by air.

The United States was now engaged in a war no one had foreseen, in a place no one had expected, against a foe no one understood.

CHAPTER 2

DOUHET'S DISCIPLES

On October 14, 1947, the leaders of the US Army Air Forces achieved the goal they had aimed for since the establishment of the US Army Air Service in 1917: recognition of the Air Force as a separate armed service on an equal footing with the Army and Navy, following passage of the National Security Act of 1947. During World War II, the USAAF had seen itself the butt of jokes by soldiers and sailors for assigning a public relations officer to every unit. However, the strategy had worked. It was an article of faith with the American public that the Air Force had made the decisive contribution to victory with the dropping of two atomic bombs that led to Japanese surrender, despite the fact there was considerable evidence to the contrary; the official government study group, the Strategic Bombing Survey, had concluded that the strategic bombing campaign had not been decisive in ending the war in Europe. But the Army Air Forces were victorious in the court of public opinion.

The leaders of the US Army Air Forces not only saw themselves the equals of the senior services, but believed air power had supplanted sea and land power as the decisive element of national military power. With the United States the sole possessor of the atomic bomb and the Air Force its only delivery system, generals Henry H. "Hap" Arnold, Carl Spaatz, Ira Eaker, and Curtis LeMay saw this power as the key to ending war forever with the threat of massive destruction to any nation that attempted to break the hard-won peace. Events since the end of World War II, which saw the increasing likelihood of a world-wide struggle for dominant power between the United States and the Soviet Union, only confirmed their belief.

Five days after the Japanese surrender on August 20, 1945, the prototype of the B-36 intercontinental bomber rolled out of the Convair factory in Fort Worth, Texas. It was the largest piston-engined bomber ever built, with a wingspan of 230 feet and length of 162 feet, a third again as large as the B-29s that had devastated Japan and delivered the atomic bombs. It was powered by six Pratt and Whitney R-4360 28-cylinder piston engines and had an unrefueled range of 10,000 miles. Carrying the "Fat Man" plutonium bomb without modification to the airframe, the B-36 was seen by the disciples of Douhet as the answer to their prayers. Bombers were the ultimate weapon and would preserve the peace. (Italian General Giulio Douhet was an air power theorist who advocated the creation of a separate air arm that would be commanded by airmen. He wrote "Rules for the Use of Airplanes in War," in 1912, through which he became the first proponent of strategic bombing in aerial warfare. He was a contemporary of air warfare advocates, including the German Walther Wever, American Billy Mitchell, and British Hugh Trenchard.)

Following the end of the war, American political leaders were anxious to return the nation to peacetime. None was more adamant about this than the new president, Harry S. Truman, who had come to the office on April 12, 1945 following the death of Franklin D. Roosevelt. Truman had made his political name as head of the wartime Truman Committee in the Senate, which rooted out "waste" in government contracts. No one was more interested in getting "more bang for fewer dollars." To Truman and his allies and enemies in Washington, American possession of the atomic bomb made such a state of affairs possible in ways no one could have foreseen prior to that morning over Hiroshima. When the atomic bombing of Nagasaki was announced by a presidential radio address on August 9, 1945, President Truman stated that because the atomic bomb "is too dangerous to be loose in a lawless world, Great Britain and the United States, who have the secret of its production, do not intend to reveal the secret until means have been found to control the bomb so as to protect ourselves and the rest of the world from the danger of total destruction."

Every physicist who heard that presidential address must have laughed; once a bomb had been successfully exploded, there was no "secret." The only limit on a nation producing a nuclear weapon was the ability to commit the necessary resources to its development; the necessary science to do so was available in any college physics textbook. By 1944, the NKVD had obtained the necessary information on the Manhattan Project and Josef Stalin had directed his scientists to commence work on a Soviet bomb that would become reality in September 1949, far earlier than anyone in the West had believed possible.

Republican Party support for rapid military demobilization was a major contributor to their electoral success in November 1946, which saw the party take control of the House of Representatives for the first time since Franklin Roosevelt's first victory in 1932. The electorate's message was received loud and clear by President Truman, and by December 1946, all wartime servicemen whose service was "for the duration" were home with their families.

The defense budget was reduced faster than the service manpower was, from a high of $90 billion on July 1, 1945 to $14 billion by July 1, 1946. The rush to demobilize saw brand-new operational equipment that had cost millions to produce scrapped or abandoned, with no funds appropriated for storage. Airplanes were left rotting on airfields or thrown overboard from aircraft carriers, while other gear was left where it had been delivered. A brand-new P-51 Mustang that had cost the government $50,000 was on sale at scrapyard airports for $500 with a full tank of fuel included; the gas was more valuable than the airplane.

In September 1945, General Henry H. "Hap" Arnold, commander of the Army Air Forces, recommended a peacetime air force of 70 combat groups, down from the wartime high of 218, with 400,000 personnel. Over the next 18 months, two blue-ribbon committees echoed Arnold's request for 70 groups. President Truman, who personally distrusted the air force leadership as "glamor boys who made wild claims," absolutely refused to agree with Arnold, setting the maximum size of the US Air Force on its separation from the Army in 1947 at 48 groups with 6,869 aircraft. By 1950, the Air Force would not even reach these minimums.

In fiscal years 1947, 1948, and 1949, the military budget faced further reductions that were spurred by an economic recession in 1945 caused by falling wartime production not being rapidly replaced by civilian production, which resulted in GDP dropping 10.6 percent by the fall of 1946. In 1949, a smaller recession resulted in GDP falling 0.5 percent while unemployment rose to 7.9 percent. In 1948, President Truman's defense budget was – in constant dollars – the smallest it had been since 1940.

During this period, the Air Force presented the argument that it was the crucial service for defense of the country. The B-36 was touted as being able to deliver an atomic bomb anywhere in the world, which would keep any potential enemy from taking action against American interests. The Air Force publicity machine made no mention of the fact that the early B-36 was clearly so underpowered that when one was sent to mile-high Denver, Colorado, in 1948 for its "hot and high" test, the airplane was unable to leave the ground for a week during a heat wave that sent the density-altitude at Stapleton Field shooting from 5,280 feet to 8,000 feet. Shortly thereafter, the B-36 program saw the airplane fitted with four J-47 jet engines below the outer wing to provide necessary takeoff power and speed over the target.

In the meantime, in 1946, former British Prime Minister Winston Churchill accepted an invitation to give a speech at Westminster College in Fulton, Missouri, titled "The Sinews of Peace." Churchill gave the speech on March 5, 1946, in the presence of President Truman. The magisterial speaker began with praise for the United States, declaring it stood "at the pinnacle of world power." Churchill's primary purpose in giving the speech was to argue for strengthening the "special relationship" between the United States and Great Britain, which he termed "the great powers of the English-speaking world." He went on to describe Soviet behavior in Eastern Europe following the end of the war, and ended by declaring, "From Stettin in the Baltic to Trieste in the Adriatic, an iron curtain has descended across the continent."

President Truman was open to Churchill's argument about an "iron curtain." Eleven days earlier, George Kennan, American charge d'affaires in Moscow, had sent an 8,000-word telegram to the US State Department that would come to be known as The Long Telegram. In it, Kennan laid out his views of the Soviet Union under Stalin's leadership and suggested US policy toward the USSR in light of that analysis. Kennan's memorandum began with his statement that the Soviet Union could not foresee "permanent peaceful coexistence" with the West. He termed this a "neurotic view of world affairs" caused by the "instinctive Russian sense of insecurity." No mention was made of the Soviet Union having suffered 20 million dead in four years of war following a Western attack, but Kennan did correctly see that as a result of that titanic struggle, the Soviets harbored deep suspicion of every non-Communist state and believed their national security could only be found in "patient but deadly struggle for total destruction of rival power."

Kennan stated his belief that the Soviets would do all they could to "weaken power and influence of Western Powers on colonial, backward, or dependent peoples"; this had indeed been Soviet policy since 1918 regarding the Western colonial empires. Kennan concluded that although the Soviet Union was "impervious to logic of reason," it was "highly sensitive to logic of force" and would back off "when strong resistance is encountered at any point." His conclusion was that the United States and its allies would have to offer that resistance. Thus was the policy of "containment" presented – it would be American policy through the next 44 years.

By the summer of 1947, Kennan's analysis was strengthened by a series of crises that swept the non-Communist world, the result of which was that all the ingredients for a new war were in place. In the United Nations, the US and USSR had locked horns since the organization's founding over recognition of Soviet-controlled governments in Poland, Hungary, Romania, and Bulgaria. The US and Britain were involved in tense negotiations with the Soviets to honor their commitment to withdraw their wartime occupation of northern Iran. In southeastern Europe, Britain had been forced in 1946 to state it was unable to maintain its armed forces in Greece that had tamped down civil war between Communists and non-Communists since the German withdrawal in 1944. With the absence of British forces to separate the opponents, the Greek civil war was heating up. Turkey was under Soviet pressure to grant naval access to the Mediterranean through the Dardanelles.

President Truman had come to see Stalin as an untrustworthy partner and potential opponent after first sizing him up as a man with whom "business could be done" during their meeting at Potsdam in July 1945. Two years later, he officially offered military aid to Greece and Turkey; this marked the first formal step to implement the policy of containment Kennan had advocated. Truman's conviction that an international Communist movement was on the advance was strengthened by the Communist *coup d'état* that overthrew the democratically elected government of Czechoslovakia in 1948, followed the next year by the victory of Communist forces led by Mao Zedong over the Nationalist government of Chiang Kai-shek in the Chinese Civil War in October 1949. He had additional impetus to adopt this policy with the hard-line anti-communism of the new Republican majority in the House of Representatives, where right-wing firebrands were intent on demonstrating the "Communist roots" of the New Deal.

The event that solidified Truman's view of the conflict was the first crisis the leaders of the new Air Force faced, eight months after having achieved independence. The first operational B-36B arrived in service in May 1948. Thirty days later, the Air Force discovered the most important airplane in the inventory was not the enormous B-36, but rather the prosaic C-54 cargo transport.

On June 24, 1948, the Soviets instituted a blockade denying the Western Allies access to railway, road, and canal routes to the sectors of Berlin controlled by the West. The political motivation for the blockade was soon apparent when the Soviets offered to stop the blockade if the Allies withdrew the newly introduced Deutsche Mark (DM) from circulation in West Berlin. The Allied sectors in West Berlin had food supplies for 36 days; coal would run out in 45 days.

The Berlin Blockade soon became the dominant event for the new Air Force. Organizing the aerial resupply of Berlin took primacy over every other activity. During the next 12 months, the USAF, along with the Royal Air Force (RAF), Royal Canadian Air Force (RCAF), Royal Australian Air Force (RAAF) Royal New Zealand Air Force (RNZAF), and the French Armee de l'Air, established the Berlin Airlift. By April 1949 more supplies arrived that month by air than had been provided by ground transport the year before. The cost was the operational sapping of each participating air force. In the summer of 1949, the Soviets relented and stopped the blockade. The first great crisis of what was starting to be called the Cold War had been successfully overcome without leading to major conflict. That fall, the North Atlantic Treaty Organization (NATO) would be founded to defend western Europe against Soviet expansion, under the umbrella of the American atomic bomb.

While the Berlin Airlift was gathering headlines, political underdog President Truman won an unexpected victory in the November 1948 presidential election. He was now seen as the valid leader of the country through election and no longer "the accidental president." With that power, he determined he would place his own stamp on presidency and nation. While a senator, he had been a strong supporter of President Roosevelt and the New Deal, but he was no Keynesian. Detroit was producing cars instead of tanks and airplanes once again; the construction industry was gearing up to meet demands of an American public that had never before had access to individual family housing, as was now the law of the land through the G.I. Bill. America was about to be transformed in ways unimaginable at the outset, and Harry S. Truman believed the duty of government was to reduce its demand for resources and get out of the way.

Possession of the atomic bomb and an air force that could deliver it anywhere in the world led the president to decide the Army and Navy could be safely reduced further than they had been in the immediate postwar demobilization. Seeing the opportunity for bureaucratic primacy, Air Force leaders argued there was no need for the Navy to have a separate air force that could not deliver the atomic bomb. Not to be outdone, the Army argued that the Navy's "army," the Marine Corps, should also become part of the Army under the new concept of "service unification" that formed the basis of the National Security Act that brought the War Department and Navy Department into the Department of Defense. Army Chief of Staff General Omar N. Bradley advocated that the Navy become a transportation service to support the Army when the inevitable war with the Soviet Union broke out in Europe, the only place American war planners believed a war could break out.

In the meantime, faced with reductions that were not as egregious as those imposed on the Army and Navy, the Air Force was forced to choose between tactical and strategic air power. Despite the lessons learned on the plains of Europe and the islands of the Pacific only a few years earlier about the value of tactical air power, the Air Force leadership decided that since such war was now "obsolete" in the atomic age, they would concentrate their resources on the B-36 and the coming generation of jet-powered bombers. By 1949, tactical aviation in the Air Force was only slightly larger than it had been at the outset of war in 1941. The newly formed Strategic Air Command (SAC) enjoyed the lion's share of defense expenditures as the nation's first line of defense.

Truman's view of the military had been opposed by James Forrestal, formerly Secretary of the Navy, who had been appointed the first Secretary of Defense. Following his death in early 1949 he was succeeded by Louis A. Johnson, whom Truman regarded as a close ally since he had been the only major Democrat to support the president's re-election and had managed the successful 1948 campaign, raising the money for the "whistle-stop" train tour that had turned things around a month before the election. Johnson was remembered by other Washington Democrats as "a wheeler-dealer, a self-made man with an inflated sense of his political abilities and possibilities." He is without a doubt the top contender for the title of worst Secretary of Defense in the history of the office.

Johnson had first gotten into politics in West Virginia before American entry into World War I, where he served as an Army captain in France in 1918. After the war, he became active in "veteran politics" and was national commander of the conservative American Legion from 1932 to 1933 before Roosevelt appointed him Assistant Secretary of War from 1937 to 1940. He became an enemy of the president when he was passed over in favor of Henry Stimson as Secretary of War. On taking office in 1949, he was an enthusiastic supporter of Truman's determination to achieve further military unification and economy of operations. Starting with FY 1948, the Department of Defense budget was capped at the FY 1947 level of $14.4 billion, with successive reductions until the president's budget set it at $13.5 billion in January 1950. Johnson was a believer in the Air Force, dating from his close association with the prewar Army Air Corps. When he was challenged by Admiral Richard L. Conolly over his decision to deactivate three *Essex*-class carriers by the end of the fiscal year, he said:

> Admiral, the Navy is on its way out. There's no reason for having a Navy and a Marine Corps. General Bradley tells me amphibious operations are a thing of the past. We'll never have any more amphibious operations. That does away with the Marine Corps. And the Air Force can do anything the Navy can do, so that does away with the Navy.

The next month, he canceled construction of the USS *United States*, the ship the Navy leadership considered essential to the future of naval air power.

While the Navy received the brunt of his reductions, the secretary ordered the Army to scrap or sell almost the entire inventory of surplus World War II tanks, radios, trucks, and small arms, and resisted Army budget requests for reserve stockpiles of small arms and antitank weapons. The Air Force was not immune, despite Johnson's liking of the airmen. He refused requests to double the number of active air wings and reduced the tactical air force budget in favor of the strategic nuclear force he saw as the answer to all problems, authorizing an increase in the procurement budget for the B-36.

Over the course of the rest of 1949, the Navy fought back in what became known as "The Revolt of the Admirals." This ultimately resulted in congressional hearings in the fall of 1949 regarding the nation's defense policy. The hearings by the House Armed Service Committee on unification and strategy opened October 6, 1949. Two weeks before the hearing opened, it had been publicly announced that the Soviet Union had exploded an atomic bomb, which ended the strategy of "atomic monopoly diplomacy." Clarification of the current implications of such a military situation revealed the general acceptance in both the political and military establishment of the belief the Soviet Union was the only possible enemy, Europe the only possible theater, and nuclear war the only outcome. The American strategic view was not lost on Josef Stalin, who would meet two months later with Kim il-Sung, the leader of the Democratic People's Republic of Korea, who would request his assistance in the forcible reunification of the nation of Korea.

The Armed Services Committee report was released on March 1, 1950. It stated that US air power consisted of Air Force, Navy, and Marine aviation and that strategic bombing was only one aspect. Additionally, the report stated that differences between the Air Force and Navy were due primarily to "fundamental professional disagreements on the art of warfare."

Four months later, payment came due for the political and military folly of the previous four years. When the North Korean People's Army crossed the 38th Parallel on June 25, 1950, the Air Force had no basic doctrine to accommodate introduction of nuclear weapons into war fighting. The service was in the midst of technological revolutions, including the transition from piston to jet power, perfecting nuclear weapons and delivery methods, and creating aerial refueling to permit the use of jet-powered bombers on long-range bombing missions. The leadership would be forced to fall back on the weapons and theory of aerial warfare from World War II.

The strategic bombing doctrine on which the Air Force based its entire *raison d'etre* would be irrelevant in this new war. North Korea was an agrarian society without an industrial base. It had no critical war industries such as power generation, armaments, shipyards, petroleum refineries or storage, or large munition or supply depots. The North

Koreans relied on rail and road connections with China to import war-fighting equipment and supplies. The electrical power-generation capability was based on hydroelectric plants near the Yalu River. These plants were immune to attack when President Truman placed a "no bomb" corridor 10 miles from the Chinese border to prevent inadvertent bombing of Chinese territory that might trigger overt Chinese involvement in the Korean "police action."

The Joint Chiefs of Staff imposed additional restrictions on bombing, ordering leaflet drops 24–48 hours prior to a bombing mission near a North Korean city to allow time for civilian evacuation. The B-29s of the two bomb groups immediately available for operations were left with few "strategic" targets other than rail yards.

General Curtis LeMay, commander of Strategic Air Command and the man who had ordered the firebombing of Japanese cities in 1945, urged General MacArthur to firebomb the five major cities in North Korea to drive home to the North Korean leaders that continuing their attack would result in the incineration of their country. MacArthur refused to order such attacks. B-29 attacks on North Korean rail yards were unsuccessful due to poor weather. The bombers that had laid waste to urban Japan were finally used to carpet bomb advancing enemy troops. By the time UN forces crossed the 38th Parallel in October 1950, there were no suitable targets for the bombers left in all of North Korea. Still, the bombing continued. By October 1950, targets were so scarce a B-29 chased a motorcycle rider, dropping single bombs until finally hitting him.

The arrival of Soviet-flown MiG-15s would force the B-29s to operate at night, with even less effectiveness. The strategic bomber, ideally suited for delivering atomic weapons over intercontinental distances, was too vulnerable and targets too lacking to fulfill its role as a war winner in a war like that in Korea, as envisioned by the disciples of Douhet.

The American people would be largely unaware of a bombing campaign that eventually knocked down nearly every structure in North Korea. The North Koreans, however, would never forget. The legacy of the bombing campaign that failed to change the outcome of a war was the unrelenting anger and hostility of those on whom the bombs fell, a legacy still felt 65 years later.

CHAPTER 3

AN AERIAL REVOLUTION

The technological revolution in aircraft design and operation that resulted from the successful development of jet engines brought about more technological change in the five years between the end of World War II and the Korean War than any other comparable time in the history of aviation from the Wright Brothers' first flight. Supersonic flight was achieved just over two years after the end of the war and the first fighter capable of controlled transonic flight saw action in Korea. The Cold War forced technological changes and by 1950 the Western nations were amazed that the Soviet Union had fielded a fighter that was competitive with the best the West had created.

The USAAF came late to the jet power revolution. While the first turbojet-powered aircraft had flown in Germany in 1939 and the British "Gloster Pioneer" flew in 1941, the USAAF only became aware of this technological development when Army Air Forces chief General H. H. "Hap" Arnold visited Britain in April 1941. The general was shown the top-secret Gloster E-28/39 jet-powered aircraft, which was powered by one of Wing Commander Frank Whittle's W2B centrifugal turbojets. Arnold was impressed with the potential of this new technology and asked if American engineers could be given blueprints of the new engine so they could manufacture it under license in the USA. Since the US government had just commenced providing increased aid to Britain through the recently passed Lend-Lease Act, the RAF readily agreed to this cooperative development. Arnold returned to his office in the then-new Pentagon determined to make up for lost time.

After the AAF Engineering Section at Wright-Patterson had examined the blueprints, Arnold met with the leaders of General Electric on September 4, 1941, and asked them to become the prime contractor for license production of the British jet engine since the company had extensive experience with turbines for various industrial and aviation applications. Fifteen Whittle engines were ordered, under the cover designation I-A, in the hope any enemy intelligence agency that discovered the project would mistakenly think it was a new turbosupercharger.

The next day Arnold met with Lawrence Bell, president of Bell Aircraft, and asked him if the company would build a fighter prototype powered by the new engines. Bell agreed to a project to design and construct three aircraft, the first to be completed eight months after the contract was approved on September 30, 1941. The serial numbers of the three prototypes were 42-108784, 42-108785, and 42-108786.

Bell's jet fighter project was assigned the designation XP-59A in hopes that if German intelligence discovered the existence of the project, it would be considered an adaptation of the totally unrelated XP-59 piston-engine pusher fighter the company was already at work on. That project was officially cancelled on December 1, 1941 and Bell concentrated their efforts on the new prototypes. On November 30, 1941, the company submitted a design for a fairly conventional aircraft using a laminar-flow, mid-mounted wing and a fully retractable tricycle landing gear, powered by two 1,400lb static thrust (S.T.). General Electric I-A jet engines, mounted under the wing roots with a high tailplane well out of the way of the turbojet exhausts, and fitted with a pressurized cockpit. Since no one was sure of exactly what stresses a jet-powered airframe might encounter, the design was conservative and featured an airframe as strong as possible. The weight of this airframe and the low power of its engines would result in a disappointing overall performance. Though the XP-59A was seen as being primarily a test-bed for jet engines, it had been given a nose-mounted armament of two 37mm cannon with 44rpg. Initial design approval was quickly given by the Wright-Patterson engineers and construction of the three prototypes commenced on January 9, 1942. In March, without waiting for the first prototype's flight, 13 service test YP-59As were ordered. These aircraft would be powered by an improved version of the General Electric engine, the I-16, which was later designated J-31, which had a rated 1,650lb thrust.

The first XP-59A was completed at Bell's factory in Buffalo, New York, in August 1942; the company gave it the name "Airacomet." On September 12 it was transported by rail to the Army's testing site at Muroc Dry Lake, California. Once on the field, the prototype was fitted with a dummy propeller to prevent the curious from asking why this aircraft didn't have a propeller. Testing began with taxiing trials at the end of the month. On October 1, 1942, while performing high-speed taxiing trials, Bell test pilot Robert Stanley "inadvertently" became airborne for a short time. The official first flight was made the next day, with a USAAF pilot at the controls. This was a remarkable achievement – for the first flight of the prototype to take place only 13 months after the development contract was awarded. The XP-59A weighed 7,320 pounds empty and 12,562 pounds in maximum-loaded condition. Wingspan was a glider-like 45 feet 6 inches with an area of 386 square feet, while length was only 28 feet 2 inches.

Testing revealed the XP-59A was far from a combat-capable aircraft. The engines were too heavy in relation to the thrust developed, while the exhaust was so hot that the turbine blades regularly overheated and often broke off with catastrophic results; fortunately the glider-like wing allowed the pilots to bring the airplane back to Muroc Field and land in one piece when these accidents happened. The engine installation under the wing resulted in an inordinate aerodynamic interference with the wing, while maximum speed was a disappointing 404mph at 25,000 feet – less than that of the standard P-47 Thunderbolt fighter that was just entering service – and the P-59 was subject to severe directional snaking, making it a poor gun platform. Nevertheless, work continued unabated, with remedies eventually found for the long list of faults.

Despite the increased power of the G.E. I-16 (later J31) turbojets, the 13 service test YP-59As demonstrated little performance increase over the prototype. Empty weight had increased to 7,626 pounds and maximum speed was only 409mph at 35,000 feet. The last four YP-59As were provided with a heavier armament of three .50-caliber machine guns and a single 37mm cannon, which was standardized for the production P-59A. The third YP-59A was sent to Britain in November 1943, in exchange for the first production Gloster Meteor I, and was assigned the RAF serial RJ362/G. Transferred to Farnborough on November 5, the airplane became a "hangar queen" because of unserviceability due to a lack of spares. From their limited tests RAF pilots found the YP-59A was badly underpowered, with an unacceptably long takeoff run. In December 1943, the US Navy got the eighth and ninth YP-59As (42-108778 and 42-100779) for use in tests.

There is a famous legend that the test pilots of the XP and YP-59s flew in gorilla suits and bowler hats, to shock other pilots of conventional aircraft that ran across them over the California desert. The facts of the tale are these: During initial flight testing, Bell personnel could be distinguished by their trademark black derby hats. Though the airspace around Muroc Dry Lake was restricted, P-38 pilots from nearby George Field would occasionally enter the restricted airspace in an attempt to see what was going on at the "secret" base. During one test flight, Bell test pilot Jack Woolams spotted one of the snoopers and decided to have a little fun. He put on a rubber gorilla mask he had brought along for such an opportunity, donned his derby, and stuck a big cigar in his mouth, then let the P-38 pull alongside. The stunned pilot took one look and quickly broke off.

Just before the first flight of the XP-59A, the USAAF placed an order with Bell for 100 P-59As. Once the performance of the service test aircraft was shown not even up to that of conventional piston-engined fighters already in service, the P-59A order was cut to 50 on October 30, 1943, with the airplanes to be used as operational trainers. A major difference with the prototypes was the reduction in wingspan by creating a squared-off wingtip in hopes of improving the roll rate. The decision to essentially abandon the P-59A was helped by the superb performance of Lockheed's XP-80, which was a combat-capable design.

Production P-59As were little different from the service test aircraft. Only the first 20 were P-59As. They were powered by J31-GE-3 turbojets, although the last five were given more powerful J31-GE-5 turbojets providing 2000lb S.T. The J31-GE-5-powered P-59A had a maximum speed of 413mph at 30,000 feet and 380mph at 5,000 feet. Range on internal fuel was 240 miles, increased to 520 miles with two 130-gallon underwing drop tanks. The aircraft could reach 10,000 feet in 3.2 minutes, and 20,000 feet in 7.4 minutes. Weights were 7,950 pounds empty, 10,822 pounds loaded, and 12,700 pounds maximum. Two 1,000lb bombs could be carried on the underwing racks, along with eight 60lb rockets mounted further outboard.

The final 30 aircraft were completed as P-59Bs, equipped with the uprated J31-GE-5 engines and having internal fuel capacity increased by 60 gallons, which increased the maximum range to 950 miles. Empty weight of the P-59B increased to 8,165 pounds with normal and maximum loaded weights being 11,049 pounds and 13,700 pounds respectively. The last P-59B was delivered in May 1945.

Most of the P-59s equipped the 412th Fighter Group, which was based at Muroc Dry Lake, where they served as operational trainers. AVG ace Col "Tex" Hill, who had only recently returned to the United States from a successful tour as CO of the 23rd Fighter Group in China, was assigned as group commander. Several P-59Bs were retained for testing at Muroc and later modified for use as drone directors or manned target aircraft with a second "open" cockpit installed forward of the main cockpit in what had been the gunbay.

While the P-59 Airacomet never saw first-line service in its intended role as a fighter, it did provide the USAAF with valuable experience in the operation of jet aircraft and furnished a nucleus of trained jet pilots who could take the service into the jet age.

With the P-59 a demonstrated operational failure by early 1943, the USAAF turned to Clarence "Kelly" Johnson and Lockheed Aircraft to solve the problem. The problem was made more urgent by the recent discovery through aerial reconnaissance of the existence of the German Me-262 fighter, which appeared ready to enter service within the next year. By this time, the AAF had been provided with the newly designed Halford H-1B engine, which would become known as the "Goblin." The engine was lighter than the Whittle powerplants and promised higher performance as it was further developed. For the Air Force, time was of the essence. Kelly's special secret design unit that combined design and engineering personnel for the rapid creation of prototypes, which was already known as "The Skunk Works," presented a concept for a single-engine air superiority fighter in April 1943. A design specification was written around the proposal and issued by the USAAF in May 1943, with Lockheed presenting its detailed proposal for Project MX-409 30 days later. A contract for a single prototype was signed on June 17, 1943. Final design and production commenced on June 26. The project was so secret only the five managers of the 130 people working on it knew they were working on the development of a jet aircraft. Security was so high that the British engineer who delivered the Goblin engine that fall was detained by police when Lockheed officials could not vouch for him. The prototype, known in the company as "The Green Hornet" for its forest green paint scheme and nicknamed "Lulu Belle," was trucked to Muroc Field from the Lockheed factory in Burbank on November 16, a remarkable 143 days from commencement of work. The engine was mated to the airframe, only to be destroyed by foreign object damage during the first run-up. There was only one other Goblin engine in existence, which delayed the first flight until it could be removed from the first deHavilland Vampire prototype and delivered from Britain.

The prototype, now known as the XP-80, was displayed to Air Force commanders at Muroc on January 8, 1944. Lockheed Chief Engineering Test Pilot Milo Burcham had the assignment of making the first flight. The jet roared down Muroc's Runway 23, lifted off, then quickly landed when the landing gear failed to retract. Lockheed's technicians quickly fixed the electrical problem and Burcham started up again and soared into the clear California winter sky. Over the next hour, he gave the assembled audience an air show in which he clearly demonstrated the wonderful flying characteristics the P-80 would become known for in service.

The second prototype, designated XP-80A, was designed for the larger General Electric I-40 engine (an improved J31, later produced by Allison as the J33). Two aircraft, 44-83021 and 44-83022, were built to test this configuration. 44-83021 was nicknamed "The Gray Ghost" for its "pearl gray" paint scheme, while 83022 was left unpainted for comparison of flight characteristics and became "The Silver Ghost." The XP-80As were testbeds for the larger, more powerful engine; the airframe was larger and 25 percent heavier than that of the XP-80. Initial opinions of the airplane were not positive. Milo Burcham commented after several flights that an aircraft he very much enjoyed when powered by the Halford engine had become a "dog." Further tests revealed the engine was not getting enough air to produce full power. Modification to the air intakes to improve boundary layer control resulted in the engine maintaining full power, which restored the flight characteristics of the Green Hornet.

While the XP-80As were under construction, an order for 13 service-test YP-80As was signed in March 1944. The first of these were delivered in September. Testing the P-80 proved very dangerous. On October 20, 1944, Burcham was killed while flying the third YP-80A (44-83025) when the engine flamed out on takeoff due to fuel starvation. His death resulted from the failure to brief him on a newly installed emergency fuel pump backup system that would have prevented the failure. On March 25, 1945, newly promoted Chief Engineering Test Pilot Tony LeVier was forced to bail out of "The Gray Ghost" when one of the engine's turbine blades broke and caused a structural failure in the aircraft's tail. LeVier broke his back when he landed hard and only returned to the test program after six months of recovery.

In February 1945, two YP-80As were sent to England, where they were kept in the open to be photographed by German Ar-234 jet-powered reconnaissance aircraft in hopes the Germans would think these were operational aircraft. Two others went on to Italy, where they were flown in operational development flights in the combat environment with the P-38-equipped 1st Fighter Group, though neither flew in any direct combat operations. The YP-80As were grounded after Air Force pilot Major Frederick Borsodi was killed when the engine of the plane he was flying caught fire during a flight demonstration at RAF Burtonwood in Britain.

Allied intelligence believed the German Me-262 was ready to enter production and the P-80's development was accelerated. Now known as the "Shooting Star," 13 YP-80As were ordered in February 1944. In March 1944, before any of the service test aircraft had been completed or flown, a production order was approved for 500 P-80As. The production P-80A had a top speed of 558mph at sea level and 492mph at 40,000 feet. Climb was 4,580fpm and an altitude of 20,000 feet could be attained in 5.5 minutes. Range on internal fuel only was 780 miles; with tip-mounted 150-gallon drop tanks, this was extended to 1,440 miles.

Jet aviation continued to create fatalities. On August 6, 1945, Major Richard Bong, the top-scoring World War II USAAF ace, was killed during the acceptance flight of a production P-80 when the engine failed on takeoff as had happened to Burcham. When the aircraft rolled inverted, Bong bailed out, but he was too close to the ground for his parachute to fully deploy. The investigation of Bong's crash found he had forgotten to switch to the emergency fuel pump, which could have prevented the accident. The pre-takeoff checklist was changed to ensure the pilot turned on the emergency pump before engine start-up.

Following the end of the war, the P-80 was tested in comparison to a captured Me-262A. The test report concluded that despite the fact the

Me-262 weighed nearly 2,000 pounds more than the P-80, the German fighter was superior in acceleration and speed and approximately the same in climb performance. The Me-262 was also found to have a higher critical Mach number of M 0.86, providing lower drag than any Army Air Force fighter. However, the P-80A was more maneuverable.

After the war, production of the P-80 was maintained at a reduced level that still was higher than other aircraft programs which were cut back or canceled, with total P-80A production at 344, down from a planned wartime total of 5,000. The USAAF first replaced the P-59s in the 412th Fighter Group with 45 P-80As in November 1945. The F-80 next re-equipped the 1st and 56th fighter groups, which were assigned to the newly formed Strategic Air Command in mid-1946. Under the command of their wartime leader, Colonel David Schilling, the 56th Group was sent to Giebelstadt, Germany, soon after their re-equipment, remaining in Europe for 18 months.

On January 27, 1946, a P-80A flown by Colonel William H. Councill made the first transcontinental jet flight, completing the 2,457-mile flight from Long Beach to New York in 4 hours 13 minutes 26 seconds at an average speed of 584mph and setting a Fédération Aéronautique Internationale record. With the British Meteor IV having recently set a world speed record, the P-80B prototype was modified as a racer with a very smooth painted finish and a lowered canopy and designated the P-80R. Colonel Albert Boyd set the world air speed record of 623.73mph on June 19, 1947.

Lockheed eventually built a total of 917 F-80As and Bs by the time production halted in 1948. These were followed by the P-80C, which began production in 1948; its designation changed on June 11 to F-80C when the newly independent Air Force changed designators to F-for-fighter rather than P-for-pursuit. This subtype differed from the P-80A and B in having a wing of thinner section and a more powerful Allison J33-A-35 giving 4,600lb S.T. dry thrust, which could be increased to 5,400lb S.T. with water injection. Top speed increased to 594mph (Mach 0.76) at sea level and rate of climb increased to 6,870fpm. The F-80C was also the first Air Force fighter to have an ejection seat installed at the factory. Production ended in 1950 with 162 P-80C-1-LO, 75 P-80C-5-LO and 561 F-80C-10-LO production blocks in addition to 129 F-80As upgraded to F-80C-11-LO standard. During the Berlin Crisis of 1948, Colonel Schilling led a squadron of the re-equipped

56th Fighter Group that accomplished the first west-to-east Atlantic crossing by single-engine jets that July, flying to Germany for a 45-day deployment in Operation *Fox Able*. Over the remainder of 1948, the 4th Fighter-Interceptor Group at Langley Air Force Base, Virginia, the 81st at Kirtland Air Force Base, New Mexico, and the 57th at Elmendorf Air Force Base, Alaska, equipped with F-80Cs. The 196th Fighter Squadron of the California Air National Guard became the first ANG unit to fly the F-80 in June 1947. Overseas, F-80s equipped the 36th Fighter Interceptor Group at Fürstenfeldbruck by March 1949, and the 51st Fighter-Interceptor Group became the first unit in the Far East to trade their F-51Ds for F-80Cs that summer. During the Korean War, 277 F-80s were lost in operations, a number that was approximately 30 percent of the existing inventory, with 113 shot down by enemy antiaircraft fire and 14 shot down by enemy aircraft. The F-80 was credited with the destruction of 17 aircraft in air-to-air combat and 24 on the ground.

One of the most important developments of the F-80 was its modification for photographic-reconnaissance. Sixty-six F-80As were modified as RF-80As, with a bulbous nose holding two to four cameras, depending on the mission, replacing the six-gun nose. The 45th Tactical Reconnaissance Squadron in Japan received its first RF-80A in early 1950. The aircraft was used for highly classified reconnaissance missions over Vladivostok and North Korea before the outbreak of war in June; these missions were so sensitive that the pilot developed his own film after them and personally delivered it to General MacArthur's headquarters in Tokyo. RF-80As were later used for missions over North Korea following the outbreak of war because they had a higher performance than any interceptor possessed by the enemy. This technological invulnerability ended with the introduction of the MiG-15 in combat, which meant that any reconnaissance mission flown into "MiG Alley" required escort by F-86 Sabres.

While production of the F-80 ended in 1950, further development of the airframe continued. Difficulty experienced by the Air Force in transitioning pilots to the single-seat F-80 resulted in Lockheed proposing development of a two-seat trainer in 1947. The design featured a fuselage extended 3 feet immediately aft of the original cockpit, with a second seat and full flight controls under an extended blown bubble canopy. Initially designated the TF-80C, the prototype first flew with Tony

Levier at the controls on March 22, 1948 and was followed by a second prototype also designated TF-80C. The extended fuselage resulted in an increased fineness ratio, which led to improved performance over the single-seat fighter. Top speed was 600mph at sea level, with a cruise of 455mph. Increased weight, however, reduced the climb speed to 4,870fpm. Designated T-33, the aircraft was ordered into production in 1949 and remained in production until 1959. Total production was 6,557 – 5,691 by Lockheed, with 210 by Kawasaki in Japan and 656 by Canadair. A total of 41 different air forces operated the T-33, with the last being retired in 1998 by the Paraguayan Air Force.

With the threat of a nuclear-armed Soviet Air Force after the explosion of the first Soviet atomic bomb in September 1949, the Air Force was confronted with a need for an all-weather jet interceptor. It had become clear in 1948 that the Curtiss XF-87 Nighthawk, which was expected to become the new Air Force's first all-weather jet interceptor, did not live up to expectations. Northrop's XF-89 had yet to fly, and when it did at the end of 1948 it would prove to need further development. Lockheed proposed an "interim" all-weather jet interceptor based on the new T-33 jet trainer, which required the least modification of any jet to perform the job. The two TF-80C prototypes were modified to what became known as the F-94. The fighter was equipped with a modified APG-33 radar developed from the radar used for the B-36 tail turret, provided an armament of four .50-caliber machine guns in the nose below the radar, and had the first afterburner to be used on an operational jet, which could increase the standard thrust of the J33-A-33 from 4,000lb S.T. to maximum of 6,000lb S.T. The first modified TF-80C flew in 1949 as the YF-94A and appeared to meet all specifications despite teething problems with the afterburner igniter and flame stabilization system. Despite the need for further development, the airplane was ordered into production in a crash program in late 1949 as the F-94A.

The 109 F-94As that appeared in 1950 did not live up to the original hope. The engine and afterburner were not reliable, leading to many pre-takeoff ground aborts; the cockpit was too tight for the crew to be able to operate successfully and exit in an emergency; and the radar needed tweaking. Pilots reported that the aircraft was unstable and hard to maneuver at high altitude. Lockheed modified the airplane to the F-94B, which entered service in January 1951. While the aircraft was outwardly almost identical to the F-94A, a number of modifications had been made to the Allison J33, which resulted in a very reliable engine. The pilot had a roomier cockpit and the canopy was replaced by one with a bow frame in the center between the two cockpits; a new Instrument Landing System (ILS) made bad weather operation much safer. Production of the F-94B ran to 356, with the surviving earlier F-94As sent to Lockheed to be re-engined and modified to F-94B standard. The upgraded F-94A/B aircraft were additionally modified with a pod under each wing for two additional 50-caliber machine guns. These modified aircraft were assigned to the Air National Guard and served until the end of the 1950s.

In 1952, when MiG-15s appeared at night over Seoul, F-94Bs were sent to Korea, where they replaced the F-82G Twin Mustangs of the 68th Fighter-Interceptor Squadron. The F-94s made several successful interceptions over the South Korean capital, ending the MiG-15 intrusions. In January 1953, the 319th FIS began operations from Suwon to provide combat air patrol protection to B-29s over North Korea when the enemy began intercepting the bombers at night with MiG-15s. Due to fear that if an F-94B was lost over North Korea its equipment would be turned over to the Soviets, the fighters only operated in certain areas. Despite this restriction, they managed to intercept and shoot down several MiG-15s, alongside the Marine F3D-2 Skyknights that also provided escort protection to the B-29s, making the F-94B the only USAF all-weather jet interceptor to ever fire its guns in anger and score victories. The F-94Bs continued in service after the Korean War with USAF and Air National Guard units until it was fully replaced by the F-86D and F-102 in 1959.

The second Air Force jet fighter ordered into development after the P-80, the P-84, was designed by Republic Aviation's chief designer, Alexander Kartveli, who had created the P-47 Thunderbolt. In early 1944, Kartveli commenced work on a turbojet-powered replacement for the P-47, initially attempting to redesign the P-47 to accommodate a jet engine. When this proved futile because of the large cross-section of early centrifugal compressor turbojets, Kartveli and his team went to work designing a new aircraft with a streamlined fuselage using an axial compressor turbojet, with fuel carried in thick unswept wings. Once he had a preliminary design, he shared it with friends at the Air Force development center at Wright-Patterson.

After meeting with Kartveli, the USAAF released General Operational Requirements on September 11, 1944, for a day fighter with a top speed of

600mph, combat radius of 705 miles, and armament of either six 0.50in. or four 0.60in. machine guns, to be powered by the General Electric TG-180 axial turbojet, which entered production as the Allison J35.

The Air Force quickly officially accepted Kartveli's AP-23 design and on November 11, 1944, ordered three prototypes of the new XP-84. Because the AP-23 promised performance superior to that of the Lockheed XP-80, and due to the fact that Republic had extensive experience in producing the P-47, there was no competition for the contract. Republic chose the emotive name "Thunderjet," to continue the tradition begun with the P-47 Thunderbolt, while emphasizing the new propulsion method. With the design quickly finalized, the USAAF expanded the order on January 4, 1945 to 25 service-test YP-84As and 75 production P-84Bs (later modified to 15 YP-84As and 85 P-84Bs), before the first prototype flight.

The design ran into problems from the outset. The General Electric turbojet was only producing some 3,000 pounds of thrust. In the meantime, the design weight escalated when the airframe was beefed up after wind tunnel testing by the National Advisory Committee for Aeronautics (NACA) revealed longitudinal instability and stabilizer skin buckling at high speeds. The results of these tests were incorporated in the third prototype, designated XP-84A, which used a more powerful J35-GE-15 engine that gave 4,000 pounds of thrust.

In January 1946, the first XP-84 was transported to Muroc airfield (later Edwards AFB). The prototype took to the air for the first time on February 28, 1946 with Major Wallace A. "Wally" Lien in the cockpit. In August, the second prototype arrived at Muroc. Both XP-84s were powered by J35-GE-7 engines producing 3,745 pounds of thrust. Flight tests revealed a limiting speed of Mach 0.80, which was quickly reached due to the thick wing. The Air Force now requested an increase in range for use as a bomber escort. Republic answered by developing jettisonable fuel tanks carried on the wingtip. The 15 YP-84As delivered for service test had the upgraded J35-A-15 engine first used in the third prototype, and were armed with a total of six .50-caliber M2 Browning machine guns, four in the nose and one in each wing root. They could carry wingtip fuel tanks with 226 US gallons each.

During the immediate postwar period, Republic ran into financial difficulties as wartime contracts were canceled. By October 1946, the company could only continue operations for three weeks and pleaded with the USAAF to begin payments on the P-84 contract, even through the first production aircraft would not be delivered until mid-1947. Payment was advanced; added to a $6 million tax refund, Republic was able to keep the Thunderjet alive. By 1947, when production P-84Bs began to roll out, the Thunderjet had only undergone limited flight tests because of delays in delivery of jet engines. In particular, the impact of the wingtip tanks on handling had not been thoroughly studied.

The production F-84B differed from the YP-84A by having faster-firing M3 guns. The Thunderjet became operational in December 1947 with 14th Fighter Group, based at Dow AFB outside Bangor, Maine. Within weeks, flight restrictions limiting maximum speed to Mach 0.8 due to control reversal, and maximum acceleration to 5.5 G due to fuselage skin wrinkling were issued. A shortage of parts and maintenance difficulties with the new type earned it the nickname "Mechanic's Nightmare." All F-84Bs were grounded on May 24, 1948, because of structural failures. This was quickly followed by the grounding of the F-84Cs just coming off the production line.

A review of the entire program later that year revealed no F-84B or F-84C Thunderjets were capable of performing any part of their intended mission. The newly independent Air Force considered program cancellation, but the airplane was saved because the new F-84D, which began entering service in early 1949, satisfactorily addressed the major faults. The wings had a thicker aluminum skin, a winterized fuel system capable of using JP-4 fuel was installed, and the F-84D was powered by the more powerful J35-A-17D engine with 5,000 pounds of thrust. Tests had revealed the original wingtip fuel tanks contributed to structural failure through induced excessive wing twist during high-G maneuvers; fitting small triangular fins on the outer side of the tanks solved this. A fly-off against the F-80 revealed that the Shooting Star had a shorter takeoff roll, better low altitude climb rate, and superior maneuverability, while the F-84 could carry a heavier bomb load and was faster, with better high-altitude performance and greater range.

The F-84E was ordered on December 29, 1948, and the first, 49-2022, which flew on May 18, 1949, was the first subtype to completely fulfill the original specifications and resulted in a production run of 843. Powered by the same J35-A-17D used in the F-84D, the wing featured a redesigned, reinforced spar, while the fuselage was lengthened 12 inches ahead of the wings and 3 inches aft, which increased the fuselage fineness ratio and increased top speed while enlarging the cockpit and avionics bay, which required the canopy be lengthened 8 inches. Most aircraft were retrofitted with F-84G-style reinforced canopies, since the large plexiglass canopy was subject to failure when the cockpit was pressurized. The fuselage stretch allowed installation of a larger fuel tank. An A-1C gunsight with an APG-30 gunlaying radar fitted in the intake splitter plate improved gun sighting. Pylons inboard of the main gear well in the wing allowed carriage of a second pair of 230-gallon drop tanks, which increased the combat radius from 850–1,000 miles to 870–1,370 miles; alternatively, each inboard pylon could carry a maximum bomb load of 2,000 pounds, greatly increasing the aircraft's capability in the fighter-bomber role it would eventually assume in Korea. Additionally, fitting rocket racks that folded flush with the wing after the rockets were fired reduced drag in comparison to the earlier racks.

However, despite these improvements, the F-84E's in-service rate remained below 50 percent at any given time, primarily due to engine spares shortages. Allison production rates had originally been set on an expected individual aircraft flight schedule of 25 hours per month. Actual flight hours in Korea were at least double this and thus rapidly outpaced the initial supply and Allison's ability to produce new engines.

The inevitable comparison to the P-47 Thunderbolt regarding the aircraft's ruggedness somewhat overstated the F-84's status. The 523rd Squadron's 1st Lt Jacob Kratt, who had flown the P-47 during the final days of World War II with the 56th Fighter Group and was the most successful Korean War F-84 pilot in aerial combat, found the F-84 dependable and capable, but unremarkable. "I didn't think it was all that superior to the F-80 or the jets the Navy flew. I flew the P-47 and the F-84, and the P-47 was a lot more rugged than the F-84. But it held its own with any other jets that were flown in Korea."

The "plank wing" F-84 began the pilot joke that "If they built a runway that ran around the equator, Republic would design an airplane that would need every foot to get off." Pilot lore regarding the Thunderjet had it that all F-84s were equipped with a "sniffer" device that, upon passing takeoff speed, would search for the dirt at the end of the runway. When the "sniffer" could detect the dirt, the flight controls would come on and allow the pilot to take off. It was suggested a bag of dirt be carried in the nose gear well. Upon reaching takeoff speed, the pilot would pull a trigger that would dump the dirt under the wheels and fool the sniffer.

In fact, the Thunderjet's takeoff performance did leave much to be desired. During the hot Korean summer, with a full combat load, the F-84 routinely required all 10,000 feet of runway for takeoff, even using four rocket-assisted take-off (RATO) bottles, each providing 1,000 pounds of thrust for 14 seconds. In such conditions, all aircraft taking off after the lead had their visibility progressively obscured by the thick rocket exhaust smoke.

Because of its thick, straight wing, at low altitude the F-84 could quickly reach its Mach 0.82 limit at full throttle. While the engine had not yet reached full power, exceeding the Mach limit at low altitude would result in a violent pitch-up and structural failure of the wings. The airplane could be flown faster above 15,000ft, at the cost of severe buffeting. Airspeed could easily be controlled, which allowed safe dive-bombing from 10,000ft. When engaged with the MiG-15, the speed limitation proved troublesome since the F-84 was slower than the enemy fighter. With a maximum instantaneous turn load limitation of only 3 G, which was followed by a rapid loss of airspeed, the airplane could not turn tight enough to get away from an attacking enemy fighter. Jacob Kratt, the only F-84 pilot to score two victories in one fight, achieved his second victory by intentionally flying his F-84 into pitch-up. The pursuing MiGs were unable to follow the violent maneuver and one crashed. Luckily for Kratt, his airplane did not disintegrate but the airframe suffered heavy warping sufficient that it was written off after he returned to Suwon.

Jet power was not limited to fighter aircraft. The Air Force saw early on that increased speed was of paramount value for bombers. Development of a jet-powered bomber began in 1944, after the USAAF became aware of the existence of the Arado Ar-234, the world's first jet-powered bomber. In response to the USAAF request for proposals, North American Aviation submitted the NA-130, which won the award of a contract for three prototypes on September 8, 1944 as the XB-45. This Air Force contract was soon followed by contracts with Convair for the XB-46, Boeing for the XB-47, and Martin for the XB-48. All these proposed aircraft were far larger than the single-seat Ar-234, and would be powered by four to six turbojets.

The XB-45 first flew in late 1946 and proved superior in performance to the Convair XB-46, leading to a contract for production of the B-45A on January 2, 1947. The B-45 was a conservative design not that different aerodynamically from conventionally powered bombers of the period, other than the powerplant. While the Air Force had initially planned to field a large force of B-45s in five bomber groups and three photo-reconnaissance groups, the performance of the revolutionary Boeing XB-47 that finally flew in late 1947 was so superior that the contract for the B-45 was cut back in the face of the technical competition from Boeing and President Truman's budget cuts. In 1948, production was cut to 190 airframes, which was reduced to 142 when further budget cuts were announced on January 7, 1949.

The RB-45C developed for photo-reconnaissance was a great improvement in strategic photo-recon capability because its increased speed made it less susceptible to interception than the RB-29. Following the introduction of the MiG-15 in the Korean War that led to the loss of several RB-29s from the 91st Strategic Reconnaissance Squadron, three RB-45Cs of the 323rd Strategic Reconnaissance Squadron of the 91st Strategic Reconnaissance Wing were deployed to Japan to operate with the RB-29s. While they were under the operational control of the 84th Bomb Squadron administratively, they received maintenance and logistical support from the 91st SRS. MiG-15s intercepted and shot down RB-45C 48-0015 on December 4, demonstrating that the aircraft was vulnerable. Despite this inauspicious beginning, the RB-45Cs continued to operate unescorted in daylight over North Korea until the summer of 1951, when one narrowly escaped another interception by MiG-15s, after which they could only operate in daylight with an F-86 escort. In late 1952, following the election of Dwight Eisenhower as president, B-45Cs capable of carrying nuclear weapons were deployed to Japan as part of the US threat to use the atomic bomb in Korea as an inducement to the Communists to come back to the negotiations at Panmunjom.

While the F-80 and F-84 performed yeoman service during the Korean War, both first-generation fighters were eclipsed by the third jet fighter ordered by the Air Force, the first of the "second generation" of jet fighters to see service.

CHAPTER 4

MESSERSCHMITT VS TANK OVER THE YALU

Between December 1950 and July 1953, an air campaign unlike any before or since raged over the northwest corner of North Korea between the Chongchon and Yalu rivers, from the shores of the Yellow Sea to the highlands of the Taebaek Mountains that form the spine of the Korean peninsula.

The battle raged in the air above this region, in a large invisible "box" between 8,000 and 50,000 feet altitude, and was fought almost exclusively by two antagonists: those flying the US Air Force's premier air superiority day-fighter, the North American F-86 Sabre, and those flying the Soviet Red Air Force's premier interceptor, the Mikoyan-Gurevich MiG-15. The Sabre's official primary mission was protection of the B-29 bombers and other UN fighter-bombers operating over North Korea, and the official primary mission of the MiG-15 was protection of the vital bridges across the Yalu by which supplies reached the front lines from Manchuria and the crucial complex hydroelectric power in North Korea that powered both that country and much of Manchuria. But both sides frequently met and contested the air space when those primary missions were not in play, in combats that had more to do with an international duel for "superiority" between two opposing political systems.

The battles over what came to be known as "MiG Alley" became similar to the battles of jousting knights from the Middle Ages, as pilots – many of whom had begun their fighting careers on both sides in the air battles of World War II – sought to hone their warrior craft and come to understand what jet-powered air warfare was about. The battles were seen as contests of "the best vs the best" to see who was truly "the very best" as the outcomes of these fights became the measure of national prestige of the two major opponents, neither of whom could otherwise directly oppose the other without the threat of planetary annihilation, and could only do so here as long as neither side publicly admitted the truth of who fought whom. However, US Air Force pilots took every opportunity they had when speaking with correspondents to say they were fighting Russians, pointing out reports that signals intelligence units had recordings of air controllers giving instructions in Russian and telling stories of "red-headed pilots" baling out of MiGs.

On the Western side, the fights over MiG Alley became the one item of interest to news media in a war that had quickly descended into a battle of attrition reminiscent of World War I, a seemingly endless tit-for-tat struggle to score points in negotiations for a cease-fire that appeared impossible to achieve during most of those years of warfare. Media coverage of the war had become nearly nonexistent in American newspapers after the first year of the war concluded with an attempt to end the conflict through negotiations that seemed permanently blocked by Communist intransigence, while public support for the fighting waned to the point the Republican candidate for president in 1952, General Dwight D. Eisenhower, coasted to victory on a promise that "If elected, I will go to Korea," implying he would take steps to end the conflict. As this went on, Air Force public affairs officers constantly fanned the flames of an "ace race" with the American media to keep the reporters coming around. In fact, these battles had little or nothing to do with the ultimate outcome of the war, and many of the "lessons learned" turned out to be irrelevant if not outright wrong in the further development of jet air combat.

By the end of the war in Europe in May 1945, Germany was head and shoulders ahead of every other country in the development and operational use of jet aircraft. The jet-powered Me-262 and the rocket-powered Me-163 had seen limited operational use, and even more advanced designs were under development. Perhaps the most important aeronautical development was the swept wing. It was not a completely new concept. German aeronautical engineer Adolf Busemann had delivered a paper at the 1935 Volta Scientific Conference regarding how swept wings would reduce drag at high speeds, which would be capable of supersonic flight with the right powerplant. The Reichsluftfahrtsministerium (RLM), the German Air Ministry, declared swept-wing research classified in 1936. A 1940 paper demonstrated that swept wings gave a firm advantage at speeds above Mach 0.9; by 1941, the concept had been successfully tested in a wind tunnel. By 1945, Messerschmitt was working on an advanced Me-262 with wings swept to 40 degrees, called the *Pfeilflügel*, or "arrow wing." Kurt Tank at Focke-Wulf was working on the Ta-183 with a similar swept wing.

The Allies paid Germany the ultimate compliment of sending technical teams in the wake of the advancing armies to winnow through the records of German aviation companies and find every scientific and engineering paper and design, and then to track down and obtain the services of every German aeronautical designer and engineer. The Western Allies offered life in the United States or United Kingdom, bringing some 1,600 German scientists and engineers to the United States under Operation *Paperclip*. The Soviet Union's Operation *Osoaviakhim* saw more than 2,000 German scientists and engineers living in the Soviet occupation zone of Germany offered a trip to Moscow or a firing squad on the night of October 22, 1946; more than 23,000 Germans, including women and children, were eventually moved to the Soviet Union.

Due to the geographic location of the factories, the Americans became inheritors of the work done by Willy Messerschmitt and the engineering and technical personnel of his company in Bavaria, as well as similar material discovered at the Focke-Wulf factory in Bremen, while the Soviets found the records of Focke-Wulf's Kurt Tank as well as those of Messerschmitt in the archives of the RLM in Berlin. Postwar jet fighter design in the United States would be influenced more by the work of Messerschmitt, while Kurt Tank's ideas regarding jet fighter design were influential in the Soviet Union.

Five years later, the differing design philosophies of Messerschmitt and Tank would meet high in the skies of northern Korea, in "MiG Alley."

Fortunately for the United States, aircraft designer Edgar Schmued of North American Aviation was among the American personnel assigned to Operation *Paperclip*. Schmued, who was 46 years old in 1945, had fallen in love with aviation when he saw an airplane fly in his native Germany when he was eight years old. From then on, he was dedicated to the idea of becoming an aviation engineer. Self-taught, he went to work as an apprentice in a small aircraft engine manufacturing company in the last year of World War I. With aviation development crippled in postwar Germany by the terms of the Versailles Treaty, Schmued left for Brazil in 1925, where he found employment in the General Aviation Company, the aviation branch of the General Motors Corporation's Brazilian operation.

Schmued quickly built a reputation for solid work at General Aviation, and in 1931 he was sponsored by General Motors to emigrate to the United States, where he went to work for the Fokker Aircraft Corporation of America, owned by General Motors, where he finally achieved his dream of becoming an aircraft designer. Three years later, GM sold Fokker to the North American Aviation holding company. North American had been founded in 1928 as a company that bought and sold interests in airlines and other aviation-related companies. The Air Mail Act of 1934 ended such holding companies, and with the acquisition of Fokker, North American became an aircraft manufacturing company. James H. "Dutch" Kindelberger was recruited from Douglas Aircraft to run the new company.

Kindelberger moved the company headquarters from Maryland to Los Angeles, California, and closed the Fokker plant in New Jersey where Schmued worked. Schmued's wife was reluctant to move across the continent, and he took a position with Bellanca Aircraft in New York. This didn't work out and after a few months, Schmued was able to rejoin North American, since Kindelberger was looking for young designers. Sadly, while driving to Los Angeles, the Schmueds were involved in an auto accident in which his wife died and he was severely injured.

Once in Los Angeles, Schmued joined the design team Kindelberger had assembled to commence work on a series of trainers for the military as a preliminary design engineer. Kindelberger had determined the competition for this work was less difficult than competing with older established companies for higher-prestige projects. Over the next several years, Schmued was involved in the design of the GA-16 trainer that became the BC-1 and led to the famous T-6 Texan trainer series, and also worked on the O-47 observation plane. These aircraft used the most modern construction techniques, which Kindelberger saw would eventually put his designers in a position to compete with the likes of

Curtiss, Boeing and Douglas. The company first demonstrated its new expertise on a bigger project when it won the competition to build the NA-40, the progenitor of the B-25; Schmued designed the bombardier nose of the aircraft. Schmued's first foray into fighter design was the NA-50, a single-seater based on the T-6 trainer, 50 of which North American sold to the Peruvian Air Force.

Kindelberger was always on the outlook for opportunity, and managed to convince the Army Air Corps to let his design team inspect and disassemble the first Messerschmitt Bf-109 to arrive in the United States following its crash and capture in the Spanish Civil War. This connection to the Bf-109, and the later similarity of the early P-51 to the German fighter, led to an "urban myth" over the years that Schmued had actually worked for Messerschmitt and brought knowledge of the Bf-109 with him when he emigrated to America.

Schmued's reputation as a fighter designer was confirmed in 1940. The British Purchasing Commission was looking for a company to build additional Curtiss P-40s under license for use by the RAF, following the fall of France. When North American was contacted, Kindelberger's response was that the company was not interested in building a semi-obsolescent design, but could produce a state-of-the-art fighter for the RAF in 120 days. In 1981, speaking at a forum held at the Planes of Fame Air Museum in California about the development history of the P-51, Schmued explained that while the prototype of what would come to be known as the P-51 Mustang was indeed built in 120 days, "I had been playing with such a design for five years." When Kindelberger made his offer to the British, he knew all about Schmued's "hobby."

Through his long friendship with Jim McGowan, a consulting sales engineer for the Aluminum Corporation of America (ALCOA) based in Germany, Schmued had continued to receive German aviation and engineering journals that allowed him to stay current with the latest work in the German aviation industry, which was at the time the most advanced in the world; he was one of those who read Busemann's paper and found the concept interesting though unusable with available technology. Indeed, Schmued's detailed knowledge of German technique had been Kindelberger's main selling point in getting access to the captured Bf-109 the year before the British came calling.

Schmued's design went on to become the premier Allied fighter of the war, considered responsible for saving the American daylight bombing campaign when the P-51 Mustang's appearance over Berlin on March 6, 1944 convinced Luftwaffe leader Hermann Göring that "the jig was up," as he later told his American interrogators. With his extensive knowledge of German aviation, Schmued was one of the first aeronautical engineers invited to join Operation *Paperclip*. It would turn out to be one of the best decisions made by anyone in the history of US aviation.

North American had become involved in the new field of jet-powered aviation in 1944. The company had won a competition of proposals with Douglas and Chance-Vought to design and produce a jet-powered fighter for the Navy, which became the XFJ-1, later known as the Fury. The design was a straight-wing airplane using a tricycle landing gear, with flying surfaces very reminiscent of the P-51D Mustang. Its lines were marred by the fat fuselage required to carry sufficient fuel for the thirsty axial-flow General Electric J35-GE-2 that provided 3,820lb of thrust (replaced in the production aircraft by the Allison J-35A-2 with 4,000lb thrust). When it commenced flight testing on September 11, 1946, the airplane revealed an undistinguished maximum speed of 547mph, with little room for further development. Schmued hadn't liked the design from the outset.

Shortly after winning the Navy's fighter design competition for the Fury, North American received a contract in mid-1944 from the US Army Air Force for the development of a medium-range, single-seat, high-altitude jet-powered day escort-fighter/fighter-bomber, contracted as the XP-86. Wind-tunnel models of the design reveal an airplane with a slimmer fuselage than that of the FJ-1, but otherwise similar. Initial design studies showed the XP-86 would be lighter and thus faster than the FJ-1, with an estimated top speed of 582mph. Unfortunately, these early studies demonstrated that XP-86 would have about the same performance as its rivals, Lockheed's XP-80 and Republic's XP-84, both of which were more advanced in development than North American's design. There was a real fear that if something different couldn't be found to leapfrog the performance of the XP-86, it would be canceled.

Schmued went to Germany in the spring of 1945, where he gained access to the Messerschmitt records. He didn't have to wait for translation of the texts and was accompanied by North American aerodynamicist Larry Greene, who could read technical German. Schmued saw the advances the Germans had made since he had read Busemann's paper, and Greene also recognized the importance of the work. The two worked for a week, translating the material for North American's chief technical engineer, Harrison "Stormy" Storms, and engineer Dale Meyers. When the four returned to Los Angeles, they believed that coupling the wing with the new jet engine seemed to be the solution North American needed. With the design of the XP-86 at an advanced stage, many engineers at North American opposed the radical redesign that was suggested. Ed Horkey, the chief aerodynamicist, was overjoyed when Storms showed him what they had, but Joe Greer, head of the aerodynamics division, said the material might be wonderful but it was too late to put it to use because the XP-86 was too far along in design. Larry Waite, head of the technical section, said, "Get rid of it! Bury it!"

With technical management opposed, Schmued and Ed Horkey took the material directly to Dutch Kindelberger and NAA Vice President Lee Atwood, who both saw the wing as the solution that would save the XP-86 from cancellation. Kindelberger shared the information unofficially with the USAAF Technical Engineering Division at Dayton, and obtained verbal approval to look further into a redesign.

Chief Engineer Ray Rice was angry he had not been consulted, but nevertheless ordered wind-tunnel tests. The results demonstrated that a redesigned XP-86 with its wing swept 35 degrees, using the NACA 0009.5–64 airfoil at the root and NACA 0008.5–64 at the tip, would be able to fly faster than 600mph. Rice took the data to Dayton and showed it to General Lawrence Craigie, chief of the Air Technical Service's Engineering Division. Redesign would add six months to the project, but Craigie gave his approval and the Air Technical Division formally approved the change on November 1, 1945. It was perhaps the most important technical decision the division had made in its existence. Dutch Kindelberger promised the prototype would fly by mid-summer 1947. Project development costs incurred on the straight-wing design were absorbed by North American.

Beginning with the Bf-108 design, Messerschmitt had solved the problem of low-speed handling of a wing designed for high-speed flight by use of the Handley-Page slat, a section of the wing leading edge that could be extended and "drooped" at low speed to change the camber of the wing while increasing area, thus providing greater lift and stability. All of Messerschmitt's jet designs used this feature, as had their piston-powered predecessors. North American carefully studied the use of slats on the Me-262, going so far as to get the Air Force to give them a complete Me-262 wing for close study. A full-span leading edge slat would be a feature of the XP-86's wing, with the three prototypes and the first four production F-86s actually using Me-262 slat rollers.

The swept wing was not the only innovation. The traditional "rib and stringer" wing structure was replaced with a double skin structure containing "hat sections" between the two skins that gave room for self-sealing fuel tanks. The wing skins themselves were tapered throughout the length and width, from .250-inch thick at the wing root to .064 inch at the outer wing skin joint, to .032 inch at the wing tip. The tapered skins were so complex their production required specially designed milling machines that took 45 minutes to finish one skin.

Crucially, Schmued and Storms chose to keep the low position of the original horizontal stabilizer, at the base of the vertical fin in the redesign. At the time they made the decision, it was merely the continuation of previous practice, since that had been the position of the horizontal stabilizer on all North American designs going back to the NA-16. This was the decision that allowed the F-86 to eventually fly faster than the speed of sound, while its contemporaries – the MiG-15 and Hawker Hunter – would both be limited to sub-Mach 1 speed due to the placement of their stabilizers high on the vertical fin in a "T" position where it would not maintain sufficient control past the limiting Mach number. Schmued's decision to adopt the electrically adjustable stabilizer that Messerschmitt had fitted to the Me-262 allowed the prototype and the F-86A that followed to exceed the limiting Mach number of 0.95 and pass Mach 1 with just enough control to slip through the "sound barrier."

Air Force tests of the Bell X-1 following its successful supersonic flight in 1947 led to the development of the "all-flying tail," in which the horizontal stabilizer assumes the role of the elevator, while the elevator becomes a trim tab; this allowed transonic speed with full control. The F-86's electrically adjustable stabilizer was easily adapted to use this feature, which first appeared on the F-86E and made the design the first operationally successful transonic airplane. The "stabilator," as the all-flying tail came to be known, was fully hydraulically operated and had an "artificial feel" built in for tactile control-force feedback to the pilot. This tail would also allow the F-86 to out-turn its eventual opponent, the MiG-15, which lacked both the all-flying tail and hydraulic control.

The XP-86 was powered by the General Electric J35-C-3, producing 4,000lb of thrust; it was a single-spool, axial-flow turbojet with an 11-stage compressor and single-stage turbine. This was the same engine that powered the Republic XP-84. The Republic prototype first flew in 1946, and on September 7, 1946, it set a US national speed record of 611mph. Two years later, on September 15, 1948, an F-86 powered by the same engine (though now built by Allison rather than Chevrolet) set a US national speed record of 671mph in similar conditions. The value of swept wings was clearly demonstrated.

The XP-86 prototype, company designation NA-140, Air Force serial number 45-59597, rolled out of the North American factory on the south side of Los Angeles' Mines Field (today's Los Angeles International – the site of the North American factory is now the cargo area for the airport) on August 8, 1947. The airplane was the result of 801,386 engineering hours and 340,594 drafting hours over the previous two years. In early September, the prototype was disassembled and trucked 75 miles up the winding Sierra Highway through Newhall Pass to Muroc Field (now Edwards AFB) on the California high desert. Reassembled and having passed all the ground tests, North American test pilot George "Wheaties" Welch first lifted off the dry lake bed runway in the early morning of October 1, 1947. Welch had already entered the history books when he just missed becoming America's first ace of World War II, shooting down four attacking Japanese aircraft over Pearl Harbor on December 7, 1941; he achieved a final victory score of 16 over two combat tours in the Pacific before being injured in a crash in 1944 that removed him from operational flying and sent him to North American as a test pilot. North American's chief test pilot Bob Chilton flew chase for Welch in the XP-82 Twin Mustang with a company photographer in the other cockpit.

The first flight lasted one hour and 18 minutes and was not without drama. Shortly after liftoff, Welch experienced difficulty getting the main landing gear to lock in the "up" position and had to recycle it twice to clean up the airframe. Ten minutes after takeoff, he reached 35,000 feet. Leveling out, the indicated airspeed accelerated to 320 knots, which Welch estimated to be 0.90 Mach. Minutes later, he rolled into a 40-degree dive and turned west. The airplane was behaving just fine, but the airspeed indicator remained unmoving at approximately 350 knots, which was unexpected. At 29,000 feet, there was a small wing rock. Welch corrected the roll and increased his dive angle. Suddenly, the airspeed indicator jumped to 410 knots and continued up. He pulled out of the dive at 25,000 feet and leveled off, reducing power. The wing rocked again, while the airspeed indicator jumped back to 390 knots. George Welch had just become the first pilot to report instrument readings that would be referred to as "Mach jump."

When Welch brought the prototype back to land on the lake bed, he was unable to get the nose gear to lock in the down position. This was potentially disastrous for the program if the prototype was lost on its first flight. Ed Horkey was in radio contact with Welch, and later remembered:

> George radioed that he would stay with the airplane and try to bring her home. But he was going to land on the dry lake bed, not on one of the runways. He made a smooth, very nose high approach. Touching down on the lake bed, George let the airplane just coast along with no brake application. As the airplane slowed and the nose started irretrievably over, the nose gear swung forward and locked into place, with George quietly exclaiming, "Lucky! Lucky!"

The North American engineers quickly discovered the source of the problem. Horkey explained:

> We found out later that someone in landing gear hydraulics wasn't impressed with the nose gear load data furnished by the wind tunnel crew. They installed a cylinder piston on the nose gear retraction system that was too small and not the one called for. Normally, nose wheels rotated down to the rear, so that air loads would force the gear down even if the hydraulics failed. However, the XP-86 nose gear rotated down to the front, against the air stream. The immediate fix on the XP-86 was to use two of the original cylinder/pistons, then we replaced them later with the correct one.

Over the years, some historians have argued that George Welch flew the XP-86 beyond Mach 1 during this flight when the airspeed indicator acted up, thus breaking the "sound barrier" two weeks before Chuck Yeager did with the Bell X-1 rocket plane. This is probably based on the fact that he did take the XF-100 Super Sabre prototype supersonic during its first flight on May 25, 1953, and subsequent tests clearly demonstrated the XP-86 could reach Mach 1.02–1.04 in a dive. While it would have been in accordance with Welch's outlook to flight testing, the US Air Force firmly states that the first supersonic flight took place on October 14, 1947. Some have argued both statements could be right, since the XP-86 would have only been able to accomplish this feat in a dive and was unable to achieve sustained supersonic flight, while the X-1 did demonstrate sustained supersonic flight. Welch died in an F-100A on October 12, 1954, and never claimed to have gone supersonic on the XP-86's first flight.

Welch experienced difficulty in raising the main gear immediately after takeoff and was ordered to take things easy for the first flight. During the next several tests, following the difficulty on the first flight, the XP-86 was flown with the gear down for safety reasons and did not fly with the gear retracted until late October, after Yeager's flight. North American's final flight reports submitted to the Air Force hint Welch flew the XP-86 past Mach 1 on November 19, 1947, and again two days later.

Officially, the XP-86 first went supersonic in a dive on April 26, 1948, which was not publicly announced due to national security. Famed British test pilot Roland Beamont flew an XP-86 prototype that day and stated in his autobiography *Testing Years* that he exceeded Mach 1 on his second dive. North American's Ed Horkey recalled:

A visiting British pilot came over and checked out in the XP-86. He was told about the phenomenon he might encounter (i.e. breaking the sonic barrier), and the secrecy restrictions. Unfortunately, he had an open radio channel and all the nearby towers got an earful when he went through Mach 1.0. The facts soon became common knowledge throughout the aviation industry. The June 14, 1948, issue of *Aviation Week* announced the XP-86 had gone supersonic.

North American's initial test flights were so successful that Phase II flight tests began in December 1947. Phase II test pilot Major Ken Chustrom recalled:

In late November 1947, North American called Colonel Al Boyd, Chief of Air Force Flight Test, recommending delay of the start of Phase II flight tests because of heavy rains at Muroc, that flooded the dry lake bed. Colonel Boyd suggested I visit Muroc and inspect the conditions to determine if I could operate from the runway at North Base. After a few days at North Base evaluating the lake bed, the runway, and the XP-86, I called Colonel Boyd and recommended we proceed.

Colonel Boyd notified North American that the Air Force would begin flying the Phase II tests of the XP-86 immediately. North American expressed concern because of the extremely short runway conditions. However, the Air Force prevailed and I made my first take off on December 2, 1947. This was a "get acquainted" flight, and since there were 110 squawks (i.e., complaints), I asked that the XP-86 be refueled for a second flight that day. This allowed for performance checks and speed points at intermediate altitudes.

I was very impressed with the XP-86's speed improvement over the Republic XP-84 which had the same engine with a straight wing. The maximum speed for the XP-84 was 615mph, while the maximum speed of the XP-86 was in excess of 650mph! Our Phase II flights were accomplished in 11 flights totaling 10 hours, 17 minutes, and all done in just six days! My conclusion to the Phase II tests, and supported by our data, was that the Air Force now had the very best jet fighter developed to this date, anywhere in the world.

The Air Force had been so eager to adopt the F-86 that an initial order for 33 of the NA-151, the P-86A, was made in November 1946, with the quantity increased to 221 the next month. The first production aircraft flew in May 1948 and the next month the Air Force changed the designation from P ("Pursuit") to F ("Fighter") and the F-86A was given the emotive name "Sabre." In February 1949, the 94th Fighter-Interceptor Squadron, Eddie Rickenbacker's "Hat in the Ring" unit, received their first F-86A-1; at the same time, 333 additional Sabres were ordered. By August 1949, the 1st Fighter Wing had 72 Sabres parked on its ramp at March AFB, California. That June, the 4th Fighter-Interceptor Wing – descended from the RAF Eagle Squadrons of World War II – received its first Sabres at Langley AFB outside Washington, DC and had all 72 present at the end of September. By the time the North Korean People's Army crossed the 38th Parallel on June 25, 1950, the US Air Force had five fighter-interceptor wings equipped with the F-86A based around the country.

While all this was going on in the United States, a far different aircraft design and development program was underway simultaneously in the Soviet Union.

The Soviet work was heavily influenced by Kurt Tank's design of a jet fighter, the Ta-183. Tank began work on the design in response to the RLM's Emergency Fighter Program announced in July 1944, which ended all development of piston-powered aircraft and accelerated designs of jet-powered aircraft. Tank's design team, led by Hans Multhopp, had commenced work in 1942 to create a jet fighter, known at the time as Focke-Wulf *Projekt VI*. Their emphasis was on creating a transonic aircraft.

By late 1944, the design was sufficiently complete that the RLM gave it the designation Ta-183. The BMW-003 turbojet was the expected initial powerplant. In order to develop as much thrust as possible for a single-engine design, the engine was fed by an annular air intake in the nose, with a short exhaust pipe to reduce loss of thrust. The intake was positioned under the cockpit floor, while the cockpit was pressurized and the pilot sat under a clear bubble canopy. Significantly, the design featured a wing swept back 40 degrees. The vertical fin was swept at 60 degrees and added about one-third to the overall length past the exhaust. A small stabilizer sat atop the vertical fin in a "T" position. What appeared to be elevators on the stabilizer were actually trim tabs, while the main pitching force was actually provided by what looked like "ailerons" on the wing. These control surfaces were well behind the center of gravity, and thus acted as "elevons" to provide both pitch and roll control, as did those on the Me-163 Komet tailless rocket fighter.

The Ta-183 "Design II" was entered in the official competition ordered by the Oberkommando der Luftwaffe (OKL) at the end of 1944. On February 28, 1945, the Junkers EF-128 was selected for further development, while the Ta-183 achieved second place. However, in late March, the OKL decided the Ta-183 was the superior design and Tank was told to arrange mockups and to plan for full production. The Ta-183 had a planned speed of 1,000km/h (620mph) at 7,000m (22,970ft) and would be armed with guided missiles or two 30mm Mk 108 cannon. A production rate of 300 aircraft per month would be achieved by the end of 1945.

First prototype flight was ordered for May, but on April 18, as British troops occupied the Focke-Wulf factory, no work had yet begun.

While little was done by the western Allies with the material seized at the factory, the design documents and a complete set of blueprints submitted to the RLM were among the records shipped to the Soviet Union following the German surrender.

Soviet work on jet aircraft had only begun weeks before the end of World War II, which put the Red Air Force well behind both the RAF and USAAF in operating jet fighters. In April 1945, the Council of People's Commissars directed the Optyno-Konstrooktorskoye Byuros (OKB – design bureau) of Aleksandr Yakovlev and that of Artem Mikoyan and Mikhail Gurevich to commence immediate work on jet fighters to be powered by captured German Jumo 004 and BMW 003 turbojets.

The Yakovlev OKB was first with the Yak-15, a very straightforward mating of the Jumo-004 engine and the engine nacelle of the Me-262 to the Yak-3 piston-engine fighter. The Yak-3 was modified by placing the jet in the nose in place of the piston engine, with the exhaust below the wing just ahead of the cockpit. Armament was to be two Nudelman NS-23 23mm cannon mounted in the upper nose above the engine. Taxi tests began in October 1945, but the heat of the jet exhaust melted the aluminum airframe behind it and set the rubber tail wheel on fire. Modifications to remedy this took until December 1945.

While Yakovlev had been ordered to create what was basically an interim design, Mikoyan and Gurevich were ordered to create a completely original design, powered by two BMW 003 turbojets. Designed as an interceptor, it was to be armed with either a 57mm or 37mm cannon and two 23mm cannons, with a top speed of 900km/h (559mph) at sea level and 910km/h (545mph) at 5,000 meters (16,470ft). The three prototypes were to be ready to fly by March 1946. The MiG bureau called it the I-300; it was later officially designated MiG-9.

The I-300 had an all-metal structure, with a straight wing layout. The engines were mounted side-by-side, low in the fuselage behind the cockpit with short exhausts that exited just behind the wing trailing edge. The cockpit was unpressurized. The armament was a single 57mm N-57 mounted in the intake splitter with 28 rounds, and two Nudelman NS-23 23mm cannon with 80 rounds. Construction of the three I-300s began in the summer of 1945 and the first prototype was completed and began manufacturer's testing on December 30. Taxi tests soon revealed that the exhaust created a low-pressure area under the rear fuselage that caused the airplane to tilt tail-down, while the rigidly mounted heatshield caused deformation of the underside of the rear fuselage since the steel and the duralumin skin each had different heat expansion characteristics. Both rear fuselage and heatshield were redesigned.

The Yak-15 and MiG-9 prototypes were trucked to Ramenskoye airfield, the main V-VS flight test center, in late March 1946. Legend has it that the Mikoyan-Gurevich and Yakovlev representatives tossed a coin on April 24, 1946 to see which would become the first Soviet jet to fly. The MiG-9 won and entered the history books with the first Soviet jet flight in a six-minute first flight. The Yak-15 took off and made one circuit before landing with an overheating engine.

Flight testing through 1946 revealed both designs were disappointing. The MiG-9 demonstrated stability problems with the airframe and vibration problems with the new heatshield. The first prototype suffered a fatal crash during a demonstration in front of high-ranking officials on July 11, due to the failure of the attachment lugs of the wing leading-edge fairings, which hit the horizontal stabilizers. The second and third prototypes commenced flight testing in August. In September, the horizontal stabilizer of the second prototype disintegrated during flight, but the pilot was able to land safely. Official state trials began December 17, 1946; the tail of the third prototype suffered a similar failure in February 1947, which forced further delay while the tail units of the two surviving prototypes were reinforced.

The Yak-15, being more conservative, was more successful, with flight tests completed by July 1946. These revealed that the top speed was limited by the thick wing inherited from the Yak-3, with a top speed of only 786km/h (488mph). The tailwheel landing gear meant that the exhaust damaged the airfield. Two more prototypes were ordered, powered by the RD-10, the Soviet reverse-engineered Jumo 004. With its low speed and short range, the Yak-15 was seen as more of a conversion trainer to introduce pilots to jet flight. The MiG-9 was scarcely better, suffering many engine problems and frequent flame-outs in flight. Neither design achieved the required performance.

In December 1946, the Council of Ministers ordered production of 50 Yak-15s and 40 MiG-9s. All were produced in time to participate in the May Day flypast over Moscow on May 1, 1947. Western observers were surprised that the Soviets had produced jets so quickly, but the designs were easily dismissed as being technologically behind both the

British Gloster Meteor and the American Lockheed F-80 Shooting Star, both of which were in first-line service. The dismissal of Soviet aircraft development and the belief these two primitive jets were the best they could come up with would lead to a nasty surprise three years later.

In March 1946, shortly after Soviet intelligence obtained performance information on the new American B-36 bomber, the Venno-Vozdushnye Sily (V-VS–the Red Air Force) issued a requirement for a jet-powered bomber interceptor capable of a top speed of 1,000km/h (621mph) and an operational ceiling of 14,000 meters (45,932 feet), able to operate from unimproved airfields. The main problem for the Soviets in achieving such performance was the lack of a modern jet engine. The Germans had been unable to successfully develop high-powered jet engines before the end of the war, which limited the Soviets in what they could do since they were restricted to using available German technology. They did get hold of early examples of the advanced axial compressor Junkers 012 and BMW 018 engines, but full development of these engines would take several years. Minister of Aviation Mikhail Khrunichev and designer Andrei S. Yakovlev suggested to Josef Stalin that an attempt be made to buy the conservative but fully developed Rolls-Royce Nene engine, which had the necessary power and could be reverse-engineered in minimum time. Stalin was said to have replied with incredulity, "What fool will sell us his secrets?"

As it turned out, the British Labour Government was foolish enough to do so. Prime Minister Clement Attlee (who had been described by Winston Churchill during the war as "a modest man of modest achievements") was keen to promote a thaw in Anglo-Soviet relations. When the Soviet ambassador let it be known that Soviet scientists and engineers would welcome an opportunity to visit the Rolls-Royce factory to learn about British design, Attlee quickly made the invitation. A three-man Soviet trade mission, which included aircraft designer Artem Mikoyan and engine designer Vladimir Klimov – both of whom were entirely unknown in the West – visited Britain. Minister of Trade Sir Stafford Cripps was more than happy to approve purchase of 25 Nenes and a license for Soviet production, with the stipulation that the engines would only be used for civil purposes, to which the Soviets easily agreed.

The design staff at Grumman Aviation, which was currently trying to get hold of the Nene to power their XF9F-2 jet fighter prototype, were incredulous when they heard of the decision, as was nearly every other American involved in aircraft development. The American ambassador protested against the decision to Attlee, who pointed to the Soviet agreement not to put the engines to military use. In the end, the Soviets never paid the license fee; when they were sued for it by Rolls-Royce, they refused payment on the grounds that both the RD-45 (the "reverse-engineered" Nene) and the Klimov VK-1 (the ultimate Soviet development of the Nene) were "essentially new" in design, and that they had never used the Nene as it was developed by Rolls-Royce, other than the 25 engines they had purchased initially.

Within a month of the arrival of the engines in the Soviet Union, Klimov and his design staff at Factory 45 were hard at work reverse-engineering the Nene for production as the RD-45. Both the Soviets and the Americans – after Grumman convinced General Electric to obtain a license to produce the Nene as the J-42 – took the largely hand-built Rolls-Royce product and modified it for mass industrial production, as Packard had done with the Merlin engine during World War II.

With a suitable powerplant at hand, Artem Mikoyan and Mikhail Gurevich were ordered to create a high-performance jet fighter to use the engine. The two designers were determined to create an airplane that was a generation ahead of the jets then being flown by Western air forces. They had the same swept-wing research Edgar Schmued had found in Germany, and had gone so far as to produce a swept-wing flying testbed in 1945, the piston-engined "pusher" layout, MiG-8 *Utka* ("Duck"). The commencement of work on what would become the MiG-15 was only several months behind North American's commencement of redesign of the XP-86.

The I-310 that emerged had a wing swept at 37 degrees (commonly described as 35 degrees since that was the sweep angle of the main spar), close to what Schmued had found optimal, with the wing mounted mid-fuselage as had been the case with the MiG-9. It bore a general likeness to Kurt Tank's Ta-183, which might have been the result of the Soviets having worked further on the wind-tunnel models of the Tank fighter that had been brought to the USSR. The fuselage had been "fattened" from the original design to make room for the centrifugal-flow Nene/RD-45 engine, which meant the airframe was less stable directionally and thus required an enlarged vertical fin and rudder from the original design; keeping the exhaust short to reduce loss of thrust meant the fin was swept at 56 degrees to put the rudder as far aft as possible to maintain directional control. This larger fin and rudder increased roll stability, reducing the ability to bank quickly, which was resolved by giving the wings two degrees of anhedral, which reduces roll stability. The one mistake made was to mount the horizontal stabilizer high on the vertical fin in the "T" position, which was done in order to place the horizontal stabilizers and elevators as far aft on the airframe as possible to increase pitching moment. The lack of the electrically adjustable stabilizer developed by Messerschmitt, and the Russian failure to discover the all-flying tail until a shot-down F-86E was studied, meant that the MiG-15 would remain subsonic.

The Soviets were well aware of the American B-36 bomber, which was the obvious carrier of atomic bombs for any attack on the USSR, and the purpose of the MiG-15 was to climb to that bomber's operating altitude of 45–48,000 feet and blow the monster apart with cannon fire. Thus, the airplane was optimized for a high rate of climb and to fly at a maximum altitude of 50,000 feet. The heavy cannon armament of an N-37D 37mm cannon and two NS-23KM 23mm cannons was optimized for destruction of bombers. It would later be found over Korea that two hits by the 37mm cannon or eight hits from the 23mm weapons were enough to bring down a B-29, and that one hit by the 37mm cannon was sufficient to knock down any F-86, F-84, F-80, F9F, or Meteor. The fighter was built strongly for operation from primitive airfields; in combat this would mean that it would stand up well to the standard USAF fighter armament of six .50-caliber machine guns carried by the F-86. In fact, the F9F Panther, with its armament of four 20mm cannon, would have greater individual success against MiG-15s, even though the first-generation Navy jet was otherwise inferior to the second-generation Soviet fighter. Navy Lt E. Royce Williams, Jr. proved this on November 18, 1952, when he shot down four MiG-15s of a formation of seven he fought flying a cannon-armed F9F-5 Panther.

Unlike Schmued, who opted for the Handley-Page slats used by Messerschmitt for low-speed handling, Mikoyan and Gurevich used wing fences that were originally developed by Kurt Tank to control airflow over the swept wings at low speed (which Tank himself used when he developed the Ta-183 as the Pulqui II in Argentina in the early 1950s). The fences were not as effective as the slats of the F-86 were at low speed, though the "hard edge" wing gave better performance at higher speeds. The F-86 would lose the slats in the later F-86F, opting for a hard edge "6-3" wing with increased area, though the slats would return on that wing in the final F-86F subtype and the Canadian-built Sabre Mk 6.

The I-310 prototype first flew at Ramenskoye on December 30, 1947, 90 days after George Welch had lifted the XP-86 off the Muroc lake bed. During that first, largely trouble-free flight, the prototype achieved a maximum speed of 1,042km/h (647mph) at 3,000 meters (9,800ft). It was the second Soviet swept-wing jet to fly, following the flight of the Lavochkin La-160, a high-speed experimental test aircraft, on June 24, 1947. Further development demonstrated the designers had achieved their goals, though the lack of an all-flying tail limited maximum speed to 0.92 Mach, and in later tests the airplane exhibited a disturbing stall-spin that was difficult for an inexperienced pilot to recover from. Over Korea, American pilots would witness MiGs enter high-speed stalls, then "swap ends" and snap end over end into a spin as they went out of control; this was caused by control reversal of the unboosted elevators due to sonic wave attachment to the high-placed tailplane, which led to "departure from controlled flight." Below 162 knots airspeed, the airplane's control became "soggy." The manually pumped pneumatic brakes faded fast and a too-fast landing would end up running out of runway as the brakes failed. Nevertheless, the MiG-15 was ordered into mass production, with the first production airplane taking flight on December 31, 1948.

The rushed development of both the engine and airframe led to initial operational problems. The "Mean Time Between Failure" of the Klimov RD-45 engine was less than ten hours. Metal for high-stress parts of both the airframe and engine was initially substandard, and production quality control in the factory was nearly nonexistent with imprecise production tolerances. Performance difficulties with individual aircraft were traced to wings that didn't exactly match. These production problems were reduced by the time the MiG-15 entered combat over Korea, but the handling problems remained. Lacking hydraulic flying controls, Soviet pilots quickly learned that if they could not shoot down a Sabre in a high-speed turning fight within the first third of the turn, the airplane would enter the deadly high-speed snap if they attempted to increase G-load and keep their turn tight enough to stay with the enemy fighter; at lower speeds, the MiG could out-turn its opponent, although if speed bled off below 330 knots the Sabre's slatted wing gave it the advantage. The lack of a G-suit meant that MiG-15 pilots could never turn as tightly as an American in his Sabre without blacking out.

In September 1949, the definitive MiG-15(SD), powered by the Klimov VK-1, an uprated Nene development producing 5,922lb thrust, completed manufacturer's flight tests. The airplane had hydraulically powered ailerons that were 21 percent larger to increase roll, though they were still hard to deploy at high speed. Redesigned speed brakes eliminated the pitch-up moment experienced on deployment of the earlier type. Official tests were completed in December 1949, and what would come to be known as the MiG-15bis began to reach operational units in the summer of 1950. The definitive MiG-15 had a thrust-to-weight ratio of 0.60:1, 30 percent better than that of the Sabre, which gave it a dramatic rate of climb: 4.62 minutes to get to 10,000 meters (32,800 ft).

As with the USAF, the V-VS assigned the first MiG-15s to elite units. The 324th IAD (Air Division) based at Kubinka outside Moscow was the first unit to get the new fighter in early 1949. Seventy-five percent of the unit's pilots were Great Patriotic War (World War II) veterans. When they flew 45 MiG-15s over Red Square in Moscow for the 1949 May Day parade, Western military observers were shocked to see an airplane in use that so obviously was the equal of the F-86 that was just entering service. When 52 MiG-15s flew over the Tushino Air Show that July, it was proof the airplane was fully in service. Ninety MiG-15s flew over Moscow on November 7 to celebrate the 32nd anniversary of the October Revolution. By the time the Korean War erupted with the North Korean invasion, three V-VS fighter divisions, each equipped with 120 MiG-15s, were in frontline service. The first units equipped with the airplane had deployed to China in the spring of 1950, where they provided air defense; the MiG-15 scored its first aerial victory on April 28, 1950, when Major Keleynikov of the 29th GvIAP (Gvardeyskiy Istrebetelnaya Aviatsonniy Polk, Guards Air Regiment) shot down a Nationalist Chinese F-5E Lightning (photo-recon version of the P-38) outside Shanghai.

One design difference between the two fighters would result in a significant difference of results in air combat – the ergonomic design of the cockpits. The Sabre's cockpit was atop the jet intake, positioning the pilot high and giving him good visibility over the nose. The fully blown plastic canopy, the sides of which were below the pilot's shoulders, conferred superb visibility, particularly to the ever-important "six o'clock," the position of choice for an attacker. The MiG-15 opted to place the pilot lower in the airframe, with the jet intake bifurcated to go to either side of the cockpit. Sitting lower in the cockpit, the MiG pilot had reduced visibility over the nose. The canopy was made of two pieces of plexiglass, reinforced with a relatively heavy frame. The canopy and seating reduced visibility to the rear. Additionally, the fact the Sabre's cockpit was pressurized while that of the MiG was not led to a significant difference in pilot ability in high-altitude combat, since the Sabre pilot could breathe more easily than could his opponent.

Overall, Sabre and MiG were well matched, with each having similar overall performance and strengths where the other had weaknesses, which controlled the way the pilot of each would fight. Soviet pilots almost always began the fight with an altitude advantage, allowing them to dive on the enemy. The Sabre could turn tighter and had better overall control, and could usually out-dive the Soviet fighter since it enjoyed the ability to go supersonic. The MiG's superior climb rate allowed the pilot to break off combat by climbing, which also put him in a superior position to turn the tables once he had outdistanced his enemy.

The two fighters were so well matched that individual pilot ability became decisive in determining the outcome of combat. The Soviet and American pilots who met each other over the Yalu in 1951 were so evenly matched in flying experience and equipment that the victory-loss ratio would be 1:1. The difference in personnel replacement policies would become decisive as the combat extended over years. American pilots served individual tours, which meant that there was always a core of combat-experienced pilots in the squadrons. Soviet pilots served their unit's tour, with a complete unit replacing the one leaving. This meant that there was a period of at least a few months after a Soviet unit entered combat where the lack of overall pilot experience meant their opponents had the edge in a fight. American pilots could always tell when they were flying against experienced Soviet pilots as opposed to the far less experienced Chinese and North Koreans who entered combat in late 1951. Still, war in the stratosphere over MiG Alley was a fraught experience for both Russians and Americans to the last day of combat.

CHAPTER 5

HOLDING THE LINE

While in Japan and Korea plans were being quickly activated for the evacuation of Americans in Korea, the first full day of the war saw frenzied activity in Washington. Secretary Acheson telephoned President Truman at 0200 hours on Sunday, June 25, at which time the decision was made to seek action by the UN Security Council, scheduled to meet in New York at 1500 hours. The US resolution calling on North Korea to cease aggression was approved in a 9-0 vote, with Yugoslavia abstaining. The vote was only possible due to the absence of the Soviet delegation, which had been boycotting the UN since January over issues involving Germany; the Soviet absence at this crucial moment would later be claimed as evidence there had been no collusion between Stalin and Kim il-Sung to invade the south.

While the vote was going on in New York City, Secretary of State Dean Acheson, Secretary of Defense Louis Johnson, Secretary of the Army Frank Pace, Chairman of the Joint Chiefs General Omar Bradley and the other joint chiefs conferred at the Pentagon all day. President Truman flew back from Missouri, arriving mid-afternoon. He, Acheson, Johnson, Pace, and Bradley conferred in Blair House, the temporary presidential residence, until midnight. There the first decisions leading to all-out American commitment in Korea were made.

Writing later in his memoirs, President Truman recalled his thoughts while flying back to Washington: how the democracies had not stopped Mussolini in Ethiopia or Japan in Manchuria, and how the British and French could have stopped Hitler at Munich with determination. After five years of what he had come to believe was Stalin's duplicity, it was clear to him that this action had been taken with Stalin's approval. The invasion of South Korea instantly placed America's prestige at stake, what Acheson described as "the shadow cast by power, which is a very important deterrent."

By 1950, President Harry S. Truman no longer felt he was living in the shadow of Franklin D. Roosevelt. When he walked into Blair House late that afternoon, he had already immediately made the critical decision after Acheson's first call. The president and his advisers were unanimous that the attack was an act of Communist aggression against the West and a violation of the UN Charter. Opposing the invasion was the only way to convince the Soviets they must avoid provoking World War III.

In New York, the Security Council adopted a resolution calling on member nations to supply such aid as necessary to the Republic of Korea in order to repel the North Korean attack. Following the vote, President Truman immediately authorized General MacArthur to employ United States air and naval forces to support South Korea, and named him Supreme Allied Commander of United Nations Forces. After dinner, further reports were received of the complete collapse of the ROK Army. American policy had always been to avoid fighting on the Asian mainland, but the situation now appeared to require at least a limited commitment of US ground forces to stabilize the situation. General Bradley counseled that such a decision should be delayed a few days to see how things worked out, which the president accepted.

The morning of June 29, a patrolling flight of F-80s shot down an Il-10 and a Yak-9 that attempted to attack Suwon. That afternoon, despite the danger from the NKPAF (North Korean People's Air Force), General MacArthur flew to Korea in his Lockheed C-121 Constellation, "Bataan," with FEAF commander General Stratemeyer and the rest of his personal staff, widely known as "the Bataan Gang" since they had served with him in the Philippines before the outbreak of the Pacific War, to receive a first-hand briefing on the situation. Due to the danger of enemy attack, the general's plane was escorted by four F-80s from the 80th Fighter-Interceptor Squadron and four F-51s that had hurriedly been recommissioned by the 8th Wing.

While MacArthur was on the field, several enemy aircraft were spotted approaching and were intercepted at low level by the F-51s. 2nd Lt Orrin R. Fox shot down two Il-10s, while 1st Lt Harry L. Sandlin was credited with an "La-7" that was most likely a misidentified Yak-9 and 1st Lt Richard L. Burns from the 35th FBS was credited with an Il-10. One of the Il-10s attempted to escape and was shot down by an F-80. General Stratemeyer later messaged the 8th Wing that MacArthur had been "very impressed" with the result.

That day, the North Koreans captured Kapyong and advanced to the north shore of the Han River. Heavy fighting raged around Kimpo airfield as the last ROK forces escaped from Seoul. MacArthur ordered strikes north of the 38th Parallel to reduce the flow of supplies to North Korean forces in South Korea. General Stratemeyer ordered air attacks on the Han River bridges and North Korean troops massing north of the river. Ten B-26s attacked the bridges, while F-80s patrolled overhead. In one of the few times when the F-82s were used in a ground support role, two flights of F-82Gs from the 86th Fighter All-Weather Squadron attacked North Korean troops along the Han River with napalm for the first time in the war.

The B-29s newly arrived at Kadena were not able to fly on June 29, due to bad weather, but on June 30, 15 Superfortresses bombed suspected North Korean troops along the north bank of the Han River, using 260lb fragmentation bombs. When the Superfortresses turned away to return to Kadena, several Yak-9s attacked the formation, and one was shot down by the B-29 gunners to score the B-29's first aerial victory of the war. American advisors were later able to examine the target and reported there were no North Korean troops or equipment in the designated bombing area. They recommended that future B-29 direct-support bombing strikes be flown only if the situation on the ground was completely hopeless.

At the same time the B-29s were flying their first wartime mission, the NKPAF returned to hit Suwon airfield south of Seoul in the early afternoon. C-54s were flying in from Japan with ammunition for the ROK troops. Four Yak-9s strafed a grounded F-82 and a B-26 Invader. Later that afternoon, another flight of Yaks caught a C-54 in the landing pattern and damaged it. They made a second pass over the field and strafed a second C-54 on the ground, which caught fire.

With MacArthur's approval to bomb targets in North Korea, 18 B-26s attacked Heijo airfield near the North Korean capital of Pyongyang and claimed 25 enemy aircraft destroyed. The 8th Tactical Reconnaissance Squadron (TRS) flew the first jet photo-reconnaissance mission when 1st Lt Bryce Poe II flew an RF-80A to photograph North Korean airfields near Pyongyang, and the 31st Strategic Reconnaissance Squadron (Photographic) flew its first RB-29 mission over Korea from Yokota AB, Japan.

The rail yards and lines around Pyongyang, Chongjin, Wonsan, Hungnam and Rashin were high-priority targets. Additionally, what passed for the North Korean aircraft and armaments industry was located in Pyongyang, while Wonsan was North Korea's most modern port and the site of oil refineries; Hungnam was the location for chemical and light metals industries, while the harbor town of Chongjin held iron foundries and rail yards. Rashin, only 60 miles from the major Soviet base at Vladivostok in Siberia, was the site of the major North Korean naval base as well as oil storage tanks and rail lines.

On July 3, the Strategic Air Command's 15th Air Force was ordered to send the 22nd and 92nd bomb wings to Japan on temporary duty. The B-29s of the 22nd Wing began to arrive at Johnson and Yokota AFBs on July 10, followed a week later by those from the 92nd. Two days earlier, on July 8, General Stratemeyer had formed FEAF Bomber Command to operate both the FEAF and SAC bomber units. Major General Emmet M. "Rosie" O'Donnell, another veteran of the B-29 campaign against Japan, was placed in command.

At 0130 hours on June 30, Ambassador Muccio reported to Acheson that "things were desperate on the peninsula," telling him furthermore that MacArthur had decided to formally request authority to commit ground troops. The Joint Chiefs received the general's cable at 0300 hours. His words were fateful: "The only assurance for holding of the present line, and the ability to regain the lost ground, is through the introduction of US ground forces into the Korean battle area. To continue to utilize the forces of our Air and Navy without an effective ground element cannot be decisive." MacArthur stated that upon approval he would send a regimental combat team to stabilize the front, followed by as many as two divisions of his forces in Japan to undertake a counteroffensive. He concluded that unless the JCS agreed, "our mission will at best be needlessly costly in life, money and prestige. At worst, it might be doomed to failure." The request was confirmed in a cable to Army Chief of Staff General J. Lawton Collins at 0430; he informed Army Secretary Pace, who in turn called the president. At 0500 hours on Friday, June 30, 1950, President Truman approved committing ground troops.

UN forces in the Far East were fortunate that the carrier USS *Valley Forge* (CV-45) had arrived at Subic Bay in the Philippines at the end of May. The carrier operated 86 aircraft of Carrier Air Group 5, the first two operational squadrons of the new jet-powered Grumman F9F-2 Panther, along with two fighter-bomber squadrons of F4U-4 Corsairs, and an attack squadron of AD-3 Skyraiders, with 14 other Skyraiders from photographic, night-attack, and radar early-warning units rounding out the complement. The air group had conducted close-support training missions with the Marines at Camp Pendleton, California, prior to their deployment. Carrier Division Five, commanded by Rear Admiral G. R. Henderson aboard *Valley Forge*, was anchored in Victoria Harbor at the Crown Colony of Hong Kong on June 25 when the admiral received notification of the attack in Korea. Orders soon arrived and the ship got underway and departed at dawn the next day, headed across the South China Sea to Subic Bay, where she provisioned and refueled on arrival on June 27. On June 26, while en route from Hong Kong, Admiral Henderson had received orders to form and command Task Force 77.

At the same time, the light fleet carrier HMS *Triumph*, with 12 obsolescent Seafire FR 47 fighters of Carrier Air Wing 13's 800 Squadron and 12 obsolete Firefly FR I attack aircraft of 827 Squadron, was preparing to depart the old Imperial Navy base in Sasebo, which was now controlled by the Royal Australian Navy as part of the Allied occupation forces in Japan. HMS *Triumph* was due to return to Britain, having completed a six-month deployment to the Far East in which her aircraft had attacked Communist insurgents in Malaya as part of Operation *Firedog*. *Triumph* left Sasebo that afternoon, headed for Hong Kong.

While *Valley Forge* prepared to depart Hong Kong, Rear Admiral Sir William G. Andrewes, RN, commander of the Royal Navy's Far Eastern Fleet in Hong Kong, ordered his ships to concentrate in Japan and await further instruction in anticipation the Admiralty would order him to participate in whatever Allied response was made to the Korean events. The Commonwealth fleet departed Hong Kong at 0130 hours on June 26, hours ahead of *Valley Forge*. Andrewes' fleet met *Triumph* in the East China Sea the next day and the fleet arrived at Kure, Japan, on June 28.

On June 29, all Commonwealth forces in the Far East as well as Canada had been ordered to participate in the UN force supporting

Korea. Task Force 77 arrived at Buckner Bay, Okinawa, from Subic Bay on June 30, where they were joined the next day by the Commonwealth fleet. That night, the joint task force departed, headed for the Yellow Sea off the west coast of North Korea.

By dawn on July 3, Task Force 77 was 150 miles off the North Korean coast, 100 miles from Chinese airfields on the Shantung Peninsula, and 200 miles from the Soviet air base at Port Arthur. At 0545 hours, HMS *Triumph* launched 12 Seafires and nine Fireflies to attack the airfield at Haeju, south of Pyonyang. At 0600 hours, *Valley Forge* launched 16 Corsairs from VF-53 and VF-54 and 12 Skyraiders from VA-55 to strike Pyongyang airfield. Forty-five minutes later, when the propeller planes had gained a head start, eight Panthers of VF-51 were launched to be the first aircraft over the target. Over the North Korean capital, the Panther pilots spotted two airborne Yak-9s and shot them down, then destroyed nine aircraft on the field in strafing attacks.

The Corsairs and Skyraiders bombed hangars and fuel storage while the British strike force destroyed hangars and buildings at nearby Haeju with a rocket attack. Antiaircraft fire was negligible, and the attackers suffered no flak damage or loss. That afternoon, *Triumph* flew a second strike against railroad lines, while *Valley Forge* struck the rail marshaling yards in Pyongyang and the bridges over the Taedong River with considerable damage to locomotives and rolling stock.

While Task Force 77 crossed the Yellow Sea, the first American ground unit, Task Force Smith, named for Lt Col Charles B. Smith, commanding officer, 1st Battalion, 21st Regiment, 24th Infantry Division, arrived in Korea on July 2. The troops had been flown in from Japan aboard C-54s from the 374th Troop Carrier Wing. The task force was composed of 406 men of the 1st Battalion, 21st Infantry Regiment, and 134 men of A Battery, 52nd Field Artillery Battalion. Smith and his men were ill-equipped and uninformed about the current situation and conditions in South Korea; the soldiers, none of whom had undergone any advanced military training while in Japan, had been issued 120 rounds and two days of C-rations each when they left Japan.

Smith's orders from 24th Infantry Division commander General William F. Dean were:

When you get to Pusan, head for Taejon. We want to stop the North Koreans as far from Pusan as we can. Block the main road as far north as possible. Make contact with General Church. If you can't find him, go to Taejon and beyond if you can. Sorry I can't give you more information – that's all I've got. Good luck, and God bless you and your men!

The next day, as the naval force struck Pyongyang, the US 34th Infantry Regiment arrived in Pusan. They were ordered to take position at Pyongtaek, southeast of Osan on the Seoul–Pusan highway. The men of the regiment had brought their summer dress uniforms with them, for the victory parade to be held in Seoul once the "gooks" had been driven out. Lt Col Harold Ayres, commander of the 1st Battalion of the 34th Infantry, told his men, "There are supposed to be North Koreans north of us. These men are poorly trained. Only about half of them have weapons and we'll have no difficulty stopping them."

Late on July 4, Lt Col Smith, who had first distinguished himself in the battle of Guadalcanal in World War II, led 540 men north of Osan. They reached position at 0300 hours on July 5, soaked by a chilling rain storm. At dawn, Sergeant Loren Chambers spotted eight T-34 tanks followed by infantry advancing down the road from Suwon, followed shortly by 25 more tanks. When the column was a mile from Task Force Smith, the Americans fired their mortars, getting a few hits with many duds. The enemy continued their advance and the Americans took them on with 57mm recoilless rifles.

The North Koreans, most of whom were battle-hardened veterans of the Chinese Civil War, kept advancing while the Americans ran out of ammunition. There was no artillery other than the 60mm mortars, which were of no use against tanks, yet still the Americans held for several hours against 5,000 enemy soldiers. Out of ammunition, Task Force Smith finally began a withdrawal that quickly turned into a rout; many dropped their weapons and took off their boots so they could move through the rice paddies faster. They left behind 150 of their fellow GIs, dead.

An hour later, the North Koreans ran up on the 34th Regiment at Pyongtaek. When Australian war correspondent Dennis Warner saw the first T-34s, he retreated and reported them to Colonel Ayres of the 1st Battalion, who responded, "We don't have any tanks," and refused to believe they were North Korean. When the T-34s showed up, Ayres ordered a withdrawal that turned into a precipitous retreat. By dawn on July 6, Pyongtaek had fallen and by day's end the North Koreans had advanced 36 miles to Chonan.

In the first direct combat, the North Koreans had destroyed two American infantry regiments, with 3,000 killed, wounded, or missing in action. The US Army left enough equipment behind to equip a North Korean regiment. The 24th Infantry Division would fight as best it could through the rest of the month to delay the onrushing North Koreans while the UN forces made a fighting retreat that only stopped after July 23 when they crossed the Naktong River, a natural barrier to the North Korean advance that allowed establishment of what came to be known as the Pusan Perimeter.

Valley Forge and *Triumph* flew additional strikes on July 4 as requested by MacArthur "in view of the deteriorating situation." *Valley Forge* aircraft destroyed two gunboats, and attacked railway bridges, locomotives, and tunnels; one bridge over the Taedong River was knocked down. The British aircraft also attacked roads and bridges. The sudden appearance of UN aircraft 400 miles from the nearest American airfield was a rude awakening for the North Koreans. More importantly, the attacks apparently deterred Josef Stalin from making a sizable commitment of Russian aircraft to support the North Korean advance, which the North Koreans had been negotiating for since the invasion. The prewar argument that aircraft carriers were obsolete was ended. For most of the rest of July, the two carriers would range up and down both coasts of the Korean peninsula, doing their best to delay the North Korean advance, which looked more and more like it could result in the expulsion of UN ground forces from Korea.

On July 6, General O'Donnell's FEAF Bomber Command flew the first "strategic" bombing mission of the war, when nine B-29s of the 22nd Wing bombed the Rising Sun oil refinery in the port of Wonsan and a chemical plant in the port of Hungnam north of Wonsan. Further strategic bombing missions were delayed as Bomber Command was diverted back to "tactical" bombing against the advancing enemy. On July 12, the Strategic Air Command's 92nd Bomb Wing flew from its base at Yokota to bomb the Seoul marshaling yards on its first mission of the war.

Due to the advancing North Korean Army units, there was a need to use the B-29s in a more tactical role to attack the invaders as the offensive moved rapidly south. On July 11, eight 19th Wing B-29s assigned to a tactical strike were able to establish radio contact with ground units and hit North Korean units in Wonju, Pyongtaek, and Chunchon, with good results.

The first B-29 (44-69866) was lost to enemy action on July 12. The airplane belonged to the 19th Wing's 28th Bomb Squadron. Navigator 1st Lt Donald Brous recalled that a North Korean Yak-9 "came out of nowhere" and hit the number three engine, which caught fire. The pilot feathered the prop but was unable to put out the fire. The bombardier made a "lone wolf" decision to bail out over enemy territory and became the first USAF POW. Lt Brous described what happened next:

We reached an altitude of about 3,000 feet, at which time we were given the bail-out signal. We were over the Yellow Sea west of Seoul, offshore from the town of Songmo-ri. One of our guys in the aft section never got out. I managed to deploy my one-man dinghy once I was in the water. Shortly thereafter, a boat came out from shore and picked me up. Most of the crew were safely in Japan within 24 hours.

B-29s from the Strategic Air Command's 22nd and 92nd bomb wings bombed the rail complex at Wonsan on July 13. The next day, the bombers were deployed against enemy troop formations that were close to overwhelming the 24th Infantry Division near Taejon. The bombers returned again the next day and reported good results. The 24th Division troops were able to withdraw in good order.

The NKAF remained active over the battlefield, despite dwindling numbers, for much of July. On July 15, the 3rd Bomb Group lost its first B-26, shot down by Yaks while attacking the bridges near Seoul. Four days later, on July 19, PFC Gene Fisher, a gunner with the 30th Squadron of the 19th Wing flying in B-29 44-61638, named "Bug's Ball Buster," flew his most memorable mission of the war. He later remembered:

We were approaching the bridges over Han River near Seoul, with 35 500lb bombs in the bomb-bay, when three Yak pilots came right up at us as we were on the bomb run ... They came in from behind, but dropped back out of range of our guns. We took hits in the bomb bay, and Captain Edenbo (the pilot) dropped them all and dived into a cloud. By then we had taken several hits from the Yaks.

From up front, someone said over the intercom that they needed the first aid kit. It was right beside me, so I grabbed it and went through the tunnel up to the front. There were bullet holes everywhere on the flight deck and we had lost pressurization. Captain Edenbo had gotten hit. I'll never forget the sight of him lying there on the flight deck with blood all over his face. I thought he was dead, but I took out the kit and tried to help him.

Going back to Kadena, we couldn't get the rear bomb-bay doors closed. The electrical systems were shot away. We had no radio. We got into a storm, but somehow that plane kept going all the way back to Kadena. We didn't know how much damage we had till we landed – they counted over 100 holes in the plane. Captain Edenbo survived, but that mission was a tough one.

On July 3, MacArthur had ordered General Stratemeyer to hit every strategic target in North Korea. Since the industries and communications complexes at the targeted cities were grouped closely together, SAC Commander Curtis LeMay suggested that these targets be hit with incendiary bombs in an area-bombing campaign to assure their complete destruction. General O'Donnell presented the kind of war plan the disciples of Douhet would approve:

It was my intention and hope that we would be able to get out there and to cash in on our psychological advantage in having gotten into the war so fast by putting a very severe blow on the North Koreans, with an advance warning, perhaps, telling them they had gone too far in what we all recognized as being an act of aggression, and then go to work burning five major cities in North Korea to the ground, and to destroy completely every one of about 18 major strategic targets.

O'Donnell's campaign was not carried out for political reasons, since President Truman did not want to face domestic opposition to using incendiaries on North Korea so soon after the destruction of Japanese cities by firebombing during World War II.

The unsuitability of the F-80 for providing close-air support over the battlefield led to a decision in early July to re-equip the 35th and 8th fighter-bomber groups with F-51 Mustangs that could operate in Korea. On July 5, nine high-time former Mustang pilots from the

F-80-equipped 12th Fighter-Bomber Squadron of the 18th Fighter-Bomber Wing at Clark AFB in the Philippines formed what came to be known as the "Dallas Squadron." After collecting Mustangs at Ashiya AFB in Japan on July 8, they moved to Taegu (K-2) airfield in South Korea, which had a PSP (pierced steel planking) runway in a valley with mountains on either side. There they operated with the volunteer instructors of Major Dean Hess' "Project Bout One," and the combined unit was designated the 51st Fighter Squadron on July 10.

Dean Hess would become one of the best-known pilots of the Korean War, due to the 1956 publishing success of his book, *Battle Hymn*, and the subsequent 1957 movie adapted from the book, which starred Rock Hudson. An ordained minister who left his ministry and volunteered for the Army Air Forces after Pearl Harbor, Hess had flown 63 missions in P-47 Thunderbolts after the Normandy invasion. Recalled to active duty in 1948, where he served with the occupation forces in Japan in the 8th Fighter-Bomber Wing, he had taken the assignment to train ROKAF pilots in late May 1950. His fame would come during the retreat out of North Korea following the intervention of Red China in the war, when he was able to organize the evacuation of several thousand Korean war orphans to safety on an offshore island.

While the Dallas Squadron was flying 426 sorties through the month of July in a desperate attempt to support UN forces in the face of the North Korean offensive, and the other fighter-bomber units worked to get up to speed in transitioning back to F-51s, Far East Air Forces put out a call to Air National Guard units in the United States to turn over their F-51s for use in the war. Mustangs were hurriedly removed from Air National Guard units throughout the continental United States and flown to the Alameda Naval Air Station in San Francisco Bay in early July.

USS *Boxer* (CV-21) had returned from her six-month deployment to the Western Pacific only days before the outbreak of war and had already departed San Diego, headed for overhaul in Bremerton, Washington. The carrier was diverted to San Francisco, where she docked at Alameda Naval Air Station on July 8. She immediately loaded the 145 Air Force F-51Ds that had been rapidly cocooned for their trans-Pacific delivery on their arrival from the ANG units, along with six Stinson L-5 Sentinels and 19 Navy aircraft. Conditions would be crowded aboard ship with the presence of 1,012 Air Force maintenance technicians and support personnel, along with 2,000 tons of crucial spare parts and ordnance.

On July 14, *Boxer* departed Alameda at 0800 hours. Once past the Golden Gate, her captain ordered the engine rooms to maintain full speed ahead for the duration of the voyage. The carrier set a trans-Pacific transit record of eight days and seven hours when she arrived at Yokosuka on July 23. The Mustangs and their service personnel and supplies were quickly off-loaded and the first F-51 flew an air-support mission a week later.

While *Boxer* was setting records delivering F-51s to Japan, the pilots of the 51st Fighter Squadron continued their fight against the enemy drive south in Korea. Major Harry H. Moreland, who had become the unit CO, remembered a mission flown shortly after arrival at Taegu in which they were requested by the Army to attack 20 railcars at Taejon filled with ammunition that had been left behind in the hasty retreat. Being unfamiliar with both the area and the Mustang after transitioning to the F-80 a year earlier, Moreland sent three two-ship flights in hopes one would find their way to the target. As it turned out, he and his wingman, 1st Lt Howard "Scrappy" Johnson, were the only ones to find their way through the valleys under the 700-foot overcast ceiling. "Once in the area, we located the railcars and proceeded to strike them with such accuracy that we managed to take out the entire lot. The resulting explosions were awesome, with the sky lit up like the Fourth of July!"

On another mission running the road between Seoul and Taejon, Moreland spotted a haystack in a field with tread marks leading up to it. When he made a low-level pass, he was able to identify the enemy tank hastily covered by the hay. Having already dropped their napalm tanks on trucks they had run across, the two Mustang pilots only had their .50-caliber machine guns, which were insufficient to harm the tank. However, their gunfire did set the hay afire. "The flames literally cooked the tank as we circled and then there was a large explosion." A few weeks later, Moreland established "Moreland's Tank Busters" within the 51st Fighter Squadron after they were able to obtain supplies of 6.5-inch tank-busting rockets capable of penetrating the armor of a T-34 tank. The flight was on call 24 hours a day and became the terror of North Korean armored units.

Among the pilots sent from the Philippines to form the "Dallas Squadron" was 1st Lt Daniel "Chappie" James, who had graduated from Tuskeegee Institute and taken flight training as one of the Tuskegee Airmen during World War II. His excellent flying skills resulted in his being held back as an instructor during the war for other African-American pilots in the program. He had served with the 332nd Fighter Group after the war until the armed services were desegregated in 1948, at which point he was sent to the Philippines to join the 18th Fighter-Bomber Wing at Clark AFB.

Moreland's wingman, 1st Lt Howard "Scrappy" Johnson – who later broke the world altitude record flying an F-104 – remembered that Captain "Spud" Taylor and "Chappie" James formed the other element in Moreland's flight in the 51st FS. On one mission during the fighting along the Naktong River in defense of the Pusan Perimeter, the flight spotted several NKPA artillery pieces on a sand bar in the river. When they dropped their napalm canisters, they failed to ignite due to bad fuses. "Every third round in our fifties was an incendiary, so we came around in a strafing run. The incendiaries set the cans off and the entire area went up in flames, completely destroying the cannons."

A major problem at this point of the war was the Korean refugees who clogged the roads. There had already been reports of North Korean troops infiltrating crowds of refugees, and UN troops had been forced to fire into refugees when fired upon by the North Korean infiltrators. Major Moreland remembered a mission in August flown with "Chappie" James to defend the airfield at Taegu, which was under threat again by the North Koreans.

> We were in contact with a Forward Air Controller (FAC) who had spotted a large body of enemy troops coming down a road. He led us to a large group of people heading south, but before we attacked I decided to take a closer look and we made a low pass over the crowd. We both saw mostly women and children, who did not run for cover. We both felt they really were refugees and decided not to attack.

At other times, other Mustang units would attack refugees when they ignored orders from UN troops to halt.

Fighter-bombers and light bombers flying in support of the early delaying actions found and strafed attacking North Korean infantry and destroyed Soviet-built tanks approaching the battlefield. On July 10, a flight of F-80s on an armed reconnaissance descended beneath the cloud layer, where they discovered a long line of North Korean T-34 tanks and trucks that had halted when they came to a demolished bridge. The pilots reported their discovery and Fifth Air Force diverted every available aircraft – F-80s, B-26s, and even F-82s – to attack the column with bombs, gunfire, and rockets. The attacking aircraft destroyed over 100 trucks and 50 T-34s.

Air combat with the NKPAF continued sporadically through the first part of July. Captain Francis B. Clark of the 8th Wing's 80th Fighter-Bomber Squadron shot down a Yak-9 on July 17 when his flight of F-80 fighter-bombers spotted four NKPAF Yaks as they strafed Taejon airfield. When the surviving Yaks fled north, the rest of Clark's flight went after them. 1st Lt Robert D. Mckee and 1st Lt Charles W. Wurster, and 2nd Lt Elwood A. Keyes, finished off the last of the Yaks in a quick fireball.

The North Koreans arrived at the Kum River, north of Taejon, the headquarters of the 24th Infantry Division, on July 12. The city was important as the major transportation hub between Seoul and Taeju, and was also the last place the ground forces could hold before they would be forced to withdraw into the still-incomplete defenses of what would come to be known as the Pusan Perimeter. With the losses suffered over the previous two weeks, the division was at about two-thirds strength, with one regiment reduced to half strength. Division commander Major General William F. Dean received an order from Eighth Army commander General Walton Walker that the city be held until July 20, to allow the 1st Cavalry and 25th Infantry divisions to take defensive positions on the Naktong River that would become the front line of the Pusan Perimeter.

Fighting on the line of the Kum River lasted until July 17, when the North Koreans were able to force their way across after inflicting serious casualties on the American units, and they entered Taejon itself on July 19. Bitter house-to-house fighting lasted until July 21. General Dean himself fought North Korean tanks, leading defenders armed with the new 3.5-inch "bazooka" and knocking out several T-34s as the Americans attempted to withdraw in the face of the attacking North Koreans. In the final evacuation, the general and his party became separated from the last unit to leave as they attempted to cross the Taejon River. Wounded, General Dean wandered in the countryside for 36 days before he was betrayed to the enemy by two Koreans pretending to guide him to safety. He was the highest-ranking American officer to be captured by the North Koreans during the war.

During the fighting, the North Korean Air Force put in an appearance over the battlefield on July 20. Captain Robert L. Lee and his wingman, 2nd Lt David H. Goodnough, pilots from the 35th Fighter-Bomber Squadron flying in the 51st "Dallas" Squadron, ran across a pair of Yak-9s over the city and shot down both in a quick fight. These would be the last aerial victories for US pilots for the next three months and marked the establishment of air superiority over the Korean peninsula by UN air units.

On July 21, Army engineer units completed their work expanding the airfield at Taegu and putting down pierced steel planking (PSP) for the runways. FEAF established Taegu as the forward headquarters in Korea, and created the Joint Operations Center to coordinate Air Force, Navy, and Marine operations over the perimeter. Fifth Air Force forward HQ was established on the field on July 24, and the F-51s of the Japan-based fighter-bomber units began using the field for temporary daylight operations.

On August 1, the 51st FS was redesignated the 12th Fighter-Bomber Squadron and was joined by the rest of the squadron when they transferred up from the Philippines to Taegu on August 3, followed soon by the 67th Fighter-Bomber Squadron and the wing HQ. Five days later, the North Korean advance forced the 18th Wing to evacuate Taegu and retreat to Ashiya AFB in Japan. F-51 flights reverted to using Taegu for daylight operations only to extend their time over the battlefield for the remainder of August during the First and Second Battles of the Naktong.

The 40th Fighter-Bomber Squadron of the 35th Fighter-Bomber Wing was the second F-51 unit committed to the war. The 35th Wing had left their Mustangs behind when they re-equipped with the F-80C in 1949, but since many pilots in the unit were qualified to fly the F-51, the 40th Squadron was hastily re-equipped with ten of the ex-ROKAF Mustangs and flew their first mission on July 16. By July 27, the unit moved from the wing's base at Johnson AFB on Honshu to Pohang (K-3), a PSP-covered landing field on the southeastern coast of South Korea. The unit found, as the "Dallas Squadron" had, that the best weapon against the surging North Koreans was napalm, followed by strafing.

Following *Boxer's* delivery of the 145 ANG F-51s, the 35th Wing's 39th FIS left their F-80s behind and were fully re-equipped with Mustangs. On August 7, they left Johnson AFB with a full ordnance load that they used on a support mission in the perimeter before landing at Pohang to join the 40th Squadron. A squadron crew chief later recalled that "Pohang was a blinding dustbowl, with stifling heat and high humidity. We lived on C-rations and drank putrid hot water out of blister bags 'flavored' by purification tablets. It truly was a hellhole." At Pohang, pilots flew two and even three missions a day, operating from dawn to dusk as the ground crews labored to service the Mustangs with fuel and ordnance in the stifling heat. Dust got into everything, and engines were constantly being torn down and cleaned out to remain operational.

While the 35th Wing changed two of its jet-equipped interceptor squadrons into fighter-bomber units flying the F-51, the 8th Fighter-Interceptor Group at Itazuke AFB also re-equipped its 35th and 36th squadrons with Mustangs, leaving only the 80th still flying Shooting Stars. With the Korean War only 46 days old, Fifth Air Force had created six fighter-bomber units capable of providing close-air support over the battlefield.

The Mustangs were just in time, as mid-August saw the First Battle of the Naktong break out, when North Korean troops were able to cross the Naktong River that formed the northeastern defensive line of the Pusan Perimeter when the river's water level dropped in the dry August weather. Had the enemy been able to break through, the entire perimeter would have been threatened with collapse. The former jet interceptor pilots now flying the Mustangs had to learn close-air support "on the job."

Fortunately, the Air Force squadrons were reinforced by the arrival of Marine F4U-4 Corsair squadrons based aboard the escort carriers USS *Sicily* (CVE-118) and USS *Badoeng Strait* (CVE-119) at the end of July. VMF-214 "Blacksheep" flew from *Sicily* while VMF-323 "Death Rattlers" operated from *Badoeng Strait*. The Marines were well versed in close-air support and so proficient at it that FACs in the Provisional Marine Brigade that arrived at the same time and entered the fighting in the perimeter on August 7 – the eighth anniversary of the landings on Guadalcanal – could call in strikes as close as 50 yards from Marine units, a capability the Air Force pilots did not have. Additionally, the two carriers could move around the coastline of the perimeter, keeping their squadrons on a ten-minute call for support against North Korean assaults. The Marine Corsairs and the

Marine infantry effectively won the First Battle of the Naktong in fierce fighting over the course of a week, while the Mustang units provided support along the rest of the line.

Operations in the Pusan Perimeter were so intense, with pilots flying multiple missions a day, that close-air support experience in the Mustang units built up quickly. By the time of the Inchon invasion, the pilots of the 35th and 36th Fighter-Bomber squadrons were regularly putting ordnance on target within 50 yards of UN lines as the Marines did. Napalm, the favored weapon, was greatly feared by the enemy; burning to death in a fire there was no way to put out was a horrible way to die. Captured enemy soldiers stated they were unafraid of UN artillery fire or infantry gunfire. The appearance overhead of Mustangs with napalm canisters, however, with the accurate delivery the pilots were now capable of, would cause even the most hardened North Korean infantrymen to break ranks and run. However, on August 13, a North Korean advance threatened Pohang airfield, and the two Mustang units were forced to withdraw to Tsuiki AFB in Japan, operating at Pohang only during daylight hours.

The Mustang was not really the right airplane for the role of battlefield close-air support. The liquid-cooled Merlin engine and the large radiator housed in the lower rear fuselage was extremely vulnerable to ground fire. While a Corsair could have one of the 18 cylinders of its R-2800 radial engine shot off and still return to its home carrier, a single hit by a .30-caliber bullet in the vulnerable cooling system meant the Merlin would overheat within minutes and either catch fire or explode. Thus, throughout its time in Korea, the Mustang suffered a higher loss rate than Marine and Navy Corsairs and Skyraiders with their dependable radials.

An example of the vulnerability of the F-51 occurred on August 5, when Major Louis J. Sebille, commander of the 67th FBS, received a hit in his engine while providing ground support over the Pusan Perimeter. Sebille dived his burning F-51 into the enemy artillery position the squadron had been ordered to attack, hitting the ammunition and setting off a large explosion. For this action "above and beyond the call of duty," Major Sebille was posthumously awarded the first Medal of Honor to a USAF member in Korea.

When the decision was made to re-equip the fighter-bomber units with Mustangs, many pilots were not excited about their prospects. The historian of the 8th Fighter-Bomber Group wrote: "A lot of pilots had seen vivid demonstrations of why the F-51 was not a ground-support fighter in the last war, and weren't exactly intrigued by the thought of playing guinea pig to prove the same thing over again." During the war, units flying the F-51 suffered the highest combat losses, losing 172 F-51s to enemy ground fire, with 164 pilots killed or missing in ground-attack operations. Colonel Bill Myers, who had flown Thunderbolts in ground attack during World War II, recalled after the war that every time he took off in his Mustang for a mission in Korea, he would pray, "Please, God, make this a Thunderbolt." The F-47's World War II combat loss rate per sortie was 0.7 percent, far better than the Mustang's 1.2 percent; more Mustangs were lost in ground strafing in the European theater than in aerial combat. One Air Force study during World War II found the Mustang was three times more vulnerable to ground fire than the Thunderbolt.

During the years since the war, many who have studied the role of the F-51 in ground support have questioned why the Air Force did not requisition the Republic F-47N Thunderbolts that equipped several Air National Guard units at the time. The Thunderbolt had clearly demonstrated its ability as a ground-attack aircraft in Europe during World War II. The airplane was much more able to survive damage from ground fire, with pilots successfully returning to base with one or more cylinders blown off its R-2800 radial engine. The reason the F-47 wasn't used in Korea lay in the postwar years during which the Air Force had concentrated on the strategic nuclear bombing mission. Only those fighters useful as bomber escorts remained in first-line service; the Mustang had established itself during World War II as the premier escort fighter, which is why the F-51 remained in the Air Force inventory while the F-47 did not. By 1950, the ANG units that were equipped with F-47s did not fly them as much as those ANG units with F-51s due to the lack of spare parts.

In April 1951, when ground fire claimed Mustangs at an alarming rate, FEAF commander General Stratemeyer asked Air Force headquarters if any F-47s were available for use in Korea, noting a tremendous increase in small-arms fire and flak along the front and stating, "All here know that the F-47 can take it." The situation was such that Stratemeyer said he would gratefully accept just 25 F-47s then operated by the Hawaii Air National Guard. In response, Air Force Chief of Staff General Hoyt S. Vandenberg stated that considering the lack of spare parts and the problems of introducing another fighter type, "we fail to see any appreciable results to be gained by the substitution." Vandenberg admitted the F-47 would likely prove less vulnerable but concluded the problem could really only be solved by replacing the F-51 with jets, since exchanging F-51s for F-47s would require a complete change in pilot training prior to flying combat missions in Korea. Unfortunately, the replacement jets came slowly; the last F-51s were not withdrawn from combat until January 22, 1953, when the 18th Fighter-Bomber Group re-equipped with the F-86F, the version of the Sabre that was finally able to undertake the ground-support mission.

While the F-51 squadrons fought desperately to support UN forces in the Pusan Perimeter, FEAF Bomber Command was finally ordered by MacArthur to turn its force loose on a strategic bombing campaign against North Korea. RB-29s of the 31st Strategic Reconnaissance Squadron had been active during April, photographing targets throughout the country. The first mission, flown on July 30, was to Hungnam, the site of an extensive nitrogen fertilizer and explosives industry. Operation *Nannie Able* targeted the Chosen Nitrogen Explosives Factory. Forty-seven B-29s of the 22nd and 92nd bomb wings unloaded 500lb bombs through thin cloud at 0950 hours, destroying or damaging 70 percent of the factory, according to later bomb damage assessment. On August 1, the Chosen Nitrogen Fertilizer Company was the target of 46 B-29s in Operation *Nannie Baker*; crews reported observing large explosions accompanied by extensive smoke and flame in the target area. Weather closed in on August 2, and Operation *Nannie Charlie* on August 3 saw 39 B-29s attack the Bogun Chemical Plant. All three raids involved precision bombing, and resulted in great damage inflicted on the largest explosives and chemical industry in Asia.

On August 6, the SAC-controlled 98th Bomb Wing arrived at Yokota, which gave FEAF Bomber Command three B-29 bomb wings. The 98th Wing flew its first mission on August 7. The next day, the SAC-controlled 305th Bomb Wing, which had arrived in Okinawa at the same time the 98th had shown up in Japan, flew its first mission. With four bomb wings, the B-29 force in the Far East was nearly two-thirds the size of the XXIst Bomber Command that had destroyed Japan five years before.

As the fighting became more difficult in the Pusan Perimeter, 98 Japan-based B-29s carpet-bombed suspected enemy troop concentrations in a 27-square-mile area near Waegwan northwest of Taegu on August 16, dropping 800 tons of 500lb bombs. It was the largest employment of strategic air power in direct support of ground forces since Operation *Cobra* at St Lo during the Normandy invasion in 1944. Later reconnaissance missions revealed little destruction of enemy troops or equipment, since they had left the area before the strike.

A seventh Mustang-equipped squadron had been in action since July 2. The Royal Australian Air Force's 77 Squadron was the first non-US unit committed to the war in Korea. Formed in 1942, the unit had flown P-40 Kittyhawk fighters and fighter-bombers over New Guinea during the war and had been assigned to occupation duty in Japan with the British Commonwealth Occupying Force (BCOF) beginning in 1946, where they flew from Iwakuni air base on the Inland Sea with F-51 Mustangs. At the time of the North Korean invasion, the squadron had reached the end of its assignment to the BCOF and was the sole remaining RAAF unit in Japan. They were about to return to Australia when MacArthur requested the squadron, which was the only unit in Japan with a full complement of F-51s, be assigned to the UN command. Led by Wing Commander Lou Spence, 77's Mustangs entered combat over South Korea on July 2, escorting C-47s evacuating casualties to Japan.

The next day, the squadron attacked what turned out to be a train full of US and South Korean troops on the main railroad between Suwon and Pyongtaek, inflicting many casualties including 29 dead. Spence had been assured by Fifth Air Force that the target was correct when he had raised concerns prior to the mission that it wasn't possible for the North Koreans to have penetrated so far south. The friendly fire incident was widely reported in American newspapers but General Stratemeyer made a public statement clearing the Australians of any blame.

On July 3, 77 Squadron escorted 17 B-26 Invaders of the 3rd Bomb Wing on a mission to bomb the Han River bridges north of Seoul. The squadron continued escorting B-26 and B-29 bombers on missions over Korea during the early weeks of the war. These missions were primarily against airfields that could be used by the NKPAF. Only the F-51 Mustang had the range to escort the bombers on missions over North Korea, which was beyond the range of Japan-based F-80s.

The squadron suffered its first combat death five days after entering combat on July 7, when Squadron Leader Graham Strout was hit and killed during a raid on Samchok to become the first Australian, and first non-American UN serviceman, to die in Korea.

Besides the pilots already in Japan, other pilots were called up for service in Korea to bring the squadron to full wartime strength. The same day the squadron flew its first combat mission, flight sergeants Ross Coburn, Robert Hunt, Jack Murray, and Lyall Klaffer received orders to join 77 in Japan. Hunt, a Pacific War veteran, found it hard to believe when he heard he was being posted to Korea. Based at Fairbairn outside the capital of Canberra when he got the news, the reality finally set in after a few beers in the sergeants' mess. When he went home to his wife, it took several hours for him to find the courage to tell her of his assignment. Next day, he and Murray left for the Richmond RAAF base near Sydney.

The sergeants left Sydney on July 6; on July 12, Coburn and Murray flew their first mission from Iwakuni to attack North Korean positions in South Korea. Eleven days later, Klaffer destroyed a tank near Hamchang, but UN troops were being pushed back toward what would become the Pusan Perimeter after the North Koreans broke through the American lines. Over the next month, the Australians flew the 200 miles from Iwakuni across the Tsushima Straits to Pusan, where they would fly a strike, land at Taegu airfield to rearm for a second strike, then return to Japan. By late July, the Mustangs were operating primarily from the forward base. On July 28, with North Korean troops approaching, the pilots were forced to make an emergency takeoff at night when it appeared the field would be overrun. Fortunately, UN troops held, and they were able to continue operating from Taegu. By then, the squadron was hitting targets in North Korea, such as a strike against the railroad at Hamhung on the northeast coast that took out several T-34s being transported south.

In the weeks leading up to the Inchon invasion, 77 Squadron flew 812 sorties in 1,745 hours of flight time, striking targets on the front lines of the perimeter. During August and the first part of September, the squadron claimed 35 tanks, 212 other vehicles, 18 railway engines or cars, and 13 ammunition and fuel dumps destroyed.

On September 3, Flight Sergeant Bill Harrop was hit by flak and forced to bail out behind enemy lines. The mission was late in the day in "iffy" weather. An HO3S-1 helicopter was launched from USS *Valley Forge* to pick him up, but the weather and loss of light forced the "Horse" to abort the rescue mission. The next day, squadron pilots could not find Horrop. Following the breakout from the perimeter in mid-September, his body was found in a shallow grave near where he had gone down. He had been executed by the North Koreans, which was a common fate for UN pilots shot down over the battlefield who could not be rescued before capture.

The flight between Korea and Japan had hazards of its own. On September 4, Coburn and Murray were returning to Iwakuni when Coburn's Mustang developed a coolant leak. As the temperature gauge rose, the airplane began to lose height and started to vibrate violently. Murray saw Coburn's Mustang plummet toward the ground but did not see him jump. Just as the Mustang crashed and exploded, Murray finally spotted the billowing parachute and saw Coburn waving from the ground. Japanese locals found Coburn and the squadron sent a truck to retrieve him. By the time they arrived at the village, "they'd given him a couple of beers and he was right as rain," Murray remembered.

On September 9, squadron CO Wing Commander Spence was killed during a napalm attack on enemy troops at Angang-ni when his Mustang was struck by enemy antiaircraft fire and failed to pull out of his attack dive. Spence was a beloved leader and his death was a serious morale blow to the squadron. In answer, Squadron Leader Richard Cresswell, 77 Squadron's original World War II commander, who had also commanded the unit in 1944 and 1945, was sent to replace Spence and assume command a third time. Cresswell was the only RAAF squadron leader not promoted to the rank of wing commander (colonel), since during World War II he had supported "the revolt of the wing leaders," when RAAF fighter commanders Clive "Killer" Caldwell and Robert "Bobby" Gibbes had attempted to resign their commissions due to their belief the commanders of the RAAF were wasting the lives of pilots on missions in the then-backwater of the Netherlands East Indies to support the government's desire to promote Australia's political position in the region after the war. The event had killed the careers of Caldwell and Gibbes and hobbled the careers of those suspected by the high command of supporting them.

Cressell arrived at Iwakuni on September 17 and immediately flew four missions during his first day of operations on September 20 in support of operations at Inchon. His inspirational leadership led to an immediate recovery of morale among the squadron pilots. Beloved by the men he led, Cresswell would command the squadron through the rest of the Korean War. His lack of rank, however, would put him at a disadvantage when dealing with USAF commanders over the role of 77 Squadron throughout the war.

September 4, 1950 saw the first successful rescue of a pilot from behind enemy lines by a helicopter. Bob Wayne, who had been the first American jet pilot to score in aerial combat when he shot down two Il-10s on the second day of the war, had been promoted to captain and gone back to flying F-51s with the rest of the 35th Squadron after picking up some of the ex-ANG Mustangs in early August. By this time, pilots of the forward units had heard stories of North Korean troops torturing and mutilating UN pilots shot down behind the lines before executing them. Capture in this war was not preferable to death in the crash.

Over Hanggan-dong, just north of the Pusan Peremieter's front lines, Wayne's Mustang was hit by enemy fire as he strafed an enemy troop column. "The first indication I'd been hit was when it felt like my right foot was on fire." When he looked down, he realized it was! Flames shot out the right side of his engine cowling. They had already eaten through the cockpit firewall and were wrapping around his feet. He jettisoned his canopy and prepared to jump, but the flames were sucked into the cockpit by the slipstream. In an instant, Bob Wayne was wrapped in flames. "I had third-degree burns on both legs and my arms. I was bleeding and my hands and legs were just a mess. My hair was gone and so were my eyebrows."

Loosening his straps, Wayne was sucked out of the cockpit when the Mustang was 400 feet over the rice paddies. He managed to open his parachute and swing once before he hit the ground, hard. The North Korean troops he had been strafing were a few hundred yards away. Overhead, the other pilots of "C" Flight saw the North Koreans fan out to go after the downed enemy pilot. Each in turn made low-level strafing passes and the soldiers went to ground, unable to move without drawing fire from above.

Wayne started moving through the paddy he was in, looking for a hiding place. When he crawled out of the paddy, he confronted an angry water buffalo. He jumped into a drainage ditch and slowly moved away from the animal. Finding another paddy, he burrowed into the insect-ridden human manure used to fertilize the paddy.

At the war's outbreak, Fifth Air Force included the 3rd Air Rescue Squadron, equipped with nine Sikorsky H-5A helicopters. Based at Ashiya, the helicopters had languished through the summer due to the fact their short range kept them from operating over Korea. In the meantime, the squadron sent a contingent of Stinson L-5 Sentinels to the Pusan Perimeter to operate in the rescue role. Unable to operate in the mountainous terrain or land in areas where there was a myriad of rice paddies, the L-5s could often not get to where they were needed.

On July 22, the nine H-5As were sent to Taegu. Over the next month, the helicopters picked up 83 wounded soldiers and delivered them to forward Mobile Army Surgical Hospital (MASH) units. Demand for their services grew. By the end of August, a further 14 H-5s were on their way to Korea. The fighter-bomber squadrons wondered if it might be possible to use the helicopters for behind-the-lines rescues of downed pilots.

While Bob Wayne burrowed into the manure, 50 miles south at Taegu, 1st Lt Paul van Bowen was called to the operations shack, where 3rd Rescue Squadron commander Captain Ray Costello told him of the downed Mustang and asked if he wanted to try a rescue. The slow, fragile, unarmed helicopter would be in extreme danger flying into a shooting war, and Costello said the mission was purely voluntary. "If you want to, you can go and take a look, but I don't want you to cross the lines. We're not required to do that." Van Bowen said yes. Minutes later, he and medic John Fuentes took off.

As the helicopter clattered north, the "C" Flight pilots were joined by another flight from the 35th Squadron and continued their efforts to hold the enemy soldiers at bay; 20 minutes later a third flight arrived on the scene. Bob Wayne knew of the helicopter detachment, and settled in for what seemed like the longest wait of his life. Ninety minutes after he went down, "C" Flight had to depart, low on fuel and out of ammunition. Soon, only one flight, led by Captain Stan White, remained overhead. Thirty minutes later, Wayne was beginning to give up hope when he heard the clatter of the approaching helicopter.

Van Bowen spotted the circling Mustangs, and went in low, circling the crashed airplane and searching for the pilot. The enemy below opened up on the helicopter and several rounds passed through the cockpit without hitting anything or anyone. Seeing the H-5, Wayne crawled out of the muck, pulled off his white T-shirt and waved it at the helicopter. As he stood there waving the shirt, a North Korean officer jumped up 100 yards away and ran through the rice paddy toward the American. Van Bowen spotted Wayne at the same moment and turned toward him. Overhead, Stan White saw the helicopter and the running North Korean. With a quick wingover, he roared in low and took aim at the figure splashing through the rice paddy toward his fellow pilot. Just as Van Bowen slowed for the pickup, White opened fire, filling the rice paddy with bullets and cutting the enemy soldier in half before flashing over the helicopter, missing it by less than 50 feet. Fuentes grabbed Wayne and pulled him aboard as Van Bowen started climbing away. The first combat helicopter rescue was a success. There would be many more.

Back at Taegu, Wayne was only able to treat his burns with several shots of bourbon before he was put aboard a C-46 headed back to Itazuke. After finally getting treated for his burns there, Wayne caught a ride to Osaka, where his wife was in the hospital having just delivered their third child. When he walked into the room with bandages over his burns, she didn't recognize him at first.

On September 8, with the Naktong Front stabilized, the 18th Fighter-Bomber Group returned to Korea, taking up residence at Pusan East airfield outside the village of Tongnae. The Mustangs were able to give all-out support against the North Korean advance south of Hajang, as they reached a point only 8 miles north of Taeju on September 9, the high point of their advance. Typhoon Kezia struck southern Japan on September 13 and the 35th and 36th squadrons relocated temporarily to Taegu so they could continue to provide support despite the adverse weather.

The Inchon invasion was MacArthur's greatest accomplishment as a general. Inchon is arguably the most difficult amphibious operation ever attempted, as regards the physical conditions that were overcome. The port had the greatest tides ever encountered in any invasion, with the LSTs (Landing Ship, Tanks) of the first wave that came ashore in the morning being left high and dry on the mud flats of the harbor floor for most of the day before the tide returned in the evening, allowing the assault craft to withdraw and be replaced by those carrying the second wave. When MacArthur first named Inchon as the place in which he would turn the war around, every expert told him it was impossible. He used that precise argument as his justification, reasoning that the enemy would see things the same way and act accordingly. This did happen, and the North Koreans were taken entirely by surprise when the 1st Marine Division landed on September 15.

Within days, the enemy forces on the Naktong were in retreat. Air power was used relentlessly against the North Korean Army. On September 18, three days after Inchon, 42 B-29s of the 92nd and 98th bomb wings carpet-bombed two 500-by-5,000-yard areas near Waegwan on the perimeter front. This second mission of direct battlefield support in Korea would go into the books as the biggest mission of its kind after Operation *Cobra*. The enemy troop concentrations were destroyed by the 1,600 260lb fragmentation bombs, opening the front for the Eighth Army offensive.

On September 21, forward air controllers flying T-6 "Mosquito" spotters discovered 30 enemy T-34s in an ambush ahead of the advancing 24th Infantry Division. The F-51s and field artillery the spotters called in destroyed 14 T-34s and forced the rest to withdraw. The next day, as North Korean resistance crumbled all along the Naktong Front, Mosquito pilot 1st Lt George W. Nelson found 200 enemy troops northeast of Kunsan and dropped a note demanding their surrender. Amazingly, the North Koreans moved to a hill Nelson designated with a smoke rocket, where they surrendered to nearby UN ground troops, the only time an enemy ground force ever surrendered to an airplane.

On September 26, units of X Corps moving out from Inchon met up with advancing Eighth Army units at Unsan. The next day the 1st Marine Division took control of the Seoul city hall. The Korean capital had been declared "secure" on September 25, despite the fact that fighting continued, so that MacArthur could say he had "ended" the North Korean invasion 90 days after its outset. As the flag was raised in Seoul, several hundred North Korean soldiers, each carrying a "safe conduct pass" that had been dropped by B-29s, surrendered north of the city.

The first South Korean unit crossed the 38th Parallel in a small operation on September 28, followed by major UN forces that crossed the border on October 9, 1950.

Fifth Air Force units moved from Japan to advanced airfields in Korea, with the 49th Fighter-Bomber Wing, which had remained at Misawa in northern Japan to counter any potential Soviet moves, bringing the F-80Cs of the 7th, 8th, and 9th Fighter-Bomber squadrons to Taegu (K-2) on October 2; the "Forty-Niners" became the first jet unit based in Korea. 77 Squadron moved permanently from Iwakuni to Pohang (K-3) and began operations under the operational control of the 35th Fighter-Bomber Wing, flying missions with the USAF squadrons as the Eighth Army and X Corps advanced into North Korea to "roll back" communism in an offensive Douglas MacArthur assured the world would be over by Christmas.

By August 14, all five strategic targets initially identified in North Korea had been hit by FEAF Bomber Command. Weather in the latter part of August restricted further missions, but Rashin was hit twice, though neither raid was considered successful. The fact Rashin was so close to the Soviet Union raised concern at the State Department that an "incident" might happen. The State Department won the argument with the Joint Chiefs and General Stratemeyer was ordered on September 1 not to make further attacks on Rashin. By early September, FEAF Bomber Command had hit all the originally identified targets except for the hydroelectric complexes built by the Japanese during World War II, located at Fusen, Chosin, Kyosen, Funei, Kongosan, and Suiho. The fact that several of these, particularly Suiho, also supplied power to Manchuria, made the decision to bomb them "political." In the end, 30 B-29s of the 92nd Bomb Wing demolished the Fusen plant near Hungnam, which was thought not to provide power to China, on September 26. Weather again intervened and by the time further missions against the hydroelectric sites were approved, UN forces were making such fast progress into North Korea that the campaign was aborted on grounds the power would be needed by the occupation forces once the war came to an end.

Between mid-July and mid-October, a force of five B-29 bomb wings had dropped over 30,000 tons of high explosives on North Korean targets, exceeding the record of XXIst Bomber Command against Japan between November 1944 and August 1945. Unlike the attacks against Japan, in which high-altitude precision bombing had been unsuccessful due to the jet stream over the country at the bombers' altitudes, which had forced a change in tactics to low-altitude area bombing fire raids at night, the North Korean campaign was characterized by a high degree of accuracy. The targets had been destroyed without the destruction of nearby urban areas where civilians lived and the relative loss of life among North Korean workers was small, since each raid had been preceded by leaflet-dropping that warned of the time and place of the attack. Rather than bomb from 33,000 feet, the B-29s had been able to operate at 16,000 feet. This was because the North Koreans did not have a large-scale antiaircraft defense, and their air force was unable to provide more than token opposition to the missions. These ideal conditions would soon change.

As all this happened, scant attention was paid that day to a newspaper report of an interview with People's Republic of China Premier Zhou En-Lai on October 3, 1950, in which he stated that the approach of UN forces to the Yalu River border between Korea and Manchuria would force the People's Republic of China to introduce Chinese troops into North Korea to stop the UN advance. When asked a week later about the Red Chinese warning, General MacArthur reminded the assembled reporters that "No Chinese army has ever successfully stood against a Western army."

CHAPTER 6

THE FATAL DECISION

The involvement of the People's Republic of China with the Korean War began when President Truman declared on June 27, 1950, that "the occupation of Formosa by Communist forces would be a direct threat to the security of the Pacific area and to US forces performing their lawful and necessary functions in that area," in answer to a question posed by a reporter at his first press conference following the North Korean invasion. Almost casually, the president had created an entirely new and firm commitment to maintaining support for Guomintang leader Chiang Kai-shek, whose defeated armies had retreated to the island in the wake of their defeat in the Civil War. The president's statement heightened traditional Chinese fears of western encirclement. The war in Korea amplified this concern, since the Korean peninsula had been a traditional invasion route into China, one that had been used twice in the previous 60 years with Japanese forces.

When North Korean leader Kim il-Sung had sought the approval and support of Josef Stalin for his proposed forcible reunification of Korea, the Soviet dictator had sent him to make a presentation to Mao Zedong, who was coincidentally in Moscow at the same time to sign the Sino-Soviet Treaty of mutual defense and cooperation. Mao had followed events in the United States during the "Revolt of the Admirals" and the congressional hearings that had exposed the American belief that war would only happen in Europe. He had also paid attention when Secretary of State Dean Acheson had stated that American defense interests in the Western Pacific ran from Japan through Okinawa to the Philippines, neglecting any mention of South Korea. Like Stalin, Mao had taken this to mean the United States had no further interest in events on the Korean peninsula. He reluctantly gave approval to Kim's proposal but cautioned that he still believed that the United States might intervene in support of South Korea.

Stalin had been surprised by the US reaction to the North Korean invasion in June. The Soviets had no expectation of President Truman seeking the approval of the United Nations for action to resist the invasion. This is evidenced by the fact the Soviets had been boycotting the UN since January over action taken in Germany to create the Bundesrepublik in West Germany following the end of the Berlin Blockade, which meant the Soviet Union was unable to veto the US resolution in the Security Council calling on UN members to provide assistance to South Korea.

History might have been different. On July 10, Secretary of State Acheson had been informed by the Indian ambassador that his government was prepared to put forward a Korean peace proposal in which the Chinese government had expressed interest. The Indian proposal began with a ceasefire, followed by both sides returning to their previous positions on the 38th Parallel, while the People's Republic would occupy the Chinese seat at the United Nations. George Kennan thought the initiative worth pursuing, advising Acheson that there would be no strategic change at the UN if the Red Chinese held the Chinese seat since the USSR already had a veto on the Security Council, and there was a future possibility of splitting the Chinese from the Russians.

Such was not to be. John Foster Dulles, a man described by Winston Churchill as "a bull who carried with him his own china closet," and who would have been Secretary of State in the Thomas E. Dewey Administration, had been appointed an advisor to the State Department on negotiations regarding the Japanese peace treaty the previous April. When he learned of the Indian proposal, he shouted down Kennan, stating that the proposal would "reward aggression" and that it would give the China Lobby the ammunition they needed to further attack the administration. Acheson never officially replied to the Indian ambassador and Kennan wrote in his diary on July 17, "I hope that some day history will record this as an instance of the damage done to the conduct of our foreign policy by the irresponsible and bigoted influence of the China Lobby and its friends in Congress."

In late July, General MacArthur had visited Chiang Kai-shek in Formosa, an event that appeared to the Red Chinese to demonstrate clear US support of their Nationalist enemies. Following this event, Mao issued orders to make preparations for possible intervention in the war. The Ninth Army of the People's Liberation Army was moved from its base of operations in South China to Manchuria, for possible use in Korea. Chinese leaders would have been even more disturbed if they had learned just how close MacArthur came to accepting the offer by Chiang Kai-shek to send 33,000 troops to Korea.

In mid-August, Politburo member Kuo Mo-Jo wrote in the official *People's Daily* newspaper that:

> The American imperialists fondly hope that their armed aggression against Taiwan will prevent us from liberating it. Around China in particular, their designs for a blockade are taking shape in the pattern of a stretched-out snake. Starting from South Korea, it stretches to Japan, the Ryukyu Islands, Taiwan and the Philippines and then turns up at Vietnam.

The Chinese Communists clearly saw the war in Korea in terms of historic Chinese national interest that had nothing to do with Communism.

Shortly after Kuo's statement, two Mustang pilots violated Manchurian airspace on August 27 and strafed an airfield near Antung, Manchuria, in the mistaken belief they were attacking the airfield at Sinuiju across the Yalu. The official *People's Daily* newspaper played this up over several issues as evidence of American intent to attack China.

A month before the success at Inchon, the Pentagon and State Department had voiced support for an invasion of North Korea. On August 17, UN ambassador Warren R. Austin issued a call at the UN for support of "establishing democratic government in the reunited Korea." In a radio broadcast on September 1, President Truman stated his support for a "free, independent, and united Korea." Shortly after, Secretary of State Acheson endorsed reunification, by force if necessary. At the same time, several influential members of parliament stated support for unification after the "liberation" of North Korea.

Kuo's *People's Daily* editorial was followed on August 20 by Premier Zhou En-Lai informing the United Nations that "Korea is China's neighbor. The Chinese people cannot but be concerned about a solution of the Korean question." This was the first indication of possible Chinese intervention in Korea. Zhou's statement was dismissed by President Truman as "a bald attempt to blackmail the UN."

MacArthur received initial approval for the Inchon operation from Chief of Naval Operations Admiral Forrest P. Sherman on August 23. Neither knew that at the same time, Mao Zedong had stated in a meeting of his political and military leaders in Beijing his belief that the United States would attempt a major military move to change the situation in Korea and that China must oppose it. Previously, his position was that liberation of Taiwan must have priority over unification of Korea.

The leaders in the Beijing meeting were then presented with a powerful briefing by Lei Yingfu, one of the ablest members of the PLA (People's Liberation Army) General Staff, regarding what this American action was likely to be. Mao had assigned Lei to study the situation in late July. Chinese intelligence was even then aware that supplies that implied an amphibious operation were arriving in Japan. Since this fitted with MacArthur's amphibious operations in the Pacific War, Lei concluded there would be a landing behind the lines to capture most of the North Korean Army. After studying six possible sites for such an operation, Lei pointed to Inchon as most likely because it was strategically the best site and also so operationally difficult that no one would expect it. MacArthur had in fact used this very argument with Admiral Sherman, citing the example of Wolff's landing at Quebec in the Seven Years' War. Following Lei's briefing, Mao gave orders for the People's Liberation Army to complete preparation for war in the event MacArthur did not stop at the 38th Parallel. Mao passed Lei's estimate to Kim il-Sung the following week; Kim was assured by his military advisors that such an operation was impossible.

On September 11, as MacArthur was finalizing the Inchon invasion plans, President Truman approved National Security Council Memorandum NSC 81/1 that authorized UN forces to cross the 38th Parallel to either force withdrawal by the North Korean Army from South Korea or inflict a decisive defeat on the NKPA.

Operation *Chromite* was an amazing success. The North Koreans were completely taken by surprise, and within a matter of days the Marines were outside Seoul, which was declared secure on September 25, day 90 of the war. The North Korean Army was routed at the Pusan

Perimeter and was retreating up the peninsula in disarray and under nearly constant air attack. On September 27, MacArthur received authorization to mount an offensive into North Korea. He had solid support from President Truman, Secretary of State Acheson, and the new Secretary of Defense, George C. Marshall: "Your military objective is the destruction of the North Korean Armed Forces." Following what was described as "some amount of inter-allied consultation," the United Kingdom, France, and some of the British Commonwealth nations backed the advance.

George C. Marshall had become Secretary of State following the president's dismissal of Louis Johnson when he had been discovered conspiring politically against the president. On September 29, Marshall sent a supportive message to MacArthur that concluded: "We want you to feel unhampered strategically and tactically to proceed north of the 38th Parallel." How Marshall – who had personally witnessed 30 years of history in which Douglas MacArthur had demonstrated his willingness to create his own reality regardless of facts – could take such a position defies all sense. The Great Man replied confidently: "I regard all of Korea open for our military operations unless and until the enemy capitulates." General Matthew Ridgway later wrote of this time:

> Complete victory now seemed in view – a golden apple that would handsomely symbolize the crowning effort of a brilliant military career. Once in reach of this prize, MacArthur would not allow himself to be delayed or admonished. Instead, he plunged northward in pursuit of a vanishing enemy, and changed his plans from week to week to accelerate this advance without regard to dark hints of possible disaster.

The rapid North Korean collapse increased the urgency for Chinese intervention. On September 19, Kim il-Sung requested assistance from Stalin and asked him to bring pressure on Mao to send troops. By the end of September, Mao had concluded it was necessary for the future of the revolution for the new China to take such a step, because not to intervene meant the new China was the same as the old, powerless when facing the West. Korean geography favored China; the American move north would require that they remain on primitive roads in difficult country because of their mechanized units, while their supply lines would be strung out in the same difficult country; thus the UN forces would be an easy target for the kind of warfare that had led to success for the PLA in the Civil War. At a meeting of the Politburo, Mao stated he did not fear attack with atomic bombs since Chinese society was rural; there was no target the Americans could bomb that would stop the enemy.

On October 2, Premier Zhou En-Lai met with the Indian ambassador to China, K. M. Panikkar. During the meeting he stated that if non-Korean armed forces crossed the 38th Parallel, China would send troops into Korea; the interview was published in Hong Kong and New Delhi the next day. No heed was paid to the Chinese warning in Tokyo or Washington. The State Department saw Panikkar as the representative of a country which was an international leader of the anticolonialist forces. The ambassador's communication of Zhou's warning was seen as the act of a "pro-Communist," even though Panikkar was well known among professional diplomatic circles as a non-Communist who deplored Mao's callous attitude about loss of life. General Walter Bedell Smith, now head of the CIA, reported that his analysts saw Panikkar as an "innocent instrument" being used by the Chinese. He stated the CIA's belief that the Chinese were not serious in their threats. Political leaders could look to a Gallup poll taken during the last week of September, which showed 64 percent of the American public supported pursuing the North Koreans across the parallel. No one knew that on October 8, Mao Zedong had ordered General Peng Dehuai, whose PLA Ninth Army had been renamed the Chinese People's Volunteer Army, to move into North Korea immediately and take position to block the UN advance.

MacArthur submitted a plan in response to the authorization to cross the parallel that foresaw an advance by Eighth Army into North Korea on the western side of the peninsula, while X Corps would take Wonsan on the east coast and proceed up the eastern side toward the Yalu. The plan drew a restraining line at the 40th Parallel, from Chongju in the west to Hungnam in the east; non-Korean forces would remain to the south, while ROK units moved to the Manchurian border.

Previously, the State Department had drawn up a proposed UN resolution which supported the new American political objectives in Korea. Because the Soviet delegation had returned in August, the US moved for adoption of the resolution in the General Assembly, where the USSR had no veto and US influence greatly outweighed the Soviets'. The debate began at the General Assembly in New York on October 4 and ended October 7 with passage of a resolution stating "(a) All appropriate steps be taken to ensure conditions of stability throughout Korea; and, (b) All constituent acts be taken, including the holding of elections, under the auspices of the United Nations, for the establishment of a unified, independent and democratic Korea." The vague language signaled a change in mission from repelling aggression to uniting Korea by force through territorial occupation. On October 9, the Joint Chiefs finally responded to Zhou's public threat of intervention and expressed further caution regarding the threat of Soviet or Chinese intervention by rephrasing their previous instructions about contact with Chinese forces: should such forces be met "anywhere in Korea," MacArthur was to continue action "so long as success seems probable."

When Ambassador Pannikar learned the UN had authorized MacArthur's move north, he wrote in his diary:

> So America has knowingly elected for war, with Britain following. It is indeed a tragic decision, for the Americans and British are well aware that a military settlement of the Korean issue will be resisted by the Chinese and that the armies now concentrated on the Yalu will intervene decisively in the fight. Probably that is what the Americans, at least some of them, want. They probably feel that this is an opportunity to have a showdown with China. In any case, MacArthur's dream has come true. I only hope that it does not turn out to be a nightmare.

At the State Department, "old China hands" John Paton Davies and Edmund O. Clubb, already excoriated by the China Lobby and the newly powerful Senator Joseph McCarthy as the traitors who had "lost China," took heed of the Chinese statements and urged caution. Davies attempted to explain what might happen, writing that "A combination of irredentism, expansionism, Soviet pressure and inducements, strategic anxieties, ideological zeal, domestic pressures and emotional anti-Americanism" could lead to Chinese intervention. Clubb, Director of the Office of Chinese Affairs, bluntly stated that China would fight if UN forces entered North Korea. Unfortunately, they were both on the way out, since Acheson had decided he did not need the continuing political grief of McCarthy's accusation that he was "soft on communism."

The possibility of accidentally expanding the war was demonstrated on October 8. A flight of four F-80Cs from the 8th Fighter-Bomber Squadron of the 49th Wing departed Taegu (K-2) to sweep the Chongjin airfield in northeast Korea. When the flight leader experienced mechanical difficulties, he and his wingman aborted and returned to Taegu while the element leader and his wingman continued on. Instead of hitting Chongjin airfield, however, they attacked Sukhaya Rechka airfield 19 miles south-west of Vladivostok and 62 miles from the Soviet–Korean border. The airfield was used by the Air Forces of the Pacific Fleet (V-VS TOF), and was occupied by the 821st Fighter Aviation Regiment (821 IAP) of the 190th Fighter Aviation Division (190 IAD), operating Bell P-63 King Cobra aircraft originally supplied during World War II under Lend-Lease. Twelve P-63s were damaged and one was burned out when the two Shooting Stars made two strafing runs before returning to their home base. On their return to Taegu, the pilots claimed it was a navigational error. General Stratemeyer quickly and publicly removed the wing commander and reassigned him to FEAF headquarters. Court-martial proceedings were instituted against the two pilots, who were quickly found not guilty of violating the rules of engagement and speedily returned to the United States. The Soviets took Stratemeyer's actions as proof the attack was not premeditated. The attack goaded Stalin to reinforce Soviet air defenses in the Far East and to confirm his commitment to the Chinese to provide active air defense of the Chinese bases in Manchuria that would support the planned Chinese intervention in North Korea.

Washington's "common wisdom" was expressed in a CIA report on October 12, four days after Mao's order to the People's Volunteer Army to enter North Korea: "despite statements by Chou En-Lai, troop movements to Manchuria, and propaganda charges of atrocities and border violations, there are no convincing indications of an actual Chinese Communist intention to resort to full-scale intervention in Korea." New Assistant Secretary of State for Far Eastern Affairs Dean Rusk told Acheson that the Red Chinese would not risk losing the chance to take their seat at the UN, that they would not want to become Soviet clients in order to wage war, and their army was not equipped to face MacArthur's armies. Acheson told the president that he found

Rusk's argument "irresistible." The United States government did not see its actions in Korea as a threat to "legitimate Chinese interests," and convinced itself the Chinese would come to the same conclusion.

In mid-October, President Truman finally met General MacArthur face to face in a meeting on Guam. Writing later of the meeting, the general stated that the possibility of intervention in the war by China came up almost casually, and that the president agreed with him that China had no intention of making such an intervention. President Truman remembered the meeting differently in his memoirs. According to the president, the threat of Chinese intervention in Korea was a prime reason for the meeting, and what he took away from Wake Island was MacArthur's assurance there was little chance the Chinese would act, that "at the most they might be able to get fifty or sixty thousand men into Korea, but since they had no air force, if they tried to get down to Pyongyang, there would be the greatest slaughter." The general went so far as to suggest that the 2nd Infantry Division, veterans of hard fighting in the Pusan Perimeter, could be transferred to Europe early in 1951.

The state of official delusion was reinforced by military events.

At sea, the fliers aboard the four aircraft carriers of Task Force 77 reported they were running out of targets. The Navy began planning to withdraw the carriers and return them to the United States. By the end of the month, only USS *Leyte* (CV-32), which had arrived in Japan at the end of September and joined the fleet in the Sea of Japan in mid-October, was still on station. No one paid much attention to the October 18 report of an RB-29 mission to the Yalu, which spotted some 75 unidentified aircraft on the airfield at Antung that had not been there two days earlier, the last time a reconnaissance flight had come close to Antung.

Four days after the president met his commanding general, 130,000 People's Volunteer Army troops crossed the Yalu between October 18 and 25, and moved into the Taebaek Mountains north and west of what UN maps called the Chosin Reservoir, its Japanese name. At the same time, a similar-sized force crossed into western North Korea and took position north of the Chongchon River.

The CIA supported what General MacArthur had told President Truman, that the Chinese would only deploy some 40,000 troops in Korea if they entered at all, and that any action would be "face saving" to support the withdrawal of surviving North Korean troops. Reconnaissance flights saw no evidence of enemy movement into the country. What they did not realize was that the army that had entered North Korea did not operate as a Western army would. There was no need for trucks to carry troops and supplies, or for the creation of supply dumps along the way. Chinese soldiers each carried 70lb packs of food and ammunition and the units moved by foot. They employed fieldcraft and camouflage to remain in the forested hills of the mountainous north, and did not rely on radio communication that could be intercepted to relay orders between units. A Chinese unit expected to move 15 miles in one night without a single cigarette smoked, then burrow into caves or hide in the deep forest during the day. By late October, the Yalu was frozen sufficiently that they did not even need to use the bridges to enter Korea, but could cross anywhere the ice was thick enough. The American leadership was unaware of any of this since not seeing anything amiss was practically a requirement for one to be taken seriously in the upper circles of both Tokyo and Washington.

On October 20, the 187th Airborne Regimental Combat Team made a combat drop 30 miles north of Pyongyang as part of a highly publicized blocking maneuver to prevent what was termed "the remnants" of the NKPA retreating north of Pyongyang, which had been taken the day before. Seventy-one C-119s and 40 C-47s from Combat Cargo Command participated in the operation, the only paratroop operation of the Korean War, which saw over 2,800 paratroopers and 300 tons of equipment and supplies dropped at Sukchon and Sunchon some 50 miles north of Pyongyang. Over the next three days, another 2,000 paratroopers would be dropped in further missions to reinforce the original contingent, with a further 600 tons of supplies also dropped, thus making this the largest airborne operation ever carried out in the Pacific, exceeding the previous combat drop by the 187th to take Corregidor in the Philippines five years earlier. The next day, MacArthur removed all restrictions on how far north American units could advance, thus allowing them to go all the way to the Yalu.

The North Korean Army had virtually melted away in the fighting after Inchon. The B-29s had run out of strategic targets to destroy, and the F-51 fighter-bomber units were facing little opposition as they moved up to Pyongyang on October 21. At the same time, F-80 Shooting

Stars from the 8th and 35th groups' remaining F-80 squadrons began operating in Korea from Suwon airfield, and the 49th Wing moved up to Kimpo from Taegu, where they were joined by the 16th and 25th Fighter-Interceptor squadrons of the 51st Fighter-Interceptor Group that moved to Korea from Okinawa. Kimpo and Suwon were the two best air bases in Korea, and positioned the short-legged F-80s to allow the jets to provide air support all the way to the Yalu.

American political and military leaders were unaware that Stalin had agreed in early October to provide "unofficial support" for China and North Korea in the event of a UN move across the 38th Parallel. Soviet support for the war was never as strong as was later made out by Americans; in fact, this lack of support would be one of the leading reasons for the eventual Sino-Soviet split following the death of Stalin, which was finally noticed in the West in 1959.

Stalin did agree to provide air defense, with limited numbers of fighters. The aircraft would carry North Korean air force insignia, the pilots would wear North Korean uniforms, and Russian would not be spoken on the radio. What this meant was that Stalin recognized in 1950 that the United States was a stronger power than the Soviet Union. His scientists had exploded an atomic bomb, but the successful production of useable nuclear weapons proceeded at a snail's pace. Additionally, while the Strategic Air Command could base their B-29s and B-50s at forward bases in Europe in the event of a war, and possessed the B-36 that could strike the USSR by flying over the North Pole from bases inside the United States, the Soviet Union possessed only a few hundred Tu-4 bombers, reverse-engineered from two B-29s that had landed in Siberia during the war; these bombers could only reach targets in America on one-way missions over the Arctic. Stalin was well aware that if World War III was to break out as a result of any action in Korea, the guaranteed loser would be the Soviet Union.

Throughout October, an increasing number of reliable reports confirmed the arrival of Chinese troops in North Korea, from airmen's reports of sighting footprints in the snow covering the ice in the Yalu to statements by North Korean refugees that they had personally seen the newcomers. MacArthur's longtime Chief of Intelligence, Major General Charles Willoughby, who had cemented his position on the general's staff back in Manila in 1941 when he provided reports that Japan had no plans for an invasion of the Philippines before the middle of 1942 – which amazingly coincided with his commander's beliefs – continued his sycophancy, "proving" the Chinese either were not present, or were there only in small numbers. Many US Army veterans who served in Korea later stated their belief that Willoughby's failure to admit the reports were accurate and move quickly to reorient toward the new enemy was directly responsible for the events of November 1950.

Ultimately, the decision to cross the 38th Parallel was influenced more by the needs of domestic politics than by any strategic military logic. The imperative for the Truman Administration was to win a mid-term election in a hostile domestic political climate where a charge of being "soft on communism" was considered fatal, as Senator Joseph McCarthy of Wisconsin used his position on the Senate Government Operations Committee to continue making charges of "Communist infiltration" of the administration. Presidential decision-making was based on the shared assumptions regarding the Cold War held by both political parties, which reinforced the fantasies of Douglas MacArthur and his yes-men in Tokyo. What the Japanese had termed "Victory Disease" in World War II was proving just as difficult to resist for Americans five years later.

CHAPTER 7

A NEW AND DIFFERENT WAR

A change in the nature of the war became apparent in late October and early November. While units of the ROK Army had reported the capture of Chinese soldiers as they advanced to the Yalu River in the final weeks of October, UN forces headquarters in Tokyo repeatedly refused to believe there was a new enemy in Korea. At best, the leaders in Tokyo would only say that there was a small force deployed to "save face" for the Chinese Communists as their North Korean comrades were inexorably defeated.

On October 31, the air war suddenly changed. That morning, pilots of the 51st Fighter-Interceptor Wing's 25th Squadron reported they had seen "silver, arrow-shaped jets" in flight over the major airfield at Antung, just across the Yalu. A few hours later, Captain Alma R. Flake led a flight of 67th Fighter-Bomber Squadron Mustangs on a sweep to the Yalu. The F-51s spotted "unknown enemy jet aircraft" on the Manchurian side of the border. Though he was unable to close the enemy fighters, Flake still fired his guns in an attempt to obtain gun camera film of the strange jets. Once his film was developed back at base, it was found Flake had gotten some fairly distinct shots of what were tentatively identified as MiG-15s, the newest Soviet jet fighter. The film went all the way to FEAF headquarters in Tokyo and eventually provided the evidence for General Stratemeyer to convince the Air Force high command to release the Sabres of the 4th Fighter-Interceptor Wing for service in Korea to meet the new threat.

On November 1, 15 F-51s of the 67th Squadron that were bombing the Yalu bridges were intercepted as they came off the target by five

MiG-15s. The Americans didn't know these enemy jets were from the 1st Squadron of the 72nd GvIAP of the V-VS, led by Hero of the Soviet Union (HSU) Major N. V. Stroykov, a 16-victory Soviet ace of the Great Patriotic War, leading senior lieutenants Guts and Kaznacheev and lieutenants Monakhov, Chizh and Sanin. At first, the Americans were able to evade the faster jets by turning sharply, a maneuver the jets couldn't follow.

Eventually, one F-51D broke from the others and Lt Chizh, a 13-victory Great Patriotic War ace, shot it down. 1st Lt Aaron Abercrombie became the first American victim of the new arrivals, though his loss was officially credited by the Air Force to ground fire until Soviet records were opened in 1992, following the end of the Cold War.

Also on November 1, the North Korean People's Air Force, now based on Chinese airfields in Manchuria, started making hit and run raids across the Yalu; they remained within sight of the international border, which allowed the pilots to dart back over the river to safety when spotted by UN aircraft. Shortly after the first Russian pilots had engaged UN aircraft, three NKPAF Yak-9Ps jumped a USAF T-6 Mosquito forward air controller and a B-26 Invader south of Sinuiju; the B-26's gunner shot down one of the Yaks.

Shortly after noon, an 8th Tactical Reconnaissance Squadron RF-80A radioed that he had spotted 15 Yak-9Ps on the Sinuiju airfield and in response General Stratemeyer ordered the 49th Wing to strike the airfield. Twelve F-80s with strict orders not to violate the Yalu border were launched to hit the airfield. Shortly after they arrived over Sinuiju at around 1545 hours, the Shooting Star pilots received a radioed warning of "bogeys" in the vicinity. Moments later, at 1550 hours, the lead flight of four Shooting Stars were hit by three MiG-15s, led by 72nd GvIAP 1st Squadron commander Major Bordunthat with Senior Lieutenant Semyon Fyodorovich Khominich and Lieutenant Sukhov, which dived out of the sun through their formation. Senior Lieutenant Khominich put the MiG's heavy armament of one 37mm and two 23mm cannon to good use by exploding the Shooting Star flown by 1st Lt Frank Van Sickle. A Soviet pilot had emerged victorious in history's first jet vs jet air combat. A Soviet ground team, sent to examine the wreckage and confirm the victory, was unable to find anything. Van Sickle's Shooting Star had either exploded in mid-air, or crashed in the Yalu River.

USAF records admitted the loss of two F-80Cs on November 1 – Van Sickle's from the 49th Fighter-Bomber Group, and another from the 51st Wing listed as lost during a rocket attack near Unsan that afternoon. These two losses were officially credited by the USAF to North Korean antiaircraft fire until Russian records that became available after the end of the Cold War revealed the truth. Initially, in the face of the pilot reports of sighting MiG-15s, FEAF intelligence believed that the Soviets might be "field testing" the jets, but considered it more likely they were being flown by Chinese or North Koreans, and that only a limited number were available. In reality, November 1 had marked the first combat for what was actually a substantial Soviet air presence that had moved into Manchuria during October.

Late in the afternoon following these other combats, Captain Flake led another flight of Mustangs on a low-level sweep of the Yalu. This time there were no MiGs, but the Mustangs did run across four North Korean-flown Yak-9s. As Flake later recalled:

Four Yaks in elements of two crossed the river on a southerly heading just east of our position. I ordered the flight to climb at maximum power and assume combat formation. Almost immediately, the first two Yaks initiated a diving attack. I brought the flight around behind the lead Yak. I fired a short burst and broke to his left. I continued in a maximum right turn and lost sight of him for just a moment. He was below me. Looking down, I spotted him and maneuvered to attack. It was obvious he had lost sight of me because he continued in a gentle climbing turn that allowed me to gain a favorable position behind and slightly inside his circle. Since I had already expended most of my ammunition on ground targets, I waited to open fire until I attained optimum range. At a distance of about 600 feet, I pulled the trigger and the Yak immediately began trailing smoke. A few seconds later the pilot leveled off and bailed out; he had a good 'chute and probably survived. The Yak spiralled down and crashed.

The wingman of the downed Yak turned north for the border and the other two enemy fighters broke off their attack before opening fire and fled across the river before Flake and his wingman, 2nd Lt "Ace"

Ausman, could catch up. "My impression was that these pilots were quite inexperienced and unskilled," Flake added.

Shortly after Flake's fight, fellow 67th Squadron pilot Captain Robert D. Thresher, a World War II combat veteran, and his flight of F-51s were called in to support an armored column that was stopped by an enemy roadblock. After knocking out the enemy position, the Mustangs hung around and in a few minutes the pilot of the forward air control T-6 "Mosquito" spotted some ox-carts loaded with supplies and called in the Mustangs.

As Thresher made his strafing run:

> Suddenly these big balls of orange fire came zipping across my wing. I started to call "flak," but suddenly an ominous shape flashed past me and climbed away. It was a Yak! I lost him in the sun. I looked over at the other planes in the flight and they were chasing a lone Yak. I shoved my throttle forward to try and catch up when the FAC called for me to watch out. I looked around and there was the Yak that had attacked me, opening fire again!

Thresher turned as tight as he could, while the enemy fighter pulled up into a loop that would put him in position for another tail pass if Thresher broke his turn. The enemy pilot made two more loops as Thresher continued to turn, and lost enough speed that at the top of his third loop he stalled out and fell into a spin. Thresher followed him down. The enemy pilot pulled out of the spin as Thresher tried to get on his tail, but the Yak pulled up in a steep climb. The Yak pilot pulled around for another dive, which Thresher countered with a tight turn. This happened twice more; the Yak pilot bled enough speed that again he stalled out and went into a spin. Thresher recalled:

> I added throttle and waited him out. I was still in my turn when he tried to pull out and I snapped off a couple of bursts. A long blue plume of smoke began to trail from his wing and he wobbled and fell off. He slowly rolled over and went into a long dive and crashed. On the way home, it was rewarding to know that after almost six years I still knew how to fight.

While the air war was changing, the ground war saw American troops confront an entirely new enemy. The night of November 1, three battalions of the 1st Cavalry Division's 8th Regiment were hit at Unsan by three divisions of the People's Volunteer Army. The Americans were quickly surrounded and the cavalrymen had to abandon their equipment the next day as small units of the survivors managed to make their way back to UN lines through the Chinese, while several hundred of their fellow troopers became prisoners of war. On November 5, the new enemy struck the Chongchon River defensive line in an attempt to gain control of the river crossing at Pakchon, but were driven back by the Commonwealth Brigade strongly supported by artillery. While the Eighth Army units completed their withdrawal by November 7, the new enemy disappeared, melting back into the forests and steep mountains of North Korea. In Tokyo, intelligence chief Major General Willoughby told reporters this was merely the work of "volunteers" who had been sent to "save face" for Mao, and that they were certainly all on their way back to China.

On November 2, Flake and his flight were again attacked by four Yaks just south of the Yalu. "This time the fight lasted longer because it was pursued with more vigor by both sides." Flake's opponent was "obviously highly-trained and eager to engage." The two opponents passed each other in a head-on pass, which Flake followed by climbing nearly vertically to get an altitude advantage as he slowed to make a quick turn. When Flake spotted the enemy, "his nose was almost on me and closing fast." Flake rolled inverted and dived straight down. "I had a most uneasy feeling that he was close behind me."

Knowing he could not out-turn the enemy fighter, Flake endeavored to keep the battle in the vertical.

The fight ended in a series of vertical turns at nine to ten thousand feet before we dived for the ground. He held the Yak in the vertical climb until it appeared to stop in mid-air, fall backwards and spin out. I could only get a few shots off when he peaked at the top; just as I got into range he would enter a spin and evade my attack. After three or four of these, I got some hits just before he reached his peak. He broke prematurely and headed straight down, then pulled out and headed north. I got into position right behind him and just as I opened fire his right wing appeared to tear away at the root. He rolled abruptly, then crashed and exploded.

Other members of the flight engaged in similar combats but were not as lucky as Flake had been. "We were all low on fuel and ammunition, so we broke off and returned to base." The 67th had a party that night to celebrate Flake's success; he never had another chance during his tour to engage the enemy in air combat.

The 67th's last air combat of 1950 took place four days later, on November 6. Captain Howard I. Price, one of the more experienced pilots in the squadron, led a flight to the Yalu. His wingman, 1st Lt George Olsen, spotted six Yak-9s below, climbing toward the Mustangs from the nine o'clock position. Price turned into the enemy fighters, and he and Olsen dived on the closest Yak; the pilot snap-rolled and dived away, leaving the two Mustangs behind. Price rolled onto the wingman and clobbered him with an accurate burst. Smoke poured from the engine and the pilot bailed out. Price then saw another Yak being pursued by a Mustang and joined the fight. He fired each of his four rockets, which all went above or below the enemy fighter. "These rockets were absolutely useless as they had been stored on Guam since 1945 and the propellant had solidified on the low side of each. Putting it in golfing terms, you didn't know whether the rockets would slice or hook!" He then closed in and got off four bursts of fire into the Yak, which caught fire. "I think one of my rounds must have killed the pilot, for he made no effort to pull out. I watched him all the way down to where he hit the ground close to Sinuiju and exploded."

The night of November 6, on the eastern side of the Korean peninsula, US Marines of the 1st Marine Division's 7th Regiment were hit by two divisions of Chinese troops at Sudong, when they advanced out of the Marines' main base at Hamhung toward the Chosin Reservoir. Unlike the cavalrymen at Unsan, the Marines held their ground and the enemy was forced to break off with heavy casualties the next day, but their commanders were the first to admit they had held on by their fingernails. What the Chinese called the First Phase Campaign had demonstrated clearly that this was a Chinese army that had to be taken seriously, regardless of MacArthur's earlier declaration that "No Chinese army has ever stood successfully against a Western army."

Douglas MacArthur was thought of by those who worked with him or confronted him during the 45 years of his career as having two speeds: "When he was good he was brilliant, and when he was bad he was terrible, and there was no in-between," as one senior officer recalled. When MacArthur's view of events and reality conflicted, as had happened when the Japanese attacked the Philippines in December 1941 after he had stated definitively that there was no possibility of their being able to attack before mid-1942, he went into a funk where his mood changed from over-optimism to panic.

After the initial Japanese attacks on December 8, 1941, MacArthur was not to be found at his Manila headquarters for two crucial weeks. Because he could not allow himself to consider that he might be wrong, he had taken no measures to provide food and ammunition on Bataan before ordering a retreat to the peninsula. There was no possibility of his men being able to hold out until reinforcements arrived, as he stated they would. Many held him personally responsible for the debacle in the Philippines and only the existence of his massive staff publicity department was able to deflect such blame and reinforce his public persona as "America's greatest general."

MacArthur had a similar reaction to the Chinese attacks in early November 1950. On November 4, MacArthur told his superiors in Washington that there was little chance of a Chinese attack on UN forces. By November 6, the general reported "men and material in large force pouring across the Yalu bridges." The air campaign, which heretofore had been fought with restrictions that required precision attacks, turned into an unrestricted bombing campaign as MacArthur ordered FEAF Bomber Command, Fifth Air Force and Task Force 77 to destroy anything and everything that might possibly be of any use to the enemy. On November 5, 30 B-29s of the 19th Bomb Group dropped 170 tons of incendiaries on Kanggye, setting fire to over half the built-up area. The response from Washington was immediate and negative, as a political firestorm was set off by news of the attack.

MacArthur cabled the Joint Chiefs that the restriction on bombing targets within 5 miles of the Yalu must be overturned and FEAF Bomber Command be turned against the Yalu bridges. President Truman and the Joint Chiefs in Washington were concerned that attacks at the Yalu risked UN incursions into Chinese air space that could expand the war and ordered the strikes be canceled. MacArthur replied that a cancelation of the B-29 missions against the bridges "might well result in a calamity of major proportions." The message ended with the statement that the air strikes were the sole means of preventing enemy reinforcement by destroying the bridges and "all installations in the north area supporting the enemy advance." He also requested authority to bomb Chinese supply bases in Manchuria and intimated he might have to request authority to employ atomic weapons.

The request to enlarge the war into Manchuria was refused. Permission was given by General Stratemeyer for the fighter-bombers to attack targets throughout North Korea, up to the Yalu, with the proviso that missions flown in close proximity to the Chinese and Soviet borders be flown by "highly experienced pilots with accurate maps of the targets they were briefed to attack." General O'Donnell was granted permission by MacArthur to bomb four North Korean cities with incendiaries; Bomber Command was ordered to burn the targeted cities "from end to end." The general charged his airmen to go "all out" for two weeks "to the point of crew exhaustion."

The first mission against the bridges was scheduled for November 7, but was canceled due to bad weather. With a forecast of better weather, the mission was rescheduled for the following day.

Major Evans G. Stephens, commander of the 16th Fighter-Interceptor Squadron of the 51st Fighter Interceptor Wing, later remembered that November 8, 1950 was remarkably bright and clear, a day different from most in Korea, where fliers regularly contended with bad weather. Flying at 18,000 feet, ceiling and visibility were unlimited, and the Korean countryside far below was already snow-covered in the outset of what would later be recorded as the coldest Korean winter in 144 years. The Yalu River border between North Korea and Manchuria was just coming into sight. Stephens stretched as best he could in the ejection seat to which he was securely strapped, and wiped sweat from his brow. The sun through the clear plexiglass canopy was hot, despite the fact that immediately on the other side of the plastic the temperature was 20 degrees below zero. He reached forward and turned up the cockpit air conditioning to fight the heat. Squadron pilot 1st Lieutenant Chester Wagner later described Stephens to historian Robert Dorr as "the best commander I ever had, a natural stick. He could handle an F-80 better than anybody I ever saw."

Stephens had begun his career as a fighter pilot in 1942, flying P-39 Airacobras in New Guinea with the 8th Fighter Group out of Three Mile Drome at Port Moresby; he exhibited the easy camaraderie of a combat veteran. He had taken command of the squadron shortly after the 51st Wing had moved to Kimpo following the success at Inchon.

His predecessor, Lt Col Converse B. Kelley, had been taken off flight operations and sent back to Japan as an inspector following the death of one of his pilots in a combat mission, the squadron's first loss, in circumstances that cast doubt on his leadership. The pilots of the 16th had all responded well to the different leadership style Stephens brought with him.

As the fighters continued toward the Yalu, Stephens glanced out at his wingman, 1st Lt Russell J. Brown, flying F-80C 49-713. Brown was normally assigned to the 25th Squadron, but was on temporary assignment to the 16th to provide the benefit of his experience for the newer pilots. A thousand yards further out beyond Stephens' four Shooting Stars was the squadron's second flight of four jets, led by Captain Eldon Neil Colby. The Shooting Stars were top cover for a strike by 70 B-29 Superfortress bombers against the border city of Sinuiju and the Yalu bridges. The clear weather today meant that the bombardiers in the Superforts should have no trouble spotting their targets.

In addition to the B-29s, F-51s of the 8th Fighter-Bomber Group and F-80Cs of the 49th Fighter-Bomber Group were assigned to attack antiaircraft gun positions near the target with rockets and bombs 30 minutes before the arrival of the main force.

Stephens later described what happened. "When I saw there was no enemy air opposition, I led my flight down to attack the enemy flak positions." He and Brown made the first run. The defending flak was heavy, and most of it was coming from across the river on the Manchurian side. "We could have got out and walked on it." Stephens and Brown climbed to cover first lieutenants Ralph N. Giel and Richard D. Escola on their attack. At that moment, they heard a call from pilots escorting the B-29s that MiG-15s had been sighted crossing the Yalu from Manchuria. Stephens quickly spotted eight MiGs approaching from the south and above, on the South Korean side of the river, and ordered Giel and Escola to break off their run and join up.

The B-29s made their attack before the MiGs could arrive, with 61 bombers dropping 580 tons of incendiaries on the city, which burned most structures to the ground, while the remaining nine bombers dropped 500lb high-explosive bombs on the Yalu bridge, though they only succeeded in damaging the road to the bridge rather than the structure itself. Their task completed, the bombers turned south and headed back to Okinawa.

Minutes later, MiG-15s flashed past Stephens' flight and he saw two of the jets pull out of their dive and head toward the Antung airfield complex across the river at the same altitude. Stephens banked sharp left to pursue them and he got the enemy flight leader in his gunsight. "I thought I could get him, but I didn't want to punch off my wing tanks for fear they might hit the two inexperienced pilots in my flight." Stephens banked sharply to the left with wingman Brown closely behind. Brown still had not spotted the enemy, and recalled afterwards, "I was looking around like mad and flying formation at the same time." As Stephens completed his turn, Brown saw the two MiGs when the wingman turned right in front of him.

The MiGs were part of a force from the 28th, 72nd, and 139th GvIAPs tasked with intercepting the bombers. They had been launched too late to hit the B-29s before they dropped their loads, and instead chose to go after the fighter-bombers that were still engaged in attacking antiaircraft positions.

The enemy leader climbed to the left to disengage, while the wingman turned right. Brown stayed tight inside his turn. Three of his six .50-caliber guns had jammed on the strafing run, but he managed to fire four short bursts that missed.

Lieutenant Kharitonov, the enemy pilot, then winged over into a dive and Brown went after him. As the two fighters hurtled straight down, Brown popped off his wingtip fuel tanks to lighten his fighter and increase its speed and closed to within 1,000 feet of the MiG. He fired one long burst during which two of his three guns jammed, following that with three short bursts from his last gun. As he did, he thought to himself, "Damn, I'm going to get him." The MiG appeared to catch fire near the engine. "It was now or never, I squeezed the trigger and held it down."

Brown's Shooting Star was buffeting as he dove at more than 600mph, nearly the F-80's limiting Mach number. He reduced the throttle and pulled back hard on the stick. With a final burst, he saw explosions on the ground. G-force streamers spread from the wing tips as the Shooting Star managed to pull out of the wild dive a hundred feet above the ground and head back for altitude.

So far as the USAF was concerned, Brown had just scored the first jet vs jet kill. He would remain in-theater until the summer of 1951, but this was his only score. The victory had been due to luck, since the enemy pilot could have easily outrun the F-80 had he climbed instead of dived and applied throttle in time.

In fact, Lieutenant Kharitonov was not splattered across the Korean countryside. As Brown had done, he had dropped his two underwing tanks in the dive to lighten his fighter. There was a light haze at this lower altitude, which limited Brown's view of the MiG, and he mistook the falling drop tanks for pieces coming off the enemy fighter. Kharitonov had just become the first Soviet pilot to release his drop tanks in combat; there were only a limited number of them available in the units at this time, which made each worth its weight in gold. Pilots were ordered to put up with inferior flight characteristics with the tanks in order to prolong their time in the combat zone.

Brown had identified the plumes of burning kerosene from the falling tanks as the MiG catching fire, reinforcing the illusion in the haze that he had mortally wounded his adversary. In truth, the MiG was so hardy that the weight of fire of one .50-caliber machine gun would only have been fatal had there been a "golden BB" hit on something vital. Kharitonov pulled out of his dive so low his exhaust rippled the trees below and he stayed low as he streaked across the Yalu. While Brown was climbing to rejoin the others and reporting his success, his opponent was lowering his landing gear and dropping onto the main runway at Antung.

The November 8 B-29 attack on Sinuiju was not successful in knocking down the bridges. The next day, the Navy joined in the effort. Between November 9 and 12, Task Force 77 hit the Yalu bridges, knocking down the two bridges upriver at Hyesanjin and the road bridge at Sinuiju, though the railway bridge there still stood. The Air Force went after other targets in a two-week air campaign that would "destroy every means of communication and every installation, factory, city and village" below the Yalu, with the exception of the hydroelectric complexes in North Korea, which supplied power to Manchuria and were considered necessary for UN forces once they occupied the country. The order prohibiting incendiary attacks on inhabited areas, which had been in effect since the outbreak of the war, was rescinded. In the event, the bombing of the bridges was "closing the barn door after the horse had escaped." The People's Volunteer Army was already in North Korea, most of the troops having crossed on the ice once the Yalu froze for the winter.

The F-86 Sabre, the USAF's first swept-wing jet fighter, made its initial flight on October 1, 1947. As a day fighter, the airplane saw service in Korea in three successive series (F-86A, E, and F). (USAF)

Pilots of 77 Squadron, RAAF – the Royal Australian Air Force entered the war in Korea in the second week of the war, providing crucial air support to UN forces in the first 90 days of combat. (Photo by Alan Lambert/The AGE/Fairfax Media via Getty Images)

Major Winton W. "Bones" Marshall, who commanded 355th Squadron in Korea at the start of the war. (USAF)

F-86E Sabres of the 4th Fighter-Interceptor Wing's 335th Squadron. (USAF/FOR ALAN/Alamy Stock Photo)

This F-82G Twin Mustang of the 68th Fighter All-Weather Squadron based at Itazuke Air Base, Japan was flown by lieutenants Hudson and Fraser on June 27, 1950, when they scored the first victory of the Korean War. (USAF)

OPPOSITE Left to right: 2nd Lt Donald H. Hooten; Captain Manuel J. Fernandez, Jr.; Lt Col Richard L. Ayersman, the flight leader; and 1st Lt Ivan J. Ely of the Fifth Air Force in Korea. (Bettmann/Getty Images)

F-51D Mustangs of the Republic of Korea Air Force in the summer of 1950.
(US Department of Defense/USAF)

An F-51D Mustang of 77 Squadron, RAAF in summer 1950.
(Australian War Memorial)

Initially the NKPAF's only fighter unit was the 56th Fighter Aviation Regiment, which, from 25 June through August 1950, flew 222 sorties, both offensive fighter sweeps and air defence operations against USAF B-26 and B-29 bombing raids and USN air attacks. Totally lacking any form of air raid warning system, the 56th FAR frequently scrambled in response to incoming American raids. (Douglas C. Dildy Collection)

A USAF P-51 Mustang, coming in at rooftop level, releases napalm canisters over a North Korean town. (Photo © CORBIS/Corbis via Getty Images)

A North Korean Ilyushin Il-10 "Shturmovik" ground-attack aircraft in a damaged hangar at Kimpo airfield, South Korea, on September 21, 1950. (NARA)

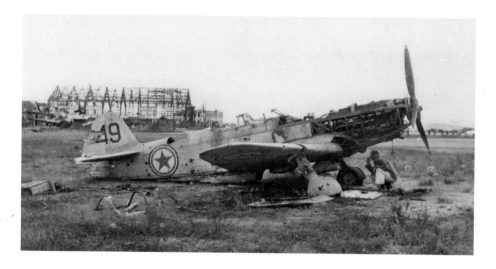

The NKPAF began the war with 79 Yak-9P fighters but lost all but one in the initial eight weeks of the conflict. This example was captured at Kimpo airfield in 1950. (R. Trebilco, Australian War Memorial)

OPPOSITE Lt Col Bruce H. Hinton of the 336th Fighter-Interceptor Squadron, 4th Fighter-Interceptor Group was credited with the first aerial victory over a MiG-15 on December 17, 1950. (Photo by John Dominis/The LIFE Picture Collection/Getty Images)

A pilot poses with the damaged North Korean Yak-9P that was captured at Kimpo airfield in 1950. (Warren Thompson)

The captured aircraft was rebuilt using pieces and parts from wrecked Yak-9Ps scattered around the airfield and was shipped back to the USA for examination, evaluation, and exploitation, primarily at Wright-Patterson AFB, Ohio. (Douglas C. Dildy Collection)

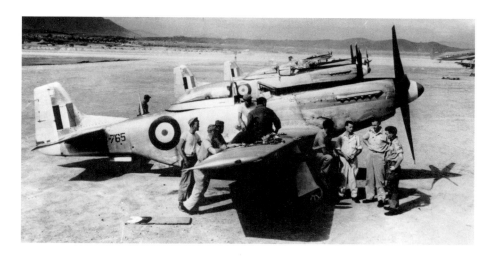

Australian fighter pilots and ground crew stand by their Mustang aircraft at their base in Korea. (Photo by Keystone/Getty Images)

LEFT F-51D Mustangs of 2 "Flying Cheetahs" Squadron, South African Air Force in Korea, fall 1950. (USAF)

BELOW The 108th Bombardment Squadron during a Korean War activation formation on April 1, 1951. (USAF)

Air Group commander Col John C. Meyer (center), the second-ranked Mustang ace of World War II, stands with a pair of unidentified fellow pilots beside an F-86 Sabre, December 1950. (Photo by John Dominis/The LIFE Picture Collection via Getty Images)

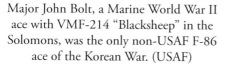

Major John Bolt, a Marine World War II ace with VMF-214 "Blacksheep" in the Solomons, was the only non-USAF F-86 ace of the Korean War. (USAF)

Captain James N. "Jabby" Jabara of the 4th Fighter-Interceptor Wing was credited as the first USAF MiG ace in May 1951. (USAF)

Captain Eddie Rickenbacker (left), the first American fighter ace of World War I, meets Captain James N. "Jabby" Jabara (center), the first American jet ace in history, on May 31, 1951. General Hoyt S. Vandenberg, Chief of Staff, US Air Force, is on the right. (USAF)

F-86 Sabres of the Fifth Air
Force in Korea in flight.
(Photo by Michael Rougier/
The LIFE Picture Collection
via Getty Images)

A flight of Lockheed F-80C Shooting Stars of the 51st Fighter-Interceptor Wing
in 1950. (Photo by Underwood Archives/Getty Images)

OPPOSITE Crews ready a group of F-86 Sabres for combat, Korea, June 1951.
(Photo by Interim Archives/Getty Images)

Husky 1,000-pound demolition bombs hurtle from this B-29 Superfort of the 19th Bombardment Group toward a Communist target somewhere beneath the cloud layers in Korea, August 1951. (USAF)

B-29s of the 98th Bombardment Group (Medium) bomb targets in North Korea in 1951. The Superfortresses would be forced to operate at night following "Black Tuesday" in October 1951. (NARA)

The North American RB-45C Tornado began reconnaissance flights over the Yalu in November 1951 following the shooting down of several RB-29s by MiG-15s. (USAF)

An F-51D Mustang on a muddy taxiway at Taegu in 1951. (NARA)

Soviet ace Senior Lieutenant Nikolai Vasilyevich Sutyagin in 1951. (Anna Rozh/ Wikimedia Commons/CC BY-SA 3.0)

Wang Hai, the leading ace in the People's Liberation Army Air Force, who later rose to become the first career aviator to command the PLAAF in 1985. (Historic Collection/Alamy Stock Photo)

A holed Soviet MiG-15 after a dogfight during the Korean War. (SPUTNIK/Alamy Stock Photo)

These attacks finally brought the MiG-15s up in force and revealed that the intelligence estimate that there was only a limited number of the jets in Manchuria was wrong. In the meantime, MacArthur recovered his nerve and announced that the "final offensive" would begin on November 24. The boys would still be victorious and home by Christmas, as promised.

At first, US Air Force commanders were not aware that the MiG-15s they were up against were flown by Soviet pilots. The main Soviet unit in operation at this early point in the conflict was the newly formed 28th IAD (Air Division), which had been formed out of the Soviet 151st GvIAD (Guards Air Division) that had been based in Manchuria at Anshan and Liaoyang airfields near Mukden since August 1950, assigned to train Chinese pilots of the People's Liberation Army Air Force on the new jet fighter. In late September, personnel from the 151st GvIAD had formed the new 67th IAP (Air Regiment) which operated with the newly arrived 139th GvIAP under control of the new 28th IAD. They were joined on operations by the 72nd IAP from the 151st Air Division to provide a force of approximately 72 MiG-15s. At this time, the Soviet units remained near Mukden, Manchuria, and did not move up to Antung as a permanent base until late November.

Between November 8 and 15, MiG-15s from these units repeatedly clashed with Air Force and Navy aircraft in the area just south of the Yalu. On November 9, an RB-29 of the 91st Strategic Reconnaissance Squadron flying just south of Sinuiju was attacked by a pair of MiG-15s after it was damaged by antiaircraft fire from the Chinese side of the river. Tail gunner Corporal Harry J. LeVene managed to shoot down one of the attackers, but the Superfortress had been badly hit. The pilot was forced to shut down one engine as the bomber returned to Japan. Attempting to land at Johnson air base, a second engine failed and the RB-29 crashed short of the runway with five of the ten crewmembers killed. FEAF was forced to end RB-29 operations in the vicinity of the Yalu during daylight hours as a result.

Later that day, Major Alexander Strulov and Senior Lieutenant Kaznachev of the 139th GvIAP encountered a flight of what they identified as F-80 Shooting Stars, which were in fact F9F-2 Panthers from *Valley Forge*'s VF-51. The Soviets made a pass on these and each claimed and was credited with an "F-80," though the only US casualty was one of the Panthers, which hit the landing barrier when it landed back aboard *Valley Forge*.

On November 10, F4U-4 Corsairs, AD Skyraiders and F9F-2 Panthers from USS *Philippine Sea* and USS *Leyte* sent to hit the Yalu bridges at Sinuiju were intercepted by seven MiGs from 139th GvIAP, followed by six from 72nd IAP. The Soviets attacked Panthers and Skyraiders they misidentified as F-80s and F-47 Thunderbolts. The intercepting pilots were credited later with shooting down three "F-80s" and one "F-47," though the only Navy loss that day was a VC-35 Skyraider that crashed landing aboard *Leyte*. It was during this action that Captain Grachov of the 139th GvIAP was shot down by VF-111 CO Lt Cdr William T. Amen, the first jet kill of the war to be confirmed by both sides.

Over the next four days, MiGs clashed with both Air Force and Navy flights. They were credited with shooting down five B-29s, five F-80s, two F-51s and an "F-47," though these claims are not supported by reported US losses. A B-29 of the newly arrived 307th Bomb Group was shot down over Uiju by MiGs on November 10; all ten crew members bailed out successfully and were quickly captured by North Korean troops, to become POWs. The Soviets recorded the loss of Senior Lieutenant Nasonov of the 28th GvIAP to an F-80 on November 11; no F-80 pilots made such a claim on that date. On November 12, a 98th Bomb Group B-29 was badly hit and just managed to limp into Kimpo. On November 14, the 98th sent B-29s to the Yalu again to hit the Sinuiju railroad bridge, and no enemy jets were spotted. The next day, a B-29 of the 19th Group and one from the 307th were badly damaged while bombing the same target. For the next eight days, no missions were flown due to bad weather over North Korea.

With the weather over North Korea deteriorating between November 15 and the end of the month, the Soviet pilots were only airborne three times during this period. A fight on November 18 saw 14 pilots of the 139th GvIAP attack 30 Navy Panthers and Skyraiders they again mistook for "F-80s" and "F-47s." Captain Pakhomov and Lieutenant Bulaev each claimed an "F-80," though the carrier pilots suffered no losses. Senior Lieutenant Arkady Tarshinov was shot down in the fight, though there were no US claims for his MiG-15.

On November 25 and 26, B-29s from the 19th and 307th wings destroyed a bridge at Manpojin and another at Chongsonjin. By this time, however, the horse was out of the barn, as the 200,000 Chinese troops in western North Korea struck at the Chongchon River, hitting the 25th and 2nd Infantry divisions after they had advanced only some 5 miles since setting out from Pyongyang on November 24, while the 180,000 troops of the Ninth Army struck every UN position in the Chosin Reservoir from Yudam-ni to Koto-ri before the Marines could advance 1,000 yards outside Yudam-ni. What would later be called by the survivors "the Big Bug-Out" was about to begin. Writing some 30 years later, British historian Sir Martin Gilbert would state, "the Chinese intervention in the Korean War was the greatest defeat of a previously-victorious army in history."

The 18th Fighter-Bomber Wing moved to Pyongyang East airfield in mid-November. The airfield at Pyongyang had been badly damaged by UN bombing during the first three months of the war, but repairs were made that allowed the F-51s to operate. At the same time, the 12th and 67th Fighter-Bomber squadrons of the 35th Fighter-Bomber Wing, along with the RAAF's 77 Squadron, moved up to Yonpo south of Hamhung on the Sea of Japan. The Mustangs were soon joined by Marine F4U Corsairs to provide air support for the First Marine Division as it moved up from Hamhung to the Chosin Reservoir to prepare for the final advance to the Yalu. The moves to Pyongyang East and Yonpo allowed the Mustang squadrons to bring tactical air power to bear on any target left in North Korea and provide air support during the advance to the Yalu.

The 18th Wing was joined at Pyongyang by the second Commonwealth squadron to enter combat. The South African Air Force's No. 2 "Flying Cheetahs" Squadron had arrived in Japan from Durban, South Africa, on September 26, 1950. The all-volunteer unit had previously flown Spitfires back in South Africa, and was equipped with the last of the 145 Mustangs ferried to the Far East by *Boxer*. After conversion training for the Mustang and operational training in the fighter-bomber role, the squadron flew its aircraft to Pusan East airfield on November 16, and from there moved up to Pyongyang East to join the 35th Fighter-Bomber Wing, with whom it would operate for the rest of the war.

The coldest winter in 144 years arrived in Korea shortly after the Mustang wings had moved to their forward positions. Neither Yonpo nor Pyongyang had facilities to perform maintenance out of the weather. Changing spark plugs was a particularly difficult job for ground crews in the bitter cold, since a mechanic had to take off his gloves to thread the plug into the engine. The days were short now, and the first flights did not get off before 0645 hours, while the last flights of the day returned by 1700 hours. With this sort of schedule, ground crews began their days at 0500 hours, working to warm up engines. With constant flight operations, armorers were at work till dark loading flights for missions. There were also problems getting supplies so far north in the bad weather.

A major reason for the UN forces' failure to detect the movement of the People's Volunteer Army into North Korea was the lack of aerial reconnaissance capability in FEAF. The RB-29s of the 31st Strategic Reconnaissance Squadron (SRS) were originally based at Kadena AFB on Okinawa. Shortly after the outbreak of war, the 91st Strategic Reconnaissance Squadron was moved from McGuire AFB, New Jersey, to Johnson and Yakota air bases in Japan, where it was joined in early August by the 31st Squadron, which was merged into the 91st SRS. The RB-29s provided the primary photo-recon capacity, along with the RF-80A Shooting Stars of the 8th Tactical Reconnaissance Squadron, which was also based at Yokota.

While the RB-29s were perfectly adequate to obtain target photography for the bombing campaign, their operational altitude was above 15,000 feet, which made detecting infantry movement difficult. The RF-80s could perform low-level reconnaissance, but their cameras did not have fast enough shutters to obtain clear photos at low level when flying at speed. Additionally, the RF-80s did not have the range to get into North Korea until late October. The 167th Tactical Reconnaissance Squadron, equipped with RB-26C Invaders, arrived in Japan in August; their specific task was night photography. The 45th Tactical Reconnaissance Squadron arrived in late September but was not able to engage in photo recon until November, when they were finally equipped with RF-51D Mustangs, the airplane best suited for the kind of battlefield tactical reconnaissance that might have detected signs of movement by the Chinese forces in October.

In September 1950, three RB-45C Tornados from Detachment "A" of the 84th Bomb Squadron, 91st Strategic Reconnaissance Wing, arrived at Yokota Air Base. After the shoot-down of the RB-29 on November 9, it was believed these jets were fast enough that they could evade defending MiG-15s and perform reconnaissance along the Yalu border. Unfortunately, the Tornado's vulnerability to the MiGs was demonstrated on December 4, when an RB-45C was shot down near Sinuiju by Soviet pilot Aleksandr F. Andrianov. Pilot Captain Charles E. McDonough and Air Force intelligence officer Colonel John R. Lovell managed to bail out and land south of the Yalu River, but co-pilot Captain Jules E. Young and navigator 1st Lt James J. Picucci were killed in the crash. McDonough and Lovell were captured the next day by the North Koreans. McDonough was tortured by North Korean and Soviet intelligence interrogators and died under torture in mid-December. Colonel Lovell survived several brutal interrogation sessions, but when he refused to provide information he was taken into a North Korean village that had been bombed and villagers were encouraged to lynch him. Lovell was the highest-ranking intelligence official lost during the Korean War.

Douglas MacArthur and all senior American leaders in Washington were convinced the coming offensive would be a "victory parade to the Yalu." MacArthur announced the offensive in an official communiqué the morning of November 24:

> The United Nations' massive compression envelopment in North Korea against the new Red Armies operating there is now approaching its decisive effort. The isolating component of the pincer, our air forces of all types, have for the past three weeks, in a sustained attack of model coordination and effectiveness, successfully interdicted enemy lines of support from the north so that further reinforcement therefrom has been sharply curtailed and essential supplies markedly limited. The eastern sector of the pincer, with noteworthy and effective naval support, has now reached commanding enveloping position, cutting in two the enemy's geographical potential. This morning the western sector of the pincer moves forward in general assault in an effort to complete the compression and close the vise. If successful, this should for all practical purposes end the war, restore peace and unity to Korea, enable the prompt withdrawal of United Nations military forces, and permit the complete assumption by the Korean people of full sovereignty and international equality. It is that for which we fight.

Eighth Army's offensive started that morning like a walk in the park. The troops crossed the Chongchon River shortly after 0800 hours. II Corps on the left moved through the coastal plain, while IX Corps advanced through the valleys of the Kuryong and Chongchon rivers.

On the extreme right flank, ROK II Corps was ordered to establish contact with X Corps at Tokchon, 70 miles to the northeast. GIs were still clad in their summer uniforms despite the fact the weather was so cold that when ordered to move out in the morning, many tankers found their vehicle's tracks frozen to the ground and were only able to move after being pushed by another tank. The soldiers of IX Corps saw ice floes in the river. Winter clothing had arrived and was in storage in supply dumps in Pyongyang, but it was considered there was not sufficient time to re-equip, which could be accomplished following the successful conclusion of the offensive in only ten more days. By dark, the force was advancing at a rate of 16,000 yards per day and forward units were outrunning their supply lines. Many GIs threw away extra equipment, believing it had no further use.

The "victory offensive" lasted less than 24 hours. Shortly after midnight on November 25, the PVA 13th Army Group, composed of 18 divisions in position in the mountains above the Chongchon River, met the advance and stopped it cold. B Company, 1/9 Infantry of the 2nd Division suddenly came under grenade and small-arms attack as they advanced on Hill 219 on the east bank of the Chongchon. At the same time ROK II Corps' three divisions were hit by five Chinese divisions and collapsed overnight; the South Koreans fell back in chaos that turned into a rout as they abandoned guns, vehicles, and equipment.

Fighting continued sporadically throughout the day of November 25. At 2200 hours, 2nd Division soldiers in positions along the Chongchon Valley heard a nightmare cacophony of bugles, whistles, drums, and rattles. Gunfire flashed as Chinese assault units smashed through non-existent perimeters and overran position after position. On 2nd Division's left, the 25th Infantry Division was also hard-pressed.

By dawn on November 26, 2nd Division had been driven back 2 miles. An 80-mile-wide chasm now existed between Eighth Army and X Corps on the other side of the Taebaek Range. The Turkish Brigade tried to move up and support the Koreans, but was stopped at Wawon, well south of what the map said was the front line. Chinese troops had bypassed UN positions and Eighth Army was in danger of being cut off and surrounded. General Walker ordered an immediate retreat.

Retreat in the face of widespread enemy attack is difficult. Colonel Paul Freeman, commander of the 23rd Regimental Combat Team, one of the few units that would come out of North Korea relatively intact after becoming the rearguard of the retreat, later described the initial attacks as a test of American strength and will. "They came tongue in cheek at first, to see what we would do. Then they found what a thin line we had, how easily the South Koreans cracked. They saw what a pushover we were. Then they became very aggressive, very bold – and stayed that way."

For 2nd Division, the order to retreat came too late. By the time the unit could be extricated from direct combat, the available escape routes had dwindled as the enemy bypassed the front lines and surrounded the division. Escape from Kunu-ri was only possible down one dirt road that led through a pass to Sunchon. The vehicle convoy quickly became a nose-to-tail traffic jam on the narrow road as the enemy poured down a storm of machine-gun and mortar fire from the high hills on either side. Trucks keeled over and caught fire. Tanks were blown up by captured bazookas. Overloaded jeeps careened into the ditches with dead drivers at the wheel. Those men not frozen in fear by the event ran for their lives. Later called "The Death Ride From Kunu-ri" by the survivors, 2nd Division's retreat was among the grimmest events in the history of the US Army. Writing of the retreat, *New York Herald Tribune* correspondent Homer Bigart called it "the biggest American defeat since Bataan" in a front-page article published in the paper's international edition on December 1.

The killing continued when daylight returned, despite repeated runs by American fighter-bombers, which had difficulty picking out targets because Americans and Chinese were so closely intermixed. With radio contact between air and ground units frequently cut off, pilots watched in frustration as surviving units drove directly into ambushes and road blocks around the next curve. Whenever possible, the F-51 pilots attacked those positions they were able to identify as enemy. Over the afternoon and night of November 29–30, 2nd Division lost 3,000 men and most of its equipment. Over the following days, the retreat became a rout as the Eighth Army retreated 120 miles south, the longest retreat in American military history. Infantryman Sam Mace of 2nd Division later recalled:

It was during the chaos after we broke contact and moved south, unable to put it all back together, that I was ashamed of my Army; not the men in my unit, or the men in my division, not after the hell they had been in, but of the men who were in charge of us. That was a moment of complete disgrace and shame.

In the face of the Chinese offensive, new tactics were brought into use by the two B-26 groups. The night of November 26–27 saw B-26s sent on night interdiction missions for the first time as 3rd Group B-26s flew 67 sorties north of the Eighth Army's Main Line of Resistance in an attempt to block advancing Chinese units. On November 28, the 452nd Group's Invaders used new radar control to make a massed bomb attack on a Chinese unit only 1,000 yards from the UN front lines.

The Mustang units at Pyongyang East soon realized they would have to evacuate. On November 27, the aircraft were hurriedly loaded with ordnance for a final strike as they left to return to Suwon, south of Seoul. Equipment that couldn't be moved was set afire on the field before the ground support personnel became part of the stream of retreating troops in what survivors of the Chinese intervention called "The Big Bug-Out."

Things were different for the 35th Fighter-Bomber Wing and 77 Squadron at Yonpo. When the enemy attacked the Marines in the Chosin Reservoir region on the night of November 26, the units held, despite the fact they were surrounded in Yudam-ni at the reservoir, at Hagaru-ri just south of Toktong Pass, and in Koto-ri at the top of Funchilin Pass. Four pilots of 77 Squadron took off at dawn on November 27, each carrying two canisters of napalm. They heard a desperate call for help from the forward air observer with Fox Company, which held the crucial position at the top of Toktong Pass that would guarantee the Marines at the reservoir the chance to retreat. The company had barely held against an attack overnight by two Chinese assault battalions, taking 50 percent casualties killed and wounded. Now, the last of the Chinese troops were massed at the foot of what became known in Marine Corps legend as "Fox Hill" for a final assault that would likely carry the day. The four Mustangs responded to the call and made a low-level pass over the hill; their napalm drop was right on target, the eight canisters incinerating several hundred Chinese infantrymen and breaking the attack.

The units at Yonpo flew missions as often as possible in horrible weather over the next 12 days. The first stage of what would come to be known as "The breakout from Chosin" began with 5th and 7th regiments abandoning Yudam-ni on December 1; they fought for 96 continuous hours in the midst of the Siberian blizzard as they advanced down the 11 miles of Toktong Pass to Hagaru-ri, arriving on December 4.

The airfield at Hagaru-ri had been completed with the engineers working under fire from attacking Chinese. It opened for business on

December 4, despite the fact it was 500 feet shorter than the operating manual required for safe operation. Fortunately, the cold air allowed C-47s to get in and out successfully. By dusk on December 5, Air Force C-47s and Marine R4Ds (the Navy designation for the C-47) had evacuated over 900 casualties in two days. The next day, 700 were flown out. On the morning of Tuesday, December 6, there were still 1,400 casualties waiting for evacuation. Aircraft flew in and out throughout the day. A four-engine Navy R5D (C-54) managed a "carrier landing" and loaded as many wounded as possible. The successful "carrier-style" takeoff was so hairy it was not attempted again. A Marine R4D wiped out its landing gear in a hard landing; it was roughly shoved aside by bulldozers. An Air Force C-47 lost an engine on takeoff and crashed outside the perimeter; fortunately, there were no casualties, but the C-47 had to be destroyed. By nightfall, all casualties had been evacuated. In five days, 3,150 Marines, 1,137 soldiers, and 25 Royal Marines, a total of 4,312 men, were air-lifted to Hamhung where they were flown on to hospitals in Japan.

The press arrived at Hagaru-ri on December 5. During his press conference, General Oliver P. Smith, the Marine commander, was asked his plans by a British correspondent, who referred to the withdrawal as a "retreat." Smith's correction – that since they were surrounded "we're advancing in a different direction" – was recorded for history as "Retreat, hell, we're just attacking in a new direction," despite the fact that pious Mormon Smith never used a swear word in his life. A television news team from CBS News photographed the casualty evacuation and interviewed General Smith. The footage was flown directly to Japan and thence across the Pacific to be broadcast in the United States four days later, the first time war news footage had been shown so closely after the event.

The Marines left Hagaru-ri on December 7, in a long line of vehicles headed across the Taebaek Plateau to Koto-ri. Famed war correspondent Marguerite Higgins, who would become the first woman to win the International Reporting Pulitzer Prize for her 1950 report of landing on Red Beach at Inchon, was one of the last to leave Hagaru-ri, flying out in a TBM-3R Avenger; she described the enormous fireworks display over the town as the Marine rearguard set fire to all equipment that could not be taken in a front page article in the *International Herald Tribune* on December 8.

The column was constantly covered by Marine Corsairs and Air Force and Australian F-51s, which bombed and rocketed enemy road blocks and successfully knocked out ambushes. There was heavy fighting throughout the day; the F7F Tigercats of VMF(N)-542 and Corsairs of VMF(N)-513 provided air cover through the night hours, during which several other attacks by Chinese units were broken up. Had it not been for the 24-hour air cover, the retreat would have been impossible.

By midnight December 8, the last Marines were safely inside the perimeter at Koto-ri. In all, 10,000 Marines and soldiers, with 1,000 vehicles, had moved 11 miles through enemy-controlled country in 38 hours, for losses of 103 dead, seven missing, and 506 wounded.

Before the final escape down Funchilin Pass could happen, the Marines had to deal with the fact that the enemy had blown a 24-foot gap in the bridge over the reservoir spillway, where the road clung to an almost-sheer cliff. The gap had to be bridged if they were to get their heavy equipment down the pass. The division engineer had determined the gap could be spanned by four sections of an M-2 "Treadway" bridge. Fortuitously, among the survivors was a detachment of the Treadway Bridge Company from the Army's 58th Engineer Battalion, with two Brockway trucks that could carry the bridge sections if they could be air-delivered.

Each section of a treadway bridge weighed 4,000lb. Eight bridge sections were located in Japan and trucked to Tachikawa Air Base, where each was loaded aboard a C-119 "Flying Boxcar" that took them to Ashiya Air Base, where the Army 2348th Quartermaster Airborne Supply and Packaging Company packed them for air drop with a 48-foot cargo parachute on each end. The C-119s then flew to Yonpo, where one section was test-dropped successfully.

At 0930 hours on December 9, the C-119s arrived over Koto-ri. Aboard each, all but one of the ropes holding the bridge section had been cut; when that was cut, a spring-loaded small parachute would deploy a larger parachute that would pull the bridge section out of the plane.

Seven of the eight C-119s dropped their bridge sections; five landed successfully, while the sixth fell into Chinese hands, and the seventh was damaged when it hit the ground.

In the last C-119, pilot Captain Jim Inks gave the drop order to his crew chief, who pulled the spring release while the assistant crew chief cut the rope. Inks later described what happened:

Unfortunately, that pilot chute mechanism failed to work, and we were past the drop zone with our load still aboard. We were in a box canyon with a loose load in the cargo compartment, and it was doubtful if I had the power to climb the overloaded aircraft over the mountains to get out of there.

Inks could dump the load if he climbed steeply, but this section was vital if the bridge was to be successfully assembled. Inks ordered the cargo crew to stay forward of the bridge section, while he, the co-pilot, and the navigator looked for a way out of the narrow canyon. "The navigator picked a canyon coming in from the east that he thought would continue downgrade, but as soon as we turned into it, we realized it was upgrade and pretty steep. We were in a hell of a spot."

The C-119 was 200 feet above the rapidly rising canyon floor; suddenly, Inks spotted another canyon beyond the ridge to the left. "We skidded into it not ten feet from the rocks and started back toward the main canyon we had just left." The C-119 headed toward the drop zone. "The crew chief managed to hit the bridge with a sledge hammer that started it on its way out, it didn't hang up, and our span of the bridge was delivered fifteen minutes late."

With the bridge successfully installed over three hours on December 9, the Marines continued down Funchilin Pass. The first units reached the bottom of the pass at Chinhung-ni at 0245 hours on Sunday, December 10. The last troops came out of the pass at 1300 hours on December 11 and reached Hamhung at 2100 hours. The most epic military retreat since Xenophon led the 10,000 Greeks out of Persia 2,500 years earlier had been carried out successfully.

On December 10, General MacArthur finally found the time to visit the front in Korea, flying into Yonpo for the first time since the Chinese attack in North Korea had commenced 17 days earlier. He complimented X Corps commander General Edward "Ned" Almond for having "tied down" six to eight Chinese divisions that would have otherwise attacked the Eighth Army.

As the Marines and the 3rd and 7th Army divisions moved into Hungnam for evacuation by sea, the airmen at Yonpo flew their last missions against the Chinese. The Marine and Air Force fliers, and their Australian allies, had flown over 1,300 missions between December 1 and 11 to cover the withdrawal. Flight conditions at Yonpo were extremely difficult for pilots, who dealt with poor charts, minimal navigational aids, and capricious radios, in addition to appalling weather. Primitive conditions and icy runways made taxiing to and from the runway for takeoff and landing dangerous. Through an all-hands effort, aircraft availability through the campaign had been 67 percent. Fortunately, only three night-fighter pilots had been lost; baling out over North Korea in winter ended in death either from the weather or at the hands of enemy troops.

The cover provided by the Mustang and Corsair squadrons was the decisive weapon in keeping four Chinese divisions and an advancing army group coming up at the rear to reinforce the pursuers at bay long enough to allow the escape. As operations wound down, C-47s arrived to evacuate ground personnel from Yonpo. The last aircraft flew out on December 14, with the Marine squadrons going to Pusan, where they were close to port facilities for re-equipment, while the Mustangs relocated to Chinhae airfield on the southeastern tip of the Korean peninsula. C-47s continued to fly into the field to evacuate casualties until December 17, when the last ground personnel were flown out.

Captured documents and prisoner interrogations confirmed the Marines and soldiers had fought at least nine and possibly all 12 divisions of the PVA Ninth Army Group. Each division had entered combat with an effective strength of about 7,500, for approximately 90,000 troops in total. The Ninth Army Group had crossed the Yalu with 150,000 troops; however, not all units had been able to fight at the reservoir.

By Christmas, the last UN units had crossed the 38th Parallel and departed North Korea. Writing later of the events of November 1950, Secretary of State Dean Acheson stated, "The Chinese intervention in Korea was the greatest defeat of American arms since the Second Battle of Bull Run."

CHAPTER 8

RED STAR OVER THE YALU

Air Force mythology has it that the F-86 pilots of the 4th Fighter-Interceptor Wing who were the first to take the Sabre to war in Korea in December 1950 were high-time Sabre pilots, with many of them experienced World War II pilots. Lt Col Bruce Hinton, commander of the 336th Fighter-Interceptor Squadron and the first Sabre pilot to shoot down a MiG-15, remembered things somewhat differently:

There has been a tendency by those who write about the Korean War to portray the American fighter pilots as highly experienced, seasoned war veterans, who faced a passel of MiG drivers made up of a polyglot of Chinese, North Korean and whatever other nationality, who had come to Korea to peck away at UN air power.

During late summer 1950, after losing a bunch of pilots to other units in Korea, I received eight replacement pilots direct from the flying schools, with several more coming to us before departing for Korea. When we left Andrews AFB outside Washington for San Diego on November 11, 1950, I had one pilot who hadn't been checked out at night flying on my wing! We accomplished that en route! We hadn't had any gunnery or bombing training since the squadron had transferred to Dover, Delaware in the summer of 1950.

This inexperience really came to a head during the early operations in Korea. In fact, while briefing my pilots in the ops tent at Kimpo on December 14, 1950, preparing for the upcoming combat operations, I told my guys that our SOP called for testing the guns over the

Pyongyang area of North Korea, inbound to our patrol area. One of the new lieutenants stood up with a question, "Sir, how can I tell if my guns go off?" Those were the "seasoned combat veterans" that we took to Korea. Later on, some of these very same green lieutenants distinguished themselves in repeated air to air actions.

The F-86 Sabre had become operational with the Air Force only some 18 months before it went to war, when the 1st Fighter-Interceptor Wing at March AFB in California took delivery of its first Sabre in March 1949. The 4th Wing, the second Sabre-equipped outfit, only became fully operational with Sabres in all three squadrons in late September 1949, barely a year before the unit went to Korea. The wing did have combat-experienced, high-time pilots in leadership positions, starting with Wing Commander Col George F. Smith and Air Group commander Col John C. Meyer, whose score of 24 victories while flying in the ETO with the 352nd Fighter Group, known as the "Blue-Nosed Bastards of Bodney," made him the second-ranked Mustang ace of the war, behind fellow "Blue-Nosed Bastard" Major George C. Preddy. Lt Col Glenn T. Eagleston, who had scored 18.5 victories as the leading ace of the 354th "Pioneer Mustang" Fighter Group, the first unit to take the Merlin-powered P-51B Mustang into combat, commanded the 334th Fighter-Interceptor Squadron. The 335th Fighter-Interceptor Squadron was led by Lt Col Benjamin Emmert, Jr., a six-victory ace with the 325th "Checkertail Clan" Fighter Group in World War II. Lt Col Bruce Hinton, who commanded the 336th Fighter-Interceptor Squadron, was the only leader in the group who did not have frontline combat experience from World War II, though he was a highly experienced pilot.

Then-2nd Lt Alonzo J. "Lon" Walter, Jr. reported to the 335th Fighter-Interceptor Squadron at Andrews AFB in early September 1950, straight out of flight school, with 75 hours of F-86 flight time in his logbook. He later recalled:

Virtually every wingman, such as myself, was fresh out of flying school. I never fired the guns of an F-86 until my first combat mission. We had faith and discipline, however, and the "old heads" were great teachers. They were the "shooters" while we were the "lookers" who watched their tails in combat.

The 4th Wing received its orders to Korea on November 9, 1950. At the time, Wing Headquarters and the 334th Squadron were based at New Castle County Airport in Delaware, while the 336th Squadron was at nearby Dover AFB, and the 335th Squadron was at the wing's official home base, Andrews AFB outside Washington, DC; they had been operating from these bases since August. 336th Squadron commander Hinton recalled how the 4th went to war:

I went into squadron ops at 0700 on November 9, to find that with a frontal passage nearing – rain, low ceilings, and gusty winds – there'd be no flying today for my squadron. It looked like a pretty quiet day. But that all changed when an unexpected phone call from 4th Wing Headquarters announced a squadron commanders meeting not later than 1100 hours.

Wing Headquarters at Newcastle was in a frenzy when we arrived. We quickly surmised that the biggest thing in our lifetime was about to happen. And so it was. The entire wing was moving overseas. Destination – Japan! All personnel, equipment, and records were to be readied for shipment. Our aircraft were to be prepared for flight to the West Coast. Many of our older Sabres would be replaced by later-production models before our departure. Most of these were delivered to us before departure by other F-86 wings, principally the 56th at Selfridge and the 33rd at Otis. As it turned out, at least six replacements were flown direct to our ports of embarkation by the lst Wing at March AFB, California.

Getting equipment ready for overseas deployment, selecting airmen and officers for specific tasks, receiving six replacement aircraft, and getting the whole outfit ready to leave in less than 48 hours was an assignment of Herculean proportions.

Choosing pilots was critically important, since there had been an influx of recent flying school graduates. To make matters worse, two veteran captains could not be included for physical reasons. But by filling many non-flying officer positions with experienced fighter pilots, we were able to achieve a ratio of two "old-timers" for each new pilot.

While the original order had been that the aircraft should arrive in San Diego by November 18, that date was bumped up on November 10 to

November 13. The next day, November 11, the Sabres departed their east coast fields. Hinton remembered:

> Our first fuel stop was Wright-Patterson. We were the third squadron to arrive, and the transient ramp was in chaos. The entire group had chosen that base for the first refueling, but no one had alerted the folks at Wright-Patterson! To make matters worse, November 11 was Armistice Day and a weekend to boot. Refueling 70-plus Sabres by the undermanned transient crew was proceeding at a snail's pace. On top of the refueling problems, one of our airplanes needed an engine change. Captain Morris "Mo" Pitts, my squadron materiel officer, discovered a flight test F-86A opened up for an engine change – with the replacement engine on a stand. After determining that the engine would work in our airplane, Pitts invoked the "Strawboss" priority code word we had been given to obtain any assistance needed during the transfer and – open sesame! – the engine was installed in our Sabre overnight by the Wright-Patterson crew.

The 336th departed the next day.

At Sheppard AFB in Wichita Falls, Texas, another of Hinton's Sabres needed a new engine. Hinton sent the rest of the squadron on to Albuquerque while he negotiated an engine change. The maintenance boss allowed that since this was an emergency on a Sunday, his crew would get on it the next day and have it finished by Tuesday. "I called the USAF Command Post and used the magic word – 'Strawboss.' Within an hour a crew showed up to perform the engine change. Magic word, indeed!"

By the time the squadron arrived at Nellis AFB in Nevada, they were expected and all servicing was performed quickly. "The flight to McClellan was relatively short, so we remained at a fairly low altitude in a wide spread formation as we passed over my home town of Stockton, California."

The 49 Sabres of the 334th and 335th squadrons flew to North Island Naval Air Station in San Diego, where they had all arrived by November 14. Once there, the Navy took two days to "cocoon" the Sabres to protect them from saltwater corrosion during the trans-Pacific trip to Japan aboard USS *Cape Esperance* (CVE-88), a *Casablanca*-class escort carrier that had recently been reactivated from the reserve fleet. The Sabres were stored on the flight and hangar decks. Though airplanes and personnel in San Diego were ready to go by November 18, they had to wait for repair of *Cape Esperance*, which had broken down during its shakedown cruise from San Francisco. Finally, the old carrier stood out past Point Loma on November 23. The trans-Pacific voyage took 17 days due to the ship having to slow due to a drive shaft problem, and because there was a need to re-route to avoid a mid-Pacific typhoon.

The 26 Sabres of the 336th Squadron flew to McClellan AFB in Sacramento. After they were "cocooned," they were sent by barge down the Sacramento River to Alameda NAS in San Francisco Bay, where they were loaded aboard four fast fleet tankers as deck cargo. The squadron pilots were bused to Fairfield-Suisun AFB (now Travis AFB) where they were flown trans-Pacific by Military Air Transport Service (MATS) to Haneda AFB, Japan. In the event, the 336th's airplanes arrived in Yokohama, Japan, aboard the tankers on December 5, while *Cape Esperance* did not arrive until December 10.

North American Tech Rep John Henderson remembered what happened after the wing arrived in Japan:

> The aircraft were off-loaded in Yokohama and barged to Kisarazu Air Base on the other side of the bay where they were cleaned, inspected and cleared for flight to Johnson Air Base, which became our rear echelon maintenance base. The F-86As loaded on the *Cape Esperance* had been coated with an anticorrosive grease on their exposed surfaces, and tape was used to close all the openings between metal surfaces to protect them against saltwater intrusion. When off-loaded at Kisarazu, it was clear, however, that saltwater corrosion had occurred. The severity of the corrosion depended upon how far forward each airplane had been on the carrier's deck. Most of the damage was due to electrolytic action between the magnesium filler strips attached to the ailerons' aluminum trailing edge. The damage that occurred en route slowed the inspection of the Sabres and decreased their availability for ferrying to Johnson Air Base, north of Tokyo.

The 4th had arrived in the middle of the greatest crisis ever to face UN forces during the war. Over the first ten days of December, the longest retreat in Army history occurred as the Eighth Army retreated 120 miles out of North Korea. Pyongyang, which the wing had expected would be their main base in Korea when they left the United States, fell to the Chinese on December 3. In the next week, the Army retreated so fast that its Chinese pursuers were unable to keep up. The speed of the retreat was fortunate, because few units could have fought successfully if they had attempted to stand; ultimately, this meant they were saved to fight again. Complete victory eluded the Chinese because they lacked a logistics system to keep units supplied with food and ammunition.

The People's Volunteer Army had suffered 40 percent casualties since the offensive began on the Chongchon River, with combat casualties wildly outnumbered by losses to frostbite and starvation. On December 7, PVA commander Marshal Peng Dehuai informed Mao the army needed at least 90 days to resupply and rebuild in order to continue the battle, and recommended the offensive stop at the 38th Parallel until spring. Mao refused his commander's advice and ordered him to continue the advance; the Chairman had fallen victim to the same "victory disease" that had struck MacArthur two months earlier. The PVA did halt on the 38th Parallel on December 10 to catch its breath before moving on.

The wing now faced the problem of where they could operate in Korea. With Pyongyang no longer an option, and with all the available air bases in South Korea filled with F-80s and F-51s from the FEAF groups, only Kimpo (K-14) could serve the Sabre's operational needs. Due to crowding on the field, only six Sabres could operate there at any time. Thus, Johnson AFB would remain the main Sabre base for heavy maintenance and repair, while detachments from the squadrons would operate in Korea at Kimpo and Suwon (K-13). Seven Sabres from the 336th Squadron, led by group commander Col Meyer and squadron commander Lt Col Hinton, departed Johnson AFB for Korea on December 13. They were delayed by weather at Itazuke AFB and eventually arrived at Kimpo on December 15.

Tech rep John Henderson recalled the arrival in Korea: "I was based in Japan for only five days when I received my orders to go on temporary duty to Korea to provide technical support to the 4th Fighter Group detachment's maintenance personnel." Henderson had won a coin toss with senior NAA tech rep Chris Christopherson to be the first Sabre tech rep in Korea the morning of December 15 when wing personnel said one of them was needed to work with the forward detachment.

I wondered what I was flying into and how everything would turn out. Perhaps I would have stayed back in Japan had I known I would go 18 days without a real bath; that the temperature and wind chill factor would drop the thermometer below freezing to the extent that a water bucket froze if left too far from a stove; that Christmas dinner was bully beef and boiled potatoes because the cook could not thaw our turkeys; that I would have chow that day with the Turkish Army Brigade soldiers who unhesitatingly used their rifle bayonets to spear bread from our table; or that I would have to talk my way onboard the last air evacuation transport in the middle of the night that was taking "walking wounded only" to avoid the possibility of being captured when our base was about to be overrun.

Over the 18 days the 336th Squadron was at Kimpo before they were forced to retreat to Japan by the Chinese offensive that began anew on New Year's Eve, Henderson would work closely with the ground crews.

From the outset of flying at Kimpo, I saw first hand the F-86A weapon system operate in the worst weather, under the most primitive and restrictive of maintenance conditions, and with probably the strongest demand for a 100 percent in-commission rate from the higher commands. We had the usual maintenance problems which were to be expected, but they were intensified during airplane turnarounds in some cases by the intense cold and lack of shelter. In retrospect, I personally believe that those first 18 days of combat operations with the F-86A were the most demanding on personnel and equipment the 4th encountered during its first year of operation with Fifth Air Force.

Within hours of the arrival of the first seven Sabres on December 14, Lt Col Hinton led a flight of four on an "orientation mission" that departed Kimpo at 1550 hours to the region of North Korea that would come to be known as "MiG Alley." The fighters each carried two 120-gallon wing tanks, giving them an effective combat radius of approximately 210 miles. Since the round trip between Kimpo and the Yalu was approximately 350 miles, the pilots were forced to economize to the maximum extent. Hinton led his four Sabres into the combat area at Mach 0.62 at 25,000 feet, the best altitude for the F-86 in terms of power and fuel consumption. On this first flight, the Sabres attracted no attention from the enemy.

Bad weather over Korea kept the Sabres grounded until late morning on December 17, 1950, when Hinton, flying F-86A-5 "Squanee" (49-1236), led the four F-86s of "Baker Flight" north to patrol near Sinuiju, across the Yalu from the Chinese air base at Antung. In order to deceive the enemy and hopefully entice the MiGs to come up and fight, Hinton used radio call signs for F-80s, while the Sabres flew patterns at lower altitudes associated with the Shooting Stars. The trick worked.

Once again conserving fuel, the Sabres arrived south of the Yalu at 25,000 feet at a speed of Mach 0.68, as they had on the first mission. Hinton recalled that "The number two pilot in our flight spotted four bogies approaching from Sinuiju, and Captain Pitts, my element lead, identified them as swept-wing types." The MiGs were at approximately 18,000 feet, climbing southeasterly. When Hinton radioed the others to release their drop tanks, he discovered his radio wasn't working. The flight did jettison their tanks, however; they dived on the enemy and closed the MiG formation at 410 knots at 20,000 feet as they pushed their throttles to maximum power. "The MiGs were in battle formation and they immediately went into a climbing right trail. We began to out-turn them while pulling about five Gs. They appeared to lose formation integrity when they spotted us as they paralleled the Yalu."

Hinton became separated from his flight when he banked too close behind the MiGs. "I picked out the lead element to attack, and when I closed to about 4,000 feet their external tanks came off. I checked my speed as I moved to six o'clock on the element and saw I was at 0.96 Mach, past the 0.95 red line for the Sabre and faster than I had ever flown an F-86." Hinton's wingman stayed with him as the second element broke off to pursue the other MiG element when they broke formation. "I closed on the enemy wingman and put my pipper squarely on where the fuel tank should be." At a range of 1,200 feet, Hinton fired a long burst and hit the second MiG-15 in its right wing and fuselage. The MiG began smoking and Hinton realized he had outrun his wingman.

"All of a sudden, the enemy pilot popped his speed brakes and then retracted them immediately, which increased my rate of closure." The MiG slowed and Hinton opened his dive brakes and throttled back. He fired a second long burst and saw fire come out of the MiG's tailpipe as smoke came out of the rest of the enemy plane. "Before I could fire again, my Sabre began bucking and twisting in his jet wash. I slid off to the inside and closed to about 800 feet."

He fired a third long burst and fire erupted over the entire rear of the MiG's fuselage. "Pieces came off and his tailpipe was filled with smoke. Seconds later a long plume of flame came out." Hinton was closing fast; he popped his speed brakes and throttled back a second time. "We hung there in the sky, turning left, with my Sabre tight against his underside in a show formation, separated by maybe five feet." A fourth long burst knocked more pieces off. "More flames exited the tailpipe and enveloped the entire plane. It flipped inverted and entered a steep dive. The smoke trail went straight to the ground, there was no explosion." The MiG crashed 10 miles southeast of the Yalu River. The F-86 Sabre had scored its first aerial victory.

Element leader "Mo" Pitts damaged another as the MiGs broke hard to get away from the new enemy. All three outran the Americans to get back across the Yalu River to Manchuria. Back at Kimpo, Hinton performed a victory roll to celebrate the Sabre's first score, to the cheers of those on the field. Within a week, 32 Sabres were at Kimpo, manned by pilots of all three squadrons.

Hinton had fired 1,200 rounds to knock down the MiG, nearly his full load of .50-caliber ammunition. The .50-caliber machine gun, the Air Force's standard fighter armament, was a fine weapon with a high rate of fire; however, it was short-ranged, and its light weight of fire as compared with the heavier cannon armament of the MiG would make knocking down a MiG-15 difficult throughout the war. Many of the MiG-15s credited to Sabre pilots as shot down on the basis of gun camera film – which would form a majority of the 792 MiG-15 kills claimed by the US Air Force in the Korean War – would in fact make it back to base, since the Communist fighter was very solidly constructed.

The MiGs Hinton's flight had engaged were from the 50th IAD (Air Division) of the 64th IAK (Air Corps). The 64th had moved from its base outside Shanghai to Anshan on November 20, after exchanging its early MiG-15s for the improved MiG-15bis. On November 24, they had removed the red stars from their aircraft and replaced them with North Korean insignia in preparation for entering combat over Korea. Their first combat happened on December 1, when six MiGs were scrambled to intercept B-29s that had been spotted south of the Yalu across from Antung. While the pilots reported only damaging two of the B-29s, senior lieutenants Orlov and Grebenkin were each credited with a B-29; USAF records recorded no B-29s lost that day.

On December 3, the 50th IAD, which included the 29th GvIAP and the 177th IAP, had moved forward from Anshan to Antung on the Yalu River border in order to provide coverage as far south as Pyongyang. On December 4, the first mission from Antung saw four MiG-15bis fighters from the 2nd Squadron of the 29th Regiment, led by Guards captain Vedensky, intercept and shoot down the RB-45C Tornado 48-0015 from Detachment "A" of the 84th Bomb Squadron, 91st Strategic Reconnaissance Wing.

Captain Stepan Naumenko, who would become the first Soviet MiG pilot credited with five victories, opened his score an hour later when he shot down what he described as two F-84s (given this was three days before the 27th Fighter-Escort Wing flew their first mission in Korea, they were most likely F-80s). During the fight Naumenko's wingman, Senior Lieutenant Rumyantsev, became the first MiG pilot to fall victim to the fighter's weak tail structure; turning sharply at high speed and low altitude as he tried to stay with Naumenko, his aircraft went out of control when its elevators buckled under the high G-loading and crashed before Rumyantsev could eject.

Hinton's four opponents on December 17 were from the 29th GvIAP, led by deputy regimental commander Major Keleynikov. Originally, six MiGs had taken off, but the third element leader had been unable to retract his gear and was forced to abort the interception with his wingman. Keleynikov's wingman was Major Yakov Efreemenko, the 50th IAD's senior MiG instructor pilot. When the first call of "four aircraft below!" was made, Efreemenko, who saw they had swept wings, radioed "those are friendly." In fact, there were two American formations in the area; the first call of enemy aircraft was when four F-80s below the MiGs were spotted; Efreemenko had looked up and seen Hinton's flight of Sabres as they entered their attack dive, which he mistook for MiG-15s from the 177th IAP.

As Keleynikov led the four MiGs in a gentle diving turn toward the F-80s, Efreemenko saw the Sabres closing from the rear, but still believed them fellow MiGs. Suddenly, Hinton opened fire. Efreemenko, who believed throughout the fight that it was a case of mistaken identity, called he was friendly as the two elements of MiGs separated. Hinton continued firing. When his plane caught fire from Hinton's second burst, Efreemenko slowed; when the third burst set fire to the engine, he prepared to eject. At the fourth burst of fire he jettisoned his canopy and ejected – unnoticed by Hinton – as the MiG rolled over and went in.

Intermittent bad weather throughout the rest of the month would affect these opening moves in MiG Alley.

Over the next five days following Hinton's victory, 4th Group pilots continued to enter MiG Alley at around 0.68–0.70 Mach as they attempted to stretch their time on patrol to the maximum. Their Soviet opponents, who always possessed a height advantage due to the MiG-15's superior high-altitude performance over the Sabre, quickly realized they could dive through the American formations in a hit and run attack and outrun them before the F-86s could accelerate to fighting speed. The tactic was used by the pilots of the two regiments of the 50th IAD on December 19 and 21, with no losses on either side.

Ten more Sabres arrived at Kimpo by December 18, while a second detachment of 16 Sabres led by Glenn Eagleston arrived at Suwon some 60 miles south of Kimpo. While both detachments were the size of a standard squadron, there were pilots from all three squadrons in both, in order to maximize the opportunity for all three squadrons to get pilots experienced in Korean combat as quickly as possible.

In response to the Soviet tactics, the Americans quickly discarded the fuel-saving tactic. It became the new rule that Sabres would accelerate to Mach 0.87 or higher before entering the combat zone. This unfortunately meant their patrol time was cut to only 20 minutes. This left little margin for high-speed aerial combat, and as the Soviets noted the time limit on the Sabre patrols, they would develop the strategy of keeping the MiG formations at high altitude north of the Yalu, jumping over the border to go after the Sabres when they were at minimum fuel.

In response, the 4th developed the strategy of utilizing a 16-aircraft patrol of four flights of four F-86s, each entering MiG Alley at five-minute intervals, at different altitudes. On the morning of December 22, the 4th took its first loss when 15 MiG-15s from the 1st Squadron of the 177th IAP led by squadron leader Captain Mikhailov used their altitude advantage to bounce the Americans. At 1125 hours, they spotted a flight of Sabres over Yomju railway station. Captain Niklay Vorobyov later described what happened:

I was first to spot the enemy, flying in a diamond formation at 12,000m (39,000 feet). I went after them while the rest of our group fell behind. I leveled off behind the trailing Sabre and closed in to about 100m from its starboard side. I fired a burst that went high, then a second burst that went low. The Sabre started banking right and I followed him. My third burst went to his right, and the fourth burst hit him when he flew into it; I must have been no more than 80 meters away. One 37mm cannon shell went into the tail pipe. Debris and wreckage sailed past me as the enemy plane caught fire and fell away. I radioed "One down! Falling down! On fire!" The three other Sabres broke and dived away. When my gun camera film was developed later, I was told by flight instructor Safronov, "I've never seen pictures with such close-ups of the enemy aircraft."

Vorobyov's victim was Captain Lawrence V. Bach, who managed to eject at low altitude successfully. He was captured almost immediately upon landing and managed to survive two and a half years of captivity as a POW. His F-86A-5 (49-1176) crashed some 25 miles southeast of Sinuiju.

The new American tactics were combat-tested on the afternoon of December 22, when group commander Col John C. Meyer led eight F-86s in two flights, with a second pair of flights led by 335th Squadron commander Glenn Eagleston. Only Meyer's formation engaged the enemy when eight MiG-15bis fighters from the 2nd Squadron of the 177th IAP attacked his force, waiting till the Sabres were coming to the end of their 20-minute patrol.

In a close-in combat that began at over 30,000 feet and extended down to the treetops, Meyer added two to his World War II score of 24, one of which was a high-angle deflection burst at a fast-flying MiG that disintegrated as his rounds hit all over the fuselage. Lt Cdr Paul E. Pugh, a Navy exchange pilot leading the second flight, claimed a MiG that was later not confirmed, while Meyers' element leader, Captain James O. Roberts from the 335th, and wingman 1st Lt Arthur L. O'Connor of the 336th, claimed one each. With fuel running low for the Sabres, the Americans turned south. As they headed home, 334th Squadron commander Eagleston and his wingman 1st Lt John Odiorne spotted two MiGs at 9,000 feet and each claimed one shot down.

The American claims of seven shot down on December 22 demonstrated that the Soviets were not the only fighter pilots to over-claim. Soviet records list the 177th IAP's flight leader, Senior Lieutenant

Barsegyan, as killed, with a second pilot successfully ejecting, while a third MiG-15bis returned to Antung with six hits in its fuselage. The remaining five MiGs landed back at base relatively unscathed. American machine-gun fire was not as effective against the MiG as the Sabre pilots believed.

The fight had demonstrated the importance of maintaining the two-plane element, since the wingmen were able to successfully call out every attempt by the MiGs to attack from the rear, with the Sabres breaking away before the enemy could open fire successfully.

Servicing the advanced F-86s at Kimpo in the face of the worst Korean winter in over a century created real challenges for the ground crews. Then 19-year-old Airman First Class Norm Kalow, who had graduated from the aircraft and engine mechanics' training course at Sheppard Field, Texas and joined the 4th Wing the previous July, recalled:

Generally, the Sabre was a great aircraft. Most repairs were easy as compared to reciprocating engine aircraft, except for a few items, such as canopy seals, and we experienced minimal servicing problems at the primitive air fields and facilities in Korea. As an example, two of us could change an engine, including the engine's run-up, at a normal working pace in under an hour with few tools. All a good crew chief needed was a screwdriver and a pair of waterpump pliers, and we could fix 90 percent of the problems! As a further example, the mounting of the J47 jet engine was secured by two ball and sockets and a forward cross pin. Elegant! This indicates an outstanding design and engineering effort by North American. The Sabre was a "crew chief's dream" from a maintenance standpoint, with our only criteria being to keep 'em flying. Inactivity was bad for the Sabre. The less it flew, the more minor problems it had. For such a comparatively complex aircraft, the Sabre was amazingly trouble-free. This included its systems, such as the hydraulics, the electricals and so forth.

All in all, the Sabre was docile, but if we were careless, it would bite. A case in point was a young crew chief; cocky, slightly careless, and sometimes unheeding of advice. When we were at Kimpo, the young man walked in front of the air intake duct of a Sabre just as it was started up. He was instantly sucked in and rammed through 12 feet of intake duct to the engine where the engine screens stopped him. He was dead by the time the engine was shut down and he was pulled out. We were always warned about the inherent dangers of the nose intake, and we treated it with great respect.

That first deployment, the cold was the thing I remember most. If you had to take your gloves off to start a screw, you'd better get it done within a minute or you'd see streaks of white on your fingers.

While the 4th was getting the measure of their enemy, back home American families were beginning to receive letters from their GI sons in Korea about how useless the war was. President Truman attempted to publicly emphasize the seriousness of the situation by declaring a state of national emergency on December 16, but the war would never again receive the public support it had before the Chinese intervention. The administration realized if they were to respond affirmatively to public sentiment to withdraw, such action would draw Republican attacks about being "soft on communism," while deciding to widen the war as General MacArthur advocated would terrify allies. There was nothing to do beyond muddle through and hope for improvement, which would become the dominant American strategy for the rest of the war.

A Sabre mission on December 24 saw the MiGs again stay high and wait to make their move at the end of the American patrol limit. Captain Stepan Naumenko claimed two F-86s shot down to become the first officially credited Soviet "ace" of the Korean War; he was made an immediate Hero of the Soviet Union on landing at Antung. The Americans admitted no losses, but two Sabres were lightly damaged.

After two days of bad weather, the biggest Sabre mission to date was flown on December 30, when all 32 Sabres from both detachments flew two 16-plane mutually supportive missions to MiG Alley in the vicinity of Sinuiju. Despite the clear weather, with ceiling and visibility unlimited, the 36 MiGs launched in response to the arrival of the Sabres remained high on their side of the Yalu. Finally, with the first group of Sabres nearing the limits of their patrol time, four MiGs dived through the formation. No damage was inflicted on the Sabres, but Captain James N. Jabara claimed one MiG damaged. He would make his reputation in MiG Alley over the next five months.

Over the last half of December 1950, the 4th Group had logged 234 sorties, during which pilots had engaged MiGs 76 times and claimed eight enemy fighters destroyed, two probables, and seven damaged, for one F-86 lost. On the other side, their Soviet opponents of the 50th IAD claimed six F-86 Sabres, two F-84 Thunderjets and two F-80 Shooting Stars shot down between December 3 and December 24, while admitting three losses.

On New Year's Eve, December 31, 1950, the People's Volunteer Army renewed its offensive by crossing the 38th Parallel. The attack was ordered that night because there was a full moon and a belief that American and European forces would be distracted by the holiday. General Matthew B. Ridgway, who had only arrived days earlier to take command of Eighth Army in the wake of General Walker's death in a traffic accident, had predicted a Chinese attack for these exact reasons, but UN forces were still surprised. The American units on the line were suffering from low morale that stemmed from "the Big Bug-Out." They had not received sufficient replacements to bring them up to full strength, and many GIs were looking forward with anticipation to leaving a country they now hated. The general lack of fighting spirit and unwillingness of the troops to maintain contact with Chinese forces by patrolling along the front contributed to the lack of warning when the new offensive began.

The Chinese assault breached the defensive line at the Imjin River, the Hantan River, and the villages of Gapyeong and Chuncheon, which were held by the ROK 1st, 2nd, 5th and 6th Infantry divisions, which led to UN collapse as the Korean units melted away in the face of the enemy. Initial progress once the South Korean divisions had been pushed aside was good. The ROK units had experienced over 45,000 casualties in North Korea in the Chinese attack and the UN retreat; the replacements they had received were raw recruits. US Army Chief of Staff General J. Lawton Collins had inspected the front just before the death of General Walker and pronounced the ROK units fit only for rear-area guard duty.

With the ROK collapse, the Chinese aimed to get into the rear of the Eighth Army and surround the Americans. Reluctantly, General Ridgway ordered the evacuation of Seoul and withdrawal south of the Han River on January 3, 1951. While Ridgway absolutely believed there would be no full-scale evacuation of the peninsula, despite the renewed panic in Tokyo, he did order that the work MacArthur had ordered in December to fortify the old Pusan Perimeter line along the Naktong River be expedited should further withdrawal be necessary.

The Chinese breakthrough along the 38th Parallel and the rapid advance toward Seoul threatened the units based at Kimpo, just south of the capital. After only 18 days in Korea, the Sabres were ordered to evacuate, fast. Kimpo was busy throughout the day as the 4th's Sabres, along with the F-80s of the 51st Wing and the RF-51Ds of the 67th Tactical Reconnaissance Squadron evacuated the field. C-47s and C-54s arrived throughout the day to evacuate personnel. The last F-86 flew back to Johnson AFB in Japan at the end of the day. That night, a C-54 arrived to pick up the remaining pilots and ground crews.

On January 3, the last Shooting Stars departed, loaded with bombs and rockets by the ground crews who had remained behind. The jets made final strikes against the enemy, rocketing, bombing and strafing advancing infantry before pointing their noses across the Sea of Japan; with US artillery, the Shooting Stars had inflicted some 700 casualties. Chinese forces entered Seoul later that day, engaging in fierce hand-to-hand combat with the US 24th and 25th Infantry divisions and the newly arrived British 29th Infantry Brigade. The 24th Division left Seoul that night, while the majority of the Commonwealth Brigade crossed the Han River shortly after dawn on January 4. All IX Corps forces were out of the city by 0740 hours; the US 27th Infantry Regiment fought on the outskirts of the city until 1400 hours.

As this went on, those UN personnel still at Kimpo set fire to the remaining supplies and blew up the unserviceable aircraft left behind. Despite the fact the enemy was now less than a mile from the field, a C-119 made a final, very dangerous flight to Kimpo to pick up remaining personnel, including North American tech rep John Henderson. Hours later, Seoul fell to the People's Volunteer Army.

The Sabres would not return to MiG Alley for two months.

The high command of the US Air Force was not happy to receive General Stratemeyer's demand that two wings of more advanced fighters be sent to Korea to face the growing Communist air threat. Most particularly, General Curtis LeMay, commander of Strategic Air Command, disliked having his force "diluted" with units diverted from their main assignments to participate in what he termed derisively a "sideshow," while he remained committed to waging nuclear war with the main enemy, the Soviet Union.

Strategic Air Command controlled five fighter-escort wings equipped with Republic F-84D and F-84E Thunderjets – the 12th Fighter-Escort

Wing, the 14th Fighter-Escort Wing that had been the first to equip with the F-84, the 27th Fighter-Escort Wing, the 31st Fighter-Escort Wing, and the 82nd Fighter-Escort Wing. These units were assigned as fighter escorts for the B-29 and B-50 units of SAC.

The 27th Fighter-Escort Wing, based at Bergstrom AFB in Texas, had begun operating the F-84 in January 1950 after re-equipping from the North American F-82E Twin Mustang, and was the only unit completely equipped with the new F-84E. The 27th FEW was commanded by Col Ashley B. Packard, while the 27th Fighter Escort Group was commanded by the legendary Col Donald J. M. Blakeslee, wartime leader of the 4th Fighter Group in England when it became the top-scoring USAAF fighter group of World War II.

The wing had deployed to Britain in the summer, demonstrating the F-84's range by flying the North Atlantic route (Labrador-Greenland-Iceland-Northern Scotland) both ways, and was preparing for a second European deployment when they received orders on November 9 to prepare to move to Korea. The aircraft departed Bergstrom on November 11. The 522nd Fighter-Escort Squadron refueled at Biggs AFB, Texas, while the 523rd Squadron did so at Kirtland AFB, New Mexico, and the 524th at Williams AFB, Arizona on the way to NAS North Island in San Diego. The Thunderjets were cocooned and the 522nd Squadron was loaded aboard USS *Bairoko* (CVE-115) on November 14, while the 523rd and 524th squadrons were loaded aboard the larger USS *Bataan* (CVL-29) on November 16.

Bairoko arrived in Japan on November 28, followed by *Bataan* the next day. Once unloaded from the carriers, the Thunderjets were barged to Kisarazu air base where the cocoons were removed. Several aircraft were found to have been damaged by salt air-induced corrosion during their trans-Pacific open-air deck shipment due to improper cocooning. Further inspection revealed corroded electrical equipment and damage to landing gear, with several flat tires. While the undamaged aircraft were flown on to Yokota AFB, several days were necessary to repair the damaged F-84s.

While this was going on, the initial ground echelon arrived at Kimpo (K-14) by air transport on November 30, to prepare for the arrival of the air group. In light of the worsening situation on the ground, FEAF decided on December 1 that the short-ranged F-86s would be based at

Kimpo while the longer-ranged F-84s would operate from Taegu (K-2). With the fall of Pyongyang on December 3 leaving planners worried about future operations in Korea, the wing was split into forward and rear echelons, with the advanced headquarters at Taegu and the main base for heavy maintenance and overhaul established at Itazuke AFB in Japan. Logistics support for the advanced echelon would be provided by the F-80-equipped 49th Fighter-Bomber Wing at Taegu, while the rear echelon was attached to the provisional 6160th Air Base Wing at Itazuke.

Don Blakeslee led the first six Thunderjets to Taegu on December 5. While the F-84s were given a primary assignment of fighter escort for B-29 strikes in North Korea, the aircraft were also equipped with special depressed gun cameras to record bomb strikes. Colonel Blakeslee led the first "armed reconnaissance" mission on December 6 over the Chinnampo River area in North Korea. That same day, the ten other F-84s of the initial advance party flew to Taegu. Like the 4th Wing, pilots from all three squadrons were assigned to spread initial combat experience. With the Chinese advance in full cry, the F-84s were committed to the fighter-bomber role to try and slow supplies to the advancing enemy. During several missions on December 7 and 8, 32 rockets and 7,200 rounds of .50-caliber ammunition were expended during "armed reconnaissance" sorties, with several locomotives claimed as damaged during a strike on the rail lines in Pyongyang.

The forward detachment suffered their first losses on December 13 when two Thunderjets were lost on a strafing mission west of Krin-ni. One Thunderjet was apparently hit by enemy antiaircraft fire and crashed. The second was lost when it was given a go-around at Taegu because of other traffic. The F-84 suddenly lost power and the pilot managed a belly landing in a dry creek bed, with the airplane written off as a result.

By early January, the remainder of the 27th Wing's aircraft were operational, but plans to send the entire fighter group to Taegu were canceled and only an advance party remained until January 6, when the F-84s were flown back to Itazuke since it appeared the enemy advance might threaten Taegu. The Thunderjet had the range to be able to continue to provide air support over the South Korean battlefield and southern North Korea from Japan.

CHAPTER 9

THE CEEGAR KID

The Third Battle of Seoul was a significant success for the People's Volunteer Army. With the loss of the South Korean capital, morale in the UN forces descended to its lowest point of the war. General Ridgway took immediate steps over the two weeks following the fall of Seoul to restore morale and fighting spirit in the Army.

By January 17, Ridgway was already planning what would become Operation *Thunderbolt,* the UN counterattack that would commence January 25. In the aftermath of the Chinese offensive, UN war goals now returned to what they had been pre-Inchon: repel aggression and push the Communist forces back north of the 38th Parallel. The official UN war policy now was restoration of the *status quo ante* of June 25, 1950. The struggle to achieve that would become the protracted campaign fought for the rest of the war. Over the next two months, UN forces re-took Seoul for the fourth and last time and Fifth Air Force units returned to their South Korean bases.

Marshal Peng's renewed offensive by the People's Volunteer Army began in late April and reached its height during May and early June 1951, and was in the end a failure; by July the battlefront ran along a line winding from below Kaesong on the west coast to north of Kansong on the shore of the Sea of Japan. In New York, the Soviet delegation to the United Nations proposed talks to bring about an armistice. The mobile phase of the Korean War was over. For the next two years, ground action would be reminiscent of the bloody trench warfare of World War I, as the opposing armies attempted to take this position or that in hopes the action would affect the peace talks.

The Sabres returned to Korea on January 17, operating in small detachments from Taegu (K-2) flying close support and armed reconnaissance missions. Taegu was too far south to allow patrols into MiG Alley. The 335th's Lon Walker remembered:

The pilots who had been sent to Kimpo in December were the most experienced in the 4th FG, and were perhaps the most combat experienced jet pilots in the world at that time. I was very lucky to be one of the pilots that went with the detachment in January. We shared quarters with some of the F-80 pilots from the 49th. It was bitterly cold, and the pot-bellied stove worked overtime to keep our huts livable.

The Sabres were only able to fly a few sorties from Taegu before returning to Japan on January 31. The PSP runway, which was torn up by all the use, proved to be "less than ideal" for F-86 operations.

The 27th Group also operated F-84s in detachments at Taegu. On January 20, the Thunderjets met the MiG-15 in combat for the first time and discovered they were as outclassed as the pilots of the F-80, though they suffered no losses in the quick encounter. The next day, the Thunderjets escorted F-80 fighter-bombers north of Pyongyang and were intercepted by MiGs. One 49th Group F-80 and one F-84 of the 523rd Squadron fell victim to the MiGs, while squadron commander Lt Col William E. "Bill" Bertram managed to tack onto the tail of the trailing MiG of the four that attacked the F-84s and shoot it down to score the Thunderjet's first MiG victory.

The 27th Group was assigned to fly cover for B-29s on a mission to Pyongyang on January 23. Wing commander Col Ashley B. Packard convinced FEAF that the best way for the wing to cover the B-29s was to attack Sinuiju, which would divert the MiGs from going after the bombers. Thirty-three F-84s from the 522nd and 523rd squadrons were assigned to the mission. Eight would strafe the airfield at Sinuiju to go after the defenses. Two flights would remain high to provide cover if the MiGs responded, while the rest would bomb the airfield.

The Antung MiGs did respond and a fierce 30-minute air battle developed. The 523rd's 1st Lt Jacob Kratt, flying element lead in the first covering flight, spotted eight MiGs that had crossed the Yalu when they attacked one of the bomber flights. Kratt and his wingman broke toward the MiGs as they closed on the others from astern. Kratt accelerated to maximum speed and flashed past the rear MiGs to open fire on the leader. His fire hit the enemy fighter solidly in its tail pipe and it blew up. This unnerved the other three, who broke off their attack. Minutes later, Kratt spotted other MiGs crossing the Yalu. He dived into this formation and hit another MiG, which went down on fire.

Kratt's flight leader, Captain Allen McGuire, and his wingman Captain William Slaughter, also engaged the MiGs, and each claimed one shot down. This engagement, with four MiG-15s claimed for no losses to the Thunderjet, was the high point of the F-84's aerial combat career in Korea. Officially only three MiGs were credited shot down, with Captain Slaughter's claim reduced to a "probable" since no one saw a crash. Kratt received the Silver Star in recognition of his achievement, while the 27th Wing was awarded the first of two Distinguished Unit Commendations for its Korean service.

The MiG pilots of the 50th IAD considered the battles between January 20 and 23 to be the toughest three days of their tour in Korea. In six fights with American jets during the month, the division claimed 15 F-84s and two F-80s destroyed. The battle over Sinuiju on January 23 was the last for the 29th GvIAP, which flew 27 MiGs north to Anshan on January 24. Two weeks later, the 50th IAD concluded its Korean tour when the 177th IAP departed Antung for Anhan. The division's MiGs were turned over to the incoming 151st GvIAD. The new unit's 28th GvIAP returned to Antung during the first week of February.

On February 5, as UN ground forces advanced near Hoengsong, northeast of Wonju, in Operation *Round-Up*, Major Arnold "Moon" Mullins of the 67th Fighter-Bomber Squadron and his wingman 1st Lt Harold J. Ausman were forced by the weather to climb above a broken cloud layer to get out of a rugged mountain valley. Just south of Seoul, they let down under the cloud layer and suddenly realized they were coming up on the tails of two piston-engine fighters, which they quickly recognized as Yak-9s. Mullins, a World War II Mustang pilot, ordered Ausman to take the one on the right while he took the one on the left. Mullins pulled in behind his target and quickly set it afire with a well-aimed burst. Ausman, however, was so surprised by the appearance of the enemy airplanes that he found himself closing too fast. He loosed a burst that struck the Yak but did no fatal harm. As he swept past, to become a target for the enemy pilot, Mullins pulled in behind the plane and set it afire before the enemy pilot could fire at Ausman. Since neither pilot saw what happened to the second Yak, Mullins only received credit for the first Yak. This was the final aerial score by a Mustang pilot during the war.

Five days later, the Eighth Army retook Inchon and Kimpo airfield. At the end of February, MacArthur ordered Brigadier General James E. Briggs, who had replaced "Rosie" O'Donnell as commander of FEAF Bomber Command, to increase pressure on Pyongyang. Briggs ordered 18 B-29s of the 98th Bomb Group to return to MiG Alley for the first time since December to bomb Kogunyong, just south of the Yalu. Twenty-two F-80Cs of the 51st Group were assigned as escorts. Unfortunately, the B-29s ran into unexpected headwinds and the waiting Shooting Stars were so low on fuel they had to abandon the mission and return to Taegu. The B-29s were forced to bomb without escort. MiGs from the 28th GvIAP, led by group commander Lt Col V. I. Kolyadin, attacked and ten B-29s were damaged, three so badly they were forced to land in South Korea. Two were claimed shot down and Colonel Kolyadin received credit for them; the Soviets admitted one MiG lost, which was credited to a B-29 gunner.

US Army engineers completed repairs to Suwon (K-13) on March 4. The 334th Squadron moved in on March 5. The single concrete runway was surrounded by a quagmire of mud; the Sabres had to land on one side of the runway and taxi back to the parking area on the other side, which called for precise operations in both directions. It would be summer before any taxiways could be constructed.

The Sabres returned to MiG Alley for the first time since December on March 6, with 16 Sabres flying a patrol that went unopposed. The number of F-86s in-theater was only just keeping pace with the attrition rate. The 334th Squadron's Captain Richard Becker recalled, "We never had more than 16 aircraft in the air at one time in the beginning. We were usually outnumbered 5:1 in a fight, and sometimes as high as 10:1. It was not unusual for four Sabres to take on 30 to 40 MiGs." FEAF experienced its only loss in air combat during March when an F-80, flown by 1st Lt Howard J. Landry of the 80th Fighter-Bomber Squadron, collided with a MiG-15; both pilots were killed in the crashes.

At the end of March, the 19th Group again went after the Yalu bridges, this time armed with the biggest bomb in the Air Force inventory. The Tarzon bomb was a development of the British Tallboy "earthquake" bomb of World War II fame. The 12,000lb bombs were so large more than half of the weapon protruded from the bomb bay. The Tarzon combined Tallboy, Range, and Azimuth Only, which described the weapon and its guidance system.

On March 29, a break in the persistent cloudy weather over North Korea allowed three Superfortresses to attempt to bomb the Sinuiju bridges. One B-29 aborted with mechanical problems, while the bomber flown by group commander Col Payne Jennings apparently ditched at sea with the loss of all aboard when he was unable to release the Tarzon. The third Superfortress successfully dropped its bomb, but missed the target. Over the next three weeks when weather allowed, 29 more Tarzons were dropped, temporarily knocking out six bridges, while another B-29 was lost attempting to ditch its bomb at sea. The bombs were so heavy and the fact they protruded into the slipstream caused handling problems in flight, which was considered responsible for the losses. At the end of April, the remaining Tarzons were returned to the United States.

In late March, the Air Force's 1st Radio Squadron, Mobile, operating in Japan, picked up Russian ground controllers in voice communication with Soviet aircraft operating over North Korea. This was an important intelligence windfall, since Soviet doctrine called for tight control of fighters by stations on the ground. This breakthrough in signals intelligence would eventually provide real-time intelligence from the Russian controllers and allow Sabre flights in MiG Alley to be warned of approaching fighters.

A weather break allowed B-29s to fly into MiG Alley on March 30, when 36 from the 19th, 98th and 307th groups were sent against the bridges. High cover was provided by eight flights of Sabres from the 334th and 335th squadrons now operating from Suwon. The 12 19th Group bombers received half-hearted MiG attacks, swooping in and out of the bomber stream. One crewmember was wounded, while other gunners were credited with two MiGs, though the Soviets listed no losses. The weather closed in again the next day.

SAC commander General LeMay had been very reluctant to release the 27th Wing for Korea; he was particularly displeased that his elite fighter escorts were used as long-range fighter-bombers and pressured General Stratemeyer to return the Thunderjets to their escort role.

The weather finally broke on April 7, and 24 B-29s from the 98th and 307th groups targeted the newly finished highway bridge at Uiju and the well-bombed railroad bridge at Sinuiju. The 27th Wing provided close escort, with the F-84s flying parallel to the bomber stream at the same altitude while four flights of Sabres provided high cover.

Thirty MiGs from the newly arrived 324th IAD opposed the mission. The 324th, led by ranking Soviet (and Allied) World War II Ace of Aces General Ivan N. Kozhedub, had been in China since February 1950 before being sent to Manchuria in March. The 324th was one of the elite units of the Red Air Force, among the first to equip with the MiG-15 at Kubinka outside Moscow in 1949. The constituent units of the 324th – the 29th GvIAP, 176th GvIAP and the 196th IAP – contained several combat veterans of the Great Patriotic War. The 196th's commander, Lt Col Yevgeny Pepelyaev, was a believer in the adage "train hard, fight easy." His pilots were experienced in dogfighting in pairs, flights, and larger formations. Pepelyaev stated, "My goal was to strive to meet the American standard, but even my pilots were not, man for man, as well trained as their American opponents." The 324th IAD and the 303rd IAD that would follow it in May were the two most dangerous units the Sabres would face in Korea. Pepelyaev scored 19 victories to emerge as the second-ranked ace of the war, while Captain Nikolai Sutyagin of the 303rd scored 21 victories and was the Ace of Aces in the Korean War.

Their first combat with the Americans took place on April 3, only 24 hours after arrival at Antung. Four MiGs of the 176th GvIAP attacked four Sabres south of the Yalu. One Sabre was claimed shot down, though the records claimed it crashed because it ran out of fuel; this would become a common way for the Air Force to reduce the number of "official" combat losses. The Sabre pilots claimed three MiGs shot down, though the 176th Regiment listed only one lost in combat, while two others returned so heavily damaged that they were scrapped; the Soviets could play the "official loss" game too.

The next day, the 196th's Captain Lev Ivanov intercepted an RB-45C Tornado escorted by four Sabres. He later reported:

We closed in a head-on course and engaged in a dogfight. We had already dropped our external tanks since we had been airborne quite some time. We made two attack runs and broke off. I was credited with an F-86. I got behind it and hit its tail. It started billowing smoke and fell out of the sky. Ground observers confirmed the crash.

American records list no such loss.

That afternoon, Senior Lieutenant Fedor Shebanov of the 196th led eight MiGs to intercept UN fighters south of the Yalu but missed them. Nearing Antung, Shebanov slowed during his approach to the field and two Sabres pounced on him but overshot. Shebanov accelerated after them and shot up the trailing Sabre. Though the USAF did not record the loss, 196th records state the Sabre was found on the ground on April 5, with 37mm and 23mm hits in the fuselage around the engine.

On April 7, MiGs from the 196th intercepted B-29s and their F-84 escorts after slipping past the 16 Sabres on high cover. Captain Serafim Subbotin and Captain Ivan Suchkov were each credited with shooting down a B-29. Senior Lieutenant Andrushko was credited with shooting down an F-84, though he was in turn shot down himself by a 27th Wing F-84. FEAF Bomber Command only listed one B-29 lost.

With the rail bridge at Sinuiju still unscathed, another mission was flown. On April 12, 48 B-29s of the 19th, 98th and 307th groups went back, escorted by 39 F-84s from the 27th Group. Nine Superfortresses aborted. As the American formation appeared on radar, the MiGs on alert at Antung were scrambled. General Kozhedub described the battle:

> When it became clear the first enemy group was headed our way, I scrambled two groups of fighters – six led by Captain Shelamnov and eight led by Captain Tkatskiy – from the 196th IAP at 0955 hours.
>
> At 1000 hours, I ordered eight MiGs of the 176th GvIAP led by Captain Konstantin Sherbetsov and six led by Captain Murashev to intercept the second group detected. At 1010 hours, our pilots reported seeing a formation of B-29s.

The 196th's Captain Lev Ivanov was already airborne and was first to spot the B-29s. Diving through the escorting F-84s, he concentrated his fire on a B-29 of the lead formation, opening fire at 600m (1,800 feet), with two short bursts that went low. He closed to 400m (1,200 feet) and fired two more bursts. The bomber emitted smoke and dropped out of the formation. Ivanov's wingman, Senior Lieutenant Kochegarov, set another B-29's wing tanks afire.

The 19th Group recorded the bombers were three minutes from "bombs away" when 30 MiGs hit the formation. They broke through the Thunderjet escorts and immediately shot down one bomber that caught fire and crashed short of the target. Six more were damaged.

Veteran navigator 1st Lt Ralph Livengood of the 19th Group's 30th Squadron described the attack:

> Only six of our twelve bombers made it back to Okinawa. One diverted to Itazuke with wounded crewmen. The pilot and bombardier of another were killed, and the co-pilot flew back to crash-land at Taegu. A third was badly hit by the MiGs and ditched in the Yellow Sea with no survivors. A fourth crash-landed at Kimpo. The fifth was shot down by the MiGs in the initial attack; there were no 'chutes. Our tail gunner, S/Sgt Lyle Patterson, was credited with shooting down a MiG, and our other gunners had one damaged and another probable. When we got back to Okinawa, we had three rounds left in our guns. After that, the strategy changed a bit. We would take off before dawn or late in the afternoon, so we would hit the targets at first light or dusk.

MiGs led by Captain Gregori Ges attacked the survivors of the 30th Squadron and claimed three more shot down in a running fight. This matches the squadron's officially stated losses, though one of the three survived to crash-land at Taegu.

Senior Lieutenant Fukin engaged the escorts, closing on the tail of an F-84 that he mistakenly identified as an F-80 and put three bursts into the airplane; the right main gear dropped and it fell off as he flew past.

The B-29s of the 307th Group approached the target independently of the other two groups, which made them vulnerable to attack. The MiGs led by captains Sherbetsov and Subbotin attacked, claiming two shot down, though the 307th Group listed one shot down and another so badly damaged it crash-landed at Suwon. The group turned away and dropped their bombs short of the target.

The crews of the 98th Group, last over the target, escaped attack. Soviet records state that the final group "encountered insufficient resistance from our fighters and managed to bomb the railway bridge." Overall, the battle had become confused, and it is likely that other reports by 324th Division pilots of attacks on B-29s may have been against formations already attacked and previously damaged.

The MiG pilots claimed 11 B-29s and two escorting fighters identified as F-80s shot down. They had flashed past the Thunderjets, which were flying throttled back to stay with the slower bombers, as if they weren't there. F-84 pilots claimed three probables and B-29 gunners were credited with seven. Soviet records record no losses.

The Sinuiju mission came to be known among FEAF Bomber Command crews as "Black Thursday." FEAF was forced to conclude that B-29s could not be flown in MiG Alley during daylight hours. While only three were listed as lost over the target, with one crash-landing in South Korea due to battle damage, 25 B-29s had been shot down or damaged by MiGs in the two missions. This was 25 percent of the total number of B-29s assigned to FEAF and far above the 10 percent loss rate deemed acceptable. General Stratemeyer banned further B-29 attacks on Sinuiju until an effective means of escort could be developed and informed Curtis LeMay that the Thunderjets were too slow and lacked the maneuverability to go against the MiG-15. From then on, whenever possible, escort missions were flown by the Sabres, while the Thunderjet went on to become the leading fighter-bomber of the war. In the event, B-29s never attacked the Sinuiju bridges again, and did not fly in MiG Alley in daylight for six months. The MiGs had won the first round.

The 27th Wing was awarded a second DUC (Distinguished Unit Citation) for missions flown between January 26 and April 21, and the Republic of Korea Presidential Unit Citation. They were replaced by the 136th Fighter-Bomber Wing, an activated Air National Guard unit that arrived in May, and stayed to assist the 49th Fighter-Bomber Wing in its transition from F-80Cs to F-84Es. During eight months in Korea, the 27th participated in three major air campaigns. They flew 12,000 sorties and lost seven pilots in combat, and 15 aircraft to all causes.

One feature of Soviet fighter aviation organization worked against them as compared with their American opponents. This was the practice in which a unit as a whole deployed to Korea for a set period; in the case of the first two air divisions, this was for approximately 90 days each. There was only a 10–14-day overlap between the arrival of a replacement unit and the departure of the previous unit, which was not enough time to pass on the experience gained. Thus, American pilots would come to recognize "experience cycles" in their opponents as an inexperienced division became operational: the MiGs would stay north of the border and only come south at high altitude to make quick attacks on patrolling Sabres, then extend combat opportunities as the pilots gained experience to the point of serious combat, only to see the cycle repeat when the unit departed. On the other hand, the 4th Fighter-Interceptor Wing, and the later 51st Fighter-Interceptor Wing, remained permanently stationed in South Korea, with individual pilots cycling in and out as they completed their 85–100-mission combat tours. Thus, experienced pilots in the unit could move up into leadership positions as the earlier leaders completed their tours and left for home. However, for the rest of 1951, the Sabres would face the 324th and 303rd divisions, which became highly experienced and dangerous enemies.

Additionally, the tactics chosen by the two opponents were different due to the differences in performance parameters between the F-86 and the MiG-15. Captain Sergei Karamenko, a 12-victory ace in the Great Patriotic War who scored 13 victories in Korea, described the situation:

> The Sabre was the most dangerous threat to my friends and me in Korean skies. Our MiG-15 and the F-86 belonged in the same class, similar types with similar performance. They differed only in that the MiG had an advantage in rate of climb at altitude, while the Sabre was superior in maneuvering, especially at low level. These advantages could not always be used, however. The fight, as a rule, was decided in the first attack. After the first pass, the MiG-15s reached for altitude, while the Sabres rushed for the ground. Each tried to reach the altitude where it held a distinct advantage, and thus the battle faded.

Captain Richard Becker, the second F-86 pilot credited with five victories, recalled:

> After our first four or five missions, combat became like a boxing match. It was either him or me while protecting my wingman, but it was a fight to the death. It was also a short fight. Sometimes during an entire day of combat, a dogfight might last only four to eight minutes, but it was so violent that we were exhausted when we landed.

While the MiG's cannon armament was slower-firing, it only took one or two hits for a MiG to shoot down a Sabre. Captain Becker explained:

It only took one or two hits to be blown up, but I do know some pilots who were hit in the tail section who came back. If we were hit in the fuselage or near the engine with an explosive shell, it was the end. We were down.

In contrast, the lighter machine-gun armament of the F-86 meant pilots had to get in close with the enemy to score killing blows. Becker recalled:

I remember one MiG I shot down when I was within 300 feet with all six .50-caliber guns firing down his tailpipe, and in a short time, he blew up. It did not take a long burst. If we fired from 1,500 feet with a deflection shot, we had a problem.

Thus, the MiG pilots favored a single pass, trying to knock down a Sabre with one or two solid hits, while the Sabre pilots favored mixing it up, depending on their superior maneuverability to get in close and open fire.

The similarity in design between Sabre and MiG led to some early mistakes when Sabre pilots were unsure whether they were closing on an enemy. In January 1951, Glenn Eagleston suggested to his former ETO flying comrade John Meyer that they create an identification similar to the black-and-white "D-Day stripes" that were used to identify Allied aircraft in 1944. Eagleston's original design for this had the fuselage stripes wrapped vertically around the fuselage aft of the wing, as his P-51 had been painted. Meyer suggested the fuselage stripes be swept forward 30 degrees. The design was finalized with three black and two white stripes on the wings just inboard from the tips, and the same stripes swept forward on the fuselage. The 4th's Sabres were painted during January and February 1951 as they rotated through Johnson AFB, in time for the air battles that spring.

On March 31, the Sabres claimed their first MiG-15 victory since December when Royal Canadian Air Force exchange pilot Flt Lt J. A. O. "Trottle" Levesque, who was flying with the 334th Squadron, shot down a MiG attempting to attack B-29s. Credited with four World

War II victories, Levesque had been shot down himself over Europe, spending three years as a POW at Stalag Luft III where he had taken part in the tunneling that led to "The Great Escape." Immediately prior to his exchange assignment with the 4th in June 1950, he had been a member of the RCAF's Blue Devils aerobatic team flying deHavilland Vampire jets. "They had wanted to send me to Britain to fly Meteors, but I didn't want to fly that old crate. I wanted to go to the US, where they had modern jets." Levesque was one of the combat-experienced pilots first sent to Korea in December; he was number four in Bruce Hinton's flight on December 17, 1950, becoming the first Canadian to fly over North Korea.

Levesque later recalled the fight:

> I was flying as wingman for Maj Ed Fletcher, leader of Red flight. Suddenly the squadron commander called out bandits coming in from the right. We all dropped our fuel tanks and Fletcher spotted two more MiGs at nine o'clock off our left wings and above us a bit.

Fletcher and Levesque turned sharply toward the two enemy fighters, which quickly split up and turned away. "My MiG pulled up into the sun, probably trying to lose me in the glare. That was an old trick the Germans used to do, but this day I had dark sunglasses on, and I kept the MiG in sight." The MiG leveled off and Levesque turned inside him. The fight had carried them from 40,000 feet to 17,000.

> I guess I was about 1,500 feet away from him. I got in a really nice deflection shot but with those six guns firing you lost 30 to 40 knots of speed, which was a hell of a lot! I aimed again and fired another burst and, all of a sudden, one flap came down on the MiG. He kept on turning and I followed him down. I started to pull up, and saw another MiG diving from above me. I climbed into the sun at full throttle and started doing barrel rolls. The MiG disappeared.

Even after evading the second MiG, Levesque was still in danger. "I went right through the B-29 formation and they all shot at me! Thank God they missed. I waggled my wings and they stopped firing, but lots of shells had just missed me." Levesque's MiG victory qualified him as an "ace" when added to his World War II score and he was awarded the US Distinguished Flying Cross.

While the Soviets had already credited two MiG-15 pilots with five victories each by the end of January, 1951, the Sabre pilots did not start to build up victory totals until April. They were able to station two squadrons at newly repaired Kimpo, while the third was back at Johnson AFB in Japan, undergoing R&R for the pilots and extended maintenance on the aircraft.

Captain James N. "Jabby" Jabara, who had been credited with a "probable" in the Kimpo detachment's last fight on December 30, 1950, scored his first credited victory on April 3, 1951, during a 12-on-12 fight with pilots from the 151st GvIAP. Jabara was a World War II veteran, having done one tour from January to October 1944, flying P-51s with the Ninth Air Force's 363rd Fighter Group, and a second tour during the last three months of the war in Europe with the Eighth Air Force's 355th Fighter Group. During his first tour, he survived two midair collisions, the first with another Mustang over England in bad weather, and the second over Normandy that summer when he collided with the Bf-109 he was dueling; both pilots bailed out and landed near each other, where they shook hands. Jabara was short even by fighter pilot standards, being only five feet five inches tall. Unlike most fighter aces, he did not have good eyesight and required glasses; one of his World War II nicknames had been "Cousin Weak Eyes." His better-known nickname as "The Ceegar Kid" came from his penchant for smoking cigars. After the war he remained in the Air Force and transitioned to the F-80 in 1948. He joined the 4th in the summer of 1950 after they re-equipped with Sabres.

A week after scoring his first victory, Jabara claimed a second MiG-15 on April 10 and a third two days later. With "iffy" weather over North Korea, he did not claim his fourth victory until April 22. While Soviet records confirmed Jabara's first victory on April 3, the records indicate there were no losses on April 10, the date of his second confirmed victory. In the big battle between B-29s and their escorts against the Antung MiGs on April 12, only one MiG was recorded lost, against four claimed by Sabre pilots; there is no certainty that Jabara scored that victory. The situation was the same on April 22, when Jabara was credited with a fourth victory, with only one MiG lost out of four claimed; again it is impossible to verify that victory was Jabara's. Even if these losses on April 12 and 22 were Jabara's, his score for April would have only been three MiGs.

By the spring of 1951, the Air Force high command wanted to proclaim an Air Force "ace" in the battle against the MiGs. By this time, the American public had soured on the war following the Chinese intervention in the previous November, and with the apparent inability to defeat the Communists in the battles being waged in the spring of 1951. The Air Force had only become independent three and a half years earlier and the junior service had always been the most publicity-conscious of the services; public-relations officers were stationed with every unit during World War II, charged with ensuring that correspondents got "the Air Force story" on every event. The commanders in Washington were no less aware of the value of good publicity now in perhaps changing the public's view of the war's conduct.

In early April, Colonel Meyer was ordered by Fifth Air Force commander General Earl Partridge to pick a pilot to become that first ace, and to position him to achieve it. Jabara was one of three Meyer identified to the general, since he had just been credited with his second victory. From that point on, Jabara was only assigned to missions where there was a strong likelihood the MiGs would come up to contest the Sabres. His next mission on April 12 saw him claim his third victory. During the ten days of poor weather over North Korea that followed, he did not fly. The next day of good weather saw him claim his fourth victory on April 22.

At the end of April, the 334th Squadron was due to rotate back to Johnson AFB in Japan. Meyer assigned Jabara to "temporary duty" with the 335th Squadron when they arrived at Suwon, to give him the opportunity to score the important fifth victory. Navy exchange pilot Lieutenant Commander Paul Pugh, who had come to Korea with the group and scored during the first deployment to Korea the previous December, had by this point scored two confirmed victories and had been appointed temporary commander of the 334th Squadron. He recalled after the war that when he suggested the tour for the entire squadron be extended, "The Air Force made it clear without exactly saying so that they were determined the first ace be Air Force and they did not want any possibility of a squid [i.e. Navy pilot] robbing them of that. We rotated back to Japan and Jabara stayed in Korea."

On May 20, the Sabres encountered MiGs for the first time since May 9, during a fighter sweep over Sinuiju in which four flights of six Sabres each hoped to lure the MiGs up for a fight. The pilots claimed the 24 Sabres fought 50 MiGs, but the 196th's records only listed 30. Lt Col Ben Emmert, commanding the 335th Squadron, was leading "Awning Purple" and "Awning White" flights when he spotted MiGs at 27,000 feet over Sinuiju, and ordered "Drop tanks!"

Determined to get a fifth MiG, "Awning Red" flight leader Jabara punched off his tanks, but only the left dropped away. Disregarding SOP (Standard Operating Procedure) to abort in such a situation, Jabara engaged a formation of MiGs in a head-on pass without scoring any hits. As he turned to pursue them, his wingman called out three MiGs behind. Turning as tightly as the unbalanced Sabre could, he started a turning duel with a MiG that dropped to 25,000 feet, where he hit the enemy fighter in the fuselage and left wing.

Jabara watched, fascinated, as the MiG-15 caught fire, snap rolled, and dived away. Halfway to the ground, the pilot bailed out and Jabara managed to photograph the parachuting pilot with his gun camera for confirmation. He lost his wingman as he climbed back to altitude, but he soon spotted six MiGs and latched onto the trailing fighter, which engaged in violent evasive maneuvers to get away. Jabara fired two bursts; the first went high, but the second hit the MiG's fuselage and it began to pour smoke and lose altitude. He followed it down to 6,000 feet.

With his attention on the vanquished enemy, Jabara suddenly found himself under attack. The hung tank impaired the Sabre's flying ability and the MiGs closed in and hit him. He was rescued by two F-86s that cleared the enemy from his tail. Jabara had flown past "bingo" fuel, which forced him to climb to 40,000 feet and turn his engine off. At that altitude, the Sabre had a 63-mile glide, which brought him over Kimpo where he turned on his engine and successfully landed. Back at Kimpo, group commander Meyer awarded him a DFC and chewed him out for getting into a fight with a hung tank.

Jabara's after-action report stated he saw the first MiG explode as a result of his gunfire, but that he only saw his second claimed victory go into a tailspin, since he was forced to break off when he was attacked by another. Soviet records recorded one MiG flown by Captain Nazarkin of the 196th IAP shot down with the pilot successfully ejecting, and two returning to their base at Antung damaged. The 196th's Senior

Lieutenant V. N. Alfeyev claimed he shot down a Sabre that still had a tank on its right wing; this could only have been Jabara. Alfeyev also reached ace status, with seven confirmed victories, including Jabara.

The Air Force proclaimed Jabara the first jet-versus-jet ace, which would be accurate if more than four of his claims could be verified through enemy records; at that point the Soviets had credited three MiG pilots with five victories each, and at least two of them claimed only jets, though the claims included F-80s and F-84s shot down, while all of Jabara's during this and his second tour were MiG-15s. Jabara later stated in an interview, "That was my bag for the day, and it made me feel pretty good to know that I was the first jet ace in the history of aerial warfare." He was actually five years behind Luftwaffe Colonel Heinz Bär, who claimed 16 victories against Allied aircraft in 1945 while flying the Messerschmitt Me-262 jet fighter, though his victories were all against piston-engined opponents.

With his claims for six victories officially confirmed, the Air Force publicity machine roared into high gear. Despite his request to remain on operations, Jabara was immediately sent home for a publicity tour. He was the first "MiG Ace" to experience how the American press would treat these first aces of the jet age as knights of the air in the way the aces of World War I had been publicly feted. The official reasoning was the same, since the pilots were achieving tangible victories over the Communists just as the ground war became more and more reminiscent of the muddy slog experienced on the Western Front.

His family's background as Lebanese immigrants and owners of a grocery store in Wichita fit the "All-American Boy" image Air Force public relations officers longed for. He was awarded the Distinguished Service Cross in Fenway Park during the seventh inning stretch at a Boston Red Sox baseball game. He and his father John made appearances on local and national radio and television, while Wichita put on a parade that had one of the largest audiences in the city's history. Capitalizing on his background, father and son were sent on a goodwill tour of the Middle East, and the new American hero gave a speech in Marjayoun, Lebanon, his father's home town. After nearly a year of touring, Jabara received an assignment to Air Training Command at Scott AFB, Illinois, where he itched to get back in the war.

Along with famed World War II ace Colonel Francis S. "Gabby" Gabreski, who arrived in Korea a month after Jabara's departure, Jabara left unfavorable memories with some of his fellow pilots, particularly wingmen who remembered him the way other wingmen recalled Gabreski. Then-1st Lt Bruno Giordano who flew as his wingman for several of his victories during his 1953 tour, recalled that Jabara seemed "to care less about what happened to his wingman and more than once put them in harm's way." Canadian Flt Lt Levesque, who flew with Jabara in 1951, remembered that he used his status to get the fastest Sabre available, and then chewed out wingmen who didn't keep up.

His 1951 commander, John C. Meyer, later related that Jabara was "a hot-shot Charlie type ... the guy who sang the loudest in the club and made more noise than the other people and dressed on the extreme side for the military." Lt Gen Earl Brown, one of two African-American pilots to fly Sabres in Korea during a 125-mission tour with the 4th in 1951, and flew as wingman for Jabara during his early missions, recalled his old element leader:

Jabara was the ultimate warrior when it came to going to the sound of the guns without orders. He would go wherever the guns were sounding, looking for some; if you're with him in a bar fight, he's just looking for a guy to punch – but if you're not careful, he might, in his excitement, punch you.

Unlike the Americans, no mention whatsoever was made in the Soviet Union about the activities of their pilots fighting in the Korean War.

The first ace of the 196th IAP, Senior Lieutenant Fedor Shebanov, was credited with his fifth victory the day following the battle with the B-29s on April 22, to become the third Soviet ace of the war. During the month of April, the 324th Division claimed 34 enemy aircraft shot down for a loss of eight MiG-15s, with two pilots killed in action. All the MiG losses were credited to Sabres. In mid-month, Kozhedub's pilots exchanged their early MiG-15s for the 151st GvIAD's 47 MiG-15bis jets. They would receive an additional 16 of the new MiGs direct from the Novosibirsk Aircraft Factory in late May when the 303rd IAD arrived as reinforcement. The fights between the MiG pilots of the 324th and 303rd IADs and their Sabre-mounted opponents throughout the rest of 1951 would be so epic and evenly matched that the Americans would name the time "The Year of the Honcho."

CHAPTER 10

YEAR OF THE HONCHO

The 324th Division's 47 MiGs were reinforced in early May by the 303rd IAD, commanded by General Georgi Lobov. The division's three regiments, the 18th GvIAP and the 177th and 523rd IAPs, had been assigned to the air defense of Moscow before their reassignment to eastern Siberia in July 1950. In October they had been alerted for duty in China, and moved to the Liaodong peninsula in December, where the 177th was replaced by the 17th IAP. The 303rd scored its first victory on December 26, 1950, when 11-victory Great Patriotic War ace Captain Stepan Bakhaev and Senior Lieutenant Kotov intercepted and shot down an RB-29 off the Chinese coast.

The 303rd arrived at Antung on May 3, 1951. Even though the weather began to improve during May, the Soviet pilots recorded the month as their lightest in terms of operations. The 303rd moved to the newly completed airfield at Tatung-kao on May 28.

June 1951 saw the air battles in MiG Alley increase. The pilots of the 4th Fighter Group reported themselves outnumbered on almost all occasions. In truth, the group was actually opposed by about twice as many MiGs as there were Sabres, but MiG formations could be appreciably larger due to their nearness to the battlefield, which allowed reinforcement as engagements happened, while the Sabres maintained their four-flight, 16-plane patrols. Both aircraft were "maintenance intensive," and both Soviets and Americans were at the end of long supply chains, which could see aircraft grounded for several weeks waiting for the arrival of spare parts. Throughout 1951, even after all three squadrons began to operate from Kimpo in the fall of 1951, the

4th never had more than 50 Sabres available for operations at any given time. Soviet figures were similar.

The 303rd opened its fight with the Sabres on June 1 when aircraft of the 18th GvIAP led by squadron leader Captain P. N. Antonov joined MiGs of the 196th IAP to intercept B-29s south of MiG Alley. Antonov's element leader, Senior Lieutenant Evgeny Stelmakh, attacked a formation of four B-29s and shot down one to open the 303rd's Korean score. He was set upon by the Sabre escort and was soon forced to eject. When Stelmakh landed, Chinese troops took him for an American, while he took them for anti-Communist guerilas. In the gunfight that broke out, Stelmakh hit three of the soldiers before shooting himself to avoid capture.

As Stelmakh was shooting it out below, his squadron mates intercepted a flight of F-51s from the 18th Group that were searching for survivors of the bomber he had shot down. Senior Lieutenant Lev Shchukin shot down one F-51 while the others evaded the MiGs. The B-29 gunners claimed two MiGs as did the Sabre escort, but Stelmakh was the only loss.

By mid-June, the 4th Fighter Group was opposed by five MiG regiments of the two air divisions based around Antung, and fights happened nearly every time the Americans entered MiG Alley. On June 17, Captain Sergei Karamenko, who would eventually rise to be the leading ace of the 176th GvIAP, fought what he later considered his most intense battle:

Our group of four took off to intercept 12 enemy aircraft. We found them immediately and I turned sharply and launched an attack, closing in on the enemy and opening fire. Suddenly, I felt something amiss; when I looked back I saw a Sabre only 80 meters (240 feet) behind me! He was already firing at me, as I saw flashes coming from his nose.

I was at an altitude of 8,000 meters (26,000 feet). I pushed the control stick and rudder pedal sharply and did a wingover into a dive. I looked back and saw three Sabres, which I hadn't seen before, as they were attacking me from above. They were heavier and started to catch me in the dive. I was thinking I had to do something else when I saw clouds below. I recovered from the dive at about 6,000 meters (19,000 feet) and flew right into the cloud, then made a 90-degree turn.

I cut through the cloud and saw the three Sabres below looking for me and I decided to attack. They saw me and split. Two headed left and down while the third started climbing to the right. I thought if I went after the pair, the one to starboard would shoot me down immediately, but if I went for him the pair would chase me. I went for the singleton.

Due to my superior height, I closed in quickly and opened fire. The Sabre immediately burst into flames, half rolled then started falling. I started to follow him, but then remembered I still had two other Sabres to deal with! I looked back and saw them on my tail. I made a climbing turn and saw they were catching me. Then I made a wingover, dived, and plunged into cloud as I tried to deceive the Americans.

The Sabre pilots were clearly combat veterans, as they didn't follow me but stayed above, waiting for me to come out of the cloud. When I did, they dropped behind me again. I then had to fight them two-to-one. I could have tried to break off by climbing, but they would have been able to shoot me if I'd flown a straight course. So I tried to maneuver my way out with slanting loops and wingovers. The Americans were seasoned pilots. My aircraft and I experienced high G-loads – the blood rushed from my head and everything went dark. My opponents were in a better position as they were wearing anti-G suits. I maneuvered toward the Yalu.

After 15 minutes of high-G maneuvering, I was almost exhausted. I thought that if I couldn't break off, the Americans would eventually get me. I decided to head for the bridge over the Yalu, which was defended by our air defense artillery. I leveled off instead of climbing and accelerated to 1,030kmh (645mph) and descended slightly. I looked back and saw the Americans lagging slightly behind as they had expected me to climb. They were about 1,000 meters (3,300 feet) behind me. I had to extend the air brakes, level off, retract the air brakes, then accelerate again. I did that again and again, accelerate into a climb, level off, accelerate again.

Naturally, the enemy fighters caught up to me and the range was about 600 meters (1,900 feet). The air defense artillery opened up as I approached the bridge and shells started exploding ahead. If I turned away, the Americans would have had me. There was no way out. I flew right into the shell bursts. The aircraft shook and was thrown from side to side as if it were taxiing on cobblestones. I gripped the stick tightly and sat there more dead than alive. I got out of the flak after about 15–20 seconds. It was sunny and calm. I saw the Americans retreating – they didn't dare follow me, and they turned towards the sea.

Close calls could happen to anyone in MiG Alley, regardless of their previous reputation or experience. Glenn Eagleston almost didn't survive to take command of the 4th Fighter Group when Colonel Meyer departed. Bruce Hinton recalled Eagleston's close call during the June battles:

It was a bright, clear, sunny day in June 1951. We had a pretty heavy commitment this day, with two squadrons involved in the mission. Lt Col Glenn Eagleston – "Eagle" – was leading the 334th Squadron, while I was leading the 336th. The mission was simple enough: a MiG sweep near the mouth of the Yalu River. On this day the MiGs came up to meet us. Part way through the patrol line we were on we encountered a large number of them. With MiGs all around us the squadrons had broken down into individual air battles involving two-ship F-86 elements against the collective bunches of MIGs.

Moving into the general area of combat, I came across a lone MiG maneuvering with the swirl of the fight. The MiG turned away from the battle, heading toward the Yalu. Using manual ranging, I began to close to within 1,500 feet range. Moving in to just under that range, leading a tad in the turn, I was ready to hammer him.

Just as I started to press the trigger an F-86 appeared between me and the MiG I was about to clobber. He was traveling 90 degrees to my direction of flight, and he was all alone – well almost. About 500 feet behind the lone F-86 was a MiG, and he was pounding the F-86 with cannon fire. Both airplanes flew directly in front of me and between myself and the MiG I had staked out. For a split second I wondered how it was possible that a midair collision did not occur. Pieces of the F-86 were flying through the air, and some were very large pieces. One unassailable rule we had in the 4th was that no MiG was worth losing an F-86. The F-86 was now on fire and I broke off my certain kill to try and beat off the MiG that was hammering the Sabre.

It's surprising how quickly situations change during aerial combat. I pulled the nose around as hard as I could toward the guy in trouble. By the time I had my nose in the direction of the shot-up F-86, he was now about 1,000 feet below me. The MiG had overshot the F-86, made a quick climbing reversal, and was now coming down in a dive to finish him off. The F-86 had lost most of his airspeed, and appeared to be just hanging there. At that moment, the MiG driver apparently saw me coming and pulled his nose up, pointing straight at me. We passed head-on with no more than a plane length between us.

We both used all we had in the crucial next turn to try and gain some advantage. We went into a Lufberry, in which I had a slight advantage. However, it wasn't enough to put me into a firing position so I started a vertical yo-yo on the far side of the circle, using the slight reduction in airspeed at the high point to increase my cornering rate. It began to work. After a few more turns around the circle I was starting to get inside of his turn on the "tight" place in the orbit. The maneuvering Gs were so extreme that my wingman left part way through, later saying that he had become airsick. As the MiG passed through my nose I held the trigger down and gave him a good burst. On the next orbit I did the same thing. This time the MiG had to fly through the spray from my six 50s. After he took that second burst, and at the far side of the circle closest to the Yalu, he suddenly broke away in a high speed dive toward the Yalu and I couldn't catch him before he crossed the river. This MiG driver had been very good. He had been waiting above all the engagements going on between the MiGs and the F-86s. It was a well-known tactic that was commonly used by a single MiG pilot that we referred to as "Casey Jones." [The name was derived from an American mythological character, "Casey Jones" the train engineer; in this case it was thought this seemingly senior experienced pilot was responsible for directing the "MiG trains."] Ol' Casey was an exceptional pilot, and definitely not an oriental. His normal procedure was to hit fast from a high perch, diving down on any F-86 that was isolated from the on-going air battle. The name came about because the MiG flights leaving Antung were referred to as bandit trains. This MiG had a significant paint job with a red nose and fuselage stripes.

I broke off to return to the stricken F-86. I found him floating for home at about 20,000 feet. The fires had gone out, but he had holes in the engine aft section, and his left gun bay door and all three .50 calibre guns were gone. The guns had absorbed most of the impact of a 37mm cannon shell and probably saved the pilot's life. I tried talking to him but another cannon shell had entered the fuselage aft of the wing root, wiping out his radio. His airplane was moving at somewhere near .7 Mach and he was steadily losing altitude.

I got the pilot's attention and signaled for him to head out toward the Yellow Sea where we could get a rescue airplane to him. I'll never forget him violently shaking his head, "No!" I was sure I had a new lieutenant in there, and couldn't figure out his disregard of a possible life-saving recommendation. We continued south, gradually losing altitude, trying to measure the angle of our flight path with the distance we had to go to see if our gradual descent angle was enough to get us over friendly territory and maybe back to Suwon.

It took forever, but we finally made it to friendly territory. I informed Suwon that we had a cripple, to clear the runway, get out the meat wagon and fire trucks, and prepare for a wheels up landing. Flying tight with the wounded F-86 around the pattern to check his airspeed indicator, I came down the final right beside him. The Sabre slowly settled to the runway, finally touching down with a jolt. I watched the pilot's head banging back and forth in the cockpit as he rode that airplane down the runway like a bucking bronco. The Sabre slid to a stop off the end of the runway in a cloud of dust.

I poured on the coal and went around. After landing, I rolled to a stop by the busted F-86. The airplane was a wreck. Not only was the engine hit, but the throttle control was smashed. The left fuselage was a sieve, with some very large holes all around the cockpit. It was then I learned that the pilot was my very close friend, Glenn Eagleston. Eagle's life had been saved by the three .50-caliber guns that took the impact from the 37mm cannon shell, which also had taken out his throttle and smashed part of the instrument panel. It had been a close call.

On June 18, the day after Karamenko's near-death experience, Captain Serafim Subottin became the 324th IAD's second ace, claiming two Sabres the hard way. Leading eight MiG-15s that intercepted 16 Sabres, Subottin closed to 100 meters behind a Sabre. His heavy cannon fire hit the enemy jet in the engine and cockpit; the Sabre went into a dive and then exploded in mid-air. Subottin spotted two F-86s closing on him.

As he turned to evade, he came across another MiG under attack by a second Sabre pair. He immediately attacked the Sabres, but seconds later his MiG shuddered as it was hit in the engine, which flamed out. Kerosene poured into the cockpit and billowing white smoke obscured his view. Subottin jettisoned his canopy and as the smoke was drawn out, he saw a pair of Sabres closing for the kill. He made a series of sharp banks as he glided down but without power he was unable to evade and the Sabres closed in.

> I went into a starboard spin. When I recovered, I was attacked twice by the Sabres. They were firing all the time. My aileron controls were damaged and they kept chasing me and firing at point-blank range. I extended my air brakes and almost immediately I felt something hit me in the rear – the impact was accompanied by a horrible grinding noise. A second later, I saw an F-86 with a torn-off wing panel on my left side. He had crashed into me! My damaged MiG started darting side-to-side, creating various G-loads, and I was thrown about inside the cockpit. When negative G lifted me out of my seat, I unstrapped and bailed out. I landed in the mountains about 12 kilometers from the town of Taisen.

Subottin was credited with both Sabres. The Americans admitted the loss of one F-86 in combat that day.

Action continued hot the next day. Senior Lieutenant Nikolai Sutyagin of the 303rd's 17th IAP, who would eventually be the Korean War's Ace of Aces with a score of 21, opened his victory ledger that day. Sutyagin was one of ten MiGs in a formation headed by the regimental commander, Majoy Gregoriy Pulov, that took off to intercept approaching UN aircraft. As the MiGs climbed through the clouds, Sutyagin spotted two Sabres maneuvering to attack. Accompanied by his wingman, Senior Lieutenant Vasily Shulev, he pulled away from the formation to engage the Americans. He closed on the trailing Sabre and opened fire; the first burst went ahead of the enemy fighter, the second behind. The American pilots immediately nosed over and ran for the Yellow Sea with the two MiGs in hot pursuit. Sutyagin fired a long-range burst at the wingman and hit him, setting the Sabre afire. It nosed over and crashed into a hillside. Sutyagin's opponent was 1st Lt Robert H. Laier, who was listed by Fifth Air Forces as missing in action.

Shulev went after the leader, diving so fast that his canopy came off from the wind pressure. He immediately throttled back and joined up with Sutyagin as they headed back across the Yalu.

The June action continued hot and heavy as Captain Gregory Ges of the 176th Regiment shot down an F-51D to score his fifth victory. He went so close in his attack that his cannon rounds tore the Mustang apart. The tail hit his MiG's tail and damaged the right stabilizer. Ges fell off, unable to maneuver, though he did manage to bank away just as four Sabres attacked him and his wingman, Senior Lieutenant Nikolayev, whose MiG was damaged by the Sabres. The two MiGs evaded the Americans and limped back to Antung. Nikolayev landed while Ges experimented at altitude to see if he could maintain control with gear and flaps down. Satisfied he could, he successfully landed the heavily damaged MiG.

While many future Soviet aces opened their scores during June, the two fighter divisions also lost eight MiG-15s in combat with four pilots killed. American records claimed 14 MiGs shot down, four by B-29 gunners and ten by Sabres.

The 334th Squadron's Captain Becker remembered combat that summer:

When I was there, the Communists had their absolutely best pilots flying. We normally arrived over MiG Alley at 45,000 feet. It looked like flying over Tucson, the Midwest or over the Rockies. It was desolate. We could see the MiG air base at Antung across the Yalu river, and the dust that was raised as they took off.

Becker's first victory claim was in April 1951, on his 19th mission.

We were flying a MiG sweep to the Yalu. I was in Jim Jabara's flight. He was Eagle Red Lead and I was the element leader, Eagle Red Three. As we entered MiG Alley, we spotted a large gaggle of MiGs above us. Jim ordered, "Drop tanks!" and the fight was on. But to my dismay, my left drop tank hung up. What to do? Standing orders were to get yourself home if you couldn't drop your tanks. I decided to fight the poor handling and stay with Jabara.

The MiGs broke down into us as we started climbing. We split their formation right in two. Jim's element took the ten MiGs to our left, my element took the ten MiGs to our right. The airplane was very heavy because of the hung tank, but the MiGs weren't getting away! I was racking the Sabre back and forth trying to get one of the MiGs in my sights. I finally got one to hold still just long enough. I pulled in behind him and gave him a long burst. The MiG stopped, smoking heavily. Then he went into a flat spin at about 18,000 feet. I followed him down to about 14,000 then had to break off due to other MiGs that were plenty mad at me.

The MiG disappeared into the cloud deck at about 5,000 feet. Two other F-86 flights were coming down to help us and saw the MiG go into the cloud deck streaming smoke and obviously out of control. But no one saw him crash.

I wrote up the report claiming a victory, and shot it off to Fifth Air Force Headquarters, confident that I would be awarded my first "kill." Wrong! A few days later the claim was returned, disallowed. It was a "probable" since no one had seen it crash. Neither I, Jabara, nor anyone else that saw that MiG going down, had any doubts it was a goner. But ...

In fact, Becker had actually shot down a MiG that day. According to Soviet records, the 72nd GvIAP lost a MiG-15 flown by Senior Lieutenant Yevgeny Savinov, who was hit in the fight and crashed to his death.

Becker's first confirmed victory came on April 22. He was again flying as element lead to Jabara, who led the four Sabres to jump four MiGs of the 196th IAP's 3rd Squadron as they climbed over the Yalu. Jabara shot down the second MiG, flown by Senior Lieutenant Y. N. Samusin, who managed to bail out while Becker attacked squadron leader Captain Nikolay Shelamonov. Becker saw the MiG begin to smoke and it entered in a spin. His claim for a victory was confirmed, but this time both Becker and Fifth Air Force were wrong. Shelamonov, a very experienced pilot who was already credited with five victories against US aircraft including the RB-45C shot down in December, was able to enter what appeared to be an uncontrolled spin and later regain control. The maneuver fooled both Becker and the intelligence officers who reviewed his gun camera film. Soviet ground crews needed several days to repair the MiG-15, and Shelamonov later admitted he had been lucky to survive. Shortly after Becker scored his first victory, the 334th Squadron rotated back to Japan.

June saw a major increase in effort by FEAF to hit airfields in North Korea with fighter-bombers after photo intelligence revealed the Communists were trying to repair the heavily bombed fields in order to operate aircraft over the battlefield to support their armies. The American effort brought a strong response from the Antung MiGs. While Becker was back in Japan, the 335th Squadron's Captain Ralph D. "Hoot" Gibson shot down two on June 18 in a fight in which he led his flight into a group of attacking MiGs and shot down the leader, which broke up the enemy formation. At that moment his gunsight failed, but he led his wingman into a further attack on the MiGs. "I closed in to where it didn't matter that I didn't have a gunsight, and let him have it." The second MiG went down and Gibson's flight pressed the fight until the enemy withdrew north of the Yalu. Gibson was awarded the Silver Star for this, the first actual US "double victory."

Gibson had joined the USAAF in 1943, but only completed flight training just before the end of World War II. He managed to amass 1,700 hours of pilot-in-command time during the postwar years, and then finagled his way into the 4th Group from the 56th Group on the basis of his logged experience when he heard they were going to transfer to Korea. His double victory made him one of the leading pilots.

As the air war heated up, General Otto P. Weyland, who had taken command of FEAF on June 10, urgently requested further fighter reinforcement in the form of two additional fighter wings from Air Force headquarters, specifically asking that one be equipped with F-86s. The Pentagon conceded an increased threat did exist, and responded to Weyland's request with one fighter wing and additional pilots and Sabres to reinforce the 4th. The F-84-equipped Air National Guard 116th Fighter Wing, which had been activated for service in Europe, was diverted to Korea. The 75 Thunderjets arrived in Japan on July 24, where it was discovered over half had been damaged by saltwater corrosion on the voyage over. The unit took up air defense duties at Misawa in northern Japan.

The Sabre reinforcements came in the form of 18 new F-86E Sabres from the 62nd Fighter-Interceptor Squadron of the 56th Fighter-Interceptor Group, led by group commander Col Francis S. "Gabby" Gabreski, who had scored 32 victories in World War II to become the Eighth Air Force's Ace of Aces. Among the 62nd Squadron pilots Gabreski brought with him was his old comrade and fellow ace from the 56th's days as "Zemke's Wolfpack," Lt Col Walker M. "Bud" Mahurin, as well as 15.5 victory ace Major William T. "Bill" Whisner, Jr., and future MiG ace and legendary Air Force test pilot 1st Lt Iven C. "Kinch" Kincheloe. They arrived in Japan in late June.

The 62nd Squadron's F-86Es had been hurriedly cocooned at North Island, as had those of the 4th Wing the previous November. The Sabres almost didn't make it when *Cape Esperance* ran into a typhoon halfway across the Pacific. The high waves swept over the jets on the flight deck and the little carrier nearly capsized. The saltwater all but destroyed the electrical systems of the exposed aircraft; subsequently, these Sabres would experience numerous in-flight emergencies once they began flying over Korea.

The 334th Squadron returned to Korea at the end of June. There was no doubt about Becker's second victory, scored on July 8. He had been promoted to flight leader, and the mission involved covering a B-29 raid against Pyongyang's airfields. Becker spotted a group of low-flying MiGs headed for the bombers that failed to spot the Sabres. He led his flight down on the MiGs and hit the leader, Captain P. P. Pavlovsky, who ejected after his MiG was set afire by Becker. The enemy fighter crashed in a ball of fire a mile south of the city.

In the same fight, Gabreski scored his first victory of the Korean War during his fifth combat mission, shooting down the MiG-15 flown by the 523rd IAP's Senior Lieutenant A. A. Obukhov, who died in the crash, a few minutes ahead of Becker. Action in MiG Alley heated up in July even more than had been the case in June, as FEAF continued its campaign against the North Korean airfields. Three days after Becker scored his second victory, Gibson scored his third on July 11.

The end of July and August saw cloudy weather return to Korea, and the operation tempo lessened. On July 21, 196th regimental commander Yevgeny Pepelyaev led a group of eight MiGs scrambled in murky conditions to intercept American fighter-bombers. When Pepelyaev spotted them, he identified them as F-94s; while the Lockheed F-94 all-weather fighter had arrived in Korea in April, the aircraft did not operate over North Korea due to fears of the enemy getting their hands on its advanced airborne radar if one was shot down. In fact, Pepelyaev's opponents were F9F-2 Panthers from VMF-311. The American aircraft had been spotted by radar, but Pepelyaev had been prevented from taking off on their first sighting due to the poor weather. By the time the MiGs got off, the Marines had made their attack on an airfield south of the Yalu and were heading toward the Yellow Sea. Pepelyaev spotted two flights of four, and went after the second, ordering his flight leader to go after the first.

> The enemy broke formation and scattered, and my pilots followed, each attacking their own targets. I engaged one from below and saw debris fly off. I saw another turning away and I shot off its tail unit while it was still turning. The debris narrowly missed me. We were already over the Yellow Sea, so I ordered the battle to be aborted. Everything would have been different if we had taken off a half-hour earlier. Our regiment was credited with seven victories. I even had to credit one of my pilots with downing two, which had collided during his attack. I didn't believe it, but the divisional command ordered me to confirm that this had indeed happened.

VMF-311 reported a single loss that day. Pepelyaev's claim was confirmed when North Korean authorities found the shot-off tail unit near Pakchong. Through July, pilots of the two air divisions were credited with shooting down 24 enemy aircraft, including seven F9Fs identified as F-94s, 13 F-86s, an F-84 and an F-89 – another misidentification that was likely an F-84. While US losses didn't match these claims, General Stratemeyer was worried by the increased losses suffered that month.

Becker's best day in combat was August 19, 1951. At 1054 hours, a big fight broke out between the Sabres of the 334th and 335th squadrons and the MiG-15s of the 18th GvIAP. Becker's flight of four joined the fight 15 minutes later.

> I spotted eight MiGs above us. We climbed behind them without being spotted. We got within 1,200 feet before they turned. I closed to 500 feet and hit the leader. He immediately snap rolled to the right and bailed out. His wingman turned straight and level. He was no problem. I hit him hard, and he blew up in my face.

Both Soviet pilots, Captain V. A. Sohan and Senior Lieutenant Y. T. Kondrashov, managed to eject from their burning MiGs. On return to Kimpo, Becker received the nickname "MiG Wrecker." With his double victory, Becker was now one ahead of Gibson, and a competition developed between the 334th and 335th squadrons as to whether Becker or Gibson would be first to follow Jabara to acedom. Gibson scored his fourth victory on September 2 and the two pilots were now tied. At nearly the same time Gibson scored his victory, Colonel Gabreski scored his second MiG-15 victory.

In September, the weather over North Korea cleared and all three Sabre squadrons began operating from Kimpo. On September 9, an estimated 70 MiG-15s attacked 22 F-86s from the 334th and 335th squadrons. The Russians were from the 17th, 196th and 523rd IAPs and the 176th GvIAP. Dick Becker recalled the fight in which he scored his fifth victory on his 82nd mission since arriving at Kimpo in the first detachment back in December:

I was leading a flight of six F-86s as Eagle Blue Leader. Ray Barton and Bob Harper were leading the other elements. We were patrolling the Sinuiju-Anju area in northwestern Korea, the heart of MiG Alley. Shortly after arriving in the area, I sighted a formation of about 30 MiGs sitting high on their perch above us.

I called my squadron CO and told him about the MiGs, then ordered my guys to drop tanks, all the while turning and climbing toward the MiG formation. As we were climbing to attack the first bunch of MiGs, I suddenly caught sight of another MiG formation that was diving on us right through their own formation!

I had my guys hold their positions as the MiGs started to bore in for the kill. They were coming at us head-on. I waited until the last second before opening fire. The MiGs broke in all directions, and my flight followed. All three elements turned and started chasing the MiGs. Barton and Harper's elements went one way, I went another.

I rolled out at 39,000 feet and began looking around. I was alone! My wingman had gotten lost somewhere in the melee. I started to make a hasty retreat since I had no wingman to cover my tail. Then I noticed another 12 MiGs entering the area about 3,000 feet below me. Without even thinking about it, I pulled around to get a little advantage, and dove on the formation.

One against twelve! Not too good of odds, I thought. But the MiGs were even more shook [sic] than I was by the way I jumped on them. They were probably thinking, "What kind of maniac is this?"

The MiGs broke in every direction, and no one was flying anyone's wing. I pulled in behind one of the MiGs that was all alone, lined him up with the pipper, and pulled the trigger. The MiG stopped suddenly, the pilot ejected, and the MiG exploded. Scratch One!

There were still plenty of MiGs around and I soon found another loner trying to get out of my way. I fired on him but missed. He dove away and headed north. I continued this pattern of jumping on any MiG in the area, squeeze off a few rounds, then break away. At about the same moment, both the MiGs and my fuel were gone.

I turned south, got as high as possible, and started for home. When I landed, there was a welcoming committee waiting for me. The kill was my fifth, making me the second ace in the Korean War.

Becker's fifth victory was the 196th's Senior Lieutenant Andriushko, who bailed out and landed safely.

Minutes after Becker scored, Gibson got his fifth MiG, on his 92nd mission. Interestingly, the Soviets only admitted one MiG lost with its pilot parachuting safely, which was Becker's claimed victory. Becker remembered:

Within an hour after we landed, we received telegrams from the Secretary of the Air Force stating we were returning to the United States. We did not have a choice. I guess the Air Force figured we were more valuable to the enemy if we were shot down. We were fighting over enemy territory the entire time.

In fact, Dick Becker was really the first Air Force ace of the Korean War according to confirmed enemy losses, since Jabara's claimed second victory on May 20, which would actually have been his fifth (assuming his second and third claims were accurate), had survived the fight. With only one MiG lost on September 9, in conditions that support Becker's claim, the fact is Gibson did not score, though the Russians do admit several MiGs returned from the fight badly damaged; one of these might have been the one Gibson claimed.

The point of going into detail about the combat careers of these three pilots who were the first to be proclaimed "MiG Aces" by the Air Force is to demonstrate how confusing air combat actually was. They all made their claims in good faith, as did their Soviet opponents.

Studies of aerial claims in all three of the air wars that have included widespread fighter-vs-fighter combat confirm that inaccurate claims by those involved directly in the fights is more the rule than the exception. In a fast-moving fight, unless the opponent explodes or catches fire when first shot, there is no way for a pilot to follow the plane he has shot to see it finally hit the ground. The Russians and Americans came to depend on gun camera film, but many times, a plane that looked like a goner actually survived to get back to base. Sabre pilots during the "Year of the Honcho" did not experience any feelings of superiority to their opponents, and in fact it is generally conceded that the two sides fought to a draw during that period.

BLACK TUESDAY

Despite the success of Becker and Gibson and their fellow pilots, the two Soviet air divisions were able to inflict serious damage on the F-51, F-80 and F-84 fighter-bombers over North Korea. In the face of these losses, General Weyland again requested reinforcement with a second Sabre wing, which was again turned down by the Pentagon. In light of the fighter-bomber losses in September, which were higher than those lost in July or August, new Fifth Air Force commander General Frank F. "Pete" Everest ordered that fighter-bombers would no longer go north of the Chongchon River into MiG Alley and would focus on the region of North Korea between the Chongchon and Pyongyang. This was a significant victory for the Soviets. The MiGs had won round two of the battle for air superiority over North Korea.

On October 2, Senior Lieutenant Lev Kirilovich Shchukin, who was credited with 17 victories in 17 air combats out of 212 sorties and had been shot down twice since his arrival in late March, was involved in an intense dogfight. He spotted the MiG flown by his friend Captain Morozov, which was under attack by a Sabre. Shchukin couldn't get there in time to save his comrade, who successfully ejected, but he caught the Sabre pilot by surprise and riddled the enemy jet at short range with cannon fire. Badly shot up and trailing a thick black smoke trail, the F-86 disengaged. Shchukin claimed the Sabre as a victory, but he had in fact badly damaged the F-86E "Lady Frances," flown by no less an opponent than Colonel Gabreski, who managed to get back to Kimpo after what he later called the most hair-raising fight he had been in. "Lady Frances," named for his wife, was written off immediately after landing – which meant the loss was not recorded by the Air Force as the result of air combat. In an incredible twist of fate, Gabreski and Shchukin would meet a second time, on January 11, 1952. This time the tables were turned and it was Gabreski who forced Shchukin to bail out. Injured in the ejection, he was able to walk again after a long rehabilitation, but was prohibited from ever flying again.

Both sides were eager to get hold of an example of the other's premier fighter for technical inspection. On October 6, Yevgeny Pepelyaev scored his fifth victory and did just that for the Soviets. Pepelyaev's flight of ten MiGs was at 8,000 meters (26,000 feet) over the Chongchon River estuary when they spotted two flights of Sabres below and immediately attacked them. After making a pass on the lead element and missing, Pepelyaev confronted two more in a head-on pass.

I was hit by the F-86 leader, and his rounds tore a big hole in my air intake. I made a tight climbing turn, then quickly reversed and followed my adversary so that when he came out of his turn, I was on his tail. As I pushed the stick forward to get him in my sight I pulled negative G and spoiled my aim. I rolled and he did the same. I had my sight on his canopy and opened fire. A 37mm round hit him just behind the cockpit and he started down. I knew he was doomed.

Pepelaev recalled that his opponent seemed "inexperienced," and he was right. He had hit 2nd Lt Bill N. Garrett's F-86A right behind the cockpit, damaging his engine and the seat ejection mechanism. Garrett was forced to ride the airplane down. With black smoke pouring from his fatally wounded Sabre, he struggled toward the Yellow Sea, where he planned to ditch and then hopefully be picked up. As he desperately tried to lengthen his glide, another MiG-15 flown by Captain Konstantin Sherbetsov attacked him. Garrett lost more altitude and barely made it to the mud flats at the mouth of the Chongchon, where he force-landed his Sabre 13 kilometers west of Pyongyang. Fortunately, his call for help had been heard, and a USAF SA-16 Albatross from the 3rd Air Rescue Squadron orbiting off the coast for just such a reason was able to pick him up from off the beach before North Korean or Chinese troops could capture him.

However, F-86A 49-1319 remained on the beach. The Sabre had been shot up and badly damaged in the forced landing, but there was still plenty there for Soviet technical experts to examine.

Using Pepelyaev's combat report, a Soviet search team that included representatives of the Mikoyan design bureau raced to capture the Sabre. They found it that night and quickly recruited 500 Chinese railroad workers to haul it off the mud flat before the tide came in. Next day, the overcast provided protection as they worked to separate the fuselage and wing. An American destroyer arrived offshore, tasked with destroying the Sabre, and opened fire on them. With MiGs in the sky, the destroyer departed. The team worked through the night of October 7 to complete the dismantling and had the Sabre on flat-bed trucks by 0400 hours on October 8 when they departed with their prize. The drive to the Yalu was slow, and they hid in tunnels during the day to avoid air attack. Engineer N. M. Chepelev, in the lead truck with the forward fuselage, stretched his luck as daylight approached and made a run for a tunnel ahead. Chepelev remembered:

The driver was already approaching the tunnel when we noticed the "night watchman," a B-26. We entered the tunnel at high speed as the B-26 fired several rockets at us. Fortunately, we were already about a hundred meters deep inside the tunnel, and the rockets could only penetrate for about 10 meters before hitting the walls.

Once at Antung, Pepelyaev and his pilots wanted to sit in the cockpit. "I sat in the cockpit. We all did. It was a well-laid-out cockpit, which created an impression that you were sitting in an expensive car." The Sabre arrived at the Air Force Research Flight-Test Institute at Zhukovsky outside Moscow at the end of October. Stalin wanted a reverse-engineered copy, but engineers from the Mikoyan, Yakovlev, Tupolev, and Sukhoi design bureaus determined the MiG-15 was already a good match and the new MiG-17 was more advanced.

Senior Lieutenant Vadim Matskevic, an engineer at the institute, was impressed by the Sabre's APG-30 radar gunsight. He eventually created a warning device that reacted to the radar signal from the gunsight. When he took his device to Manchuria in 1952 and experimentally installed it in ten MiG-15s, pilots were initially suspicious. When a regimental commander flew with it and was able to escape attack by two Sabres in cloudy conditions where he could not see them till they were nearly on top of him, the device was "sold." Matskevic received the Order of the Red Banner for his invention, developments of which are still found on Russian fighters.

The Soviet effort to obtain advanced US aviation technology scored a major accomplishment in May, 1952, when "Bud" Mahurin crash-landed his F-86E in North Korea. It too was taken to the Soviet Union where the all-flying tail was examined and tested on Soviet aircraft. It was adopted on the MiG-19 and all subsequent Soviet fighters.

While the struggle for technological superiority continued, the USAF continued the antiairfield campaign to prevent Communist air forces from advancing south of the Yalu. FEAF intelligence discovered a previously unknown North Korean airfield at Saamcham when a reconnaissance pilot returned with photos of the field on September 27. Revetments for antiaircraft artillery ringed the 7,000-foot runway, which was in the process of being paved. The field length and surface meant one thing: the enemy was planning to base MiG-15s south of the Yalu. On succeeding days, two more similar airfields were discovered at Taechon and Namsi, west of Saamcham and within a 20-mile radius of each other, right in MiG Alley. If the fields were completed, MiGs would be able to operate south of Pyongyang, endangering all tactical air support over the main battle line.

Postwar studies have revealed that the units destined to operate from these airfields would have come from the North Korean and Chinese air forces rather than the Red Air Force. These pilots were later found not to be as qualified as their Soviet allies, but this fact was unknown to Air Force planners at the time. Based on the experience of the air battles over the summer, the new threat was ominous.

Fighter-bomber attacks against airfields in the three previous months had not stopped the effort to repair existing fields and construct new ones in North Korea on the part of the Communists. The B-29s were the obvious means of attack, but the bombers had been withdrawn from daylight operations in MiG Alley after the losses suffered in April. FEAF Bomber Command decided to send the bombers at night to attack the new airfields. On October 13, only two of 12 B-29s from the 307th were able to successfully find and bomb Saamchan airfield, releasing 276 bombs, of which only 24 hit the runway. Over the next several days, single B-29s guided by radar from the offshore islands still controlled by UN forces attempted to hit the airfields, but results were disappointing. There was now no choice but to send the bombers back into MiG Alley in daylight.

The 19th Group was assigned to hit Saamcham, while the 98th Wing would go to Taechon and the 307th drew Namsi. Each mission would involve nine B-29s in three flights of three, with the bombers given the heaviest possible fighter escort. With the shortage of Sabres, only two missions could be flown each day, the first before 1000 hours, the second after 1500 hours, in order for the Sabres to return to Kimpo and refuel between each strike after flying barrier CAP (Combat Air Patrol) along the Yalu. The bombers would receive close escort from the F-84s of the 49th and 136th groups.

The first raid saw the 19th Group hit Saamcham on the morning of October 18 with a successful strike that dropped 306 bombs on the runway and put it out of action. Crews were relieved when no MiGs appeared to contest the mission. That afternoon, the 98th Group went to Taechon, but missed the rendezvous with the Thunderjet escorts; the B-29s aborted the mission and bombed a secondary target outside MiG Alley. A second mission to Taechon on October 21 saw the B-29s and F-84s again fail to rendezvous, with the bombers diverting to their secondary target.

On the afternoon of October 22, the 19th Group's B-29s were sent against Taechon for a third attempt to hit the target. The bombers made the rendezvous with 24 F-84s from the 49th Group as scheduled and headed for the airfield. This time, the enemy responded.

Forty MiG-15s were scrambled from Antung to intercept the bombers. Flak over Taechon had already damaged one B-29 when the bombers released their loads over the field. As the Superfortresses began to turn away for home, three MiGs dropped out of the clouds. They went after the damaged B-29 and hit it hard. The bomber managed to survive long enough to get to the coast, where the crew bailed out. The other MiGs hit the formation, with the Soviet pilots ignoring the F-84s as they desperately turned into the attackers. Nearly all the B-29s returned to Okinawa with some damage.

Everyone was expecting the worst the next day, October 23, 1951, which would be a maximum effort, flown against still-unbombed Namsi airfield. Captain Earl McGill, who was flying his first mission that day, later recalled, "It was my first mission, and we were briefed for heavy MiG interception. I was more scared on that day than I've ever been frightened since." The briefing in the ready room had been filled with black humor. "The guy who briefed the navigation route had been an undertaker. He delivered the briefing in an undertaker's stove-pipe hat." McGill recalled there was no radio chatter between the crews as he taxied his bomber to the runway at Yokota AFB for takeoff.

The 307th Bomb Group put up nine Superfortresses, flying at 22,000 feet to put them above the lighter flak, but still low enough to get good coverage when they bombed the runway at Namsi. The 7th, 8th and 9th squadrons of "The 49ers" provided low close escort, flying at the bomber's altitude, while the 111th, 154th and 182nd squadrons of the 136th Wing flew high; the bombers were surrounded by no fewer than 55 Thunderjets, as well as 16 Gloster Meteor F.8s flown by the Australian 77 Squadron. The barrier at the Yalu was provided by 34 F-86s from the 335th and 336th squadrons of the 4th Group. Sixteen Sabres of the 334th Squadron were over the bomber formation at their maximum altitude of 40,000 feet, flying a "racetrack" course to stay back with the slower bombers yet keep their speed up to counter an attack.

The B-29s, flying in arrow-shaped flights of three Superfortresses each – Able, Baker and Charlie – crossed the South Korean coast near Kwanju at 0745 hours. They were two hours from the target. With a weather forecast of low clouds over the target, the plan was to use SHORAN (Short Range Navigation), a system that allowed the bombers to drop accurately without seeing the target. However, use of SHORAN required each individual aircraft to fly a prescribed arc through the bomb run, with no allowance for evasive maneuvers. Such an attack increased the risk of midair collision, and the bombers spread out as they closed on the target. It was impossible for the close escort to give adequate coverage to the B-29s during this all-important moment of the mission. Without the fighters, the bombers were sitting ducks.

Forty-five miles east of Namsi, each Superfortress banked left to take up the SHORAN path. Pilots moved their controls to keep the needle centered on the calibrated instrument display of the SHORAN gear. Each B-29 flew toward the target alone.

At 0935 hours, the four F-84s of George Flight from the 136th Group spotted the first MiGs high overhead. They had used their superior high-altitude performance to evade the Sabre barrier at the Yalu and were 10,000 feet above the 16 orbiting Sabre escorts.

The 303rd and 324th IADs put up a maximum effort, with 58 MiG-15s of the 303rd assigned to attack the bombers, while 26 MiGs from the 324th reinforced them and covered their escape. At 0940 hours, Lt Col Aleksandr P. Smorchkov, commander of the 18th GvIAP, ordered 14 of his MiGs to tackle the Sabres below. Smorchkov led six MiGs that tore past the F-86s and through the 136th Group's top cover Thunderjets.

Eight Sabres engaged the 18th Regiment MiGs. Moments later, the other eight had all they could do to handle another 18 from the 523rd IAP coming down right after Smorchkov's group.

Again, six MiGs ignored the Sabres and Thunderjets and went straight for the B-29s. Spotting the Australian-flown Meteors, some of the Russian pilots called them out, tempted to go after the easy targets, but 523rd Regiment commander Nikolai Volkov radioed: "We're going after the big ones."

The MiGs tore into the Superfortresses. Some attacked vertically from below while others raked the bombers from above. Earl McGill recalled that his first encounter with the MiGs was typically brief. "One of the gunners called him out. He was a small silhouette. That's when I saw him. The gunners were shooting at him."

Smorchkov's target was "Charlie Lead" in the third formation, flown by 1st Lt Tom Shields, who abandoned the bomb run as he tried to maneuver, but cannon rounds struck the bomber's wings and the B-29 failed to respond. "Salvo the bombs!" he ordered. "Lower the nose wheel! Get ready to bail out!" A moment later, it seemed control returned and he canceled the bail out order. The right blister gunner called, "Right wing and number three engine on fire!" Charlie Lead fell off in a spiraling dive. When the altimeter registered 18,000 feet, Shields ordered the crew out. Below, Smorchkov pulled out of his dive and saw the parachutes blossom above.

MiG-15 pilot Porfiriy Ovsyannikov was on the other end of the B-29 guns. "When they fired at us, they smoked, and you think, 'Is the bomber burning, or is it machine gun smoke?'" MiG pilots were able to open fire from about 2,000 feet away, out of range of the bomber's defensive fire. "They could savage a B-29 formation in one pass," recalled McGill.

B-29 "Sit 'n Git" held first position as Able Lead, the same position she had flown in April on the mission that came to be known as "Black

Thursday." Navigator 1st Lt Fred Meier looked out of the glass nose as the bombardier called "bombs away" and saw MiGs that seemed to flash past in every direction. Left blister gunner S/Sgt Rolland Miller opened fire at an incoming MiG as he saw flames erupt from Able Three; the B-29 fell off and vanished into the clouds; two parachute canopies blossomed just before the bomber disappeared. Damaged, "Sit 'n' Git" managed to make it back to Kimpo. She never flew again.

Aboard Charlie Two, Bombardier John Wagenhalls remembered:

> The bomb doors on the right side of the aircraft were shattered from cannon fire, while those on the opposite side suffered only minor damage. I was able to wire the pieces of the bomb bay doors in the up position sufficiently to allow us to fly the aircraft. We were the only plane that made it all the way home to Kadena.
>
> Fortunately no one aboard the aircraft was injured in the melee. During and after the attack it seemed that the B29s were scattered, as not one of the flights remained intact. It was almost as if each airplane was on its own, since at least one aircraft from each flight was destroyed almost immediately in the first attack. Our firepower effectiveness was severely reduced as, basically, no formation still existed. I believe we were the first crew to get back from Korea that fateful day. If the MiGs would have continued their attacks they could have shot us all down.

Major William Griner's B-29, "Baker Lead," was badly hit. Sergeant Paul Dickerson, a gunner aboard Griner's aircraft, remembered:

> We took the shell in number three main fuel tank and fuel started pouring out over the wing and down the right side over my blister. When the fuel went over the blister it made the blister milky and I could not see out of it anymore. I went off interphone and took care of Lt Thorton, who had shrapnel in his arm.

Griner managed to bring the badly damaged B-29 as far south as Kimpo, where he gave the crew the option to bail out before landing. None did. Sergeant Dewell Turner remembered the landing:

> Major Griner gave us the option of baling out, but all the regular crew wanted to stay with the plane, probably because the radar operator

was wounded and could not jump and they did not want to leave him. I wasn't about to jump alone. Everyone had great confidence in Major Griner and he did a fantastic job getting us down safely. I saw the tires blow out upon our landing when Major Griner locked the brakes to stop us. I also recall that a bomb hung up and had to be manually jettisoned before we landed. The first thing the gunners did after landing was to clear the guns. When we looked for the lower forward turret cover to remount it, we could never find it. No telling what happened to it. Someone probably thought it would never be needed again. They were right.

B-29 44-61816, the third bomber to crash-land at Kimpo, had over 500 holes in it and never flew again.

In 15 minutes over Namsi, the MiG pilots claimed the destruction of ten B-29s and four F-84s; FEAF admitted the loss of three bombers, which at 33 percent of the attacking force was the highest percentage of US bombers ever lost on any bombing mission in any war. The Soviets admitted the loss of one MiG. *Stars & Stripes* reported an estimated 150 MiG-15s had attacked the B-29s, which was nearly twice the number of MiGs involved. FEAF Bomber Command claimed 18 MiGs shot down, five by B-29 gunners. The five B-29s and one F-84 that returned seriously damaged and were later written off were listed as "operational accidents" since they made it back to their bases. If these "operational accidents" are added to the admitted combat losses, then eight B-29s and two F-84s tabulates closely with Soviet claims. By October 27, FEAF admitted the loss of five B-29s.

Earl McGill, who later flew B-52s for Strategic Air Command and participated in the last major bomber battle of history, the "Christmas Bombing" of Hanoi, recalled, "In percentages, Black Tuesday marked the greatest loss on any major bombing mission in any war the United States has ever engaged in, and the ensuing battle in a chunk of sky called MiG Alley still ranks as perhaps the greatest jet air battle of all time." To make matters worse, the mission failed to do any damage to Namsi airfield.

The B-29s returned the next day to bomb a railway bridge near Songchan. The eight Superfortresses were given a heavy escort of Sabres, Thunderjets, and Meteors. Again Lt Col Smorchkov led all three regiments of the 303rd's MiGs. By the time the MiGs reached the target, the bombers had already unloaded over the bridge and were headed toward the coast. They were right at the Pyongyang-Wonsan line, the southern limit for the MiGs. Alone of the MiG pilots, Smorchkov closed and shot down one Superfortress. The Soviets claimed four F-86s and four Meteors also shot down. USAF losses admitted the B-29 and two Sabres, with two other Sabres and four Meteors damaged.

Over the three raids, Lt Col Smorchkov was credited with the destruction of B-29s in each raid. His claims are supported by USAF loss records. He was made a Hero of the Soviet Union at the end of October for his leadership and performance.

Former Sabre pilot Lt Gen Charles "Chick" Cleveland stated in 2007: "You have to remember that the little MiG-15 in Korea was successful doing what all the Focke-Wulfs and Messerschmitts of World War II were never able to do: drive the United States bomber force right out the sky." Combined FEAF B-29 losses during the month of October were 14. After October 28, 1951, the B-29s were restricted to nighttime bombing for the rest of the war. The MiGs had won the 1951 battle for air superiority.

By the fall of 1951, it was clear that the 4th Fighter Group could not meet the increased MiG threat in North Korea, with only 89 Sabres available for operations; outside of the F-86Es transferred in June with Colonel Gabreski's detachment from the 56th, these were all war-weary F-86As. Aerial reconnaissance identified a new airfield in the Antung complex at Takishan, and MiG-15s of a new fighter aviation regiment were confirmed based there by mid-September. The Americans were unaware that this was the first MiG-equipped fighter regiment of China's People's Liberation Air Force, which would join the experienced Soviet pilots of the 324th and 303rd air divisions. Intelligence estimated the total number of MiG-15s in the MiG Alley region at 290. In fact, it would be later determined the Communist air forces included 400 MiG-15s by the end of 1951.

F-80 losses to enemy ground fire were such that a decision was made in October 1951 to concentrate the type in the squadrons of the 8th Fighter-Bomber Wing, following the re-equipment of the 49th Fighter-Bomber Wing with F-84 Thunderjets in June 1951 and the concentration of surviving F-51s in the 35th Wing. Air Force Headquarters in Washington finally approved the transfer of 75 new

F-86E Sabres to Korea on October 22, 1951, to re-equip the 16th and 25th squadrons of the 51st Fighter-Interceptor Group, which would hand over their Shooting Stars to the 8th. The new Sabres were scheduled to arrive at Suwon in December after their trans-Pacific voyage aboard the *Cape Esperance* and USS *Sitkoh Bay* (CVE-86), with half the Sabres departing San Diego on November 1 aboard *Cape Esperance* and the others on November 6 aboard *Sitkoh Bay*. This time, the new F-86Es were properly cocooned.

Colonel Harrison R. Thyng became wing commander of the 4th in early November. Awarded his Army Aviator's wings in 1940, Thyng had commanded the 309th Fighter Squadron of the 31st Fighter Group when the group went to England in the summer of 1942, and had first seen combat during the Dieppe Raid that August. Flying Spitfires in North Africa after the invasion, he was officially credited with five victories including a Vichy French Dewoitine D.520 for his first victory on his first day in theater. He had completed his World War II service leading the P-47Ns of the 413th Fighter Group over Japan in 1945. He would be one of the few wing commanders to fly regular combat missions and become an ace in a second war.

By the time he assumed command of the wing, Thyng had already demonstrated what kind of commander he would be by flying five "orientation missions" over seven days after his arrival, then leading a flight into MiG Alley on October 24, during which he attacked a formation of 11 MiGs and scored his first victory in his second war when he hit the leader, who ejected. Captain James A. Horowitz, who flew as his regular wingman in 1952, remembered that the colonel reminded him of a "fading jockey" for his short stature. Horowitz, who would gain recognition as one of America's finest novelists under the name James Salter, later confessed that he had based the character of "Colonel Dutch Imil" on Colonel Thyng in his novel of fighter pilots in Korea, *The Hunters*.

Following the decision to re-equip the 51st Wing, Colonel Gabreski and the group of experienced Sabre pilots he had brought to Korea from the 56th were transferred from the 4th at Kimpo to the 51st at Suwon. He took command of the 51st Fighter-Interceptor Group on November 6, 1951.

1st Lt Joseph "Joe" Cannon was among the 56th Group pilots Gabreski brought with him and would fly 40 missions in Korea as

Gabreski's wingman in both the 4th and 51st groups. He later recalled the difference between the F-86A and F-86E.

In early 1951, Iven Kincheloe and I were assigned to ferry the group's F-86As from Chicago O'Hare where we were operating to the North American factory in Los Angeles and bring back the new F-86Es. Kinch and I used to argue with each other about which of us had more time in the airplane. It didn't take long for all of us to realize just how much better the F-86E was in comparison with the F-86A. Its improved handling, thanks to its all-hydraulic controls, really came to the fore during our mock dogfights over Lake Michigan. For example, it was very easy to "Split-S" in the new model at 40,000 feet and pull out of a vertical dive while exceeding Mach 1. This was done with ease through light back pressure on the stick, and we didn't witness any of the violent rolling tendencies that afflicted the F-86A. This was due to the "all-flying" tail. The more powerful J-47GE-13 engine, which produced an extra 600 pounds of thrust, was also a great asset in a dogfight, as was the radar-ranging A-1CM gunsight.

Gabreski was an excellent choice to bring the 51st up to speed as an air-superiority fighter wing. He was an aggressive commander who promoted a fierce rivalry between the two Sabre wings, a continuation of the keen rivalry that had existed between the 4th and 56th fighter groups in World War II, when they became the two top-scoring USAAF fighter groups. In later years, however, he would be criticized about having a poor attitude toward his wingmen. Six of the junior pilots in the 51st Wing who flew with him later claimed he always flew the fastest F-86 available and paid no attention if his slower wingmen failed to keep up. The 4th Group's Captain Robert W. "Smitty" Smith remembered:

I never forgot his response, when someone asked about the problem of wingmen staying with leaders. He replied, "Wingmen are to absorb firepower," and I never knew him well enough to judge whether he had a dry sense of humor, but he made the right choice.

"Joe" Cannon called Gabreski "my kind of pilot." 1st Lt Harry Shumate, who also flew multiple missions as wingman to the colonel, recalled a mission where he was flying wing in Gabreski's flight and was first to call out a MiG-15. "Colonel Gabreski told me to go get him and he covered me." 1st Lt Anthony Kulengosky, who first flew with Gabreski in the 4th, observed:

> I moved up in the world of wingmen by flying Colonel Gabreski's wing. I was absolutely thrilled to fly with this legend. He was a tiger and went on to become an ace again. When asked who I looked up to the most as a pilot and a gentleman in all my flying, I still have to say it was Gabby Gabreski. When he took over the 51st Wing, he asked me to move over as a flight leader.

The pilots of the 324th and 303rd divisions were showing signs of combat fatigue by late December 1951. Yevgeny Pepelyaev and Nikolai Sutyagin had seen their best scores in November, with Pepelyaev shooting down three F-86s and three F-84s through the month, raising his score to 14. The 51st Wing began operating two squadrons of Sabres from Suwon while the 4th now had three squadrons at Kimpo. With Sabre strength now at 127, the Soviet pilots found combat difficult, with increased Sabre screens protecting the fighter-bombers. In January 1952, losses of experienced flight and element leaders among the Soviet units increased, due to pilot fatigue and the increase in enemy aircraft.

On January 6, five-victory ace Senior Lieutenant Viktor I. Stepanov was killed when his damaged MiG crashed at Antung and burst into fire. The next day, the 196th's deputy commander, five-victory ace Captain Boris Abakumov, ejected from his MiG when it was set afire by a Sabre. He would be permanently grounded by the wounds he suffered in the fight. On January 11, 15-victory ace Captain Lev Shchukin was shot down. He ejected but was injured and did not fly again. Sergei Karamenko was forced to bail out on January 17. He was able to convince an old North Korean farmer that he was Russian and not American by shouting the names of Stalin, Mao and Kim il-Sung while smiling, and was returned to Antung. By the end of the month, the 64th IAK had an admitted loss of 11 MiGs with four pilots killed, their heaviest losses since entering combat ten months earlier.

At 1617 hours on January 20, 1952, six 196th IAP MiGs led by Major Alexey Mitusov took off in company with eight MiGs from the newly arrived 148th GvIAP, on what would prove to be the 324th

Division's last mission of the war. On January 31, the division's pilots left for the Soviet Union, followed by the 303rd Division on February 15. The "Honchos" of the first year of the war were gone.

During 1951, the "Year of the Honcho" (Japanese for "the boss"), as the Sabre pilots who served in Korea remembered the time, the Soviets claimed to have shot down or damaged beyond repair 142 UN aircraft against 68 losses, an overall 2:1 kill ratio. Their most successful month was October 1951, when Soviet-flown MiG-15s claimed seven F-86s, six F-84Es, two RF-80As, one F-80C, one Meteor and ten B-29s for a loss of eight MiGs. During the period between March 1951 and February 1952, when the 324th and 303rd regiments opposed the Americans, 30 pilots were recognized as aces, among them Nikolai Sutyagin (21), Yevgeny Pepelyaev (19), Lev Shchukin (17), Sergei Karamenko (13), Mikhail Ponomaryev (11), and Dmitri Samoylov (10). Most of the claims made by the four top-scoring aces – Sutyagin, Pepelyaev, Shchukin and Karamenko – were shown to be very reliable once the USAF practice of minimizing combat losses by assigning non-combat causes to actual combat losses was taken into account.

How could the Soviets do this, when American aces in that same period only scored five to six victories and only four aces did so in 1951? Were the Russians two to three times better as fighter pilots than their American opponents, as the claimed scores might imply?

One major reason is that in 1951 they were using better tactics. Soviet fighters were guided to the air battlefield by ground control, which directed them to the most advantageous position. The MiG-15s always operated in pairs, as part of a team called "the sword and the shield," with an attacking leader ("the sword") covered by a wingman ("the shield"). The squadrons operated in six-plane groups, divided in three pairs, each composed of a leader and a wingman: the first pair ("the sword pair") attacked the enemy while the second pair ("the shield pair") protected the first pair. The third pair remained above, with a panoramic view of how the battle evolved, providing support for the "sword pair" or the "shield pair" depending on the situation. This third pair had more freedom than the others, because they could also attack targets of opportunity, such as lone Sabres that had lost their wingmen. This tactic is likely where the "urban legend" among Sabre pilots of an enemy "Casey Jones" who attacked lone Sabres from above came from.

Experience was also a key factor. Most of the regimental and squadron commanders in the 324th and 303rd air divisions were Great Patriotic War aces, such as Georgi Lobov (19), Aleksandr Vasko (15), Aleksandr Kumanichkin (30), and Grigori Ohay (6). The Russians were at least as experienced as the American World War II aces in the 4th Group, such as John Meyer (24), Glenn "Eagle" Eagleston (18), Francis "Gabby" Gabreski (32), Walker "Bud" Mahurin (19), and William "Bill" Whisner, Jr. (15).

For the Soviets, Korea was a "target-rich environment." In April and May 1951 there was only one air division of MiG-15s in Manchuria, with a total of 72 MiGs, despite USAF reports of 200 MiGs in China at that time. They faced about 700 UN aircraft, odds of 10:1. The arrival of the three regiments of the 303rd IAD in June lowered the odds to 4:1. The Soviet units never enjoyed the numerical superiority so often mentioned in US sources, though they could put up larger formations over MiG Alley due to their close proximity. Taking into account such figures, it is clear the Russians always found the Korean skies full of American aircraft, which is why scores of 15, 10 or 8 were not uncommon.

An additional reason for the score differences is that the Soviets were going after piston-engined F-51s and B-29s and first-generation F-80, F-84 and F9F-2 jets, which they completely out-performed. The Sabre pilots on the other hand had only one enemy: the MiG-15, which was their equal.

CHAPTER 12

OUR ONLY ASSET WAS OUR COURAGE

Unknown to the US Air Force, a new air force entered combat over MiG Alley in the summer and fall of 1951 to join its Soviet Allies. Yang Guoxiang, who later became the famed test pilot who dropped the first Chinese H-bomb in January 1972, recalled that when the Chinese People's Liberation Army Air Force (PLAAF) was sent into combat the first time, he and his fellow pilots knew they were outclassed by an enemy whose pilots had thousands of flying hours while the Chinese pilots had on average less than 200 flying hours each.

On July 9, when Dick Becker claimed his second victory, the 4th Group claimed three MiGs shot down, including a MiG-15 claimed by Captain Milton Nelson, who reported that the enemy pilot ejected. Communist sources only admit one loss that day. The pilot who ejected was Commander Fang Ziyi, leader of the 12th Fighter Aviation Regiment of the 4th Fighter Aviation Division, the first unit of the Chinese People's Liberation Army Air Force equipped with the MiG-15 to enter combat over North Korea. The regiment had arrived at Antung in mid-June and had flown its first missions against the Americans on July 6. Following the loss of the commander's MiG-15 after only three days, the regiment was pulled off operations and returned to China with the rest of the 4th Division for an additional two months' training before it was declared fit to return to combat.

The US Air Force had believed that the MiG-15s it first encountered in November 1950 were likely flown by Chinese pilots. It was not until the spring of 1951, when radio intercepts of controllers speaking

Russian confirmed pilot rumors that the Sabres were actually flying against the Red Air Force, that this belief changed. In fact, there would be no Chinese pilots in the MiGs until the arrival of the 4th FAD that summer for its brief encounter with the Sabres, and the second unit would not appear over MiG Alley until that fall.

That the PLAAF had deployed any MiG-15s in 1951 signaled a remarkable achievement for an air force that had not existed two years earlier. The People's Liberation Army's first organized air unit was only formed in July 1949 at Beijing Nanyuan Airport. That unit's equipment consisted of six P-51 Mustangs, two DeHavilland Mosquito F.B.6s, and two Fairchild PT-19 Cornell trainers, all previously operated by the Republic of China Air Force (ROCAF) and abandoned on the field during the Kuomintang retreats. Liu Yalou, commander of the 14th Bingtuan (Army), was appointed Chief of Air Force in the People's Liberation Army on October 11, 1949, the day after the People's Republic of China was proclaimed. A month later, on November 11, the PLAAF was officially formed from the headquarters of Liu Yalou's army.

While the USAF only accepted pilot candidates who were college graduates, making the service primarily upper-middle class in terms of background in a time when only 10–15 percent of American high school graduates went on to college, the PLAAF looked to its revolutionary background in determining who should sit in the cockpit of a MiG-15. Historian Xioming Zhang wrote that at the PLAAF's beginning, all candidates were required to be party and youth league members who were known to be politically reliable and had a background as platoon or company officers who had combat experience; additionally, they should be elementary school graduates (which was as small a percentage of the Chinese population at this time as college graduates were in the United States), be between 18 and 24 years old, and physically fit. These were formal requirements issued by the Chinese Communist Party's Central Military Commission. From a Communist perspective, a background from peasant and worker origins combined with infantry experience meant that the candidate would already have the qualities of bravery, adaptability, and toughness considered essential for aviation.

In his memoirs, General Liu Zhen recalled he considered the entire subject of air power a mystery at the time he was appointed commander of the Air Force of the Chinese People's Volunteers on the eve of China's military intervention in the Korean War. He knew that as an infantry officer, he had no experience in commanding aircraft formations; since all other officers assigned to the new PLAAF shared a similar background, their level of understanding regarding air strategy, tactics, and technology was far below that of their enemy. As with many senior Chinese Communist commanders at the time, he drew inspiration for what he was required to accomplish from the history of how the People's Liberation Army had developed and grown through its struggle against unbelievable odds on the battlefield during the Civil War, learning to defeat its enemies through a painful process of trial and error. This attitude was found throughout the leadership of the new armed force. This meant that there would be acceptance of high losses during training, in the expectation that those who survived would be the best and most capable of learning what was required and thus speeding operational development and competence in the long run.

What would eventually become the PLAAF came to life before its formal creation. After the defeat of the Japanese in 1945, the People's Liberation Army found itself in possession of aircraft previously operated by the Japanese, as well as a number of Japanese pilots who were now POWs. Over the next several years of civil war, as the Communists advanced through the rest of the country, they captured aircraft of the Republic of China Air Force left behind by retreating Kuomintang forces.

One of the first trainees was Wang Hai, who would eventually become the first career aviator to command the People's Liberation Army Air Force in 1985. Born on January 19, 1926 in Yantai, Shandong Province, Wang joined the Communist Party of China in September 1945 while he was a student at Weihai High School. Following graduation, he studied at Linyi People's Revolutionary University in Shandong before becoming one of the very first trainees assigned to Mudanjiang Aviator School in Hunan Province, the first flight training school of the Communist Party, in June 1946. After training with the Soviet 106th IAD in the spring of 1950, he became a fighter pilot in May 1950, initially flying the Lavochkin La-11 piston-engine fighter.

Another "original" was Liu Yudi. Born in Cang County, Hebei Province, on September 17, 1923, Liu joined the Eighth Route Army at age 15 in 1938, a few years after Mao's army arrived in Hunan Province following the Long March, and became a member of the Communist Party of China the following year. In 1939, he was sent to the

From top left: 1st Lt Archie P. Buie, Jr. of the USAF; an unidentified Sabre pilot in the cockpit; flight leader Allen F. Jenkins of the British RAF; and Major Edward W. Sullivan of the USMC. Jenkins and Sullivan were on exchange duty with the 51st Fighter-Interceptor Wing, whereas Buie was assigned to the unit. (Bettmann/Getty Images)

The Douglas B-26 Invader light bomber was the primary USAF night intruder aircraft in the Korean War. (USAF)

A North American F-86A in flight, 1951. It had been shipped to Japan in December 1950 with the 4th Fighter-Interceptor Wing and flown in Korea. Most of its combat missions against MiG-15s were flown from Kimpo Air Base near Seoul. (USAF)

An F-84 Thunderjet of the 27th Fighter Escort Group takes off past another in 1951. (Photo © CORBIS/Corbis via Getty Images)

An F-80C Shooting Star of the 35th Fighter-Bomber Wing takes off carrying two 75-gallon napalm tanks in 1951. (Everett Collection Historical/Alamy Stock Photo)

Retired Lt Gen Charles "Chick" Cleveland (third from right) was deployed to South Korea in March 1952, where he flew F-86s as a flight commander with the 4th Fighter-Interceptor Wing. Fifty-five years after the Korean War, the Air Force has recognized General Cleveland as a fighter ace for his accomplishments of five MiG-15 kills and one probable. (USAF/Staff Sgt Bennie J. Davis III)

A flight of F-80C Shooting Stars of the 8th Fighter-Bomber Wing in 1952. (Photo © CORBIS/Corbis via Getty Images)

Major George Davis, the first USAF pilot to push his score beyond ten, was also the only USAF ace to die in air combat in Korea. (USAF)

Col Francis "Gabby" Gabreski, the top-scoring pilot of the Eighth Air Force in World War II and a MiG ace in Korea where he commanded the 51st Fighter-Interceptor Wing in 1952. (USAF)

Major William T. Whisner, Jr., a World War II ace in the European Theater of Operations with the 352nd Fighter Group, became the first ace of the 51st Fighter-Interceptor Wing in 1952. (USAF)

Captain Harold E. "Hal" Fischer scored ten victories over MiG-15s before being shot down in February 1953. Imprisoned as a POW in the People's Republic of China, he was finally released in 1955. (USAF)

Col Harrison Thyng, commander of the 4th Fighter-Interceptor Wing, seen here in 1952. (USAF)

Gun camera film records strikes on a MiG-15 in MiG Alley combat in 1952. (USAF)

North American F-86E Sabres of the 51st Fighter-Interceptor Wing in 1952. (NARA)

OPPOSITE Captain Robinson "Robbie" Risner of the 4th Fighter-Interceptor Wing was one of several pilots to score the majority of his eight victories north of the Yalu. (USAF)

51st Fighter-Interceptor Wing commander Col Francis "Gabby" Gabreski (left) congratulates Major William T. Whisner, Jr. (center) on becoming the first ace of the wing in 1952. Both had been World War II aces in the European Theater of Operations and became aces in Korea. (USAF)

Captain Joseph C. McConnell, Jr., a pilot with the 51st Fighter-Interceptor Wing, talks with his crew chief while in the cockpit of his F-86 Sabre, "BEAUTEOUS BUTCH II." Captain McConnell became the 27th jet ace of the Korean conflict on March 9, 1953. (USAF)

Two F-86 pilots wearing what was called the "poopysuit." This survival suit provided protection in the winter seas of the Yellow Sea or Sea of Japan for ten minutes before the pilot froze to death. (USAF)

ABOVE Captain Joseph C. McConnell, Jr. returns from his final mission in May 1953. (USAF via Thompson)

RIGHT Portraits of the 39 jet aces who wreaked havoc in MiG Alley. The total kills claimed by each pilot are indicated beneath the photos. (PJF Military Collection/ Alamy Stock Photo)

OPPOSITE Captain Lonnie R. Moore, ten-victory MiG ace of the 335th Fighter-Interceptor Squadron of the 4th Fighter-Interceptor Wing, in 1952. (USAF/Seymour Johnson AFB Library Digital Collections)

A huge jet of flame shoots from the tail pipe of this USAF Lockheed F-94B-5-LO Starfire and splits the blackness of the Korean night as the pilot tests his afterburner before takeoff, July 1953. (NARA)

RIGHT Lieutenant No Kum Sok of the NKPAF after delivering his MiG-15bis to the US forces in September 1953. (USAF)

OPPOSITE Captain Manuel J. "Pete" Fernandez, Jr. of the 34th Fighter-Interceptor Wing became the war's 28th US ace when he scored his fifth and sixth victories on February 18, 1953. (USAF)

Captain Joseph C. McConnell, Jr., credited with 16 victories in 1953, was the top-scoring USAF pilot of the Korean War. (USAF)

A Korean War-era photograph of Major John F. Bolt exiting his F-86 Sabre. Assigned to the 1st Marine Aircraft Wing, Major Bolt was the USMC's first jet ace. (NARA)

Major John Glenn of the USMC flew F9F Panthers with VMF-315 in 1952 and F-86s with the 51st Fighter-Interceptor Wing in 1953, where he shot down three MiG-15s in the summer of that year just before the end of the war. (Courtesy of the Ohio Congressional Archives)

Captain Richard J. Love, seen here in 1953, was a ten-victory MiG ace. (Photo by Los Angeles Examiner/USC Libraries/Corbis via Getty Images)

The F86F, seen here in 1953, would solidify the Sabre's reputation as the last of the great dogfighters. (USAF)

A USAF Lockheed F-80C-10-LO Shooting Star in Korea. The official description refers to the aircraft as a reconnaissance plane photographed in June 1954. However, although the gunports are sealed over, no camera windows are visible. The plane also appears to wear the markings of the 35th Fighter-Interceptor Wing, which flew the F-80C in Korea in 1950 and 1951. (NARA)

Counter-Japanese Military and Political University in Yan'an, graduating in 1940 and assigned as a squad leader in the 358th Infantry Brigade of the 120th Infantry Division of the Eighth Route Army. Shortly after this assignment, he participated in the Hundred Regiments Offensive led by Zhu De and Peng Dehuai (who would later command the People's Volunteer Army in the Korean War) in Hebei and Shanxi provinces.

Liu was accepted to the Northeast People's Liberation Army Aviation School in Manchuria in October 1946 and graduated in September 1948, after which he was assigned as a pilot in the North China Military District, flying captured C-47 transports to support the army. In June 1950, he joined the newly created PLAAF 4th Mixed Brigade as a deputy battalion chief. He transitioned to the MiG-15 in 1951 and went to war as a member of the 3rd Fighter Division, where he achieved ace status that fall with a score of six.

One of the most highly acclaimed Chinese fighter pilots of the Korean War was Zhang Jihui. Born at Rongcheng in Shandong Province in January 1927 and raised in a family of poor peasants by a father who was a member of the Communist Party, Zhang joined the Eighth Route Army in 1944. After the Japanese surrender, he was one of the first students sent to the Northeast People's Liberation Army Aviation School in Manchuria in 1945, graduating three months ahead of Liu Yudi. One of the first pilots trained to fly the MiG-15 in 1950, Zhang became a group leader of the 4th Fighter Aviation Division and flew with the unit during its first deployment to the front in the summer of 1951, returning in February 1952 to replace the 3rd FAD at Antung for a second tour. Zhang claimed four victories during his service in Korea and was awarded the title Combat Hero, 1st Class. He was publicly acclaimed throughout China after he was officially credited with having shot down the 4th Fighter Group's Major George A. Davis, Jr., who was the leading US Air Force ace of the war with 14 victories when he was killed on February 10, 1952.

Zhang remained in the PLAAF after the war and became deputy commander in 1973. Following the overthrow of the "Gang of Four" by Deng Xiaoping's faction of the Communist Party, Zhang was stripped of his rank and imprisoned in June 1978. Following his release from prison in 1980, he became deputy mayor of the town of Yantai. In July 1990, he was restored to his former rank by the PLA Central Military Commission and allowed to retire with a state pension. He died in 2015.

Han Decai was one of the PLAAF's first generation of pilots following the service's official founding. He became a five-victory ace and national hero during the Korean War and later became a lieutenant general when the PLA reinstituted formal military ranks in 1988. Born in the poverty-stricken village of Fengyang in Anhui Province in 1933, he lived there for 15 years, during which he received one year of education. He worked on a farm as a laborer and was also a beggar. He was 16 when the Communists liberated the town in February 1949, at which time he joined the People's Liberation Army. When Chairman Mao announced the founding of the PLAAF, he was one of many PLA soldiers who volunteered to become pilots.

Han was initially sent to a preparatory school run by the PLA to receive academic training, but his education stopped in December 1950 when he was assigned to the air academy for training as a pilot. He later remembered that when China joined the Korean War, the Chinese air force did not have one operational unit that could be put into the air. The training consisted of a single month to learn the theory of flight and three months of flight training. By the time he was assigned to a combat unit in July 1951, he had a total of 60 hours' flying time, which included 15 hours in the MiG-15. Han Decai was declared a national hero when he was credited with shooting down 51st Fighter Group ace "Hal" Fischer in February 1953.

Yang Guoxiang left his home during middle school after he came in contact with the underground Communist Party and joined a Communist youth group. He took part in an armed uprising against the Kuomintang government in November 1948 and had to flee into the mountains, where he became a guerrilla and formally joined the PLA in 1949.

By the time the People's Republic of China was founded in October 1949, Yang was the political commissar of a horse and mule transportation team in Yunnan Province. He was one of six young PLA members who volunteered for flight training after the creation of the PLAAF who was accepted in the first trainee class and sent to Beijing in February 1950 for initial processing before he was sent to the aviation school at Mudanjian, where most of the instructors were former Japanese POWs and former Kuomintang pilots who had joined the victorious side. They were trained on ex-Kuomintang PT-17s and the Japanese Type 99. With the outbreak of the Korean War that summer, the training was cut to three months before the trainees were sent to operational units. With a total of 70 flight hours, Yang was sent to fly the Russian Ilyushin Il-10, and to the 22nd Division, and later to the 11th Division. Inasmuch as the ground-attack aircraft did not participate in the war in Korea, Yang transitioned to the MiG-15 in late 1952 and flew in combat during 1953.

Once a student was assigned to a fighter air division, they made the transition to the MiG-15 under the guidance of Soviet instructors after they gained some 15–20 flying hours in the Yak-17UTI, a first-generation two-seat version of the Yak-17 single seat fighter that had been developed from the original Yak-15 and featured a nosewheel undercarriage. After they had successfully demonstrated the ability to fly this trainer, they moved on to the MiG-15, in which they were given an additional 30 hours, before they moved with their unit to an advanced airfield at the front.

After the Chinese units were committed to combat, the pilots were independent of Russian control. During late 1951 and early 1952, Russian pilots were always airborne when the Chinese were, but flew in their own formations as cover flights behind the Chinese. US pilots began to recognize what they came to call "MiG trains," large formations of MiG-15s that remained at high altitude on the Manchurian side of the Yalu and only rarely ventured across the river, while smaller units composed of Soviet pilots engaged in combat with the Sabres.

Reflecting on his experience fighting over MiG Alley, Han came to believe that a Chinese fighter pilot's success in combat depended on how quickly he recognized his disadvantages and dealt with them. Chinese pilots had a low level of flight experience, and the aircraft they flew were outperformed by their opponents. He learned that he had to take advantage of the situation to use any mistakes the Americans made against them. Of his five credited victories, he stated that in four of the combats he was able to take advantage of a mistake the pilot made.

The 4th FAD, with 55 MiG-15s and 56 pilots, arrived at Antung on September 12, 1951. They were assigned to operate from Langtou airfield and placed under the control of the 64th IAK that controlled the 324th and 303rd IADs, though they were to fly missions independently of the Soviets. After a week of orientation flights at altitude over MiG Alley, they entered their first combat with the US Air Force on September 25.

Soviet radar picked up a formation of 20 Sabres flying cover for 13 F-80s in the Sinuiju area. Sixteen MiGs from the 12th Regiment, led by deputy regimental commander Li Wenmo, joined eight Soviet MiGs from the 196th Regiment to intercept the Americans. The Chinese pilots had already flown two missions that morning, but had not been able to contact the enemy formations they were sent after, due to their inexperience.

After assembly, the three six-MiG flights crossed the Yalu, heading for the area of the Chongchon River. The six MiGs led by Li Yongtai, commander of the 1st Flying Group, brought up the rear of the formation. Over Anju, he spotted eight F-80s below. He informed Li Wenmo of the enemy and ordered his pilots to drop their tanks, then led two pairs down toward the Shooting Stars, leaving the third as cover. He pulled out of the dive out of position for attack. His wingman and the other pair fired wildly as they flashed past the F-80s, which broke away from the attackers.

Li suddenly felt the impact of bullets and realized he was under attack, finally spotting the eight Sabres that were bouncing his formation with a flight of four from either side. When a second burst hit his MiG, Li pulled up and used his superior climb to lose the enemy fighters at 12,000 meters (4,500 feet). When he landed at Langtou, the ground crews counted 30 hits in his fuselage, wings, landing gear, and canopy.

Li's third pair, led by Li Han, became involved in a furious fight with six Sabres. His wingman was hit solidly and attempted to bail out, but he was too low for his parachute to deploy before he hit the ground. Li Han managed to hit an F-86 with a solid burst and claimed it shot down, making him the first Chinese Communist pilot to shoot down an American airplane; FEAF recorded that the Sabre made it back to Kimpo, heavily damaged, where it was subsequently written off. Li Han's victory was solid.

Over the next two days, the pilots of the 4th FAD fought two consecutive large air battles, in which they lost several MiGs due to the pilots' inexperience. They were able to redeem themselves on October 5, when the division sent 42 MiGs to cover ground troops crossing the Chongchon. At 1155 hours, the 10th Regiment's 18 MiGs caught what they identified as eight F-80s (they were actually F-84s) just as the American fighter-bombers pulled away from a bombing run southeast of Sinanju. The Chinese swarmed the enemy, flying with good discipline as leaders and wingmen, and claimed three destroyed and one damaged for the loss of one MiG.

On October 10, Hua Longyi of the 2nd Flying Group of the 10th Regiment took off at 1530 hours to reinforce other MiGs of the regiment that were involved in a fight over Anju. Hua's flight spotted four F-84s headed for the Yellow Sea. He dived after the enemy leader and opened fire, but the Thunderjet was able to break clear of his attack. Hua continued his attack and caught the F-84, which caught fire with his second burst in the engine area. His wingman reported the American streamed smoke as he went down and impacted a hill. Hua then chased the wingman and caught him with a blast of fire into the fuselage that caused smoke. Breaking away in a climb, Hua saw the second Thunderjet go down. He was the first Chinese pilot to score a multiple victory, but these would be his only victories in the war.

The 4th Division flew 508 sorties between September 12 and October 19, engaging the enemy ten times, eight of these being major air battles involving more than 100 aircraft. The pilots of the division claimed 20 enemy planes shot down and ten damaged, for a loss of 14 MiGs. Overall, the 4th Division lost two MiGs in each engagement, and the pilots were exhausted by the time they returned to Shenyang for rest and reorganization on October 20.

The 3rd Fighter Division, which was the most successful of any PLAAF fighter unit in the war, was originally commissioned on November 11, 1949, when it was created out of the 209th PLA Infantry Division. It was organized with the 7th Fighter Air Regiment, which was formed from personnel from the 625th Infantry Regiment, the 8th Fighter Air Regiment, formed from the 626th Infantry Regiment, and the 9th Fighter Air Regiment, formed from the 627th Infantry Regiment.

The 3rd Division was the first unit of the PLAAF to transition to the MiG-15 in November 1950. After the Soviet instructors passed the unit's pilots, the division engaged in an intense training program, with pilots flying every day and becoming experienced with formation flying, aerobatics, and simulated dogfights. By October 1951 when they deployed to Antung, the 3rd FAD included 3,183 personnel, of whom 59 were pilots and 280 were ground crew; they were equipped with 59 MiG-15s and two Ilyushin Il-12 transports. The pilots averaged 70 hours each of advanced flight training in their MiGs beyond their initial training. Once at their base, the pilots received an additional

20 flying hours of operational training and regional familiarization, receiving lectures from Soviet pilots and pilots of the 4th Division about their experience against the Americans, before they entered combat with the USAF that November. Among the senior pilots in the division was Wang Hai, who had been one of the first Chinese pilots to transition to the MiG-15 the year before, and was assigned to the unit as a senior flight leader.

The division adopted a strategy of seeking small engagements with American fighter-bombers while initially avoiding the Sabres. They flew into MiG Alley for the first time on November 2. Between then and November 10, they engaged five times with small enemy formations, claiming five UN fighter-bombers shot down and three damaged for no losses. During their tour from November 1951 to January 1952, the 3rd FAD produced six aces, including top ace Wang Hai, while the unit as a whole was credited with 29 victories.

Wang Hai's acclaim in the Korean War rests on his demonstrated leadership and commitment to teamwork, which resulted in the flying group he led achieving a victory-loss rate of 15:0 during their tour at the front. He first saw the value of teamwork in his first combat on November 9, when his flight of four MiG-15s caught a lone Australian Meteor F.8. Being inexperienced, they all opened fire at too great a range, attacking in an undisciplined manner that resulted in their getting in each other's way. Finally, Wang's number four wingman reported the Meteor had caught fire. In the end, all four pilots were credited with the victory; it was the result of Wang training his flying group members to stick together and protect each other in combat.

On November 18, Wang's group sighted two flights of Thunderjet fighter-bombers headed for the Chongchon River bridge, and engaged in a fierce dogfight with the Americans. As Wang's pilots attacked, the F-84s went into a defensive Lufbery circle. Wang ordered the flight to make vertical attacks on the Americans, diving through their formation, to negate the value of the maneuver, which allowed each pilot to protect the tail of the one in front. Wang claimed two F-84s shot down, as did his wingman, while the element leader claimed one. Wang was later awarded the Combat Hero Medal First Class, and his flying group received the designation "Hero Flying Group." The MiG-15bis Wang flew in Korea is exhibited today in the Military Museum of the Chinese People's Revolution in Beijing.

After the war, Wang Hai remained in the PLAAF and was promoted to command an air division just prior to Mao's Cultural Revolution. Surviving the disruptions of the Cultural Revolution, he was named commander of the Guangzhou Military Region Air Force in 1979. In 1985, he became the first aviator promoted to Commander of the People's Liberation Army Air Force. When the PLA re-instituted military ranks, he was awarded the rank of lieutenant general in September 1988 and remained in command until his retirement in 1992. Since then, all PLAAF commanders have been career aviators. As the most famous Chinese pilot of the Korean War, there is even a diecast statue of him and a model of his MiG-15 which is still given to children in China.

Zhao Baotong, who had joined the PLAAF in 1949 and graduated from flight training in October 1950, became a qualified MiG-15 pilot in February 1951. His demonstrated flying talent and diligence resulted in his being promoted to deputy leader of the 3rd Flying Group of the 7th Regiment in July 1951.

The morning of November 4, 1951, Zhao flew as second element leader of the six-MiG covering flight when 24 MiGs led by 7th Regiment deputy commander Meng Jin intercepted F-80 and F-84 fighter-bombers over Kaechon. Arriving at the limits of their operating area, Meng led the 18 MiGs back north without spotting the enemy. Zhao's flight, which was at the rear of the formation, continued on south. The flight leader spotted 24 F-84s heading south after their attack. He ordered an immediate attack and the six MiGs dived on the enemy formation; the surprised Thunderjets broke in every direction. In the chaotic battle that ensued, Zhao pulled so tight onto the tail of an enemy fighter that he blacked out momentarily. When he came to, he realized he'd lost his wingman. He continued the attack, squeezing off two short bursts before breaking from other F-84s so tightly he went into a spin. He recovered in time to see his victory hit the ground below. He continued on despite being alone and attacked another pair of Thunderjets, setting one afire. Called to return, Zhao circled the battleground and saw one F-84 burning on a hillside and the second with its nose plunged deep in the sand of the Yellow Sea shoreline. Over the next three months, Zhao would score seven victories and two damaged. On December 2, in a battle in which he claimed two F-86s shot down, he was himself shot down and forced to bail out of his flaming MiG.

Liu Yuti, another 3rd FAD pilot, was credited with shooting down four Thunderjets in one fight on November 23. Leading two four-MiG flights, Lieu spotted two flights of F-84s headed toward the Yellow Sea after bombing a village. The Thunderjets spotted the incoming MiGs and broke wildly. Liu chased the leader and wingman at low altitude over the sea. The enemy leader pulled up as he got too close to the water's surface, and Liu hit him in the engine with a single burst of cannon fire. As the leader went straight in, the wingman managed to turn in front of Liu, who caught him with two bursts in the cockpit and engine. Liu and his wingman avoided the other American jets and headed back toward the Yalu. Spotting another formation of Thunderjets, he shot down the trailing one after losing his wingman. Heading for home, he found four other F-84s headed south. Dropping low behind them, he used his superior climb and hit the wingman as he climbed away from the others. American records only list two F-84s badly damaged and two others slightly damaged, but the PLAAF recognized Liu's claim when the wreckage of several Thunderjets was found in the area where the fights had happened.

With these successes in November and December, Chinese Communist leaders directed that the 3rd FAD should switch from intercepting fighter-bomber formations to seeking combat with the Sabres. When they followed this direction in January, their relative lack of skill as pilots put them at a disadvantage. That month, the division recorded the loss of 16 MiGs and several pilots including the deputy division commander. In the face of these losses, the 3rd FAD was withdrawn from combat in February 1952. In their time of fighting in MiG Alley, the Chinese pilots flew 2,319 sorties and engaged in 23 engagements between October 21, 1951 and January 14, 1952. They claimed 55 UN aircraft including 17 Sabres. On their return to China on February 1, the pilots received a personal message from Chairman Mao saying that he wholeheartedly saluted and congratulated the 3rd Fighter Aviation Division.

In addition to Wang Hai, seven other PLAAF pilots were credited as leading aces during the Korean War, all but one serving in the 3rd FAD. They are: Zhao Baotong, the first Chinese pilot credited as an ace and tied with Wang Hai as the PLAAF "ace of aces," with a score of nine; Li Han (8), the first Chinese pilot credited with shooting down an American aircraft in September 1951, who flew with the 4th FAD; Lu Min (8), who flew with the 12th FAD, as did Liu Yudi (6). The other two leading aces did not survive the war. Fan Wanzhang (8) was killed in action, on August 8, 1952, while Song Shenglu (6) was killed in action on December 3, 1952.

The Air Force of the People's Volunteer Army was originally created to provide air support to the army at the front. Thus, bomber aviation divisions operating Ilyushin Il-10 attack bombers and Tupolev Tu-2 battlefield bombers were created at the same time as the fighter aviation divisions. The original planning had been that these units would operate from airfields in North Korea, but the UN air campaign against the North Korean airfields had demonstrated these forces would not be able to operate in the country without sustaining crippling losses.

The 8th and 10th bomber divisions, equipped with the Ilyushin Tu-2, had been assigned to the PLAAF in March, 1951. A twin-engine bomber with a crew of three, powered by two Ash-82FN radial piston engines each providing 1,850 horsepower, the Tu-2 had been introduced into the Red Air Force in 1942 as a high-speed frontline bomber and dive-bomber that was comparable in its multirole capability to the German Ju-88. It was second in importance in the V-VS behind the Petlyakov Pe-2. The airplane had remained in production following the end of the Great Patriotic War, and by the time production ceased in 1951, some 3,000 Tu-2s had been constructed. It was provided to the Eastern European satellite air forces, and 311 of these bombers were provided to the PLAAF following the Sino-Soviet treaty of cooperation signed in December 1949.

When the Chinese military leaders were forced to admit in September 1951 that it was unlikely the piston-engine battlefield attack aircraft would be based in North Korea, the PVA's bombing force was assigned to knock out the island bases off the coast of North Korea that were controlled by ROK forces. Among these, Taewha-do Island, just south of the mouth of the Yalu River, was given first priority for attack. The island was garrisoned by 1,200 ROK troops. Radar installations on the island provided early warning of Communist aerial activity over MiG Alley, while the radio intercept station was responsible for listening in to air controllers at Antung who guided the MiGs onto UN aerial formations over North Korea. The island was also used offensively by commando forces that supplied anti-Communist guerillas in the north and carried out sabotage raids on the coastal railroad. A decision was made in late October to mount an amphibious operation using troops from the PVA 50th Army to take Taewha-do and the surrounding smaller islands, Ka-do and Sohwado. An aerial bombing campaign would precede the invasion.

Reconnaissance missions on November 1 by MiG-15s and La-11s obtained photos of the defenses. On the night of November 5, North Korean artillery opened fire on the island from positions on the coast, firing for three hours. At 1435 hours on November 6, nine Tu-2s of the 8th Division took off from Yuhongton airfield near Shenyang to bomb Taewha-do. They rendezvoused with 16 La-11s of the 2nd Fighter Aviation Division at 1516 hours as they crossed the Yalu. At 1538 hours, 24 MiG-15s of the 3rd FAD took a blocking position between Sonchon and Sinmi-do Island to intercept any UN aircraft sent to oppose the raid. At the same time the MiGs took position, the bombers arrived at their drop point over the island and dropped 81 250-kilogram bombs, including nine incendiaries. The command post and the food and ammo storage sites were destroyed. There was no UN aerial opposition and the bombers were unscathed by the island's antiaircraft defenses. They landed at Antung 40 minutes later.

Bad weather delayed the deployment of the invasion force, and the operation was put off to the end of November. In the meantime, FEAF had established a plan to defend the island. On the night of November 29–30, a few Chinese bombers attempted to bomb the island again, and the next day US Army radio intelligence listening posts learned there would be a second daylight attack and let the Kimpo Sabres know. The 4th Group laid on a special afternoon mission to meet the bombers. The idea of intercepting piston-engined opponents thrilled the pilots when they were briefed for the mission.

Group commander Colonel Benjamin S. Preston, Jr. led 31 Sabres from all three squadrons, at the head of the first flight of 336th Squadron Sabres, with the second led by Major Al Simmons. The recently promoted Lt Col George A. Davis, Jr., a seven-victory World War II ace with the 348th Fighter Group in the Southwest Pacific who had already scored two victories since taking command of the 334th Squadron in mid-October, led two flights of Sabres in the low position, while Major Winton "Bones" Marshall, a six-month combat veteran with four MiG Alley victories, led two Sabre flights of the 335th Squadron as high cover. The formation flew out over the Yellow Sea to avoid being spotted and reported by Communist ground forces.

At 1550, Preston ordered the six "Dignity Red Flight" Sabres to drop their tanks as they turned toward Taewha-do Island. Simmons' Dignity White Flight followed. At the head of Dignity Able and Dignity Baker, George Davis and his pilots punched off theirs. "Bones" Marshall's Sabres kept theirs a bit longer as they stayed high to keep watch for intruding MiGs. Eighteen F-86s headed for their Combat Air Patrol position over the island.

To the north, Chinese bomber formation leader Gao Yueming checked his planes – nine Tu-2s flying in a Vee-of-Vees formation at 380kph (180mph), escorted by 16 La-11s from the 2nd FAD. They were five minutes away from the target. He wasn't aware that by taking off from Yuhongton airfield one minute early, and then making an early turn to the southeast to cross the Yalu, he was now five minutes ahead of his scheduled rendezvous with the covering MiG force. At Antung, the MiG-15s from the 3rd FAD had taken off on schedule. When Gao spotted the swept-wing jets headed toward him, he thought they were his covering MiGs.

At 1607 hours, Colonel Preston saw the shapes in the distance resolve themselves as the enemy aircraft the Sabres were there to meet, low on his starboard beam. The Sabres were dangerously short on fuel now, and there wasn't time to maneuver for the best attack position.

Calling out "Tally-Ho!" he led Dignity Red Flight in a diving right turn that put the Sabres on a head-on attack. The closing speed was over 750mph, and he had seconds to fire. Flying down the formation as they fired, the Sabres missed. Preston then spotted an La-11 behind the bombers as it turned in front of him. His burst caught the enemy fighter in the engine and it fell away afire to crash at 1609 hours. Low on fuel, Preston and his wingman turned for Kimpo. His element leader and wingman had become separated in the lunge at the enemy.

Major Simmons followed Preston in a front-quarter attack on the bombers. He and his wingman, 1st Lt Robert Akin, opened fire on the bombers. Flashing past too fast for accurate shooting, Simmons chandelled up away from them and spotted the MiG-15s as they arrived overhead, losing Akin in the process. Pulling behind the last one, he got one burst before his guns jammed. He dove away, found Akin, and headed for Kimpo.

Akin's aim had been better than his leader's. Captain Buford Hammond, Simmons' element leader, saw the trailing Tu-2 catch fire as Akin flew past it, hammering the bomber as its left engine began smoking. Hammond's wingman, 2nd Lt Leonard Merook, missed the bombers and came around for a second run. Dodging an La-11 that attempted to intercept him, he opened fire on the same Tu-2, with his gun camera confirming Akin's victory. He looked up to see the MiGs overhead as they punched off their tanks. They were three minutes too late.

1st Lt Doug Evans, Dignity Red Three element lead in Preston's flight, banked his wings vertical as he and Dignity Red Four, 1st Lt Dave Freeland, made their pass. They were three minutes past "Bingo" fuel. He pulled his nose onto the Tu-2 in the right-hand Vee and opened fire. The bomber was hit, but it wasn't fatal. Evans pulled up and went around again, bingo fuel be damned. He lined up and his shots went into the right engine.

The first moment Gao Yueming knew he was under attack was when his right wingman's right engine caught fire, with the fire spreading to the wing as the bomber fell out of formation. He didn't know it was Evans and Freeland flying the two Sabres that flashed through the formation. Gao turned the formation to the southeast, banking away from the target ahead. More Sabres fell on the bombers. He saw four of them concentrate on his wingman until his fuel tanks finally detonated. Fire engulfed the bomber, and Gao saw no parachutes appear as it fell toward the water below.

Evans and Freeland came around again, but now the sky was full of Sabres savaging the bombers "like a school of sharks going after whales," as he later recalled. There was no chance for another attack and it was now doubtful if they would get home. Reluctantly, he soared up, away from the flight, and the two Sabres began coasting for Kimpo; when he landed, Evans would find there were only 15 gallons left in the fuel tanks.

The Sabres that disrupted Evans and Freeland were George Davis' Dignity Able and Baker flights. Davis had maneuvered his planes for a favorable attack position, and they came down on the bombers from the rear, slowing the closing speed and giving him time to aim. His bullets hit the leader of the third Vee, whipsawing the bomber as it caught fire and fell away. It was 1616 hours and he was desperately short of fuel, but he gave no thought to leaving as he arced up with his wingman to come around again.

He closed rapidly on the Tu-2 ahead, holding fire till he got close. A short burst ignited the fuel tank in the left wing. As it fell away, the fire reached the bomb bay and the enemy bomber exploded when it hit the water at 1618 hours. Davis wasn't aware he had lost his wingman in the maneuver. Dignity Able Two departed for Kimpo and Davis was alone. He figured he had fuel for one more pass and came up directly astern of the next Tu-2 in the formation. He ignored the tracers as the enemy rear gunner opened up on him. Closing to within 100 yards of the target, his second burst set the bomber afire and he saw the three crewmen take to their parachutes. The third Tu-2 hit the Yellow Sea at 1619 hours. George Davis had just become the fifth Air Force ace and the first World War II ace to achieve acedom in a second war.

His fuel state was such that he now had to leave regardless. As he climbed for altitude, he heard Dignity Able Three, his element leader, call for help. Captain Ray Barton had followed Davis in his attack, not knowing he had lost his wingman until he discovered the hard way that the swept-wing fighter on his tail was a MiG, not a Sabre! As he evaded that attacker, four more came down around him. He turned and turned, banking as tightly as possible as he turned to face each attack run and called for help. He broke from them and turned south, only to have two more catch him. He broke away from them and found himself low over the water when he spotted yet another MiG-15.

Davis arrived off the southern end of Taewha-do Island to find Barton running for home 500ft above the water with a MiG on his tail. Creeping up on the two, Davis dived onto the MiG's tail and opened fire, striking it in the tailpipe and engine. The MiG caught fire and went into the water just off the island's southern tip. Linking up with Barton, the two Sabres climbed for altitude. In the end, both of them landed dead-stick at Kimpo, out of fuel. George Davis had just shot down four enemy aircraft and was the leading American ace in Korea with a score of six.

"Bones" Marshall thought he and his two flights would be out of the battle, but as he pulled away from the formation, Preston called, "Bones, come on down and get 'em." Marshall didn't have to be told twice as he punched off his tanks and dove into the fight. High and to the rear, the 335th Squadron Sabres arrowed down on the enemy formation. Marshall picked out a trailing Tu-2 and opened fire. The bomber caught fire and he saw the crew bail out as he pulled up from his attack and took position on a second bomber. He clobbered it hard, but before he could take the time to see the final result, two La-11s came in on him. He aimed at one head-on, and it exploded when his bullets hit the engine. The second La-11 turned in on him and opened fire just as he heard his wingman, 1st Lt John Honaker, yell to break. He pulled the stick in his gut and rolled away. He was just in time not to be killed by the burst of fire from the La-11's three 23mm cannon, but his Sabre was hit so badly that pilot Wang Tingbao claimed it as a victory on his return to Antung when he saw the smoking Sabre enter a spin headed toward the sea below.

Wang's fire had hit Marshall's Sabre in the wingroot and the canopy, with the cannon shell impacting against the back of his ejection seat, which knocked him unconscious. He regained consciousness with the altimeter reading 3,000 feet in a spin, and managed to pull out with less than 200 feet of air between his Sabre and a watery grave. He started climbing as he heard Honaker calling for him. When the two joined up, Marshall discovered his radio system had been damaged – he could receive but not transmit. He checked himself over and discovered that his parachute was riddled with shrapnel. With an inoperable seat and a shredded parachute, he gave thought to a forced landing on the beach and a ride home in a helicopter, but decided as long as the Sabre was working he would stay with it.

When they arrived over Kimpo, Marshall let his wingman land ahead and then set up for landing. He was about to lower his gear, moments from touchdown, when another Sabre flashed past and cut in front of him, dropping onto the runway. The engine responded as he quickly throttled up and he was able to narrowly miss George Davis, who landed dead-stick. As Marshall went around and then finally landed, he was not aware that with the two Tu-2s he'd shot down, he'd become the sixth MiG ace, only a minute behind Davis.

As the Sabres flew away, Gao Yueming, in the only Tu-2 that hadn't been hit by the Sabres, turned what was left of his formation away from Taewha-do Island as he jettisoned his bombs on the beach below.

The Taewha-do mission was a disaster for the Chinese. The Americans claimed eight Tu-2s destroyed; the actual count was four Tu-2s, three La-11s and a MiG-15, with 15 bomber crewmen and the pilots of all four fighters lost. The PLAAF would attempt no more offensive missions for the rest of the war, concentrating their effort on training their MiG pilots and engaging the Sabres over MiG Alley.

CHAPTER 13

SHOOTING STARS, THUNDERJETS, AND METEORS

In the summer of 1951, following a year of mobile warfare that ranged up and down the Korean peninsula, the Communists were fought to a draw by a strengthened UN ground army by the end of June. At the United Nations, the Soviets suggested talks to bring about an armistice and a peace agreement, a sign that the other side was now as exhausted as the UN and that both sides now recognized that complete victory by either was not possible. The beginning of the armistice talks in July and August dominated the news in the United States and the negotiations at Kaesong were taken domestically in the United States as a promise that an imminent end to the fighting was at hand.

This optimism was short-lived. The first days of negotiations were dominated by the efforts of the UN delegation to limit Communist propaganda activity surrounding the negotiations, disagreement regarding administration of the neutral area around the site of the talks, and arguments regarding the procedure of the talks themselves. After two weeks of tension, the two sides were able to adopt an agenda that addressed the proposed ceasefire.

Even this did not last. There were repeated Communist violations of the neutral zone, which led General Ridgway to suspend the talks. After a week, meetings resumed, but this was quickly followed in late August by an incident fabricated by the Communists that "proved" UN aircraft had bombed Kaesong and they in turn suspended further negotiations. The negotiation site was changed in late October to Panmunjom. By November, there were reports that both sides were willing to consider the existing battle line, which ran more or less roughly along the 38th Parallel, as the final armistice line.

The hope that this agreement meant the talks would quickly reach a successful conclusion was dashed over the issue of the return of prisoners of war. The West knew of the terrible fate of Soviet POWs who were returned to the USSR at the end of World War II, where most were executed or ended up in the gulag. Thus, the UN forces opposed any forced repatriation. This was met by an equal determination by the Communists for nothing less. They were unwilling to allow a possibility of the spectacle of their soldiers and citizens refusing to return to the "worker's paradises" and the damage such events would create in the Cold War court of world public opinion. This issue of POW return would stymie further negotiations for the next 21 months.

There was every possibility that the Chinese and North Koreans might again rethink their strategy and attempt to resolve the Korean conflict by force. In an attempt to prevent this, FEAF began searching for a way to convince the other side such a decision would never work. James Michener's fictional Admiral Tarrent in *The Bridges At Toko-ri* would put words to this strategy:

> I believe without question that some morning a bunch of Communist generals and commissars will be holding a meeting to discuss the future of the war. And a messenger will run in with news that the Americans have knocked out even the bridges at Toko-ri. And that little thing will convince the Reds that we'll never stop, never give in, never weaken in our purpose.

This would be the rationale for the air war waged over North Korea for the next two years. FEAF Bomber Command had already leveled every target in the country that could be remotely considered "strategic" by the month after the Inchon invasion, yet the loss of such factories and transportation centers had no effect on the execution of the war by the Communists.

In December 1950, the Air Force had developed Operation *Strangle* as a way to deny necessary supplies to the frontline armies. It had not proven successful during the fighting in the first six months of 1951, but the Air Force could find no alternative strategy that carried the slightest hope of "bringing the enemy to his senses."

The Navy had learned during the Battle of Carlson's Canyon in March 1951 that the enemy could keep transportation infrastructure operational regardless of repeated air attacks. The outstanding "lesson" of the Korean War and the greatest surprise to the disciples of Douhet would be the limited effectiveness of "air power" in bringing the war to a politically acceptable conclusion. Despite the fact that UN forces had near-total air superiority throughout the first year of war, air power had been powerless to prevent battlefield reverses at the outset or, following the intervention of China, to detect large-scale movement of enemy forces as the People's Volunteer Army entered North Korea, or effectively isolate the battlefield.

Tactical air power had been decisive in preventing North Korean victory at the Pusan Perimeter and Chinese victory following the expulsion of UN forces from North Korea, and tactical air power along the Main Line of Resistance prevented the enemy from achieving more than very limited successes here and there as the stalemated ground struggle dragged on. Strategic air power in the form of the B-29 had been driven from the daylight skies of North Korea by the end of 1951, and tactical air power was only able to re-enter the northern part of North Korea at the end of the year because of the additional two squadrons of F-86s from the re-equipped 51st Fighter Interceptor Wing, giving the UN flyers just enough of an edge to keep the MiGs at bay.

The Air Force planners saw the North Korean rail system as the part of the supply transportation system most vulnerable to air attack. The railroads were the most efficient method of getting supplies into the rear areas of the front lines, whence ox carts and even coolie gangs could get the supplies to the front, and so the Air Force contribution to Operation *Strangle* centered on the railroad that ran down western North Korea from the Chinese border to Pyongyang. Railway bridges were the primary targets, and required repeat missions to keep them knocked out in the face of the work done by Communist repair crews; eventually, the Chinese and North Koreans would employ over 100,000 peasants from both countries as dragooned labor for this effort. Throughout 1951–53, the fighter-bomber squadrons would hit many North Korean transportation targets repeatedly in a never-ending struggle to keep targets out of action in the face of enemy repair activity in an interdiction effort that would never achieve full success.

The 8th Group war diary history for November–December 1951 states: "With deadly monotony and a somewhat creeping paralysis of enthusiasm, the group returned again and again to hit a piece of terrain that became as familiar as Main Street, USA." The target was critically important, a 25-mile stretch of winding, twisting railway between Kunu-ri and Sunchon. The war diary continues:

> Despite the almost undivided efforts of this peerless fighter-bomber group, Communist repair troops filled bomb craters as fast as the pilots could make them. From the outset of the Operation *Strangle* attacks, the Reds have managed to repair rail cuts very quickly. No doubt assisted by frozen ground which caused some delayed-fused bombs to skip off the target and reduced the dimensions of bomb craters of those that hit the target, the Reds seldom left rail cuts unrepaired for more than twenty-four hours in November. When it appeared that the battered Kunu-ri to Sunchon track defied further repair, the Reds redoubled their efforts in December.

The 8th Group's bleak assessment was echoed by Fifth Air Force intelligence in the status report for December 1951, which acknowledged that "Red railway repairmen and bridge builders 'have broken our railroad blockade of Pyongyang and won the use of all key rail arteries.'"

In the spring of 1952 FEAF's commander General Everest made efforts to eliminate the use of the term *Strangle* when he explained to newsmen on April 12, 1952 that Operation *Strangle* had been the name for a short-lived highway-interdiction program and that the aerial interdiction campaign against North Korea's railroads was properly termed the "Rail Interdiction Program." A year before, Air Force leaders had confidently informed war correspondents that Operation *Strangle* would win the war.

The war the fighter-bombers engaged in was a bloody one, a war unrelieved by opportunities for the kind of public acclaim the Sabre pilots received. Typically, fighter-bomber pilots suffered higher casualties since they flew lower-performance planes and were exposed to more hostile ground fire than the typical fighter-interceptor pilot. While only 147 Air Force planes were lost in air-to-air combat, over 816 fighter-bombers were shot down by ground fire. Raymond Sturgeon, a pilot with the 35th Squadron of the 8th Group, recalled that he had friends who flew Sabres who never saw an enemy fighter in their entire tour, but that fighter-bomber pilots got fired on every mission, with his squadron losing a pilot or two every week, which was not considered unusual. Perrin Gower, another pilot in Sturgeon's squadron, claimed that five of the ten pilots he shared his hut with were killed, and Howard Heiner, a pilot in the 12th Squadron of the 18th Wing, remembered one week when seven pilots in his squadron were shot down:

Far and away the greatest danger to the fighter-bomber were antiaircraft (AA) weapons. The Communist AA effort was concentrated to cover the areas south of the Chongchon River that the MiGs did not patrol. Bridges were especially well defended, but even along standard stretches of track, the Communist forces deployed antiaircraft emplacements every four miles. However, the weapons that pilots feared most were not these big guns, but small-caliber 37-millimeter automatic weapons operated by regular Chinese and North Korean troops. Small caliber antiaircraft weapons presented such a dangerous threat for the fighter-bomber because they were indiscriminate and easily hidden in so-called flak traps. Regional militia and repair troops would guard important interdiction routes by creating large barriers of small-arms fire. These troops also strung wire cables between hills to thwart low-level attack, and created elaborate ambushes using tanks as bait to lure UN aircraft into carefully configured "kill zones of automatic weapons."

Superior flying could not warn you of hidden flak, nor could it necessarily save you in a typical bomb run. All a pilot could do was minimize his exposure to fire by employing a steep angle of attack in a bomb run; however, exposure was still unavoidable. Such daily, involuntary risk-taking made fighter-bombers much more fatalistic than their fighter-interceptor brethren; they lived a life of uncertainty, praying every day that their luck would hold out.

In addition to ground fire, slower planes and dangerous payloads made the life of the fighter-bomber pilot more hazardous than that of the fighter-interceptor. The first generation of combat jet aircraft had more than a few bugs in them, and fighter-bomber detachments received the oldest and least mechanically sound aircraft in the inventory.

In addition to the difficulties of life as a fighter-bomber pilot during a mission, life on the ground was only better in that one was not being shot at. One pilot of the 8th Group recalled life at Suwon in the winter of 1951–52:

> We lived in Quonset huts that had never been painted and had no insulation or covering of any kind on the inside walls; all you saw or felt was the cold, corrugated steel. There was one flight of four pilots to a hut. The hut was heated with fuel oil furnaces made of 55-gallon fuel drums, two of them in each hut. We slept on canvas Army cots with lots of blankets. The only women on base were either Korean or a few nurses. The nurses had their own hut of course, inside a fenced-in compound with one other house that was used by the group commander and hospital commander. The bath house sat off by itself about 100 yards from our hut (we were the closest) and it had the commodes too. There was nothing like taking a hot shower and then running 100 yards through snow and zero-degree weather to get back to your warm hut.

Fortunately for the hard-pressed Shooting Star pilots in the 8th Wing, they were led by one of the best pilots in the Air Force. Colonel Levi Chase is not as well known in histories of the Korean War as other pilots and leaders of his generation due to the fact he did not spend his days polishing his own apple or blowing his own horn.

Born in Cortland, NY, on December 23, 1917, Levi R. Chase dropped out of Syracuse University in his junior year and became an Army aviation cadet in November 1940. A member of Class 41-G, he received his pilot wings and commission as a second lieutenant in September 1941 at Maxwell Field, Alabama, and was assigned to the 33rd Fighter Group flying the P-40F Warhawk and commanded by then-Captain Phil Cochran.

He participated in Operation *Torch*, the American landings in French North Africa, flying off the escort carrier USS *Chenango* (CVE-28). Between December 18, 1942 and April 5, 1943, Chase shot down eight Bf-109s, a Ju-88, and a Macchi C.202 to become the top-ranked USAAF ace in the Northwestern African Theater and rise to command the 60th Fighter Squadron.

In 1944–45, he rejoined Group Commander Cochran and old friend Johnny Alison as group operations officer for the 2nd Air Commando Group in the China-Burma-India Theater, where he planned and led the longest fighter mission of the war, flying P-51s from Cox's Bazaar, India, to attack the Don Muang airfield in Bangkok, Thailand, an 1,800-mile round trip across the Bay of Bengal, during which he shot down two JAAF (Japanese Army Air Force) Oscars to become one of three USAAF aces to score against all three Axis enemies. Cochran's Air Commandos were later the inspiration for the Al Capp cartoon series "Terry and The Pirates."

Chase was recalled from the Air Force Reserves to active military duty in April 1951. He served successively as deputy commander of the 1st Fighter Group at Griffiss AFB, New York; executive officer of the 56th Fighter-Interceptor Wing; and commander of the 63rd Fighter-Interceptor Squadron at Selfridge AFB, Michigan, where he flew the F-86 Sabre. In November 1951, he was assigned to Korea as group operations officer of the 51st Fighter-Interceptor Wing, flying F-80C Shooting Stars. When the decision was made to re-equip the 51st Wing with F-86s and concentrate the F-80s in the 8th Fighter-Bomber Wing, he was made wing commander and led the 8th Wing through the fighter-bomber campaign in 1951 and 1952.

Chase's most important combat missions were a series of low-level bombing attacks he led on the North Korean capital of Pyongyang on July 11, 1952, during which the group flew three wing-strength missions through intense flak with no loss of pilots or aircraft to inflict serious damage on several of the Pyongyang airfields and the railroad marshaling yards. For this, Chase was awarded a second oak leaf cluster to his Silver Star and a second bar to his Distinguished Flying Cross. He also led the wing's attacks on the Suiho Dam and the North Korean hydroelectric complex on June 23–24 and June 26–27, 1952, and was awarded both a fourth Silver Star and a fourth DFC for his leadership in these dangerous and important missions. Colonel Chase completed his tour as commander in October 1952, during which he had led over 100 missions, including every "hot" mission the 8th Wing was assigned.

The most well-known pilot in the 8th Wing at this time was Major Charles Loring. A World War II veteran who had flown P-47 Thunderbolt fighter-bombers during the Normandy invasion and the subsequent campaign across Northwestern Europe, Loring chose to make the Air Force a career after the war. Stuck in non-flying jobs during the postwar years, he had been an instructor at the Army Information School in Pennsylvania for two years when the Korean War broke out. He requested assignment to a combat unit, but had to wait two years to go to war.

When Loring reported to the 8th Fighter-Bomber Wing, he was initially assigned to Headquarters and Headquarters Squadron, where he was put in charge of training and indoctrinating replacement pilots. He held the position for 30 days before he began flying combat missions and became squadron operations officer in the 80th Fighter-Bomber Squadron. The missions were the same kind he had flown eight years earlier.

In early November 1952, Communist forces recaptured Triangle Hill after it was taken by US infantry in October, and were threatening US ground units at Sniper Ridge. The morning of November 22, 1952, Major Loring flew his 51st mission. His four F-80s were tasked with attacking enemy units on Triangle Hill. Contacting the "Mosquito" FAC, he was directed to dive-bomb artillery positions that were firing on Sniper Ridge. As was now usual, ground fire was heavy.

Locating the target, Loring rolled into his bomb run. Enemy antiaircraft fire exploded around his F-80. The other members of the flight saw Loring's Shooting Star take severe hits and waited for him to pull out of his dive and break away. Instead, when the airplane was at approximately 4,000 feet, Loring deliberately changed course, turning the F-80 45 degrees left as he pulled up in a controlled maneuver, took aim at Communist gun emplacements on a ridge northwest of his briefed target, and dived directly into them. The resulting explosion knocked out the artillery position. On their return to Suwon, the surviving pilots stated there had been no indication from Loring that he had been hit or that his aircraft was too heavily damaged to escape.

On the testimony of the three pilots who had witnessed his act, Major Charles Loring was nominated for the Medal of Honor. In a White House ceremony on May 5, 1954, President Dwight D. Eisenhower presented the medal to his widow. Limestone AFB, located in Limestone, Maine, was renamed Loring AFB in the Maine native's honor on October 1, 1954.

By 1951, the F-84 Thunderjet had replaced the F-80 as the most important fighter-bomber type used by the Air Force in Korea. In June 1951, the 49th Fighter-Bomber Wing handed over its Shooting Stars to the 8th Wing and began converting to F-84E Thunderjets once the Air Force had approved the transfer of 75 F-84s to Korea. The Thunderjet force continued to grow. The 136th Fighter-Bomber Wing, an Air National Guard unit from Texas, had arrived in Korea in May. They were followed by the 116th Fighter-Bomber Wing, composed of squadrons from the Georgia, Florida, and California Air National Guard in July. Strategic Air Command regained control of the 27th Fighter-Escort Wing following their departure from Korea at the end of June; before they left, the 27th provided transition training for the 49th Wing and operational training for both the 49ers and the pilots of the 136th Wing.

Air Force Chief of Staff General Hoyt S. Vandenberg warned General Stratemeyer that these F-84 reinforcements would be the last FEAF would see for the foreseeable future, since aircraft shortages throughout the USAF resulting from the prewar parsimony prevented FEAF receiving the 50 percent theater reserve of fighters Stratemeyer had requested; FEAF would be lucky to have a 10 percent reserve over the next year until increased aircraft production ordered in the aftermath of the war's outbreak caught up with demand.

Upon arrival in Japan, the 116th Wing found that 33 of 75 aircraft had structural damage or corrosion problems from their trans-Pacific trip. Several weeks were spent straightening out these problems while the pilots trained on the remaining 42 Thunderjets. Surprisingly, the 116th Wing was initially assigned to air defense duties in Japan based at Misawa AFB on Hokkaido and charged with preventing any aerial incursion from the USSR. Air defense was a singularly inappropriate mission for the F-84. By November, the 116th Group began deploying a squadron at a time to Korea to supplement the two F-84 wings based at Taegu, and the wing would participate in the first long-range missions that took advantage of aerial refueling. When the 116th Wing designation reverted to the Air National Guard in June 1952, the unit was redesignated the 474th Fighter-Bomber Wing.

The 136th began combat operations as quickly as possible, aided by the fact its airplanes had been better-cocooned and did not need repairs once they arrived in Japan. The group flew its first mission on May

24, 1951. A month later, on June 26, the Thunderjets were providing close escort to Superfortresses attacking Yongyu airfield. When the MiG-15s of the Chinese 4th FAD attacked the formation, Captain Harry Underwood and his wingman, 1st Lt Arthur E. Olinger, shared credit for destroying a MiG-15 that made it past the F-86 screen for the first victory by Air National Guard pilots. After a year of active service, the 136th Wing was returned to the Texas Air National Guard and the unit became the 58th Fighter-Bomber Wing in the regular Air Force.

On September 19, 1951, 16 F-84E Thunderjets from the 9th Fighter-Bomber Squadron of the veteran 49th Fighter-Bomber Group were headed north from their base at Taegu (K-2) at 12,000 feet, each airplane loaded with two 500lb bombs. The 9th FBS, alongside sister squadrons the 7th and 8th, was briefed to dive-bomb the main rail line between Sinanju and Pyongyang at a "choke point" just south of Sukchon where the line went through a marshy area between two hills, making it the most difficult place for the enemy to make repairs. The target was right in the middle of MiG Alley.

Leading the 9th's Purple Flight was Major Willie Williams, the squadron commander. One of the most experienced pilots in the 49ers, Williams had joined the 49th shortly after the Inchon landings in September 1950. Williams' element leader, Purple Three, was Major James F. Sprinkle, with Captain Kenneth L. Skeen, the 9th's new squadron executive officer, flying his third F-84 mission as Sprinkle's wingman, Purple Four. Williams recalled, "We had transitioned to the Thunderjet by late August, and had been back in Korea for about a week at the time of this mission."

As the Thunderjets crossed the bomb line north of the Main Line of Resistance along the 38th Parallel, the weather changed from the clear skies in the south to broken clouds that became a heavy undercast by the time the 48 F-84Es passed east of Pyongyang.

I heard the group commander call out MiGs above us at seven o'clock, and saw the contrails. I told the rest of the squadron not to pickle their bombs if they made a pass on us unless it was life and death. At our altitude, the MiG was not that good, and I was pretty sure we could turn away from them with our ordnance. I knew they wouldn't stick around that low with 48 of us wanting to take a crack at them.

While the MiG-15 had demonstrated its superiority over the Thunderjet in air-to-air combat, with an experienced pilot in the cockpit the big Republic fighter could hold its own at lower altitudes against the lesser-trained Communist pilots. By the fall of 1951, the 49th Fighter-Bomber Group was a collection of highly experienced flyers, with most pilots having flown at least 50 combat missions.

> I watched the MiGs above us, and saw them head down. They were coming right after the four of us in the lead, so I very reluctantly called for Purple Flight to salvo their bombs. I broke hard to the right as I saw them set up on their firing pass and they overshot. I reversed the turn to the left, and saw Ken Skeen pulling up high to my left and falling behind as I came around into the MiGs before they could get away to set up another pass. I got off some shots at two of them, and then warned Jim Sprinkle that he had one on his tail. Suddenly the MiG on Jim's tail caught fire and was trailing smoke. Then Ken Skeen called to break right, because I had another one on me. Ken had shot the one on Sprinkle's tail, and he kept at it till it blew up.

While the mission was unsuccessful, inasmuch as the MiGs had managed to catch the 49ers without their Sabre escort, forcing them to jettison all bombs in the melee that resulted, there was an appropriate celebration back at Taegu that night, since Skeen had scored the group's first MiG kill with the F-84. "The next day, I had each airplane in the 9th painted with a red star to celebrate that kill. It became part of the squadron insignia for the rest of the war."

By this stage of the war, sobering knowledge of the enemy dictated Air Force strategy, most particularly use of the two wings of long-range F-84 Thunderjet bombers that had become the most important tactical aircraft of the war besides the F-86 Sabre. The People's Volunteer Army had approximately 60 divisions in Korea, which each required 40 tons of supplies per day for effective operation. Rail traffic had been reduced to a minimum by the air interdiction campaign, though the situation was only maintained by repeated attacks against sections of the rail lines like the group's target on September 19. This meant that 6,000 trucks per day had to deliver their supplies to the front lines for the Communists to maintain their position against the United Nations forces.

The MiGs were tasked with intercepting the fighter-bomber formations when they went north of Pyongyang. When F-84s inbound for a strike passed between Sonchon south of Pyongyang and Sinanju, the Communists would get word of the formation size. The MiGs would climb to their ceiling of 50,000 feet and overfly the F-86 patrols south of the Yalu, to hit the Thunderjets north of Sinanju before they struck their targets, with the objective of making them jettison their bombs and defend themselves against the superior MiGs. While only a few F-84s were shot down, the Communists gained their goal with the first pass when the Thunderjets salvoed their bombs. Combined with the great increase in AA weapons between Sonchon and the Main Line of Resistance, FEAF air intelligence would estimate in December 1951 that only seven percent of bombs dropped were hitting their intended targets.

In October 1951, the Thunderjets were concentrating on enemy truck convoys. With 70 operational F-84s, the 49ers flew 1,727 sorties that month, mostly deep-penetration raids. These attacks were so effective that by mid-November, any strike north of Pyongyang could expect to be intercepted by MiGs, and FEAF was only able to continue such missions due to the increase in defending F-86 squadrons when the 51st Wing transitioned from the Shooting Star to the Sabre. Williams recalled, "We kept our losses down with our tactics. We maintained close formations, and we always turned into the MiGs once they committed to their gunnery run. Our ability to out-turn them at our operational altitude was crucial to survival."

At the end of November, Williams was detached from the 9th Squadron and reported to Misawa AFB in Japan to work with the 116th Wing on the development of procedures and pilot training for what would ultimately be known as Operation *High Tide*.

During 1950, F-84Es had been used to develop air-to-air refueling techniques based on the Royal Air Force's probe-and-drogue system, and two Thunderjets had made a trans-Atlantic crossing from Britain to the United States on September 22, 1950, refueling three times for an elapsed flight time of 10 hours and 2 minutes. Following the successful demonstration, B-29 Superfortresses were modified as tankers and sent to Japan at the end of 1951, where the activated 116th Fighter Group was assigned to learn use of the technique.

"We had 77 pilots qualified for air-to-air refueling by early March, 1952. We wanted to put it to operational use, but the aircraft were diverted to Korea for close support missions in late March and all through April. Finally, we got the go-ahead in May," Williams recalled. On May 28, 1952, 16 F-84s left Misawa, Japan for Itazuke, where they would undertake a strike across the Sea of Japan against Sariwon, in North Korea.

> We carried two 500lb bombs each, and flew directly across the Sea of Japan to the target, which took the Communists by surprise, since we were coming from a direction they weren't expecting. After dropping our ordnance we headed south and refueled from B-29 tankers in the vicinity of Taegu before returning to Japan.

The mission was successful, and three more missions were flown on June 7 and 22, and July 4, with all three squadrons of the 116th Fighter-Bomber Wing participating. Operation *High Tide* had successfully demonstrated that tactical fighter-bombers could be used on very long-range missions.

Following this success, Williams returned to the 49ers and took up his old command. He had flown 300 missions in two years, the equivalent of three complete tours, but had no plans to leave.

> I knew Don Blakeslee, and I knew how he had doctored his books in England during World War II, listing any mission that didn't contact the enemy as a training flight, any mission flown with another unit as orientation, things like that. I did the same thing myself. I know it may not sound particularly right, but the flying we were doing in Korea was very satisfying to me and I didn't want to stop. I'd worked damn hard to finally get into fighters after they made me a recon pilot back in World War II, and I wasn't about to give it up.

Aircraft attrition in early 1952 was so bad that in April 1952 the 49ers only had 41 operational aircraft. Production of the "definitive" F-84G fighter-bomber with a more powerful engine and in-flight refueling capability had been delayed, and the fighter-bomber units fighting the Korean War were hamstrung throughout 1952 by lack of aircraft availability. The situation became so bad that the only way the Air Force could make up the combat attrition was to send 102 old F-84Ds to the far east. The units in Korea did not see this as progress. In order to reduce maintenance problems, the 136th Wing handed over all its remaining F-84Es to the 49th Wing and began operating the D-model Thunderjets. The crisis eased in the summer of 1952, when the 49ers took delivery of their first F-84Gs in July. They were fully equipped with the "definitive" Thunderjet fighter-bomber by October 1952.

Williams was also involved in the final development of Thunderjet tactics in the Korean War, the use of the airplane as a night intruder over the north.

The Douglas B-26 was the workhorse over the north at night, but the Communists were getting used to them, to the speed with which they could make an attack, and the gun crews were starting to hit them more often. We figured that with the Thunderjet, we could hit them fast enough the gun crews would be firing at our engine sound, which would be behind us.

The F-84 was not designed for night operation, and modifications had to be made to the instrument panel lighting. "Even then, it was bright enough that to check the panel you needed to close one eye and put your hand over it before you looked down, so you'd still have night vision." The Thunderjets carried two 1,000lb bombs for these missions, set with proximity fuses so they would explode 50–100 feet above ground. "Our plan was to harass the crews who were working on the trucks, repairing the roads, things like that."

Flying over North Korea at night was far different than what the pilots encountered during daylight. "In the daytime, you could fly over the whole country and never see anything moving, but at night you'd be at 30,000 feet and you could see every major supply route up there completely lit up with truck headlights!" Once they began operations, the mere presence of F-84s over North Korea at night had its own effect on the enemy, as Williams recalled:

When we got on station and they could hear us on the ground, all those lights would go out, and you knew they were reduced to about walking speed, if they could move at all, and they sure weren't getting any repairs made with no light. Our biggest problem would be if a searchlight got lucky and lit up the cockpit. If that happened, it would be pretty easy to fly into a mountainside and never see a thing.

Spotting trains was also easier at night, Williams remembered:

I came up with the tactic of getting down low, where you could see the reflected moonlight on the tracks. When you lost the reflection, you knew there was a train there and you could swing in on an attack before they could run it into a tunnel to hide it. One of our guys found an ammo train as I was coming up to relieve him on station, and he got lucky with both his bombs. I was around 100 miles away when that thing went up and it was the biggest fireworks display I ever saw anywhere!

With the 49ers having demonstrated the success of Thunderjet night operations over North Korea, they were joined by the 474th Wing in this effort in November 1952.

By the end of the Korean War in July 1953, Willie Williams was the high-time Air Force pilot of the war in terms of missions flown and hours logged over the course of nearly three years of combat flying. Looking back on two years of combat in the Thunderjet, Williams liked the airplane.

It was a maintenance hog, and the TBO [Time Between Overhaul] on the engine was horrible until we got to the G-model. Everything you've ever heard about the airplane taking every inch of runway to get airborne is true. But as far as jets were concerned, it was about as rugged as the old Thunderbolt. We got chewed up by flak, and by MiGs, and brought them home with some pretty big holes in them. The ground crews managed to put them back together and they kept on flying. I never knew a pilot who didn't think the Thunderjet would get him home as long as the wing hadn't been shot off.

The RAAF's 77 Squadron, which had been attached to the 35th Fighter-Bomber Wing in the fall of 1950, moved on from flying the Mustang in early 1951. The Australian government wanted the squadron employed "on the front line" and equipped with jets. Squadron personnel were unanimous in recommending that the RAAF obtain F-86 Sabres. However, Sabre production was still catching up with American demand in 1951, and the Australians were informed that the earliest they could obtain Sabres would be 1954. The Australian government decided they would obtain the best British fighter, the Gloster Meteor F.8. The first of four Meteor T.7 two-seat trainers arrived at Iwakuni AFB in Japan in March 1951 for conversion training to commence and 77 Squadron re-equipped with the Meteor F.8 between April and July 1951.

The pilots were not happy to be assigned the Meteor. The aircraft was the first RAF jet fighter, and was even earlier in design than the Lockheed F-80 Shooting Star. The basic airframe had been modernized in 1947 to increase the limiting Mach number, with the fuselage extended 30 inches, providing an additional 50 gallons of fuel. A Martin-Baker Mk. 2 ejection seat was fitted under a more streamlined canopy. The Meteor's handling was vastly improved when the original tail unit was replaced by the modern tail unit of the canceled Gloster E.1/44. With modified engine nacelles that improved airflow enclosing upgraded Derwent 8 centrifugal turbojets, maximum speed was raised to 590mph. By the time the first Meteor F.8 arrived in an RAF squadron in December 1949, the second-generation F-86A Sabre and the MiG-15 were entering squadron service; the first-generation F.8 was obsolescent if not completely obsolete from its first day of service. While the pilots found that the Meteor was more maneuverable than either the F-80 or F-84 below 20,000 feet, they knew they would be at a distinct disadvantage when meeting the MiG-15 at the altitudes combat usually took place at over North Korea.

The squadron was ready to take its Meteors operational at the end of July 1951, and 22 F.8s were deployed to Kimpo air base on July 29, where they were assigned to operate under the control of the USAAF 4th Fighter-Interceptor Wing. They flew their first escort mission for B-29s on August 5. The Meteors first engaged MiG-15s on August 25, with no losses on either side. Four days later, eight Meteors and 16 Sabres fought 12 MiG-15s. One RAAF pilot ejected when his aircraft was shot down, and a second Meteor was badly damaged. On September 4, another Meteor suffered severe damage in a dogfight with

MiGs. The Soviet pilots considered the Meteor their least-dangerous adversary.

On September 26, Flt Lt "Smoky" Dawson made 77 Squadron's first jet victory claim when he damaged a MiG-15 during an escort mission near Anju, North Korea. The next day, Flying Officer Les Reading was credited with damaging another MiG-15 while covering B-29s over Sinanju; the claim was subsequently confirmed as destroyed, making it the squadron's first MiG "kill." 77 Squadron was awarded the Republic of Korea Presidential Unit Citation for "exceptionally meritorious service and heroism" on November 1.

All of the Meteor's shortcomings as an air-superiority fighter were demonstrated on December 1, 1951, in a battle over Sunchon. Twenty Russian-flown MiG-15s from the 176th GvIAP attacked 16 Meteors flying in four 4-plane flights. Twenty MiG-15s were split into a 12-MiG attack force led by six-victory ace Lt Col Sergei Vishnyakov, with a six-MiG covering force led by 13-victory ace Captain Sergei Karamenko. Karamenko later described the action:

I saw the enemy to the left, some ten kilometers distant. Our group began a right turn. We then dived down to attack them, dropping behind the Australians. We closed in on the rear flight of Meteors and I ordered my wingman to "Take the right one – the left is mine!" I opened fire and saw my shell bursts dancing all over the enemy aircraft; its right engine flamed. I noticed the Meteor wingman's tail flying off as the result of a burst by my wingman. We passed over the falling aircraft and went into a steep climb.

As I looked around me, the battle literally surrounded us. Our MiGs were shooting at the Glosters. The Australians spread out and individual aircraft were left on their own. Now there were eight left out of 16 aircraft. I saw a Meteor leaving the battle; we overtook him and attacked. Seeing us, he turned, but too slowly. I managed to frame him in my sights and opened fire. My shells burst on the Meteor's wings and the pilot bailed out. Then I noticed another Meteor hurrying back to his comrades. I was nearly out of ammunition, so I ordered my wingman to attack, but his speed was too high and he overshot. I decided to let the Meteor pilot fly home and tell them about the battle – two kills were enough for me. We turned back and headed for our airfield.

Both sides overestimated the scale of battle and damage inflicted on their opponents. The Russians claimed nine destroyed, though only three Meteors were lost with one pilot killed and two POWs, while the Australians claimed one MiG-15 shot down and another damaged, though Russian sources state that all the MiGs returned to base. Following this, in a controversial decision, the Meteors were withdrawn from combat and assigned as standing alert air defense for Kimpo, since they were considered outclassed by the MiG-15.

In early 1952, 77 Squadron was reassigned to a primary mission of ground attack, since the Meteor was capable of carrying up to 16 rocket projectiles. The Meteor was relatively silent on approach to a target, which allowed the attackers to surprise their targets, while the airplane's excellent low-altitude acceleration and maneuverability gave it good survival chances in the battlefield environment. 77 Squadron continued to operate mainly in the ground-attack role until the end of the war, losing approximately 25 percent of assigned pilots either killed or captured as a result of the dangerous antiaircraft environment in which they flew. Flt Sgt George Hale was credited with a MiG-15 damaged on May 4, 1952 and one destroyed on May 8 during missions near Pyongyang for the final aerial victories credited to the Meteor.

CHAPTER 14

MiG MADNESS

The year 1952 began with the Sabres of the two wings taking on different markings. 51st Fighter Group commander Lt Col George C. Jones believed the unit needed markings that would distinguish the unit's Sabres not only from enemy MiGs but from their rivals in the 4th. Group materiel officer Captain Ed Matczak came up with a design utilizing a 28-inch-wide yellow diagonal stripe on the fuselage, with 36-inch yellow stripes on the wingtips that had 4-inch black borders. Once the stripes were applied, it was realized they were far easier to see than the black-and-white stripes the 4th used, and Fifth Air Force directed both units to utilize the identity stripes. Something else had to be done to distinguish the competitors. The 51st's 25th Squadron had adopted black checkerboards on its vertical fins as a squadron marking, which was soon adopted as a group marking. The 4th would stick with the yellow stripes and black borders, painting a 36-inch yellow stripe across its vertical fins. As Sabres spread to other units later in 1952, the yellow-and-black identity stripes were maintained on all those in Korea.

After the departure of the 64th IAK's two veteran air divisions, the 324th IAD and 303rd IAD, and the PLAAF's 3rd FAD early in 1952, the Communist aviators made no further attempts to achieve air supremacy over North Korea. Like the rest of the war, the air war over North Korea settled into a stalemate that lasted until the final months of the war. The two wings of F-86 Sabres were always outnumbered by the Antung MiGs, but American pilots continued to be better-trained for combat than their opponents, and the US policy of individual replacements rather than unit replacements meant the two units only became more experienced as they remained in Korea. The replacement pilots coming to the units were better-trained for the war they would fight in than their predecessors had been, since the US Air Force's training command was now populated by experienced Korean War combat veterans who passed on to their trainees the lessons they had learned the hard way over MiG Alley.

Frustration over the lack of progress to a conclusion of the war only grew stronger in 1952. For the Air Force, the only "bright light" in the tunnel was the achievements of the Sabre pilots, which were trumpeted by the Air Force publicity machine to the American media. As a later frustrating war would lead to the "body count" being the measure of "success," the "MiG count" became the measure of individual and group success here. Men who went home "aces," or with at least a few victories over the MiGs in their records, would see better promotion possibilities, while the promotion of those in leadership positions was dependent on the record created by those whom they led.

This constant emphasis on the victory count would lead to what came to be known as "MiG Madness," as individual pilots and their leaders concentrated on scores. It would lead to the loss of at least one leading Air Force ace, and to an unofficially sanctioned violation of the Rules of Engagement regarding intrusions in Manchurian air space; when this situation became public, it led to a major shake-up in command and to the termination of promotion prospects for those leaders who had countenanced it. In the case of Colonel Francis Gabreski, his opportunity for promotion past colonel was canceled in the aftermath of the Yalu violations becoming public knowledge that embarrassed the Air Force in 1953, since he had not only allowed such violations but had actively promoted them and participated in them personally.

The veteran Soviet units were replaced by the 97th IAD, which had previously been assigned to the air defense of Moscow, and the 190th IAD joined them. The unit flying personnel arrived in Manchuria in early January 1952, where they took over the aircraft and ground crews of the two IADs they replaced. The two units would not experience the success their predecessors had. This was for two reasons: first, the addition of the Sabres of the 51st Wing meant they had more opponents; when scrambled to attack fighter-bombers, it was more likely the MiGs would become engaged with the stronger and more numerous patrols of Sabres. The second reason was the lack of experience on the part of the

Soviet pilots. The large formations of MiGs worked against them now; the leaders were reluctant to break their formations into smaller, more maneuverable formations, and pilots who lagged from the formations were picked off by their Sabre opponents operating in two- and four-plane units. The pilots lacked experience in high-speed, high-altitude fighter operations, and thus were forced to pay more attention to simply flying their aircraft than keeping watch for their enemies. This problem continued through the spring of 1952.

The 51st Fighter-Interceptor Group flew its first missions on December 1, 1951, operating from Suwon, which was 60 miles south of Kimpo, where the group would remain for the rest of the war. The first victory was scored by 1st Lt Paul E. Roach, who bagged a MiG on December 2. The 4th Wing remained the primary MiG killers, scoring nine MiGs in the first week of December. With Colonel Gabreski as wing commander and his old 56th Fighter Group fellow ace Lt Col Walker "Bud" Mahurin as deputy wing commander, the two aces fostered the kind of morale that had been common in "Zemke's Wolfpack." The 51st Fighter Group commander Lt Col George Jones, who had seen combat in the Southwest Pacific flying P-47s, and 15-victory World War II ace Major William T. "Bill" Whisner, Jr. commanding the 25th Fighter Squadron brought a similar World War II "can-do" attitude.

The 4th's Major George A. Davis, Jr., who had scored three Tu-2s and a MiG-15 shot down in combat with the PLAAF on November 3, claimed two more victories on December 5. Leading the 334th to cover an attack by F-84s, he spotted two MiG-15s over Sinanju at 1555 hours. He came up on the number two MiG and opened fire. As the enemy jet blew up, its pilot, Senior Lieutenant Anatoly I. Baturov of the 18th GvIAP, ejected. Unfortunately they were at low altitude, and Baturov's parachute did not deploy in time. Flying back to Kimpo, Davis spotted a MiG chasing another F-86, and claimed it shot down, with the pilot also ejecting, though this claim is not backed by Russian loss records, as is Baturov. In addition to Davis' claimed victories, "Bones" Marshall of the 335th Squadron shot down the MiG flown by the 196th regiment's Senior Lieutenant Aleksandr Ryzhkov, who was wounded and crashed to his death. However, the F-84s still took losses when Lt Col Sergei Vishnyakov, CO of the 176th GvIAP, shot down the F-84E flown by 1st Lt Hugh Larkin, who was listed MIA, while Captain Vasily Stepanov of the 18th GvIAP shot down 1st Lt Horace Carman, who became a POW.

The biggest battle of the last month of 1951 occurred on December 13, when some 150 MiGs challenged the 4th's morning and afternoon sweeps over Sinanju. About noon, Davis' 334th Squadron ran across MiGs from the 18th GvIAP; in a hard-fought battle, Davis claimed two MiGs, though Soviet loss records only confirm the loss of Senior Lieutenant I. A. Gorsky. That afternoon the 334th and the 336th squadrons flew a second sweep. At 1552 hours, Davis spotted a large gaggle of MiG-15s; these were flown by pilots from the Chinese 40th Fighter Air Regiment of the newly arrived 4th FAD, and most of the pilots were novices. The Sabres quickly claimed ten of them, including two by Davis. The PLAAF admitted the loss of seven, with two heavily damaged that were later repaired. The Chinese records confirm the two victories claimed by Davis, shot down between 1552 and 1553 hours.

Moments later, MiGs from the 18th GvIAP and the 176th GvIAP arrived on the scene. The 18th's Captain Aleksey Kaliuzhny shot up the F-86A flown by 1st Lt Ken Chandler, who later reported he thought his engine was damaged by debris from the Chinese-flown MiG he was shooting at after he was forced to bail out over Cho-do Island and be rescued. Captain Pavel S. Milaushkin, an ace of the 176th, shot down one of Davis' 334th Squadron pilots, 1st Lt Charles D. Hogue, who was listed MIA. Short of fuel, the Sabres withdrew, having shot down eight MiGs according to Soviet and Chinese records, for an admitted loss of two.

Davis' claim of four shot down for the day was confirmed by Fifth Air Force, making him officially the top-scoring American pilot of the Korean War to date, with 12 credited victories, the first American pilot to have a double-digit score. Scoring four victories in a day was not unheard-of during World War II, but it was highly unusual in Korea. This was due to the high-speed nature of jet combat, which was so fast and so violent that a pilot was lucky to line up on one opponent long enough to score. Davis had done so twice, and was the only American pilot to score four in a fight in Korea other than Navy Lt E. Royce Williams, whose amazing score of four Soviet MiG-15s shot down on November 18, 1952 in a 7:1 fight while flying an F9F-5 Panther was never acknowledged until the Russians published the names of the four pilots shot down and killed following the end of the Cold War in 1992.

As the new year began, maintenance problems and a lack of spare parts contributed to high out-of-commission rates for the Sabres, which rose to an amazing rate of 45 percent in January 1952. Fortunately, this was the worst point of this problem during the war. With two wings now flying Sabres on almost daily combat missions, the demand for external drop-tanks soared. By the end of January 1952 the stockpile of tanks was almost exhausted and through February and early March pilots often had to fly missions carrying only one tank, which cut the time that could be spent in MiG Alley to less than ten minutes. Eventually, drop-tank production in the US would be supplemented by tanks made in Japan known as "Misawa tanks." The problem would never really go away as operations only increased.

It became common for pilots to extend their time by flying past "bingo" fuel, then climbing to 35–40,000 feet where they would shut down their engine and glide back to South Korea. Sabres from the 51st Wing would often dead-stick into Kimpo for refueling before flying home to Suwon. The F-86 could glide 69 miles from an altitude of 30,000 feet and more from 40,000. The practice became so widespread that one 4th Group squadron commander noted his pilots made up to a dozen dead-stick landings each week in 1951 and 1952. The senior squadron, group and wing leaders did not punish pilots for flying past bingo fuel, no matter the fact it was a violation of official Air Force policy to do such a thing. Pilots who did this were celebrated by their commanders, with multiple such returns in their record recorded as a sign they were an aggressive fighter pilot who pushed the flight envelope. Promotions came to those who engaged in this kind of risky behavior, since they were the ones who were "defeating Communism" in an otherwise forgotten war.

Coming back out of fuel or unable to re-start one's engine could lead to some hairy events at busy Kimpo airfield. Captain Karl Dittmer of the 335th Squadron recalled one memorable event in 1952 when he was pulling duty at the mobile control unit at the north end of Kimpo's airstrip. Traffic from a returning mission had pretty well quit when he heard a pilot call he was 30 miles out at 15,000 feet, flamed out, and cleared him to land. "Then I saw three Marine Corsairs start to taxi onto the main runway. I called Kimpo Tower to get them to stop, that we had a flamed-out F-86 coming in, but they continued onto the runway despite my repeated call." The three Corsairs proceeded to go through their pre-flight checks as Dittmer screamed at the tower to stop the takeoff. The leader took his time checking his magnetos, then added power and accelerated down the runway. Once he was close to take off, the number two Corsair finished his mag check and accelerated down the runway. "Number two had just taken off and number three was ready to go when the flamed-out Sabre swooshed past him and set down on the runway ahead of him. Then, as if nothing had happened, he accelerated down the runway past the stopped Sabre and took off."

In February, the use of "MiG trains" by the newly arrived Russian units increased. This was due to the inexperience of the newly arrived pilots. They would commonly form up over Manchuria, with those from Antung crossing south over Sinanju, while those operating from Tatung-kao would enter North Korea over the Suiho Reservoir. These formations frequently contained as many as 100 MiGs. Flying above 45,000 feet where they were untouchable by the Sabres, they would fly as far south as Pyongyang before turning back north. Despite their growing numbers, the Sabre pilots noted that their opponents often demonstrated little desire to engage in combat.

A competition grew between the two American Sabre units. In January 1952, the 51st claimed 27 victories while the 4th only claimed five. This was undoubtedly due to the fact the 51st was flying new F-86Es with improved flight controls and a new radar-ranging fire-control system, while the 4th continued on with its increasingly weary F-86A Sabres. While maintenance and spares problems continued to plague the two American units, fewer missions were flown in February, and only seven MiGs were credited to the 4th and ten to the 51st. These successes were overshadowed by the loss of the top Sabre ace of the war at that time, Major George A. Davis, Jr., on February 10, 1952. 1st Lt Alfred W. Dymock, who flew as element lead with Davis on some missions, later recalled his friend's state of mind at that time. "George's main goal in life was to shoot down MiGs. He was dwelling on his score a lot, about how he hadn't scored since December." Davis was recalled by others as being more willing to take risks than other pilots in the squadron, which was considered remarkable given his status as a World War II ace and an older pilot. "Bones" Marshall remembered him as "the best deflection shooter in the air force." Dymock and 1st Lt Charlie Mitson, who had flown with Davis before the war as well as in the 4th, both recalled that after the four-victory mission of December 13, Davis became increasingly contemptuous of the enemy, saying they were nowhere as good as the Japanese pilots he had flown against in New Guinea. "He'd come to believe no MiG pilot could shoot him down," Mitson remembered.

"It wasn't a good attitude, because there were some good pilots on the other side." Some in the squadron compared Davis with the impetuous ace Frank Luke of World War I fame. Other pilots in the squadron took quiet bets on when Davis would "get himself killed."

On February 10, 1952, Davis led 18 334th Squadron F-86s as screen for an attack on Kuni-ri by Thunderjets from the 49ers. With no enemy aircraft in sight, he broke formation and took his flight up to the Yalu, looking for action. The decision was remarkable, since he was the mission commander responsible for the screen. It is even more remarkable when put in the context of the time – F-86s did not operate in MiG Alley in formations of less than three flights, since the MiG formations were so large they could overwhelm their American opponents with sheer numbers. Just before entering MiG Alley, Davis' element leader reported his oxygen system had failed and he aborted with his wingman, leaving Davis with only his wingman, 1st Lt William W. Littlefield, as he flew into the area most likely to have MiGs in it.

Moments after his formation was halved, Littlefield later remembered they spotted five MiGs milling about north of the Yalu. Davis led them around and spotted a formation of ten MiG-15s ahead and below at 32,000 feet. On that day, the weather was such that the MiGs at high altitude were not leaving contrails, which meant they might not have spotted all the MiGs in the vicinity. Despite being outnumbered 10:1, Davis bounced the MiGs and flew directly into the enemy formation as he opened fire. The MiGs immediately broke and scattered, but one hesitated just long enough for Davis to pounce and score victory number 13. Davis had the speed to continue his dive and get away from the enemy, but he chose instead to rack around after another MiG, sacrificing speed and energy in the turn. He got behind what would become his 14th and final victory and opened fire in a steep bank, hitting the MiG in its wingroot and engine. It caught fire and went down while Davis continued his turn, bleeding off more energy and speed, as he sought a third victory. As he did, an unseen MiG closed on his tail and opened fire. Littlefield saw cannon shells rip the Sabre just below the cockpit canopy; they were almost certain to have killed him. The Sabre spun out of control and fell from 32,000 feet to crash in the mountains below as Littlefield followed him down, calling for help.

When he returned to Kimpo, Littlefield was mercilessly grilled by the group leadership, who intimated they believed Davis had been lost due to Littlefield's failure to provide proper cover. "They were looking for a scapegoat since George was a national hero," Dymock later commented. According to others in the unit, Littlefield was shattered by the incident and sick at heart that he might have failed his leader. "It took him months to recover," said Mitson.

It took Fifth Air Force two days before they admitted the loss of Davis. Of the three MiGs claimed by US pilots the morning of his loss, two were officially credited to him despite the lack of any evidence that they were in fact the MiGs Littlefield claimed his leader shot down, and the fact that two of the claims – for "damaged" – were made by Major Donald D. Rodewald and his wingman, 1st Lt James R. Ross, of the 51st Wing's 25th Squadron. According to the 25th FIS squadron history, Rodewald claimed a "probable" at 0800 hours and Ross a "damaged" at 0810 hours, 28 and 18 minutes respectively before the time Davis initiated his attack at 0828 hours after breaking away from his squadron at 0803 hours.

George Davis, the only American ace to be killed in combat in Korea, was posthumously promoted to lieutenant colonel and was awarded the Medal of Honor. The citation reads in part:

> Major Davis' bold attack completely disrupted the enemy formation, permitting the friendly fighter-bombers to successfully complete their interdiction mission. Major Davis, by his indomitable fighting spirit, heroic aggressiveness, and superb courage in engaging the enemy against formidable odds, exemplified valor at its highest.

This part of the citation is undoubtedly true, since the Chinese and Russian MiG formations never made it far enough south to break up the Thunderjet attack that day.

Fellow ace and 336th Squadron commander Major Dick Creighton said of Davis, "He had more guts than the law allows."

When it was announced that the leading American ace had been lost in combat, the Chinese examined their records and determined that 36 MiG-15s from the 4th Fighter Aviation Division had been involved in the fight in which Davis was killed. Zhang Jihui, a flight leader in the 12th FAR, reported after the battle that while the MiGs were en route to intercept Davis' group, he and his wingman became separated from the main formation. As they tried to rejoin the formation, he spotted eight F-86s in the area between Taechon and Chongye at 0740 hours. The two then got on the tails of two Sabres and opened fire. Zhang claimed that he shot down both Sabres, but other Sabres had shot down his MiG, forcing him to bail out, and killing his wingman. In the absence of gun camera film, the 4th FAD sent out two search teams on February 16 and 18, which found wreckage of an F-86E, in addition to Davis' body and personal effects. They also determined the crash site was 500 meters from where Zhang had bailed out, and that Zhang's 12th Regiment was the only unit operating near the area at the time. Additional testimony was taken from Chinese troops on the ground about what they saw of the combat above. As a result, Zhang was credited by the PLAAF with shooting down Davis, whose dog tag is presently on display at the Memorial of the War to Resist US Aggression and Aid Korea in Dandong, China. A MiG-15 in Zhang's Korean War markings is displayed at the entrance of the museum.

Doubts about Zhang's claim were raised after the Chinese announcement, due to Littlefield's recollection of the event being inconsistent with Zhang's account. The lack of gun-camera footage meant Zhang's claim hinged on his own recollection of the event. Just to make things more complicated, following the end of the Cold War when Soviet records were opened to researchers, the claim was made that Davis was actually shot down by Senior Lieutenant Mikhail Akimovich Averin of the 148th GvIAP. According to testimony at the time from the pilots of the Soviet 64th IAK, both Zhang and his wingman were probably shot down by Davis, who was in turn surprised and shot down by Averin scrambling to save the Chinese MiGs. Lt Gen Georgi Lobov, commander of the 64th IAK, also noted in his memoir that Davis was killed by a Soviet pilot.

During the war, Zhang became a household name in China. His victory is one of the few proud moments in the PLAAF's underwhelming performance in Korea and is now a "fact of state" in China. He was awarded the title "Combat Hero, 1st Class" for his accomplishment.

Ten days after Davis' loss, on February 20, Gabreski, "Bud" Mahurin, and "Bill" Whisner, Jr. were involved in the first mission in which an F-86 pilot deliberately turned off his IFF (Identification Friend or Foe) equipment and crossed into Manchurian air space on the other side of the Yalu. At the time, Gabreski and Whisner were each credited with four MiGs destroyed. Catching a flight of MiGs south of the river,

Gabreski attacked and severely damaged one that broke away and fled back across the Yalu into China. With his own airplane damaged in the fight, Gabreski broke off and returned to Suwon, where he claimed the MiG as a "probable."

When Gabreski broke off, Whisner switched off his IFF and trailed the enemy fighter into Manchuria to confirm Gabreski's kill, where he finished off the damaged MiG and returned to confirm the kill for Gabreski, which would give Gabreski his fifth victory. Gabreski angrily ordered Whisner to change his report, confirming his role in the kill, which Whisner refused to do. Later, Gabreski recanted his anger and the report was rewritten to have the two men share the claim. On February 23, Whisner shot down his fifth MiG to become the first pilot in the 51st ranked an ace.

In February, 17 MiGs were claimed by Sabre pilots against the loss of two F-86s. In March, the 4th Wing received an upgrade when 60 F-86Es built in Canada by Canadair arrived in Korea, which allowed the wing to retire most of the war-weary F-86As and even the competition with the 51st. The pilots of the two wings claimed 37 MiGs in March and 44 in April, for a loss of six Sabres during the two months. By the end of April the Air Force was able to celebrate 12 "MiG aces," including Col Francis Gabreski, who claimed his fifth MiG on April 1, and Iven C. Kincheloe, Jr., now a captain, who claimed number five on April 6. By this point in the war, the fights over MiG Alley were the only place Americans seemed to be winning over the Communist enemy, and the exploits of the Sabre pilots filled the papers back home, as had the exploits of their forebears 35 years earlier in World War I when the military needed to find "winners" in an otherwise-fruitless struggle.

Beginning in March, the new Soviet pilots began to become more aggressive as they felt themselves experienced enough to confront the Sabres. Over the course of the month, the Soviets engaged in 89 air combats. Captain Vladimir Zabelin of the 821st IAP, who would become the most successful Soviet pilot in the 1952–53 fighting with an eventual score of nine, was credited with his first victory on March 16. He hit the Sabre he claimed from close range with repeated bursts that resulted in the American fighter emitting smoke as it headed down, though the USAF listed no losses that day. Five days later, future ace Captain Anatoly Bashman of the 148th GvIAP scored the first of his five credited victories. Over the course of March, the pilots of the 97th and

190th IADs were credited with 43 Sabres and four F-80s shot down, though few of these claims can be matched to American losses. Their American opponents claimed 39 MiGs shot down, while the 64th IAK recorded only 16 MiGs and four pilots lost, with 43 MiGs returning to their bases damaged.

Captain Zabelin scored his second Sabre victory on April 2 when he spotted an enemy fighter, which had crossed the Yalu, attacking another MiG with its landing gear extended on final approach in the landing pattern at Antung. He closed on the Sabre and hit it solidly. The 51st Group F-86E managed to get back across the Yalu before it crashed near Dadonggang in North Korea at 1710 hours. By April 12, Zabelin had claimed two more Sabres, while Captain Bashman was credited with his fifth victory on that date. The next day, Zabelin became the first of the new pilots to reach five victories when he shot down another 51st Group F-86E which was listed as missing by the Americans.

335th Squadron commander Major "Bones" Marshall fought what he later considered "the battle of my life" in March. As he recalled, "We flew into MiG Alley and someone in one of the other squadrons called out that 'Casey Jones' was aboard. There he was, a single contrail sitting high above all the other MiG formations." Sabre pilots had given the name "Casey Jones" to what was believed to be the MiG tactical commander who directed all the "bandit trains" out of Antung; most pilots were convinced "Casey" was a Russian. "He flew in a single MiG, well above all the MiG flights, directing the air battle. With him aboard we knew we could expect a hell of an air battle."

At this point in the air war, the MiG pilots were not as aggressive as they had been in 1951, preferring to remain in their large formations at high altitude. With an airborne fighter director, smaller formations of MiGs could be directed to drop out of the formation when there was a favorable set-up. Marshall explained:

With this direct control, the MiGs put emphasis on coordinated high-side attacks, in conjunction with their normal 6 o'clock passes. While you were turning into the pair making the high-angle attack, two more were coming up your tailpipe. They were attacking in groups of four to six aircraft, which was more than the two-ship F-86 element could cope with. Interestingly enough, even with these tactics, we were still maintaining the large kill ratio that we'd had from the beginning. But now we were having to do a hell of a lot more fighting than in the past.

Marshall counted over 70 contrails above his formation. Suddenly he heard calls that they were coming down.

We had just rolled out from breaking into two attacking MiGs, when almost immediately my cockpit was surrounded by a hail of bright tracers that looked the size of oranges as they went by! They were from the cannons of a MiG on my tail! My wingman had said nothing. I jerked the stick back so hard that I easily exceeded the Sabre's "G" limit. The MiG went one direction and my wingman the other. I had lost them both.

Now separated and alone, Marshall was the kind of victim "Casey Jones" was known to look for.

Before I could take a breath, I was again the target of a stream of tracers, but they were a lot closer this time. There was a second MiG sitting right on my tail! Again, I slammed the stick back, trying to "split S" out of there. I did it so hard, it produced spectacular results. My Sabre snap rolled and I was in an inverted spin with zero speed. This was a great evasive maneuver, I thought. No attacker could have stayed with me through that.

Time seemed to stand still as Marshall entered what Sabre ace Ralph Parr once described as "the fifth level of the brain," where fear is pumping adrenaline so fast the mind enters what seems like another dimension where time has no meaning.

When I looked out my canopy, there was a MiG! We were both spinning together, canopy to canopy. We had ended up in a flat spin, with very little speed, in a nose-up attitude, with his nose almost pointing at me. I expected him to start firing at any moment.

Marshall executed a rapid spin recovery, only to realize the enemy pilot had done the same.

"He was still with me, so I again slammed the sloppy stick to one side, kicking the rudders as hard as I could. It worked! I was off in another spin, slower but more controllable this time." Marshall glanced outside. "The impossible had happened! There was the MiG, also spinning down! We were fast losing too much altitude, so I again made a recovery." Again, the MiG recovered right beside Marshall, except that this time he had ended up directly in front of Marshall's Sabre. "It was a simple task to open fire. I must have hit something vital as the MiG suddenly caught fire and exploded."

When told back at base by another pilot that the MiG that had attacked him had dropped on his tail alone from higher altitude, Marshall was convinced he had fought "Casey Jones" himself, who was known to make such attacks on lone Sabres.

It was just Lady Luck riding with me, that he ended up in the dead center of my gunsight. Otherwise, I don't know. That fight had probably lasted little more than five minutes, but it seemed like a lifetime. I had been shot at twice, exceeded the airplane's "G" limits with my maneuvers, had snap-rolled and spun twice. All the time being together in formation with an enemy aircraft, until I recovered in a position to shoot him out of the sky. What an air battle! I half regretted the loss of such a great pilot, even though he was on the other side. I would have loved to have sat down for a beer or vodka at the O-club with that guy, trading fighter pilot stories together.

Beginning in March 1952, the practice of "crossing the Yalu" became common as the Sabre pilots and their leaders became increasingly frustrated that their enemy was accorded the privilege of a sanctuary to take off and form up before entering a fight. Missions known by the clandestine code words "Maple Special" were deliberately flown to catch the MiGs at takeoff and landing at Antung, their most vulnerable moments. More than one gun-camera film supposedly exists that shows MiGs with their landing gear down approaching an airfield, with numerous parked fighters clearly visible.

Among Sabre pilots known to have crossed the Yalu were Gabreski, Lt Col George Jones, Major William T. Whisner, Jr. and Col "Bud" Mahurin. Twenty-six of the 39 American jet aces admitted after the war that they crossed the Yalu, including the three leading aces, Joseph

McConnell, Jr. (16), James Jabara (15) and Manuel Fernandez, Jr. (14). Eight of the 11 pilots who scored ten or more kills admitted after the war that they had gone into Manchuria. Air Force General John Roberts remarked after the war, "There were a lot of airplanes shot down in Korea by guys who did not necessarily play by the rules." In the spring of 1953, as the air war heated up, Fifth Air Force commander General Glenn Barcus officially gave pilots a "fig leaf" with which to cover such actions when he approved a policy of "hot pursuit" into Manchuria of airplanes that were already "heavily damaged." He was quoted officially telling pilots in a briefing, "Screw the Yalu!"

The pilots were encouraged in this incredibly provocative action by the lax attitude of senior leaders, who they rightly expected would wink at border violations. After watching two F-86 pilots twice circle a Chinese airfield 100 miles inside Manchuria on a recording from the Cho-do radar control site, General Frank Everest, commander of Fifth Air Force between June 1951 and May 1952, angrily stormed into the post-flight debrief of the two pilots and threatened them with court-martial. He then stomped back out of the room, slamming the door behind him for emphasis. Moments later, the door opened and Everest poked his head back in, saying "And furthermore, if you are going to violate the Manchurian border, for God's sake turn off the damn IFF!"

Not only did commanders permit and encourage such border violations, but many engaged in the practice themselves. 2nd Lt Michael DeArmond, a young F-86 pilot in the 51st Wing, recalled his squadron commander stating before a mission that if any pilot was caught north of the border, he would be subject to a court-martial. During the mission, the commander led four Sabres deep into Manchuria and shot down a MiG. On return to Suwon, he asked DeArmond where the shootdown had occurred, to which DeArmond answered, "Somewhere around the mouth of the Yalu." As he recalled, "The colonel responded, 'Son, you have a bright future in the Air Force.'"

Francis Gabreski was perhaps the most senior officer to actively violate the rule against crossing the Yalu. On one mission, he chased a MiG over the main runway at Antung and shot it down, then executed a victory roll over the airfield. When queried by Col David Jones, then a Fifth Air Force staff officer and later Air Force chief of staff, Gabreski admitted that the 51st Wing frequently crossed into China. When Jones expressed dismay, Gabreski suggested he was free to fly to the

Yalu and write down tail numbers, declaring that "If the Fifth Air Force wants 'to kick ass' for the border violations, they should start with my own." Nothing was done, but Gabreski's career stalled at colonel and he retired from the Air Force five years later.

Colonel Harrison Thyng, who led the 4th Wing at the time, ordered future RAF Air Marshal Sir John M. Nicholls KCB CBE DFC AFC, then a flight lieutenant exchange pilot in the 335th Squadron, to buzz Antung airfield's main runway at an altitude of 10–15 feet at Mach 0.9, "to stir them up," then shot down a MiG-15 that took off in reaction just after it retracted its gear. Lt Gen Charles Cleveland, then a first lieutenant in the 335th, was in a flight led by Thyng that resulted in the colonel shooting down his fourth MiG north of Mukden, nearly 100 miles inside Manchuria, although the submitted victory claim placed the location at the mouth of the Yalu River. After he scored his fifth credited victory on May 20, 1952 and became the 16th USAF jet ace of the war, pilots recalled the 4th's wing commander shooting down "at least five more" MiGs, which he credited to his wingmen before he completed his tour in October.

The 51st's 1st Lt Bill Ginther returned to Suwon in May with gun-camera film that showed a MiG-15 with its landing gear extended, with other enemy planes plainly visible in the background, parked on the tarmac of Antung airfield. Understandably, this type of incriminating evidence tended to get "lost" or destroyed; Ginther personally burned his after a one-time-only "private screening" for other inductees to the "Maple Special Club."

One thing the Sabre pilots didn't do was strafe MiGs on the ground, in recognition of the example that had been made of the two unlucky 51st Group F-80 pilots who were court-martialed following a mission in which they became lost and shot up a Soviet airfield in October 1950. Soviet General Georgi Lobov, commander of the 64th IAK, stated after the end of the Cold War that "Americans were constantly crossing the border." Twenty-six MiGs were lost over their own airfields during the first six months of 1952.

At the end of April, General Lobov ordered his pilots to stop flying in regimental-size formations. The Soviet pilots began flying in four- or six-plane formations, maintaining radio silence while they were guided by ground control in a search for fighter-bomber formations in MiG Alley. On April 30, a flight of six MiGs from the 16th IAP was guided onto a formation of F-80s that was attacking ground targets north of the Chongchon River. Captain Boytsov spotted what he identified as three groups of four Shooting Stars near Anju. When the MiGs attacked, the fighter-bombers went into a defensive Lufbery, but Captain Petr Minervin still managed to claim two in separate attacks, while Major Tokarev also claimed two and Boytsov claimed one. Two of the American pilots were seen to eject and the Shooting Star formation broke up as the Americans headed south in disarray. The combat had taken place at low altitude, and the MiGs were so short of fuel afterwards that Boytsov and his wingman were forced to make an emergency landing at Sinuiju to refuel before returning to Antung that evening. All six pilots were awarded the Order of the Red Banner for the action. The 8th Fighter-Bomber Wing recorded the loss of three F-80Cs, with several others returning heavily damaged.

From then on, the MiGs operated in smaller units throughout the rest of 1952, which led to numerous air battles. By the fall, the Americans had credited 16 pilots as aces over the previous year, while the Soviets listed ten over the summer.

The Sabre pilots didn't need to cross the Yalu to see that the Communists were assembling a large force of MiG-15s on their Manchurian fields. In addition to the Soviet 64th IAK, the PLAAF sent three more fighter aviation divisions to Manchuria that spring. On April 13, American reconnaissance missions recorded between 400 and 500 MiG-15s parked just at Antung airfield.

With the Communists using effective radar control to allow the MiGs to evade Sabre patrols and go after the vulnerable fighter-bombers, Fifth Air Force established a radar direction center on Cho-do Island off the mouth of the Yalu in the Yellow Sea in April that began operations in May, with radar coverage extended all the way to the Yalu. SA-16 Albatross rescue amphibians were also based on the island, as well as H-5 and H-19 helicopters. Although Cho-do was not fully operational in May, the American controllers were able to assist the Sabres in shooting down six of the 27 MiGs claimed destroyed that month. However, these victories came at a cost: Fifth Air Force recorded the loss of an F-51, three F-84s, and five F-86s in May, all shot down by MiGs. A sixth important F-86 loss was scored by enemy antiaircraft fire.

"Bud" Mahurin had transferred back to the 4th from the 51st in March, to become 4th Fighter Group commander under wing commander Colonel Thyng. During his two months in that position, he flew with

Captain James Horowitz frequently, and would be the model for the character of Colonel Monk Moncavage in *The Hunters*. On May 13, 1952, while on an experimental fighter-bomber mission, Mahurin was hit by North Korean ground fire while strafing a truck. He broke his arm in the crash-landing and was captured by the North Koreans. During 16 months as a POW, he was tortured by his North Korean captors, fed only enough to keep him alive and forced to endure sub-freezing conditions with minimal clothing, while undergoing all-night interrogations in which he was repeatedly threatened with execution if he failed to answer questions. The Communists' goal was to get him to sign a confession that he had engaged in "germ warfare," their latest charge against UN forces. After surviving weeks of this, he believed he was losing control and attempted suicide, barely surviving a serious blood loss before he was discovered.

The Chinese then took control of Mahurin and attempted to gain his cooperation with better treatment. At last, Mahurin agreed to write and sign a confession. It was full of inaccuracies and implausible information, in an attempt to let any Western reader know it was forced. Nevertheless, Mahurin was condemned by Senator Richard S. Russell, Jr. and others due to the confession after he was released two months after the armistice in July 1953. His experience led to a modification of the official code of conduct that had been adopted after the war; a POW would be allowed to write such a fake confession when he believed he had come to the end of his ability to resist.

Mahurin was replaced as group commander by Lt Col Royal N. Baker, who had flown with Thyng in the 31st Fighter Group in North Africa, where he had scored 3.5 victories against the Luftwaffe flying Spitfires with the 308th Squadron. Baker had flown a second World War II tour, commanding a Thunderbolt fighter-bomber squadron in the ETO, and was another group commander who believed in leadership by example. By the time he left Korea nine months later, his score of 13 would put him one shy of George Davis' record.

In June, "Gabby" Gabreski finished his tour, and was replaced as the 51st's wing commander by Col John Mitchell. Mitchell had led the mission that intercepted and killed Japanese Admiral Yamamoto on April 18, 1943. He would add four MiGs to his World War II score of 11 to become a triple ace.

CHAPTER 15

STALEMATE

At about the same time that Gabreski went home, the 51st Wing received reinforcement when Fifth Air Force commander General Everest decided to take the F-51-equipped 39th Fighter-Bomber Squadron and assign it to the 51st. This coincided with the arrival of the first new F-86F Sabres in Japan, and the new Sabre squadron found itself the proud operators of the best Sabre of all, which would give the pilots a great advantage when they entered combat.

Based on Korean combat experience, the F-86F would solidify the Sabre's reputation as the last of the great dogfighters. While the new model weighed the same as the F-86E, it was powered by the more powerful J47-GE-27, providing 200lb more thrust than the J47-GE-13 in the F-86E, giving it a top speed of 695mph and a maximum Mach 1.05 in a dive. Additionally, it could carry drop tanks filled with 200 gallons of fuel as opposed to the 120-gallon tanks the earlier Sabres used; this doubled the time the new fighter could spend in MiG Alley.

What really changed the F-86F was its modified wing. North American had experimented with an F-86E by closing the slats to give a higher top speed. Additionally, the wing's leading edge was changed to increase chord 6 inches at the fuselage and 3 inches at the tip. The "6-3" wing increased wing area from 288 square feet to 302 square feet, which improved high-altitude performance, giving the Sabre a maximum ceiling of 55,000 feet and finally ending the MiG-15's altitude advantage. As more F-86Fs appeared in theater through the fall, the stage would be set for a major change in the air war. In the meantime, pilots in F-86Es continued to fight the MiGs over North Korea.

In late July 1952, the pilots of the 190th Air Division were replaced by the 216th IAD, with the 518th and 878th IAPs based at Tatung-kao and the 676th at nearby Dapu. Three weeks later, the 32nd IAD relieved the 97th Air Division, basing the 224th, 525th, and 913th IAPs at Anshan airfield, where they joined the three regiments of the 133rd IAD at Antung main airfield. Significantly, the assignment of the 32nd IAD was to provide air defense over the Antung airfield complexes to protect the MiGs from Sabres crossing the Yalu. Over the course of August, these newly arrived MiG pilots would claim 16 Sabres shot down while admitting the loss of 18 MiGs and seven pilots, with a further 33 damaged.

On May 30, 1952, 25-year-old 2nd Lt Cecil G. Foster arrived at Suwon to join the 51st Fighter Wing, where he was assigned to the 16th Fighter-Interceptor Squadron, commanded by Major Edwin L. "Ed" Heller, a 5.5-victory World War II ace who had flown two tours with the 352nd Fighter Group in the European Theater during which he'd destroyed a further 14 aircraft and 14 locomotives by strafing. The name on his Sabre, "HELL-ER BUST," which he had painted on his P-51s in World War II, was an indication of his attitude toward aerial combat. Cecil Foster had joined the Army in 1943 and served in Europe, returning after the war to attend college on the G.I. Bill and then joining the Air Force in 1949. After completing flight training in 1951 and being assigned to fly the F-86, he considered himself fortunate to have been given advance training at Nellis AFB by recently returned Korean War combat veterans. Foster's opponents would be the newly arrived Soviet pilots as well as Chinese pilots of the PLAAF.

Assigned by Major Heller to "D" Flight, Foster flew 35 missions that summer as a wingman, demonstrating sufficient promise to be checked out as an element leader in early September shortly after his promotion to first lieutenant. On September 7, he was enjoying a rare day off operations and decided to take his camera to the flight line to photograph the group's Sabres as they returned from a maximum effort mission.

I wanted to watch for planes with "black noses" from the gunsmoke they emitted when their .50-caliber guns were fired in combat. Arriving early, I entered our operations building and saw Lieutenant Sands, our A Flight commander, briefing three newly assigned pilots on combat theater procedures. Captain Charles T. Weaver, our operations officer, was behind the counter when the field telephone from Headquarters jangled. I overheard him confirm we had four in-commission Sabres available.

Weaver asked Sands if he could man the four alert flight Sabres. When Sands replied that he didn't have a qualified element leader available, Foster volunteered. Weaver demurred because Foster had the day off, but that changed when a second phone call directed him to man the alert flight as quickly as possible.

Now assigned to the mission, Foster sprinted to the equipment building to don flight gear.

Captain Weaver yelled "Scramble!" and activity exploded! I rapidly donned my flying suit and boots, grabbed my helmet and parachute, and I was given an airplane number as I ran for the revetments. Another new pilot followed me up the side of my Sabre and straddled the nose backwards. He then reached into the cockpit and started my engine as I was strapping in while aided by a crew chief. Two other pilots performed my exterior pre-flight check for me, gave the OK signal, and off I went!

Foster took off behind Sands, who immediately aborted when he found his gear wouldn't retract. "This left me airborne leading two new pilots whom I had never met to accomplish an entirely unplanned mission." Foster received a quick radio briefing that he was to cover the withdrawal of the main force, which was low on fuel with many MiGs airborne. Over Cho-do Island, he released one of the two accompanying pilots and flew into MiG Alley with 2nd Lt Les Erickson flying wing.

As we approached the Yalu at 38,000 feet, I spotted eight MiGs flying two abreast with elements in trail. We jettisoned our drop tanks and bounced them from their seven o'clock position. As I closed to 2,000 feet, Les called a second flight of eight MiGs attacking at our six o'clock! The first MiG flight began a left climbing turn to evade. I fired a quick burst at one and then broke left. This caused the second MiG flight to overshoot. I reversed and rolled back into the stern position on the second flight. As I was positioning on their number seven man, they also climbed rapidly and continued a left turn. Les then called out another flight of eight MiGs lining up on our stern to fire at us! Meanwhile, I fired a long burst into the seventh MiG-15 of flight number two. We broke hard left and again were able to reverse and roll into the stern position of the third flight. By now, we had three flights of 24 MiGs, as well as our two F-86s, in a high-altitude Lufberry! I felt we had the advantage because we could shoot at anybody, but they had to select the right plane before they fired!

Foster and Erickson continued dueling the MiGs over the next 45 minutes. "We took turns covering and shooting whenever we could. We alternated between being the hunter and the target!" Suddenly, Erickson called out a single MiG to the right.

I made a quick pull up and roll to the right, ending a thousand feet dead astern of the MiG. I fired my remaining ammunition in several bursts. Les and I both saw sparkles on the MiG as my bullets struck. Its wings remained level, but the MiG entered a slow descent, heading to sea. Les then called that one MiG flight was in our six o'clock position firing at me! We were at our bingo fuel and I was out of ammo, so it was time to exit. We did a modified split-S and turned home at max speed. It was a relief that none of the MiGs followed!

On return to Suwon, the two pilots each put in a claim for a damaged MiG because that was all each could confirm for the other. Two weeks after this first MiG combat, Foster was made commander of D Flight when the previous flight commander was promoted to assistant squadron operations officer. Five days later on September 26, he was informed the Claims Board had upgraded his claim for one damaged to one shot down for his first victory. On the same day he received credit for his first victory, he put in solid claims for victories two and three.

The same week that Foster scored his first victory, two first lieutenants arrived in Seoul on the same flight. At Fifth Air Force headquarters, 1st Lt Manuel "Pete" Fernandez, Jr. was assigned to the 334th Squadron of the 4th Wing at Kimpo, while his friend 1st Lt Joseph C. McConnell, Jr. received orders to join Foster's 16th Squadron at Kimpo, where he commenced flying as a wingman that October. Both fliers had been trying to get into the war since the outset. Fernandez had been kept at Nellis because of his skill as an advanced flight training instructor until he turned himself into such a "problem officer" that he was finally "thrown in the briar patch" with an assignment to Korea. McConnell, who had been one of Fernandez's last students at Nellis, had been originally refused for service in Korea in 1950 because he was deemed "too old" at 28 to fly combat.

On September 26, D Flight was ordered to fly a combat air patrol. Though Foster had been promoted to command the flight a few days earlier, Captain Bartholomew, the previous flight commander, was designated as flight leader; Foster flew element lead with wingman 2nd Lt Al Crenz, who was flying his first mission. "We flew to the mouth of the Yalu where we turned east northeast, just south of the river. We were flying at 40,000 feet with the sun at our six o'clock. There were no contrails at our altitude, although we observed many to the north." Bartholomew suddenly spotted two MiGs ahead crossing from left to right, slightly low. The four Sabres punched off their wing tanks. "We began a descending hard right turn toward the MiGs' stern position, which would result in my element being out of position to cover, so I began a climbing left turn followed by a rapid reversal to a covering position on our flight leader."

As he did so, Foster was startled to see six pairs of white puffs, which were caused by fuel spills when the MiGs above dropped their tanks. Mistaken, Foster called "Flak!" which was immediately followed by, "No! they're MiGs!" He made a reversal to the right.

I saw the MIGs flying with elements in trail. The flight leader was in a hard left turn so we entered a scissors maneuver. He fired much too early. I rolled level as I called my flight leader that I was in a scissors with six MiGs, and could use a little help. As I called, I estimated my lead on the first MiG and fired a one-second burst. I watched my tracers fly toward the MiG in what seemed like slow motion. My tracers passed just aft of the lead MiG's tail, and the bullets subsequently stitched a row of hits along the fuselage of his wingman. At that same instant the lead MiG exploded in a very large black and orange fireball! The wingman's aircraft was emitting brown and black smoke as I pulled up sharply to miss the others.

I kept my eyes on the second MiG as it seemed to stop in the air, and my nose climbed almost to the vertical. I continued with a rolling pull over and nearly entered a vertical dive following the crippled, inverted MiG. I fired a short burst, but then I suddenly realized I was about to have a mid-air collision! I rotated my aircraft about a quarter turn counterclockwise as my right wing passed between the MiG's wing and fuselage, close enough that the scare aged me about ten years! This was followed by an immediate pull up and hard turn back toward the damaged MiG. It was falling like a leaf, still inverted. I then saw the MiG pilot floating with his parachute fully opened. I then flew toward the enemy pilot to take a picture with my gun camera after placing my guns in the safe position. I wanted my wingman's confirmation for both kills.

In contrast to my September 7 mission, this combat lasted only seconds. From the time I first spotted the MiGs dropping their tanks to when the second MiG was disabled, about six seconds had elapsed. When I looked at my gun camera film later, I saw that when I nearly collided with the second MiG, it had already lost its horizontal stabilizer and was therefore uncontrollable.

Foster had been surprised when the lead MiG exploded when his tracers had passed behind. The Sabre had been recently delivered to Suwon and had not had time yet for the ground crews to boresight its guns. When it was boresighted a day later, "One gun that hadn't been loaded with tracers was firing considerably left from where the gunsight aimed. That was the one that hit the lead MiG. Sometimes one just cannot improve on dumb luck."

September had been tough on the Russian pilots at Antung, as they lost 41 MiG-15s and 13 pilots killed. Of these losses, 19 happened over the home airfields, with all the 13 pilots killed lost during takeoff and landing, when they had virtually no chance of getting out of their airplane successfully before crashing. The two Sabre wings had claimed 64 MiGs shot down. While the Russian pilots claimed 40 Sabres and 18 Thunderjets shot down, the Air Force admitted loss of eight F-86s and four F-84s. Captain Mikhail Mikhin, whose score of nine would make him the leading Soviet ace of the period, claimed his second Sabre when he found it attacking one of his pilots who was attempting to land at Antung. "I fired at the fuselage. The Sabre started smoking and dived into the bay. The pilot, a first lieutenant, ejected and was taken prisoner by the Chinese."

By October 16, Foster was firmly established as leader of D Flight, with West Pointer 1st Lt Herbert Leichty as element leader. That day, the flight was assigned a combat air patrol near the Suiho Dam, which was being hit again by the fighter-bombers.

I was the flight leader with 1st Lt Wilton B. "Bing" Crosby on my wing. Herb was element lead with 1st Lt Edmund Hepner as number four. The air was crisp and cool, like football weather at home, and we were expecting contrails above 33,000 feet. We were filled with high expectations as we had four combat-experienced people, and we had flown together enough to know what each would do in combat.

The four Sabres test-fired their guns after crossing the bomb line north of the Main Line of Resistance and assumed the combat spread formation.

We heard other flights on the radio as we flew north. As we reached the Suiho Dam, we paralleled the Yalu and flew an elongated racetrack pattern. We patrolled until we saw eight MiGs flying southwest over the Yalu.

I attacked the stern MiG as the leader entered a hard left turn. We were slightly high and reached maximum speed rapidly. I began to overshoot, so I pulled up to reduce my speed and keep an altitude advantage to then return to a good shooting position. At this time, Herb called out eight more MiGs trying to enter a firing position on us. This made 16 MiGs and four F-86s maneuvering into firing positions in a roller coaster engagement. I got inside the number eight MiG which decided not to maintain its position with its element leader. It was like cutting a cow away from a herd! As I forced the MiG away, he became desperate and headed for the sun. I lined my radar ranging gunsight up his tailpipe and fired a long burst. When my bullets hit, he emitted a large doughnut smoke ring, followed by continuous smoke. I fired a second burst, with my hits evidenced by successive smoke rings. He continued flying toward the sun. I bounced around as I flew through the engine exhaust.

After seven or eight machine-gun bursts. the MiG was still flying, but I was out of ammunition. Fuel was also at bingo, so I called that I had a MiG crippled, and anyone who could reach it could have it. The MiG was easy to spot as its heavy smoke looked like a contrail. A flight leader from the 39th Squadron later told me that after I broke off, my burning MiG made a 90-degree left turn toward South Korea and then a flaming descent through another flight of F-86s! The MiG's crash was observed by this second F-86 flight.

Foster now had a score of four.

The Americans had stopped their blockade of the Antung airfields in October, with the result that only two of nine MiG-15s lost were shot down near their bases, while the other seven were lost in air battles against the Sabres over MiG Alley.

November 22, 1952 was a cold, clear day at K-13. Foster had just returned the day before from taking an F-86 back to Johnson AFB for rear-echelon maintenance and a two-week R&R in Tokyo, where he'd been able to call home and discover he was the proud father of a fourth son, born on November 13. He now planned to change the name on his Sabre from "Three Kings" to "Four Kings and a Queen." Immediately on his return, he found he was assigned as mission leader for the next day. The mission was to provide cover for an RF-80 on a bomb-damage assessment of the Suiho Dam near the Yalu. 1st Lt Ed Hepner was Foster's wingman for the mission. "The other flights in the mission had already gone north while we stayed with the RF-80, flying S-turns to keep with it."

Just prior to entering MiG Alley, Foster called for the flight to drop their empty wing tanks, at which point he found his wouldn't separate. Standard procedure in such a situation was to abort the mission with his wingman. "We headed south. I was so frustrated I could have screamed! I went through the procedures again, pushing and pulling circuit breakers. For some reason, on the umpteenth try after resetting the breaker, the tanks separated! I turned north and called our group that I would rejoin."

The two Sabres entered the combat zone, but were unable to rejoin the mission.

As Ed and I reached the Yalu and turned toward the Yellow Sea, we spotted eight MiGs. I initiated an attack, but I soon found we had engaged some very experienced pilots! The ensuing action was both at full throttle and at maximum aircraft performance. There was shooting by both sides, but no one could get a good position, and no visible hits were scored.

Hitting "bingo" fuel, Foster and his wingman headed for home at maximum speed.

The MiGs, however, were not ready to quit, and were soon in our stern position, 4,000 to 5,000 feet behind. We kept watching them gain.

One MiG lined up on Ed and one on me. When they closed to 2,000 to 3,000 feet, the MiG behind Ed fired. I told Ed to break right as I also broke right to shake the MiG, but my call was blocked when Ed called me that he was breaking left. Then a cannon shell hit Ed's Sabre near his canopy. Ed lost his canopy and most of his instrument panel in the explosion, and he was unable to hear any further transmissions. I rolled up and over Ed and the attacking MiG to pull out underneath and behind. I fired a burst directly up the MiG's tail while my aircraft was buffeted in the exhaust. The MiG stopped in mid-air after losing its engine. I went to idle with my speed brakes extended, and I returned to a stern firing position behind the MiG and gave it another good burst into its engine. I was still overrunning the MiG, so I pulled up and rolled inverted, but then I saw the MiG pilot eject.

Fearing Hepner had been shot down while he concentrated on the MiG, Foster was trying to locate him on the ground when he heard Hepner call that he was near Cho-do Island and would eject as he had no instruments and did not know how much fuel he had.

I returned to K-13 without incident. Ed was rescued after only 30 seconds in the water. But when my film pack was removed from my 86, my camera had taken no pictures! There was no confirming evidence of my fifth kill! I was immensely relieved that Ed was recovered with only a slight head wound, but I was also chagrined that I had a kill but no proof. Our intelligence officer said he was going to Fifth Air Force Headquarters the next day and for me not to give up hope.

On November 26 Foster was informed his fifth victory had been confirmed, and he was now officially the 23rd American jet ace.

Perhaps the most egregious violation of the border was by eight-victory ace Captain Robinson "Robbie" Risner, who would later be a prominent Hanoi Hilton POW during the Vietnam War. Known as one of the most aggressive pilots in the Air Force, Risner had originally come to Korea as a recon pilot and had managed to convince the assignment officer in Seoul to send him to the 51st Wing, where he was at first not accepted as a "real" fighter pilot. On October 22, 1952, he demonstrated his qualifications as a fighter pilot by becoming an ace during a wild fight.

That day, while assigned to escort fighter-bombers on a mission near the Yalu, Risner chased four MiGs across the river and finally caught the fourth deep in Manchuria, firing a burst that shattered the enemy's canopy. Attempting to escape, the MiG pilot entered a split-S and managed to pull out 10 feet above a dry riverbed, so low that Risner saw the exhaust kick up dust. Risner later described the fight. "He was not in very good shape, but he was a great pilot, and he was fighting like a cornered rat!" The MiG pilot pulled his throttle to idle and extended his air brakes to get Risner to overshoot, but he rolled over the enemy fighter and came down on the other side next to his wingtip.

> We were both at idle with our speed brakes out, just coasting. He looked over at me, raised his hand, and shook his fist. I thought, "This is like a movie. This can't be happening!" He had on a leather helmet, and I could see the stitching in it.

The chase continued with the enemy pilot valiantly evading Risner all the way back to Tatung-kou airfield, which was 35 miles inside Manchuria. Once over the field, Risner and his wingman, 1st Lt Joe Logan, doggedly pursued the MiG as it flew between two hangars. Finally, Risner got in a shot and blasted off part of the enemy's wing; it crashed alongside the runway.

During the high-speed pass between the hangars, Logan's fuel tank was punctured by Chinese antiaircraft fire. With jet fuel pouring out of his Sabre, Risner told him to shut down his engine and tried to push the Sabre to safety by putting the nose of his F-86 into Logan's jet pipe. Risner was forced to back off after two attempts when venting fuel and hydraulic fluid covered his canopy. Logan ejected near Cho-do Island, but drowned when the wind entangled him in his parachute. Returning to Kimpo, Risner ran out of gas, but he managed to glide home and make a successful dead-stick landing.

During November, the 64th IAK admitted the loss of six MiGs in high-altitude combat over MiG Alley, while the Sabre pilots claimed 29 MiGs destroyed. The Soviet claim of 21 Sabres was matched by admitted US loss of three F-86s.

December saw Korea again blanketed with snow, though the cold was not as terrible as the winter of 1950. For much of the month, aircraft of both sides remained on the ground during several major snowstorms. Having been proclaimed an ace and promoted to captain, Foster knew his tour would be up soon. "I had promised Ed Hepner he would fly as our flight leader until he avenged his being shot down on the day I scored my fifth victory. Besides, I was training him to take over as our flight commander when I rotated home." On December 7, Foster took position as element lead for a sweep to the Yalu. "This day showed promise as the MiGs had been flying in large numbers. There was much chatter on the radio as other flights spotted the enemy. There were numerous contrails, both active and inactive."

Arriving south of the Yalu, the four Sabres set up a racetrack pattern and searched for enemy fighters. "We finally spotted a lone MG-15 near Sinuiju, heading toward Manchuria. Ed made an excellent attack and scored hits all over the MIG which then went into a spin. He continued his attack until near the ground when we observed the MiG's crash." As the four pulled away, Foster spotted two more MiGs flying in trail and headed north. As he climbed to cut them off and closed in on their tails, he was surprised when the trailing MiG fired a burst of gunfire into the leader, then spun out of control and entered a spiral, spinning toward the earth! "I latched on to the damaged MiG, firing every time it flew into my gunsight and scored several hits. All of a sudden, my wingman called to pull out before I hit the ground!" Foster immediately leveled his wings and pulled back on the stick. Contrails coiled off his wingtips as he pulled maximum Gs to recover. "I was unable to watch the MiG explode as it crashed near Namsi-dong, North Korea, but my flight members confirmed my sixth kill." The entire fight, from Hepner's first victory, had lasted three minutes.

The third January of the war saw temperatures so cold the Sabre pilots were issued "poopysuits" for cold-water survival. Now nearly at the end of his tour, Foster was assigned as an instructor for pilots recently arrived in the group, providing ground school and theater checkouts as well as flying a first combat mission as their leader. He recorded these missions as training flights since they were unlikely to result in combat. On January 22, 1953, he was on the schedule for a combat air patrol in MiG Alley, his 95th combat mission.

Once again taking position as element leader to give experience to Hepner as flight leader, Foster's four Sabres flew over the snow-covered hills of North Korea as they entered MiG Alley and set up the now-standard racetrack pattern as they looked for the enemy.

The MiGs had another class of pilots engaging us who had started operating at our altitude over the past several missions. We spotted many contrails north of the Yalu and were eager to find a target. Several minutes later, we saw a large formation at 11 o'clock crossing our path at a right angle as they came south of the river.

As he turned toward the enemy to approach from their six o'clock, Foster guessed there were more than 20 MiGs in the widely spread formation.

I was at full power when we saw the MiGs. I entered a shallow dive and nearly reached compressibility before I eased my nose up and allowed my radar ranging gun sight to lock onto a MiG. When I was 3,000 feet away, I began shooting. I saw several hits, but they did not slow the MiG.

He turned slightly and fired at a second MiG with the same result, then dived and fired again at another MiG. Closing the range on the third MiG, he fired again and the enemy fighter emitted smoke.

As the MiG formation began a sweeping right turn, we were attacked by six MiGs that dove on us. We broke left, but as quickly as the MiGs appeared, they were gone and no one was hit. We returned to the hunt, but targets were not found.

Back at Suwon, Foster claimed three damaged, but then a pilot from another flight confirmed that his third MiG had caught fire, fell off into a dive and crashed. Foster now had seven credited victories.

On the next day's mission, Foster came up empty, but the next day he flew two memorable missions that would prove to be his last before going home.

"On January 24, my flight was scheduled for morning and afternoon missions. Captain Dolph Overton, another flight commander who had scored his fourth victory the day before, requested we fly together. His wingman was Captain Irish and mine was Ed Hepner." Shortly after the foursome arrived in MiG Alley, the two elements separated to attack different MiG formations they spotted. With both experienced Soviet pilots and novice Chinese pilots opposing the Sabres, it was anyone's guess when they entered a fight as to what kind of opposition they would find. Foster and Hepner ran across Russians. "We tangled with some mighty good MiG pilots, but the result for my element was a standoff." Minutes later, he spotted what was likely a Chinese formation, since the MiGs were flying high and didn't spot the Sabres as Foster slid up from below and fired a long burst into the trailing MiG's tailpipe from a range of 2,000 feet. Though firing his guns while climbing dropped his speed and he was unable to stay in a firing position, what he had fired paid off when the enemy jet caught fire and fell off on one wing to leave a smoky trail across the sky till it impacted in the hills below. While Foster was scoring number eight, Overton scored number five to become the 25th MiG ace.

On the afternoon mission, Foster expected to do no shooting since he was flying as number four in order to check out a young lieutenant as an element leader. However, once they were over the Yalu, they came across a formation of 16–20 MiGs.

Our flight leader attacked, and half the MiGs entered a hard right turn with the other half swinging wide. I guided my element leader onto the rear two MiGs, but when one swung wide to attack him, I told him to shoot at something while I held off the MiG. The trailing MiG was very agitated, but it would not pull in to shoot as I faked toward it, and my element leader didn't shoot. I took the initiative and told him to cover while I attacked the trailing MiG. When I did, this MiG broke away immediately, so I turned toward the others and lined up 2,000 feet behind one. I fired several bursts and scored hits, but he didn't seem hurt. I fired a final burst and suddenly the MiG entered a spin and crashed.

Back at Suwon with his ninth victory confirmed, Foster was told he could call it a war if he wanted. "I decided that nine was enough! My war was over, and I went home." His nine victories made Cecil Foster the top-scoring ace to fly with the 16th Fighter-Interceptor Squadron in the war.

CHAPTER 16

WILL THEY EVER SAY "ENOUGH"?

The outstanding missions flown by the Air Force fighter-bombers were the strikes against the North Korean hydroelectric complex in 1952. Accomplished in coordination with Navy squadrons operating from four aircraft carriers of Task Force 77, the strikes were an attempt to break the impasse at the Panmunjom peace talks. During the "strategic campaign" by the B-29s in 1950, the hydroelectric targets had been untouched since the UN high command determined they would be necessary for the UN occupation of North Korea that fall. In the end, though the strikes were successful in destroying all of North Korea's electrical power, they did not succeed in bringing the Communists back to the negotiating table.

In the spring of 1952, intelligence sources stated that the Communists were stockpiling supplies to attempt another offensive in the summer. In some UN quarters, this was seen as an opportunity to finish the fight that had been stopped the year before when the Communists first proposed peace negotiations, since an offensive would bring the enemy into the open where they could be bombed by a UN air force that was even better than it had been in 1951. Air Force planners proposed concentrating on maintaining air superiority in MiG Alley and increasing fighter-bomber strikes to maximize the cost of war to the Communists. With the Thunderjets of the 116th Wing now capable of undertaking long-range strikes from Japan into North Korea, a mission was flown from Itazuke to the transportation center of Sariwon in North Korea. The enemy was surprised by the appearance of the 48 F-84s, which successfully dive-bombed the target. With the tactic proven, Air Force planners started looking for other likely targets.

Newly named Commander Seventh Fleet on May 20, 1952, the aggressive Vice Admiral J. J. "Jocko" Clark's first act in command was to confer with the new CinCFE (Commander in Chief Far East), General Mark W. Clark, where he advocated that UN air forces hit the North Korean hydroelectric complex. The Joint Chiefs had blocked the requests made by FEAF for such a campaign for over a year, on the ground the generators supplied electricity to China. General Ridgway had refused the Air Force pleas to attack the hydroelectric facilities in 1951 since he still believed it possible the UN forces would again advance into North Korea. Admiral Clark pointed out to General Clark that since American policy now excluded any advance into the north, the denial no longer made sense, while destroying electrical power in North Korea and Manchuria might bring progress in the long-stalled negotiations. With the Communists having rejected a revised UN peace proposal on April 29, 1952, there was new desire to break the stalemate.

General Clark agreed. Instead of asking permission from Washington, he held a press conference and announced the campaign. Not wishing to contradict the new commander publicly, the Joint Chiefs approved the operation.

The proposed strikes were considered "strategic," which placed responsibility for the attack with the Air Force. However, B-29s were now limited to night operations only and the generators were not suitable targets for night attack. With only two groups of F-84s in Korea backed up by the 116th Wing in Japan for long-range missions, the strikes would have to be a joint Army-Navy operation. Fifth Air Force commander General Glenn Barcus agreed that Navy Skyraider dive-bombers were the best weapons for the attack.

The Suiho complex, located on the Yalu River in western North Korea right in the middle of MiG Alley, was the world's fourth largest hydroelectric plant. The Japanese had built the complex in 1941. The dam was the largest in Asia: 2,800 feet long, 300 feet thick at the base, and 60 feet wide at the crest, with a height of 525 feet. Six turbine generators with a capacity of 100,000 kilowatts each provided power for western North Korea and the Port Arthur and Dairen regions of northeast China.

While Navy Skyraiders would dive-bomb the dam, the Air Force would fly a maximum effort follow-up strike with the F-84s of the 49th and 136th wings and the F-80Cs of the 8th Wing, while the Sabres of the 4th and 51st wings would fly a barrier patrol against incursions by the Antung MiGs.

On June 23, the carriers *Boxer*, *Princeton*, and *Philippine Sea* in the Sea of Japan prepared to launch 35 Skyraiders at 0800 hours, to hit Suiho at 0930 hours. The launch preparations halted at 0730 hours when the Air Force canceled the mission because of a forecast for bad weather. By midday, the heavy clouds over the Yalu moved south; H-Hour was re-set for 1600 hours to use the heavy broken clouds for cover. At 1410 hours, 35 Skyraiders, each carrying three heavy armor-piercing 1,600lb bombs, left the carriers.

At precisely 1600 hours, 16 F9F Panthers struck the aircraft defenses surrounding the complex. As the Panthers pulled off their runs, the Skyraiders entered their dives. Over two-and-a-half minutes, 81 tons of bombs set the power house afire and secondary explosions were reported. Antiaircraft fire was moderate and there were no losses since the defenses had been overwhelmed.

At 1610 hours, 79 F-84Es of the 49th and 136th wings and 49 8th Wing F-80Cs dropped 145 tons of bombs on the burning complex. The 84 Sabres in MiG Alley found no opponents because 160 of the 250 MiGs at Antung had flown into the Manchurian interior, fearing an attack on their base. Five minutes later, Navy and Marine fighter-bombers and Air Force F-51s struck the power plants at the Chosin, Fusen, and Kyosen reservoirs. Photo-recon missions showed heavy damage to the Suiho, Chosin, Fusen, and Kyosen No. 1 and 2 plants. The power generator at Suiho was totally destroyed in a strike by F-84s of the two fighter-bomber wings and Skyraiders from *Bon Homme Richard*. F-51Ds of the 18th Wing bombed the unscathed Chosin No. 1 and 2 power generators and the Kyosen No. 4 plant was destroyed by Navy aircraft. All remaining smaller power plants throughout eastern North Korea were struck by carrier air strikes that afternoon.

The weather closed in on June 25. F-84s and F-80s bombed the Chosin and Fusen plants on June 26 and 27. During the four days of strikes, the Air Force flew 730 sorties while Task Force 77 launched 546 sorties. The 4th and 51st fighter wings flew 238 combat air patrol sorties that prevented the Antung MiGs from intervening. A total of five aircraft were lost: two F4U-4 Corsairs that crashed at sea with the pilots rescued, while two F-80s and an F-84 were written off in crash landings when they returned to their bases. No pilots were lost.

The strikes knocked out 90 percent of North Korean power production capability, with 11 of 13 generators destroyed completely and major damage to the remaining two. Northeast China lost 23 percent of electrical power and 60 percent of industries in Dairen failed to meet production quotas that month. North Korea was totally dark for two weeks.

However, the strikes did not achieve the hoped-for success. China and the Soviet Union sent technicians to North Korea and, over the course of the summer of 1952, repairs were made to most generators and some were rebuilt. By September, 10 percent of the pre-strike capacity was restored with thermoelectric plants brought on line. The Chinese and North Korean negotiators did not budge at Panmunjom.

In another attempt to bring pressure on the other side to return to negotiations, Operation *Pressure Pump*, flown on July 11, saw 106 Navy aircraft lead 822 Air Force, Marine, and Navy planes from every operational unit in Korea to bomb defensive gun positions, troop and supply sites, and factories in Pyongyang. Destruction of the targets was extensive. Radio Pyongyang went off the air for 48 hours. When it came back on, the North Koreans stated 1,500 buildings had been destroyed with 7,000 people killed. The Communist negotiators at Panmunjom maintained their boycott.

Elsewhere in the world, reaction to the strikes was strongly negative, particularly in Britain. Labour Party leaders Clement Attlee and Aneurin Bevan said the strikes risked instigating World War III. The Churchill government was particularly criticized for the fact there had been no "consultation" with the Truman Administration before the strikes. A vote of censure of the government failed when US Secretary of State Dean Acheson stated the Truman Administration had been wrong not to consult the British government "as a courtesy." A British officer was appointed deputy chief of staff to the UN Commander at the end of July.

Reaction in Washington was the opposite. Congressional critics asked why approval of the attacks had taken two years since they were so successful. The hydroelectric campaign was now forced to continue through the rest of 1952 to keep the enemy from repairing the system and re-establishing power in the region. Enemy antiaircraft defenses around the complexes were strengthened and losses mounted.

Pyongyang was hit by the largest air raid of the war on August 29, with the objective of giving the Chinese and Soviets "food for thought" while Chinese Prime Minister Zhou En-Lai was meeting Soviet leaders in Moscow. Warning leaflets were dropped on August 28 and the next day 1,802 Air Force, Navy, Marine, British Commonwealth, and ROK aircraft bombed the city in three raids. For all intents and purposes Pyongyang was of no further military value for the rest of the war. Again, there was no change in the Communists' boycott of the peace negotiations.

During the night of September 12–13, 1952, Suiho was bombed again by a strike force composed of flak/searchlight suppression flights of B-26 Invaders from the 17th Bomb Group (Light) and Navy aircraft from the carrier *Princeton*. Four specially modified B-29s used ECM (Electronic Countermeasures) to jam Soviet antiaircraft radars and radio communication, while 25 B-29s from the 19th and 307th wings used Short Range Navigation (SHORAN) to locate and bomb the complex. The ECM B-29s were not able to completely jam the defenses, while the B-26 flak-suppression force was only able to locate and attack eight searchlights. An unexpected cold front created icing conditions for the B-29s, causing one 19th Wing Superfortress to stall and crash with a loss of all but one of the crew. The B-29s were met by intense flak over Suiho, and one 307th Wing bomber was shot down; the Communists claimed it had been shot down by a MiG-15, but one survivor stated they were shot down by flak. Two other B-29s were damaged by flak so badly they were forced to make emergency landings at Taegu. The overall bombing accuracy was poor due to the intense defensive reaction. The dam, the operational turbines, the generators, and the other transformers were not damaged. Photos taken the next day showed the generator still in operation, demonstrated by the flow of tailrace water from two turbines.

In October 1952, UN negotiators conceded the Communists would not change their position regarding the forced repatriation of prisoners of war. The negotiations were stalemated. A recess in the negotiations was announced, with the statement there would be no return to the peace table until the other side presented "constructive new proposals."

In early 1953, the 8th Fighter-Bomber Wing was able to get rid of their war-weary F-80s, and the 18th Fighter-Bomber Wing was finally able to retire the F-51 Mustang. The worn-out fighter-bombers were replaced with the new F-86F-20 Sabre. The final subtype of the

Sabre to see combat in Korea, the F-86F-20 had provision for another underwing hardpoint inboard of the drop tank pylons, ahead of the main landing gear. The Sabre could now carry two 1,000lb bombs and still have the range to fly into North Korea. Putting the Sabre to use as a fighter-bomber in MiG Alley ended the MiGs' superiority over the UN fighter-bombers.

2nd Lt Bob Rawlings completed Air Force flight training in Class 52-F in the summer of 1952 at Bryan AFB in Texas.

I next went to Nellis for fighter gunnery training in the F-86A. My most memorable experience at Nellis as a student pilot was flying a mock intercept mission one day and having Jimmy Jabara and Iven Kincheloe as our leaders in two four-man flights. As I remember it, I was just happy to land in one piece that day!

From Nellis, it was on to Korea in late December 1952. I arrived in Suwon where I found myself assigned to the 80th Fighter-Bomber Squadron. I remember being initially disappointed, as the 80th was the only squadron in Korea still flying F-80s. My disappointment was short-lived however when I found the 80th was flying many more missions than the 35th and 36th squadrons. They were busy with training after having recently converted to F-86s. Fortunately, I was able to fly 34 combat missions in the old Shooting Star during the period January to April 1953. All these missions were air-to-ground. Targets were bridges, rail yards, and tank and artillery positions. My most noteworthy action during this time occurred on April 24, when I flew five combat missions in one 24-hour period. It was amazing how well our ground crews could turn our aircraft around for repeated missions.

At the end of April, the 80th said good-bye to the Shooting Star as their F-86s finally arrived at Suwon.

I flew 58 additional combat missions in the F-86F. When our 24 brand new F-86Fs arrived, each had logged only ten hours or so of flight time. We were like kids with new toys! The F-86F proved to be an effective fighter-bomber with the ability to get into and away from a target with much more speed than the F-80. Our element of surprise was a big advantage. The F-86F became a real workhorse for air-to-ground work.

My most memorable mission flying the F-86F came on June 13, 1953. It was my 53rd combat mission, and by now I was a flight leader. Reporting to the flight line that morning, full of confidence and cockiness, I noticed the name "Stone" had been filled in as the Number Four man in my flight. Not knowing anyone in my squadron named Stone, I figured it must be a new guy. Upon inquiring around, I was told that Brigadier General Stone, the base commander, had signed on for the flight that morning! What had been confidence soon turned into nervousness and anxiety. What was a 22-year-old doing leading a general into combat? Our target that day was the railroad marshaling yards in the Wonsan Valley. I had never been there before, and I was told by our intelligence section that it was heavily defended with antiaircraft batteries. My concern was more with the general's safety than about my ability. At our preflight briefing, General Stone was full of questions, as he had flown infrequently, and seemed rather unsure of himself.

Our flight at 15,000 feet to the target area was uneventful. We were carrying two 500lb bombs under each wing, and were going to dive in a trail formation and then reform at 10,000 feet for our flight home. While I was busily engaged in identifying the target and talking with a T-6 spotter plane, I was amazed at the amount of ack-ack fire randomly put up at us as we circled our target. Characteristically, the first Sabre into a target usually surprises the defenders so that their return fire is often quite a distance behind the divebombing plane. As the second man comes in, the return fire is closer but still behind the plane, and so on until the fourth man comes in. By this time the ack-ack begins to zero in, and it becomes a hairy ride for the fourth plane. So it was again that day. I attracted a tremendous amount of fire as our first man in, but the bursts of smoke were well behind my flight path. As I pulled off the target at about 500 feet and started to climb, zig-zagging all the way, I could see a pattern of intense ground fire. The second and third Sabres were being closely targeted, but they toggled their bombs away and climbed up safely. General Stone seemed to wait a little too long before starting his dive. When he did, he encountered as much ack-ack fire as I have ever seen. I was now up to 4,000 feet, and I remember saying to myself, "Please let him make it." Fortunately he made it off the target safely, though he took some superficial hits, and rejoined for the trip home. I was immensely relieved. I will never forget the look on the general's face as he expressed his happiness to me with getting back in one piece. I felt great when he said we had all done a good job.

The 8th Wing was preceded in upgrading to the Sabre by the 18th Fighter-Bomber Wing, which had operated the F-51 Mustang since the opening weeks of the war. By the spring of 1953, the antiaircraft environment was such that the Mustang was ever more a sitting target, especially with its vulnerable liquid-cooled Merlin engine.

Captain Howard R. "Ebe" Ebersole arrived in Korea in August 1952.

I was assigned to the 18th Fighter-Bomber Group, and I went to the 12th Fighter-Bomber Squadron as a replacement pilot flying the F-51 Mustang. As a captain, my total flight time was about 1,800 hours of which approximately 135 were in jets in F-80s and F-84s. I had also flown over 500 hours in B-24s, including 16 missions over Europe with the Eighth Air Force during World War II. But by 1952, I was a bonafide, practicing, fully converted fighter pilot with over 1,000 hours of single engine time, who wanted no part ever again of bomber flying!

The 18th Wing, which was by then based at Hoengsong air base in South Korea, had three squadrons: the South African Air Force No. 2 Squadron, the "Springboks," the 12th FBS, called the "Fightin' Foxey Few," and the "Fightin' Cocks" of the 67th FBS. The 39th FBS had been transferred to the 51st Fighter-Interceptor Wing at the end of May 1952 to bring the 51st to full wing strength, reverting to its original designation as a fighter-interceptor squadron.

In late September 1952, with five F-51 missions to his credit, Captain Ebersole was sent to the 51st Wing's 39th Squadron at Suwon on temporary duty for checkout in the F-86, since he had recent jet experience. After flying ten missions with the 39th he was returned to the 12th FBS as an instructor pilot for the squadron's transition to the F-86.

I managed to change the "fly ten missions" assignment with the 51st to "at least ten missions" and had 15 in my logbook when they caught up with me and sent me back to the spam cans in the 18th.

By the end of December, when the T-33s showed up to give conversion training to the rest of the wing's flying personnel, I had 30 F-51 missions completed.

The 18th Wing trained on T-33s and then F-86s during January and February 1953, with pilots receiving approximately 30 hours' training from F-86 pilots sent over from the 4th and 51st wings. Ebersole's assignment was to supervise the training of the South Africans of No. 2 Squadron. The wing flew its first combat mission on February 22, when the wing commander and squadron commanders made a Yalu sweep with the 51st Wing. Before the wing went fully operational, FEAF decided that all F-51 pilots who were not flight leaders or above would be replaced with pilots fresh from jet training in the United States. Ebersole recalled:

> Those with 75 missions or more were sent back to the States. The others were transferred to Mosquito squadrons to fly T-6s as forward air controllers or sent as instructor pilots to the South Koreans who were still using the F-51. March 2 was "Black Monday" in the group and that night there were several .45-caliber bullet holes made in the barracks huts by a bunch of very upset Mustang pilots.

By April 1953, the squadrons of the 18th Wing were engaged in fighter-bomber missions, but over the final months of the war there were opportunities to fly air-superiority missions up to MiG Alley, and Major James Hagerstrom, commander of the 12th FBS, became an ace with five victories credited.

In April 1953, the peace negotiations at Panmunjom recommenced. Intelligence learned that the People's Volunteer Army hoped to go on the offensive in the summer, to change the "facts on the ground" and influence the outcome of the negotiations. Bombing sorties against the transportation system were increased in May and June, which resulted in the planned Chinese offensive being delayed until mid-June. With negotiations hanging up on the riots happening in South Korean prisoner-of-war camps and the decision by the South Koreans to allow the Communist prisoners to escape from the camps, the outcome of the war was on a knife edge. The main thrust of the attack broke through the Eighth Army's defensive lines and threatened a breakthrough that could end with a third fall of Seoul. The army did not have the reserves to stop the Chinese and action was limited to attempting to close the hole and blunt the enemy spearhead. A second Chinese attack in the west to push on toward Seoul and Inchon was expected any day.

On the night of July 15–16, 1953, the Sabre fighter-bombers of the 18th Wing took part in a mission that did affect the final outcome of the war, one that the Fifth Air Force would deny had ever happened, until Flamm D. "Dee" Harper of the 18th Fighter-Bomber Group told the story for the record in 1992.

Captain Harper had been shot down over North Korea and injured in his ejection three weeks earlier and had been assigned a ground job as group operations officer, which carried with it a spot promotion to major. On July 15, 1953, with both 18th Wing commander Col Frank Perego and 18th Group commander Col Maurice Martin attending a conference in Tokyo, Deputy Group Commander Lt Col Glenn Stell was the acting group commander. By 1700 hours the wing had completed all missions assigned for the day by Fifth Air Force's Joint Operations Center, responsible for coordinating air support operations over the front. Harper recalled:

> Two flights were still north of the Main Line of Resistance, but at the Combat Operations Center, we were putting the day's activities to bed. Lt Col Harry Evans, commander of the 12th Squadron, who was leading a flight still north of the MLR, contacted us and said he had located about 100 enemy boxcars in a marshaling yard near the front. Everything they shot exploded, which indicated munitions! He also said another nearby marshaling yard was also loaded with boxcars and gave the map coordinates. We finally had a real target!
>
> Night was rapidly approaching and we were a day fighter outfit. I knew that by morning the munitions would be dispersed and this prime target would no longer exist. Instant action was required. While the duty officer relayed the scramble order and target data to our two alert flights, I contacted the duty officer in the Combat Operations Center at Fifth Air Force Headquarters. I gave the data on the targets and I stressed the need for immediate action. I advised I would launch our alert flights against these targets while he obtained the necessary authority.

Considering the seriousness of the situation, I never once thought we might not receive such authority. The duty officer at the Combat Operations Center at Fifth Air Force was also advised we would load and man all available aircraft for immediate strikes against these targets.

Within 15 minutes we were ready to launch 16 additional aircraft. Again I contacted the duty officer at Fifth Air Force for authority, and was advised that General Barcus, the commanding general, was at dinner, and they did not want to disturb him. Again, I advised the duty officer that we would launch the flights that were ready. Meanwhile we would turn everything around upon landing as well as augment the force as rapidly as possible. He agreed to work on the necessary authority for conducting our operation.

By now this had become a major operation. Bombs were moved from the dump to the flight line. Every organization on base was putting on a maximum effort. I was the only one on base who knew that none of this had been authorized or directed by Fifth Air Force.

We continued launching flights. The sun set and darkness arrived. I was advised by the commanders of the 67th and 12th squadrons that the fires within the targets were so extensive our pilots could read their instruments without their cockpit lights.

Lt Col Evans later recalled, "The whole valley in the target area looked like daylight. We did not need maps or photos. We just headed north, and when we got to 6,000 feet, we could see the fires on the horizon." Lt Col Carroll L. "Stan" Stanton, who commanded the 67th Squadron, remembered:

When my flight arrived over the train, Harry's was just leaving. It was now almost pitch dark. It was obvious we were setting ourselves up for a mid-air collision. That would have really ripped it! I took control and assigned holding quadrants, then called individual aircraft in and out of the target area. Let me say, I've never seen a fireworks display that comes close to the show that night. Burning ammo flew thousands of feet into the air, and secondary explosions were everywhere!

As the night wore on, clouds moved in between the 18th's base at K-55, and the target and pilots were logging 40 minutes of weather on each sortie. After several hours of sustained attacks, a C-47 with a forward air-control team arrived to take charge.

Major Harper continued:

Due to the press of events, I had not advised Colonel Stell we lacked authority for the sorties, a serious breach of command authority, because up to this time I had not considered Fifth Air Force approval to be a problem. In my mind, I knew approval was imminent. I was just busy doing my job hacking through the red tape. I continued contacting the Combat Operations Center at Fifth Air Force Headquarters for authority. At one point I requested they order me to stop or else obtain authority, but neither occurred! In my opinion, the response from the 18th had been so fast and of such a magnitude that after General Barcus completed dinner, no one wanted to tell him he had missed the war! In my defense, we were striking the only real target I had seen during the seven months I was in combat. I was also aware that after going this far, I had better finish the job. I made the personal decision to remain silent about the authority. There was no need for anyone else to be open for court martial. Operations continued.

Shortly after midnight, ground fire claimed two Sabres and 1st Lt Don Forbes was down in No Man's Land.

Because of these losses, I knew our operation could not be swept under the carpet. We shut down shortly thereafter feeling assured our target had been destroyed. For the day, the 18th Fighter-Bomber Wing produced 212 sorties, of which 120 had not been authorized.

Harper realized the upper echelons of Air Force command were upset at 0300 hours, when he saw a copy of an order to colonels Perego and Martin directing them to return to Fifth Air Force Headquarters immediately. "After the day's events, I was totally exhausted and extremely shaken, considering that I was not in good physical shape to begin. With visions of a court martial and a possible sentence in Leavenworth, I went into shock prior to falling asleep."

The next day, Colonel Martin walked into Harper's office in the group operations office at 1430 hours. Harper was officially informed that he would not be court-martialed for his audacity and would receive no citation. "After a considerable pause, Colonel Martin continued. 'As Air Force officers we are all required to make decisions. Yesterday, you made the right decision. If you never make another decision, you have earned your pay for the rest of your career.'"

Following the destruction of the ammunition trains, the Communist offensive ground to a halt as the expected second assault failed to take place. The hope of James Michener's fictional Admiral Tarrent in *The Bridges At Toko-ri* that the negotiations would someday be moved by the news that "they have even bombed the bridges at Toko-ri" had happened, and the Air Force couldn't officially claim its victory because staff aides had been reluctant to interrupt General Barcus' dinner in order to obtain proper bureaucratic approval of a one-time-only opportunity. The man who had consistently "pushed the envelope" during his time in command in an unceasing effort to achieve this result would never be able to claim his victory.

Throughout 18 months of a stalemated war, air power had not been able to conclusively affect the outcome, but the Sabres of the 18th Wing had saved the conclusion of the Korean War by stopping the planned Chinese attack on the western end of the battlefield in its tracks before it could begin. The armistice that ended the fighting was signed ten days later.

CHAPTER 17

THE ACE RACE

By the end of 1952, it was clear the Communists had given up on being able to bring air power to bear on the battlefield. While the UN force's fighter-bombers were unable to make more than quick hit and run raids into MiG Alley, the fact they were able to attack in the region at all was the result of the protection provided by the two outnumbered Sabre wings. Targets in MiG Alley were limited to airfields, to keep the Communist construction troops from repairing them sufficiently to allow any movement of aircraft to bases south of the Yalu.

However, in December, the North Korean People's Air Force had increased their night-time attacks on UN air bases. The NKPAF had first begun these "nuisance" raids in June 1951, when a Polikarpov Po-2 biplane trainer bombed Kimpo on the night of June 21 and destroyed or damaged more Sabres than were lost that month in MiG Alley. The ungainly biplanes had first been used in the role of night-time harasser by the Red Air Force on the Eastern Front during World War II, where a squadron of women known as "The Night Witches" made a lasting impression on the Wehrmacht. Built of wood and fabric, the biplanes were virtually invisible on radar, and with a maximum speed of 70mph there was no Western night-fighter that could stay with them long enough to shoot them down without the possibility of stalling out and spinning in. At the low altitude the North Koreans flew at, this would be fatal. In 1952, a Marine F7F-3N Tigercat night-fighter managed to shoot down one of the intruders, and a second fell to the crew of a B-26B Invader who were guided to the vicinity of the enemy airplane by ground radar, after which they were able to spot it visually and shoot it down. Now, the North Koreans introduced Yak-18 trainers. With a metal airframe covered by fabric, they were slightly easier to pick up on radar and were faster, with a speed of around 100mph, but their agility again made them a difficult target. On January 31, an F-94B of the 319th Fighter All-Weather Squadron flown by Captain Ben Fithian with radar operator 1st Lt Sam Lyons in back dropped gear and flaps and slowed the engine to idle in order to shoot down what was later identified as a Lavochkin La-11; however, the jet stalled and spun at low altitude when Fithian opened fire, killing both in the subsequent crash. The inability of the Air Force to end the night-time raids was an embarrassment to Fifth Air Force that would only be ended in July when they asked for a Navy night-fighter to go after the Yaks and Navy Lt Guy P. Bordelon brought his F4U-5N to Kimpo, where he shot down five intruders over ten days and stopped the raids just before the end of the war.

After 1952, the number of Soviet units committed to the Korean air war was reduced, while the number of Chinese units expanded in early 1953 as a result of the increased training program begun in 1952. The Communist Party Military Commission had determined in 1952 that the war was likely to continue beyond that year, and directed the PLAAF to rotate as many units into combat as possible to spread combat experience through the air force.

While the PLAAF leadership had no knowledge of aerial warfare, they strongly supported programs to improve pilot effectiveness by trying different tactics and adjusting operations as the usefulness of these changes was confirmed or not. The inexperienced Chinese pilots were sent against the UN fighter-bomber missions as much as possible, while the more experienced Soviet units engaged in direct combat with the Sabres, with the Chinese flying at high altitude to avoid the Sabres, operating in large formations in line with Soviet doctrine from World War II. By mid-1952 this strategy was modified and the Chinese started flying smaller formations. A unit's tour at the front was 90 days, and the Sabre pilots noticed the regular changes between large numbers of what they termed "students" arriving every few months, with the students gradually becoming more proficient. However, 90 days was not enough time for Chinese pilots to become really proficient in combat. In late 1952, American pilots reported an increase in aggressive tactics by Chinese pilots.

Over the first four months of 1953, Chinese pilots flew more sorties than had been flown in 1952. This increase in air activity by less-experienced pilots would lead to the big air battles waged by the Sabres in the final months of the war. While the 3rd and 4th FADs had been the most effective fighter units in 1951 and 1952, they were replaced by the 12th and 15th FADs as the best units of the PLAAF, though the new units were not as capable as the earlier units, which Mao had personally ordered be withdrawn to keep their experienced pilots for future air force expansion. With the disappearance of the F-51 and F-80 fighter-bombers and their replacement by F-86s in the two US fighter-bomber wings, the air war continued to favor the Americans, particularly since the new fighter-bombers could be as dangerous as the Sabres of the 4th and 51st groups, once rid of their ordnance. Beginning in April, the Soviets withdrew 40 percent of their aircraft and pilots from frontline operations, in response to the increase in US fighter operations north of the Yalu that put the MiGs at risk during takeoff and landing.

By the beginning of January 1953, the F-86F was fast becoming the standard jet fighter in the two units, and F-86Es were being upgraded with field modification kits to give them the "6-3" wing. While they did not have the power of the F-86 and could not reach the higher altitudes the latest Sabre was capable of, they were able to take on the MiGs at higher altitude than before. The pilots at the controls of these Sabres now included younger men who had benefitted from the Korean veterans who provided realistic training before they went overseas. They were also fully trained in the use of the radar gunsight and able to make the most of its increased accuracy.

In December 1952, Col Robert Baldwin arrived at Suwon. Shortly after the new year, he took command of the 51st Fighter Group, a position he would hold till the end of the war. A graduate of Class 40-C at Kelly Field in the summer of 1940, he had eventually commanded the 71st Fighter Squadron of the 1st Fighter Group, flying P-38s on air-to-ground missions and bomber escort over Germany and Austria from Italy late in the war, after spending the three previous years as a flight instructor and test pilot. After the war he returned to flight test for two years, then transferred to the 56th Fighter Group at Selfridge Field as their wing operations officer. Baldwin had first flown the F-86A in 1950 when the 56th re-equipped. He later recalled:

When I was notified I was going to Korea, I checked with the Pentagon to find out which assignment I was getting. It was to be with the 18th, flying F-51s. I did not want that. I had a friend at Nellis who was conducting training for Korea. I called and asked, "I am heading for Korea. Can I get some refresher training in the F-86?" I was there for ten days flying training missions. I received a good indoctrination into air-to-air combat because the people running the program were all ex-Korean War combat personnel. When I arrived in Korea, I was sent to Fifth Air Force Personnel. The general in charge asked where I'd come from and I said, "Nellis." I didn't tell him it was not the full 90-day course. He said, "F-86s! We are looking for an F-86 group commander." "Great!" I said, "I'll take it." That is how I got the 51st. I then flew three missions on the wing of the previous group commander and took command of the group after those three missions.

While Baldwin would fly 85 missions and become an ace, he didn't see that as his primary purpose.

As group commander, I flew with all three squadrons in all positions. As group commander, my job was to get everyone experienced in air-to-air combat tactics because this was the world's last eyeball-to-eyeball combat where the pilot aimed the airplane to direct its weapons. By the end of the war, the 51st had as good a kill ratio as the 4th. We had as many kills, but we lost fewer pilots. And while I was there, we lost only two in my group. We recovered one pilot. We lost the other in the Yellow Sea.

Recalling combat in early 1953, Baldwin related:

There was one period during which the MiGs' tactics had us stopped. No one was able to successfully engage them. Every time we engaged a flight of four MiGs, within about three minutes four more MiGs joined the fight. If we chose to stay and fight with these odds, in a few more minutes, four more MiGs joined the fight. At that point it was smart to head for the deck and leave the fight for another time. Our group operations analyst was a second lieutenant ROTC graduate from MIT who majored in mathematics. He figured out what was happening. The Communists flew flights of four MiGs south from Antung to the Chongchon River, made a wide turn, and flew back across the Yalu at the Suiho Reservoir. Their flights followed this track at three minute intervals. If we engaged a flight of MiGs, we became badly outnumbered in short order.

In order to counter this, we changed tactics. We laid out a "racetrack" pattern directly across their "railroad." We flew flights of six F-86s at three minute intervals. The results were astounding, and the number of aircraft involved in these engagements was unbelievable! For a period of ten days, we were the only ones getting kills. Everyone wanted to fly the number five or six positions in the flights as they were unexpected by the MiGs and therefore the most successful.

Like most pilots, Colonel Baldwin had no problem remembering his first MiG victory.

We were at high altitude, patrolling the Yalu River. I looked to my left and saw a flight of four MiGs two miles away. We were crossing ahead of them. They looked like they were on a training mission. I called my flight. "Heads up! We are turning back on these guys." We made a right turn heading north in their direction, and they ended behind us. This is an indication of the poor maneuverability at that altitude.

As we headed north, it was like walking on eggs with the MiGs alongside about a quarter mile away. They were preoccupied while we were flying alongside. We then gradually moved behind. Now they were at our maximum gun range. We had been two miles ahead, made our turn and moved behind them by 2,000 feet. It was a long shot, but the radar gunsight ranged a little better.

I picked the last MiG in the flight and gave a short burst. We had tracers loaded one in every ten rounds. Nothing happened. I raised the gunsight more and gave another short burst. Again nothing happened. I raised my gunsight a little more. Now I began slowing down because I was pulling my F-86's nose up. With that burst, I hit the MiG. Then I gave a good long burst, and hit the saddle tank beneath the engine. It flamed like a big skyrocket and down it went.

Baldwin's final victory was the most difficult.

I put 10 Gs on the airplane for my fifth MiG kill. We were in and out of the clouds between 25,000 to 30,000 feet. We encountered a flight of MiGs flying in our direction almost directly below us. We were too close to nose over, so I did a loose barrel roll and ended up about 100 feet behind the leader. I fired at the MiG, which immediately started to burn. The MiG pilot dove into the clouds, and I trailed him through the clouds by tracking the black smoke. As soon as we broke out of the clouds, I fired again. That happened four times. In the process of tracking the smoke, I became disoriented. The next time we broke out, we both were in a vertical dive at 12,000 feet near Mach 1! I made a reflexive pullout as the ground was coming up fast! The pull out was hard enough to force my helmet blast shield and my head down. I was looking at the floor and everything was dark! I could not pull my head up to see if I was going to make it. I had to ease up on the pull out at the proper time, because in my blinded condition I was eventually going to hit the ground. Eventually, I relaxed my pull and raised my head. I was in a canyon. Very soon I was going straight up. I looked at the "G" meter, and it was pegged at 10!

The MiG went straight in. I lost my wingman when I followed the MiG into the clouds. My gun camera film showed the MiG burning like a torch, but I could not confirm its impact. Fortunately the pullout happened in front of one of my other flights. The flight leader said the MiG never tried to pull out. It hit the ground so hard it did not even burn. I called the tech representative when I returned and told him, "I bent your airplane!" They flew a crew in from Tokyo to set the Sabre on jigs. They found it was perfectly alright with nothing wrong!

Baldwin remembered MiG Alley as mostly open country with a few small villages.

It was not highly populated. The weather was generally good. On rare occasions we had clouds that interfered. The MiGs as a rule did not fly through overcast, and those were the days we worked below it. There were beautiful days where everyone left contrails. Very soon, the sky looked like a plate of spaghetti! There were no mountains, only rolling hills. It was semi-agricultural, with small plots of land and open brush.

Baldwin's opposite number in the 4th was Lt Col Royal N. Baker, one of the oldest pilots, at 34, to fly in Korea. The month he became group commander of the 4th, he scored his first victory on June 20, 1952, when he, Captain Frederick C. "Boots" Blesse and 1st Lt George J. Woods ran across a flight of piston-engine La-11 night-fighters of the 351st IAP and each shot down one of the old fighters; the Communist night-fighters had achieved some success over the previous month against night-flying B-29s. Throughout the summer and fall of 1952, Baker had scored regularly. He was credited with his fifth victory on October 25 and his tenth on February 14, 1953. Shortly after Baldwin scored his third victory, Baker shot down his 13th MiG. Having completed his tour, he left Korea as the second-ranking Air Force ace after Major George Davis, with a score of 13 to Davis' 14, achieved over 127 missions. Under his command over nine months, the 4th Fighter-Interceptor Group became the top scorers in the competition with Baldwin's group.

Equipped with the F-86F from the time the unit entered combat, the 39th Squadron quickly became the 51st Wing's top scorers. The squadron was led by Lt Col George I. Ruddell, who had scored 2.5 victories in World War II flying P-40s in the Aleutians with the 11th Fighter Squadron of the 343rd Fighter Group, commanded by Col John Chennault, son of the legendary General Claire Chennault. He would score eight MiGs in Korea by the end of the war and was well remembered by those who served under him as an aggressive and demanding leader who worried about his pilots.

When the 39th Squadron re-equipped with Sabres, the F-51 pilots were transferred out and sent to the Mustang squadrons in the 18th Fighter-Bomber group. With news that a sudden need to fill a large number of jet-fighter pilot slots existed, experienced pilots who had been shut out of flying Sabres till now put in for transfers, hoping the fact of their previous combat experience would give them an edge in getting an assignment to the new squadron.

Among those who made the cut was 1st Lt Harold E. "Hal" Fischer. Born on a farm near Lone Rock, Iowa, on May 8, 1925, Fischer had grown up reading about the flyers of World War I and building model airplanes he flew from the roof of his family's barn. Once out of high school he joined the Navy and served at sea briefly before the end of the Pacific War. Returning home he went to Iowa State University for two years on the GI Bill, then joined the Army in 1948. Transferring to the Air Force in 1950, he went through flight training at Williams AFB before being assigned to the 49th Fighter-Bomber Wing, where he flew 108 missions in the F-80C Shooting Star.

Following the end of his tour:

> I volunteered to go to Headquarters, Far East Command, to work as a personnel officer in the Combat Crew Branch. After I was there for a while, the lure of air combat and all the talk of "jet aces" began to excite me. One day, Bill Whisner stopped by my office. He told me experienced pilots were needed desperately in his unit. When he saw my positive response, he said he thought I could be an ace. I applied quickly for another combat tour and made several visits over to Korea to "court" the F-86 units there. This paid off, and I soon received orders to the 51st Fighter-Interceptor Wing at Suwon.

Assigned to the new 39th Squadron, he was cleared as an element leader for combat missions following six hours and 45 minutes of checkout in the F-86F.

The 39th began flying operations into MiG Alley at the end of September 1952. Fischer later recalled that:

> After a few missions, I was assigned as element leader to a flight commanded by an RCAF exchange officer, Squadron Leader Douglas Lindsay. He was one of those rare individuals who was truly dedicated to getting the job done. And because of his beliefs – that the results are more important than the methods – he was viewed with disfavor by some. But without a doubt, he was the best fighter pilot I had ever seen or flown with. As my mission total increased, so did my desire to get a kill. Soon the moment came that I had been dreaming about. On my fifth mission, I was number three with Lindsay, when the sky was suddenly filled with MiGs everywhere. I called that I was going to make a "bounce," turned to the left and surveyed the scene for a moment.
>
> I saw two MiGs heading north, about 1,500 feet below me. I eased down and fell in behind them, about a mile in trail. I don't think they saw me, and I pulled up the nose of my aircraft, moved the radar gun sight to manual and fired several long bursts. Just as I was going to break off the attack, the wingman began a slow descent. I called Lindsay that I had one going down. I followed and when I caught up

to the MiG, I rolled around him and got one of the biggest surprises of my life. The canopy was missing and the pilot was gone! When the MIG crashed I knew there was no positive verification on the gun-camera film, so I strafed the wreckage for confirmation purposes. That evening, Lindsay told me that it would probably be impossible to sleep. He said that after his first kill in Spitfires during WWII in England, he couldn't sleep a wink. He was right.

Fischer's second victory came several weeks later, without actually hitting his opponent.

I made an attack on a MiG by positioning myself about 600 feet directly behind him at 40,000ft. Before I could fire, he entered and completed a perfect loop. I floundered over the top, and he proceeded into a series of loops. With each successive loop, my advantage increased slightly because of the "flop" at the top. This way, I was squaring a corner of our circle, and the flying tail helped out at the bottom. I had presence of mind to fire only short bursts, so as not to dissipate air speed at that altitude. Over the Yalu, he straightened out for a moment and I prepared to fire a long burst when I observed an object going by my canopy. It was the MiG's canopy, followed shortly by the pilot in his ejection seat! When the gun camera film was processed, the seat could be seen going by.

Over the next 30 days, Fischer scored numbers three and four. He named his Sabre, F-86F-10NA, 51-12958, "Paper Tiger" and painted a tiger mouth around the intake, in reply to the Chinese Communist assertion that the United States was an over-rated "paper tiger." His fourth victory was remembered as his most difficult to date.

When I commenced my attack on him, the closure rate was so great that I had to execute a displacement roll around him to maintain nose-to-tail separation. As I rolled, I hit his exhaust. The jolt was so great that my binoculars hit the stick grip and were broken – binoculars were carried by all serious students of MiG killing, just for the chance to get a "first sighting."
    As I tried to recover the aircraft and myself, the gunsight quit while I was firing and the guns also stopped. For a heartbeat, I thought

of ramming, striking the horizontal tail which I could see was just inboard of my left wing. I missed by about six inches. Rolling over the MiG, which was rapidly losing airspeed, I recycled the gun switch to "guns, sight, and camera" and everything came back on. I popped the speed brakes, squeezed the trigger, and literally blasted the MiG out of the sky.

On January 24, 1953, "Hal" Fischer became the 25th US jet ace of the war. The fifth victory stood out in memory for the rest of his life.

The fifth kill was one of both anguish and jubilation. I ended up in a tail chase about 4000 feet from the MiG. Again, I turned off the radar computing gunsight, elevated the nose and fired. The tracers made a small halo around the MiG. Gradually a fire began to grow in the rear of the MiG, and about the time I had closed to an ideal firing range there was no need to expend any more ammunition. It was a dying aircraft, with the entire fuselage serving as a flame holder.

I pulled up alongside. The pilot was beating on the canopy, trying to escape. Seeing me, he tried to turn and ram me. I thought the humane thing to do was to put the pilot out of his misery, so I slid my Sabre back onto his tail. Molten metal from the MiG rained on my aircraft. Firing a few short bursts, the sounds suddenly changed. Three of my guns quit firing, my left rudder pedal went to the firewall, and I thought for sure I had been hit. I disengaged and cautiously returned home to find after landing that the intense heat from the burning MiG had caused a misfire of a .50-cal. round. The exploding cartridge shut down the guns, severed the rudder cable, and subsequently dumped my pressurization.

Victories six and seven came ten days later.

The next two kills were in the best fighter tradition of Mannock, Udet, Nungesser, and other heroes of the first dogfights in World War I. I found myself and the MiG at the same airspeed, altitude, and going in the same direction. Immediately we got into a flat scissors maneuver trying to get on the other's tail. Dropping my speed brakes and using aerodynamic braking, I fell in behind the MiG at a range of about 600 feet. This time the radar gunsight was working marvelously and the first burst of a few seconds caused my opponent's aircraft to light up almost wingtip to wingtip. Before I could fire again, the canopy went by, followed by the pilot.

As we were leaving MiG Alley, my flight had to break to avoid an attack. I fell in trail behind my wingman and told him to take us home. As we climbed out, I spotted a MiG closing behind my wingman at about 3000 feet. I dropped in behind him at about the same range but he must've seen me. He turned left and I zoomed into a yo-yo. He continued and I ended up behind him at about 300 feet almost in full stall. I fired a burst that struck right behind the canopy and the MIG immediately snapped into a spin. There was nothing else to do but spin with him. Both of us entered the spin at about 30,000ft. I would take short bursts when my F-86 pointed at him. He spun all the way into the ground.

Fischer remembered victory number eight as the one that held the most danger and which was fraught with the most mistakes.

It began with a new wingman, who had been a professional musician and could play a mean clarinet. Our flight was late getting into the area and battles had already begun. The fight was taking place about 50 miles northeast of the mouth of the Yalu River. We came into the area climbing through 40,000 feet, dropped our tanks, and spotted four MiGs in a fingertip formation. There were four F-86s behind them at a great distance. As we jockeyed for position, we almost collided with the other Sabres, since neither formation wanted to give way and lose the advantage. No one was firing because the range was so great, but the MiGs appeared to be aware of us.

We were now over China. We were above a solid layer of clouds and they were letting down into it. Guessing where they were going, I continued down with my element and occasionally could see them going in and out of cloud layers. Then we all broke out. They were to our left and in a turn. We could've joined up with them. In fact, my join-up with the number two MiG was too good, and I was too close to open fire effectively. My wingman called me clear to fire, and as I got into position, a volley of cannon tracers went by my right wing and canopy. Immediately my wingman called me clear again, and I thought he had negated whoever was shooting at me.

I continued my attack, but once again a burst of fireworks passed my right wing and canopy before I could fire. Still I didn't look back, and once more my wingman called me clear. I was very nervous by now, but not once did I look around to my six o'clock. I suspect the reason I wasn't nailed was because I was so close to the MiG in front of me that his buddy couldn't get a good shot at me without hitting his friend. Finally I thought I was clear to fire, and it was no problem to dispatch the aircraft in front of me, once I got my mind settled down. A few good bursts and the battle was over. The MiG was on fire and the pilot ejected.

Fischer's tenth victory on April 6, 1953 was his easiest of all, and he became a double ace. "I saw a MiG firing on an F-86 and dove on him. I fired and got his attention. He disengaged and headed north. I fell in behind him and easily got him burning. The pilot bailed out."

On April 7, Fischer flew his final mission. As he recalled:

My last mission of the war was both successful and unsuccessful. I set up a pass on two MiGs in formation. My speed was such that I rolled over the number two man and fired a long burst that stopped his engine. Devoting my attention to the leader, I fired from about 1,200 feet and this tore apart the MiG. Debris came back at my aircraft in large pieces. I instinctively ducked as parts came by my canopy. Some of them went into my engine and it came to a stop. I smelled smoke and stepped over the side and into captivity.

It was later determined that Fischer had been shot down by Han Decai of the PLAAF, who hit him at the same time he hit the wreckage of his 12th victim. After the end of the Cold War, Fischer discovered he had also been claimed as a victory by Major Dimitri Yermakov, a WWII ace with 26 victories, who claimed "Paper Tiger" as one of two F-86s he was credited with in the Korean War. Fischer corresponded with Yermakov and met then-General Decai during a visit to Shanghai in 1997.

Fischer had ejected on the wrong side of the Yalu River; his captivity lasted two years past the end of the Korean War on July 27, 1953, along with three other Sabre pilots who were captured in Manchuria. Nine months into his captivity, he was captured during an attempted escape.

After that, he was routinely tortured and ultimately admitted to charges he had been ordered to enter Manchuria and had participated in germ warfare. Fischer and the three other pilots, Major Edwin L. Heller, 1st Lt Lyle W. Cameron and 1st Lt Roland W. Parks, were tried in Beijing on May 24, 1955, and found guilty of violating Chinese territory by flying across the border while on missions over North Korea. They were sentenced to be deported and the three of them walked across Freedom Bridge at Panmunjom the next day.

Ten days before "Hal" Fischer became an ace, 1st Lt Joseph C. McConnell, Jr. finally scored his first victory.

Born on January 30, 1922 in Dover, New Hampshire, McConnell had enlisted in the Army Medical Corps after graduating from high school in 1941 and entered the Aviation Cadet Program in 1943, hoping to achieve his lifelong dream of becoming a pilot. Too many demerits during basic training resulted in his being assigned to navigator training rather than flight school. He completed his training and became a second lieutenant on September 18, 1944. After completing combat crew training for the B-24 Liberator, he was assigned to the 448th Bomber Group in England in January 1945, where he flew 60 missions by the end of the war.

Electing to remain in the Army Air Forces after the war, he was finally accepted for flight training in 1947 and achieved his lifelong goal and his pilot wings in the new United States Air Force on February 25, 1948 at Williams. McConnell was sent to Alaska, where he flew F-80s with the Air Defense Command. When the Korean War broke out, he volunteered for assignment overseas, but was told that, at age 28, he was "too old." McConnell was persistent in his requests for overseas assignment, and finally in 1952 he was ordered to Nellis AFB for advanced flight training in the F-86.

Upon his arrival at Suwon, McConnell had been assigned to the 16th Fighter Squadron where he flew as a wingman for the rest of the year. Squadron commander Major Ed Heller believed in giving promising pilots the opportunity to advance, and the fact that McConnell's excellent eyesight had made him a good defensive wingman led to his promotion to element leader in late November, with several opportunities during December to lead a flight.

On Heller's recommendation, McConnell was assigned to the 39th Squadron in early January, flying as a flight leader assigned to command

D Flight. Within two weeks of his arrival, he shot down his first MiG-15 on January 14, 1953. By February 16, he had scored his fifth victory to become the 27th US ace of the war.

McConnell's friend "Pete" Fernandez, Jr., who had been his gunnery instructor at Nellis and arrived in Korea with him in September 1952, had been assigned to the 334th Fighter Squadron at Kimpo. Like McConnell, Fernandez had also been a lifelong "airplane nut," building model airplanes as a child growing up in Miami, Florida, and selling newspapers to raise the money to obtain his pilot's license when he was 15. Fernandez was supported in his enthusiasm for flying by his father, an early amateur radio enthusiast who became chief radio operator for Pan American World Airways.

He graduated from Andrew Jackson High School in Miami in January 1943 and enlisted in the USAAF's Aviation Cadet program on February 23, 1943, having passed the entrance examination high enough that the requirement to have two years of college was waived. He began flight training on November 5, 1943 and was commissioned a second lieutenant and awarded his pilot wings on November 20, 1944. He was assigned as a flight instructor in Midland, Texas, then sent to San José, Guatemala to train pilots of the Guatemalan air force.

In November 1946, Fernandez was assigned to the 23rd Fighter Squadron, 36th Fighter Group at Howard Field in Panama. In 1947, the unit transferred to the United States where they converted to the F-80 Shooting Star. Following the imposition of the Soviet blockade of Berlin in June 1948, the 36th's Shooting Stars were loaded aboard USS *Sicily* (CVE-118) and sent to Glasgow, Scotland. Once refurbished from the sea voyage, the group moved to Fürstenfeldbruck air base in Germany to provide fighter cover for C-47s and C-54s involved in the Berlin Airlift.

Returning to the United States, Fernandez was again assigned as a flight instructor for new F-80 pilots at Randolph AFB in Texas. A year later he was checked out in the F-86 and assigned as a gunnery instructor at Nellis AFB. He developed a reputation as a crack marksman and one of the best deflection shooters in the Air Force at the time. When war broke out in Korea, he volunteered for a combat assignment but was told his skills as a gunnery instructor were too valuable to let him go. Frustrated by repeated denials of his request for combat duty, Fernandez began a disobedience program, showing up at 0500 hours late, drunk, or on occasion AWOL. Eventually, his superiors were forced to choose between court-martialing him or sending him to Korea.

While McConnell started in the 51st as a wingman, Fernandez's experience earned him assignment as a flight leader in the 334th from the outset. He was credited with his first victory within ten days of his arrival in the squadron on October 4, 1952. On February 18, 1953, two days after McConnell had become an ace, "Pete" Fernandez became the war's 28th US ace when he scored his fifth and sixth victories.

The new year 1953 also saw the return of first Korean ace Major James Jabara on a second tour that January. It would be nearly four months before he scored his seventh credited victory, after which he would become "red hot" in his pursuit of the honor of becoming the war's top ace.

Major Ed Heller regularly took his flights of 16th Squadron F-86s north of the Yalu throughout 1952 and early 1953. One of the most successful pilots over Manchuria was Captain Dolphin D. "Dolph" Overton, who became the 24th US ace the same day "Hal" Fischer became number 25. Like Fischer, Overton had flown a 102-mission tour in F-84 fighter-bombers before wangling a transfer to the 51st. At the time he scored his fifth victory, he was on the "hottest streak" of any Sabre pilot, having scored all five victories in four missions over a ten-day period. Everyone knew he was going north of the river, because the MiGs weren't that common south of the border to allow such a score. One officer recalled that Heller's pilots were coming back with "blackened noses" after every flight. "That meant they were shooting at MiGs every time they went up. That couldn't happen unless they were on the wrong side of the border."

Heller was shot down over Manchuria on January 27, 1953 when a burst of fire from a MiG-15 hit his cockpit and broke his arm, severing his control stick and disabling his ejection seat. Falling from 40,000 feet to less than 2,000 feet, Heller saw an 8-inch hole in his canopy overhead. He forced his way through the canopy and was sucked out low enough that his parachute only swung once before landing. He was quickly captured. Since he was 150 miles north of the Yalu, no attempt was made to rescue him. There was no way for the Air Force to hush this up, since the fight and Heller's bail out had been witnessed by Communist peace negotiators on a train traveling to Panmunjom to re-open negotiations.

Overton had flown the same mission and returned to Suwon to claim his sixth and seventh victories. He was met by wing commander Col John Mitchell, who was, as one witness later recalled, "madder than any colonel I've ever seen." Overton was immediately confined to quarters. The next day, General Barcus arrived to confer with Mitchell and it was decided that Overton, who had graduated from West Point in the class of 1949 and had followed orders like everyone else in the squadron when he crossed the border with Heller, would be the scapegoat. 4th Group commander Colonel Brooks was ordered to inform Overton he was being stripped of ace status and shipped out of Korea immediately. In the event, Air Force headquarters refused to go along with completely stripping Overton of his status, but his final two victories were never awarded. Ironically, it was likely the success of the January air battles that had taken place north of the Yalu that broke the logjam and restarted negotiations.

The air war continued to heat up during the spring of 1953. "Hal" Fischer, "Pete" Fernandez, and Joe McConnell were building double-digit scores. The Air Force found that the air battles in MiG Alley were the one thing that attracted the correspondents who were bored over the still-slow pace of the now-resumed peace talks at Panmunjom. Fifth Air Force's public relations department decided to create an "ace race" to generate more favorable publicity. In the wake of the "Heller incident," General Barcus had given approval in February to an official policy of "hot pursuit" that would allow the Sabres to chase MiGs across the Yalu when the enemy jet had been hit in combat south of the border. The real result was that the new policy gave a semiofficial "wink and a nod" approval to pilots who went hunting in the skies of Manchuria as Heller and Overton had done, and cross-border violations reached an all-time high over the rest of the war. All of the top-scoring aces of this period scored many of their victories north of the Yalu.

On March 21, "Pete" Fernandez led a flight to the Yalu. Cho-do radar warned him of MiGs in the area. Just at that moment, his element leader suffered a mechanical malfunction and was forced to abort with his wingman. When Fernandez ordered his wingman to drop their tanks, one of his tanks hung up. At that moment the MiGs appeared. Fernandez should have aborted, but instead he flew into the enemy formation of 30–40 MiGs. He closed behind the last two and opened fire on the wingman, who took hits in the fuselage and immediately ejected. Fernandez closed to within 200 yards of the leader and opened fire. The MiG caught fire as the pilot slumped in his cockpit, then fell off in a vertical dive to smash into the fields below. Fernandez was now a double ace with ten victories.

When he reported to the 39th Squadron, Joe McConnell met Flt Lt Roy French, an RAF exchange pilot. French had volunteered for assignment to Korea after seeing an F-86 perform in Britain. "It was completely clear from the first time I saw one," he recalled years later, "that the Sabre represented the ultimate in what would interest a fighter pilot: it looked right, it flew right, it was right." On the Suwon flight line, French was distinguished by his white helmet with RAF roundels painted over the earphones. The two men hit it off, and French flew McConnell's wing through most of his scoring missions that spring.

French had great reason to remember the mission of April 12, 1953. "While we were suiting up, Joe asked to borrow my helmet, and I decided 'why not?' As it turned out, I would regret that decision." The fight McConnell got into that day was one of the epic encounters of Sabre and MiG. While he would score his eighth victory against a Soviet ace, McConnell was shot down himself – by the pilot he shot down!

The MiG-15s that D Flight went up against were from the 913rd IAP of the 32nd IAD. Captain Semen Alexeievich Fedorets scored early in the fight, claiming his fifth victory against another Sabre pilot, killing 1st Lt Robert Niemann when he hit the Sabre in the forward fuselage. He then saw what turned out to be McConnell's Sabre, chasing another MiG. Fedorets performed a wingover and put himself slightly below, on the Sabre's tail. Roy French spotted the MiG and called to McConnell to break, but when McConnell glanced back he couldn't see Fedorets.

Seconds later, Fedorets fired a burst that smashed into McConnell's Sabre, nearly severing the right wing and hitting the engine. Despite the damage Fedorets' fire had caused, McConnell managed to force his Sabre into a barrel roll, which resulted in Fedorets overtaking him so that McConnel came out of the roll on his opponent's tail without Fedorets being aware of what had happened. With the tables turned, McConnell opened fire on Fedorets' MiG, which caught fire. Fedorets immediately ejected. McConnell's Sabre was smoking, the engine could only provide half power, and the radio was out. However, the crippled Sabre was still controllable. McConnell stayed with his airplane.

Fedorets later described the fight:

My number three and number four, Aleksandrov and Shorin, lost track of me during my sharp maneuvers, but my wingman Yefremov stayed with me. When I was closing on this Sabre I heard Yefremov say "A flight of Sabres behind." He then went away to the left, leaving me alone without cover. As soon as I stopped looking through the gunsight and I turned my head, a short burst struck my cockpit from the right and above.

I sharply broke to the right underneath the Sabre, getting out of the line of fire. The Sabre went forward, and ended up in front of me at my right. The American pilot turned his head, saw me and lowered his air brakes, with the intent to slow down, to let me pass forward and to riddle me at short range. I realized his maneuver, and sharply broke left, while firing a burst at the Sabre without aiming. The burst struck the base of the right wing, close to the fuselage. A huge hole, about one square meter, appeared in the Sabre's wing. He broke to the right and fell downwards. That was my second enemy aircraft destroyed in that combat.

As soon as I got my plane out of the attack, I was hit by a machine gun burst. I sharply pushed the stick, and tried to disengage. The cockpit filled with smoke and kerosene, the instrument panel was destroyed, and finally the new pair of Sabres [Fedorets was unaware of McConnell's maneuver] knocked out my controls. Using the trimmer I leveled my plane, and decided to bail out. With a tremendous effort I was able to eject the canopy, and successfully ejected out of my damaged plane at 11,000 meters altitude.

Followed by Roy French and element leader 1st Lt Harold Chitwood and his wingman, McConnell headed south, toward the Yellow Sea. His Sabre was still smoking, but not burning. Chitwood contacted Cho-do control and called for air-sea rescue. Once far enough offshore, and with the approaching H-19 rescue chopper in sight, McConnell ejected and parachuted into the water. "And of course, when he hit the water, he lost my helmet!" French remembered.

The air-sea rescue teams at Cho-do were so well organized that McConnell was in the water less than five minutes before he was winched to safety. In a letter home to his sister, McConnell joked, "I barely got wet." On April 24, he scored his tenth victory. Fernandez scored number 11 a day later. Fifth Air Force public affairs had their "ace race."

The two friends were remembered in much the same way by those they flew with. Fernandez stalked MiGs with stealth and cunning rather than attacking impetuously. He held his fire until he attained an optimum firing position. Unlike aces such as Gabreski and Jabara, Fernandez had a reputation for not being reckless with his wingman's safety in pursuit of air victories. Roy French remembered that McConnell was:

> the best shot I ever saw. He got in close, which was the only way to be sure you got a MiG with the Sabre's light armament. We wingmen liked flying with him because he paid attention to what was going on and never had a problem with breaking off from an attack to protect us if we got into trouble.

During the first half of May, Fernandez added three and a half victories to his score, to pass George Davis' score of 14. These last victories were most likely scored over Manchuria, though they were "officially" reported as taking place just south of the Yalu. Now the leading ace in Korea, Fernandez was ordered home on May 13, with the official reason given that he had "overstayed his tour" with 125 missions. In fact, after the loss of "Hal" Fischer, General Barcus wanted to make sure his heroes got home to their hero's welcome. When Fernandez got home to Miami, he was the star of a parade down Biscayne Avenue and received the key to the city from the mayor.

At the time Fernandez made his score, McConnell's score was 13. On May 16, three days after Fernandez' departure, Major James Jabara, now the executive officer of the 4th Wing's 334th Squadron, finally scored victory number seven to end his four-month "drought." That afternoon, Jabara scored a double to bring him to nine.

Two days of bad weather over North Korea slowed the air battles. On May 18, the weather over North Korea cleared and the Sabres headed north.

McConnell and wingman 1st Lt Dean Abbott spotted an enemy formation. When the two MiGs they were chasing flew across the Yalu River into Manchuria, they followed in "hot pursuit." As McConnell closed in on the trailing MiG, a large formation of MiGs showed up. The two Americans were hard-pressed to out-fly their opponents. McConnell shot a MiG off Abbott's tail for his first score. The two Sabres kept up their evasive scissors and moments later McConnell shot another MiG off Abbott's tail. The staff back at K-13 heard Abbott call that he thought there were 30 MiGs. McConnell replied, "Yeah, and we've got 'em all to ourselves." Minutes later as the MiGs ganged up on the two Sabres, they hit "bingo" fuel and dove away south of the Yalu. The MiGs broke off their pursuit and the pair landed safely back at Suwon.

McConnell was scheduled for a second mission that afternoon, and he begged Colonel Baldwin not to inform FEAF that he now had 15. He took the mission and got his third kill of the day, just south of the Yalu. When General Barcus was informed that McConnell now had 16 and was the first "triple jet ace," it was reported the general said, "I want that man on his way back home to the USA before you hear the period at the end of this sentence."

McConnell was replaced as "D" Flight Commander by his element leader, Major John Bolt, USMC, of the famed "Black Sheep" VMF-214, who had been flying with the wing since March when he completed his combat tour flying Panthers with VMF-124. Over the two months of combat left before the armistice, Bolt became the only Marine ace of the Korean War, shooting down six MiGs, all north of the Yalu.

McConnell arrived home only days after his friend "Pete" Fernandez. The two aces were welcomed at the White House by President Eisenhower, who had requested a "personal briefing" from the two men. Two months later, McConnell stood as best man for his friend's wedding.

CHAPTER 18

THE FINAL MONTHS

Throughout the war, the Sabre pilots had complained about the light armament they had to use against the hardy MiGs and repeatedly requested that the fighter be rearmed with 20mm cannon. In 1952, Air Force headquarters ordered North American to modify four F-86E-10s and six F-86F-1s on the production line with four T-160 20mm cannons, a design based on the excellent German MG 151 cannon. The Sabres were designated F-86F-2s. After testing at Eglin AFB and Edwards AFB, eight were sent to Korea in early 1953 and issued to a special group of pilots in the 4th Group's 335th Squadron for combat evaluation as part of Operation *Gunval*.

Lt Col George C. Jones, who had commanded the 51st Fighter Group in 1952, returned to Korea with the cannon-armed Sabres as head of the *Gunval* evaluation team. On March 29, 1953, flying a *Gunval* Sabre as element leader in a flight of normal Sabres, he flew a fighter sweep to the Yalu he would describe 40 years later as:

one that remains vivid in my memory. I remember it so well because it was a mission whose outcome pivoted around the reactions of two wingmen in a combat situation – my wingman and his enemy counterpart in a MiG-15.

Originally, we had a flight of four aircraft scheduled for the mission. But somewhere along the line, two of the flight didn't get off, and my wingman, Major Wendall Brady, and I proceeded with the mission as a flight of two.

The two Sabres entered MiG Alley at 42,000 feet, with the contrail level at 30–38,000 feet.

Flicking my left wing down for the crossover signal, I moved my wingman to the left side and gave him the "Heads Up!" signal. I knew there were plenty of MiGs in the area and I wanted no surprises. Rather selfishly, we hoped that the large formation of Sabres behind us would be the focal point of attention on the enemy radar scopes. Our small flight might have a good chance to make a surprise "bounce" on the MiGs trying to intercept the north-bound flights.

As we approached the Yalu, I spotted a glint in the sky high above us and to the right. I waggled the stick, rocking my wings to get my wingman's attention. I silently signaled "Drop tanks!" Again a silent signal to push up the throttle, and we started a slow turn under the "glint" above. Now we could see many other flashes in the sun up ahead. All of a sudden I saw them. First there was nothing in front, then they jumped into focus. A flight of eight MiGs in loose trail, climbing as they crossed the Yalu heading south. Ever so gently, we increased our rate of turn and started an easy climb behind them. I swung in behind their last man, but still too far out to shoot. We had to close on them.

I watched the range dial unroll. We were closing on them, but slow. I glanced behind. Bad news! Coming in from below, almost in position for an attack on me, was a MiG! I realized now that I had cut between the leader and his wingman! Jerking around I looked to my right for my wingman. He was right there. As I watched, he dropped his wing as if to start a firing pass on the MiG coming up.

I snapped my head around to the left. The MiG that had tilted his wing down for the start of a slanting pass at me suddenly straightened up and leveled out. No attack this time. Evidently, he realized if he jumped me, Wendall would swing in behind him for a firing pass.

By now we were climbing through 40,000 feet. The MiG I was chasing was closer. The range was 1,800 feet. I wanted 800 feet, but I wasn't sure how long the game between the two wingmen would keep up. Each feinting an attack, one at me, one at the other.

In the back of my mind I remembered the engine compressor stalls which had been occurring when we fired the new cannons at high altitude, a stall which robbed the engine of power, leaving you a sitting duck unless you could recover by diving to a lower altitude for a try at an air start. I dismissed the thought – "Shoot first! Worry about the stall later."

Now the range dial on the gunsight indicated 1,000 feet. The MiG at my rear was getting frantic. Wendall broke radio silence: "I can't hold him much longer. Get out of there! Get out of there!" "Watch him," I replied, "Call if he turns in." I eased my nose up, the pipper was just under the MiG. "A little more. Up a little, easy, don't lose air speed."

Finally, the pipper was on his tailpipe and the range was 800 feet. The little orange-colored diamonds of the sight reflected on my windscreen and circled the MiG perfectly. I pressed the trigger. Instantly a stream of incandescent flashes exploded in rapid succession on the MiG and it seemed to stop in mid-air as it burst in flame and smoke. I was momentarily fascinated by the sight. Then with an awful start, I realized that I was about to run into him.

Before I could do anything, I was completely enveloped in smoke. I felt there was a solid wall of debris ahead in the darkness. Instinctively I retarded the throttle, my thumb jerking back the speed brake switch to slow down. Now I could only pull back on the stick and try rolling upside down in a barrel roll, hoping to get out of the way. Suddenly, I was out of the smoke. Looking through the canopy, I saw the MiG. The canopy was gone, the cockpit empty. It was starting down with debris, smoke and flames trailing behind. I rolled upright.

It was then I first noticed the sound of my engine in a compressor stall – a roaring, buzzing noise that vibrated the whole airplane. I wasn't too worried. I knew what to do – point her nose down. In the past, we usually recovered from these stalls around 30,000 feet. However, when I passed through 30,000 with the engine still stalling, I began to worry. At 25,000 nothing had changed.

The stall really had my attention now. I remember thinking, "At 18,000 feet I'll have to pull out. Maybe I can glide out to the Yellow Sea." Then I noticed my speed brake switch had broken off, and the brakes were still open, and still slowing me down. I pushed my index finger down between the thumb guard to the nub of the switch and edged it forward. All at once, the brakes closed and I felt the aircraft accelerate. With the increased speed the buzzing stopped, the engine smoothed, and the compressor stall broke. I eased the power on. It was 18,000 feet. I took a deep breath.

Now I felt better about the situation and looked around for my wingman. There he was, just off my right wing, staring through the oil-smeared canopy at me. I couldn't have been happier. I started to relax a little and gave him a signal that meant, "Let's get the hell out of here! I'll buy the drinks tonight!" For the second time during the entire flight, he broke radio silence: "You're all heart, Lead!" He was "there" all the way, a great wingman. Major Wendall Brady was an accomplished flier to whom the flick of a wing tip spoke volumes. If not for a great wingman today, I would not have been able to make "ace."

Over the course of the next two months, Jones would score 6.5 victories in the *Gunval* Sabre and prove the value of the 20mm cannon. No other Air Force fighter after the F-86 would be armed with machine guns.

For the PLAAF, the month of May, when the air war became "white hot," saw losses so high that the political leadership in Beijing became appalled when they learned the actual figures. Wang Bingzhang, First Deputy Commander of the PLAAF, was sent to Antung to determine what the cause of the problem was. He concluded that fundamentally the problem was due to the inexperience and poor proficiency of pilots in terms of intelligence, coordination, tactics and marksmanship.

Beginning at the end of May, the dank weather of the Korean monsoon reduced the tempo of air operations over North Korea. Even with its poor weather, June saw the Sabre pilots scoring fast and furious, since the cloudy conditions forced the MiGs to operate beneath them, at the Sabre's best operating altitude. By June 10, Jabara was credited with his tenth victory, but was also mired in a controversy within the Air Force.

On a patrol in MiG Alley, Jabara spotted four jets headed south that crossed the Yalu. It was a moment when his notoriously poor eyesight would get him in trouble, since he failed to recognize that the four swept-wing fighters he was closing on all had the yellow fuselage bands and wing stripes of F-86s. Rather than the flight of MiGs he thought he was engaging, Jabara was in fact taking aim at 1st Lt Dick Frailey, a 64-mission veteran of the 334th Squadron, who was flying Jabara's usual Sabre and had frequently flown Jabara's wing.

Jabara closed in on the number four airplane and opened fire on Frailey, who recognized his opponent. "Jabara, you're shooting at me!" he screamed over the radio, but Jabara continued and fired seven more bursts of machine-gun fire from a range of 3,000 feet. The bullets smashed the left wing, engine and canopy of Frailey's Sabre, while several rounds passed close by Frailey's arm and chest and ripped his instrument panel.

Frailey's engine started to smoke and the Sabre rolled over into a dive. With his controls badly damaged, he managed to temporarily recover control of the fatally damaged Sabre and head toward the Yellow Sea, where he might have a chance of rescue. By this point, Jabara had realized his mistake and was accompanying his erstwhile wingman. Just over the coast, the damaged Sabre gave up the ghost and Frailey was forced to bail out close enough to shore to be in range of Communist artillery. He had trouble getting out of his seat and was only able to deploy his parachute moments before hitting the water. The parachute dropped on top of him and he had to use his knife to escape the web of tangle shroud lines. When he tried to inflate his dinghy, he discovered one of Jabara's bullets had punctured it.

With the Communists shooting at him, Frailey was rescued by an SA-16 Albatross whose pilot braved the barrage to pluck him from the water. Jabara was quickly sent on a week's R&R in Japan despite his protests that he was close to breaking the record to keep him away from any reporters who might hear rumors of the event.

Jabara returned to combat in the last week of June, and scored his 14th victory on June 30, putting him half a kill behind Fernandez. He scored his 15th and final victory on July 15, to come in at second place in the "ace race."

Jabara wasn't the only high-scoring pilot at this time. 4th Group commander Lt Col Vermont Garrison had flown P-51s with the unit in England during World War II, where he scored one victory in 92 missions. Garrison came to the 4th Group in November 1952, to take command until the end of the war. By February 28, 1953, he had scored his fifth victory. As group commander, he could pick and choose his missions, and took those that were more promising of action. He scored his tenth and final victory on June 30.

The fastest-scoring double ace of the war was Captain Ralph Parr of the 335th Squadron, who scored his ten victories during 30 missions flown in the final two months of the war. Parr had flown P-38s in the final six months of the war in the Pacific with the 49th Fighter Group, but had had no opportunity to engage the enemy. Returning to the 49ers in 1950, he flew 165 fighter-bomber missions in F-80s. After honing his skills in the F-86 flying in the 1st Fighter-Interceptor Wing with Korean War ace "Boots" Blesse, Parr arrived in Korea in mid-May, assigned to the 4th, where he became squadron operations officer in the 334th. He engaged MiGs on June 3 while flying an orientation flight as a wingman, where he discovered he had opened fire at too great a range. All of his ten kills, starting with the first two scored during his 16th mission on June 7, would be confirmed on his gun camera film.

Parr recalled after the war that his most exciting fight was his first, in which he scored two victories on June 7, 1953. John Shark Flight of the 335th Squadron was at 43,000 feet, 20 miles south of the Yalu. Flying lead was 1st Lt Mervin Ricker, with Col Robert Dixon on his wing, accompanied by element leader 2nd Lt Al Cox with wingman Captain Ralph Parr on his final "wingman" mission. The sky was a deep blue with ceiling and visibility unlimited.

When "Dentist," the radar controller on Cho-do, called "bandit tracks," Ricker called "Drop tanks!" On their second swing to the northeast, Parr spotted four MiGs closing from the left. "John Shark, break left! MiGs close and firing!" Fortunately, the MiGs flew through the formation without hitting anyone. Ricker and Dixon turned after them, but they disappeared. With the two flights now separated, Ricker ordered Cox to withdraw. Cox completed a final orbit and nursed the two Sabres back up to 41,000 feet.

Glancing down at the Yalu to his right, Parr noticed movement and called it out. Cox radioed back, "I can't see it! You take it, I've got you covered." Parr rolled into a split-S at full power, and headed straight down to intercept what he thought were two MiGs going south. Cox asked which way Parr had gone. He replied, "Straight down. Come on down and find me."

Pulling out of his near-sonic dive at 500 feet under maximum G with his G-suit inflated to maximum, Parr closed on the MiGs. "I had found my MiG ... two ... nope, four ... Whoops – eight! No! Sixteen!" He was alone in the middle of an angry hornet's nest. Rapidly gaining on eight MiGs in two flights, Parr thought to himself, "This may be my last chance with the war winding down. So as long as I'm going to do it, I may as well take the leader and turn the peasants loose!" He lined up on the apparent leader as he closed within 3,000 feet. Out the corner of his eye he saw another eight to his left, then the eight in front broke in all directions.

Still closing fast, Parr jerked the throttle to idle, popped the speed brakes, and tracked the leader as he pulled the trigger while pulling Gs for all he was worth. Before he let off, the gunsight fuse blew at 9 Gs; he now had no working gunsight.

The MiG leader did a reverse that put him and Parr canopy-to-canopy in a rolling scissors, each looking straight at the other. The MIG pilot made a slight change and Parr slid behind so close he feared collision. Now on the deck and ten feet behind the quarry, he pulled the trigger. Gunsight or no gunsight, he couldn't miss. But with each burst, the Sabre stalled due to the tight turn and gun vibration.

On the fifth burst, Parr's Sabre was soaked with the MiG's fuel as he stalled through the turn. With the next burst, flame shot back from the MiG around the F-86, then its engine quit. Parr shot past as his opponent hit the ground. He rolled into a left turn just as another MiG closed in from the left. The MiG overshot and Parr reversed. He held the trigger down and walked tracers through the MiG before it could get out of range. Looking to his right, he saw five MiGs trying to cut inside. He pulled a hard left turn that kept them at bay, but he was hosed with cannon fire as each started shooting. "There were five of them firing at me and coming close!" Shooting at anything he saw as he turned and maneuvered, flat on the deck, another MiG spun and exploded when it hit the ground. Moments later, Cox showed up and the four survivors broke for the Yalu.

On the way back to Kimpo, Cox remarked that Parr's Sabre had sustained no damage, despite being shot at by seven MiGs. After review of Parr's gun camera film and Cox's report of the battle, Parr was credited with two MiGs destroyed and one damaged.

1st Lt Hank Buttelmann, who had arrived in Korea on December 23, 1952 and was assigned as a wingman in the 25th Squadron of the 51st Wing, finally achieved element lead status in June.

I was checked out as an element leader with 57 missions on June 19, 1953. June and July turned out to be the two months where more MiGs were shot down than any other time in the war. From January

15, 1953, when I flew my first mission, until mid-June, I saw the MiGs only twice, and on both cases, there were no engagements. From mid-June through July 1953, I saw MiGs on 80 percent of my missions.

After graduation from Aviation Cadet training in August 1952, Buttelmann was sent to advanced gunnery school at Nellis where he first flew F-80s and then both the F-86A and F-86E under the watchful eyes of Korean War veterans. Shortly after his 23rd birthday, he received orders to Korea. He recalled his seven months of war. "I have yet to meet any F-86 pilot who did not say that his one year in Korea was probably the high point of his life."

On June 19, 1953, on his first mission as an element leader, Buttelmann saw his first MiG and shot it down.

We were in MiG Alley on a normal patrol when I noticed a flight of MiGs. They were very low. Most of their flying during that time was usually at lower altitudes. We patrolled at altitude. After we punched our tanks off, I saw these MiGs heading home. I called the leader, and he rolled in after them. We were high and they were low. I was behind my leader as he went in on his bounce. He had his speed brakes down and came in fast. Unfortunately, he misjudged and rolled out way behind the MIGs. He obviously was not closing on them. I popped my speed brakes in and slid behind one MiG. I gave several short bursts when suddenly his canopy blew off. He was still flying. Then I gave him two more short bursts, and the pilot ejected. I was very fortunate. I never believed they saw us. The odd part about the kill was that after we rolled in, the MiG pilot never rolled his wings more than ten or fifteen degrees from straight and level. We came in behind and I hit him with several bursts. I saw an explosion which must have been in a critical area. Even with that, the guy never made a single turn! It was an easy kill.

Combat was so furious in June and early July that in eight missions, Buttelmann scored seven victories. He scored his fifth victory on June 30 to become the war's 36th Sabre ace.

The most difficult kill came when our flight got involved with two flights of MiGs. I had just shot down one MiG when I looked back and saw another MiG firing at me. I was lucky because he was a little out of range. I broke into him, and at that instant, I was hit underneath my fuselage about one foot behind my burner cans. I immediately got two fire warning lights. I pulled my power back to about 90 percent and kept turning into the MiG. At this point he broke off. Had he stayed, he would have done alright! As he broke, I rolled out. Again I was extremely fortunate because there were thunderstorms in the area and I got into the weather and stayed there. That saved me. Had it not been for the poor weather, I would have been in real trouble! I climbed through the weather and worked my way home. I was fortunate enough to bring the aircraft back.

On July 19, 1953, Buttelmann flew as element leader with Marine exchange pilot and future astronaut Major John Glenn leading the flight. Buttelmann's wingman, 1st Lt John Boyd, who would 30 years later become the "guru" of air combat strategy, was forced to abort due to a fuel feed problem. Buttelmann should have aborted with him, but he and Glenn, and Glenn's wingman 1st Lt Jerry Parker, elected to continue the mission. Glenn spotted four MiGs; as he closed on them, a flight of four Sabres and 12 more MiGs joined the fight. Glenn lost his wingman, and then Buttelmann, and overshot his target to become the MiG's target. Fortunately Parker swung in behind the MiG and shot it down, but Parker's Sabre was damaged by ingesting parts from the exploding MiG.

The two Sabres turned south, with Glenn escorting Parker. South of the Chongchon, six MiGs swept in to attack. Glenn turned into them and opened fire out of range, scaring them off. Glenn tacked onto the sixth MiG and shot it down for his second victory in the ten days he had been flying combat with the 51st. Buttelmann, who scored his seventh and final victory in the fight, later recalled that "if the MiGs had kept coming up in the last two weeks of July like they had during the first two weeks and the month of June, John Glenn would have become an ace at the rate he was going." As it was, on July 22, Glenn led another flight into MiG Alley where he spotted two MiGs and attacked with wingman Sam Young. Glenn shot down the leader for his third victory and Young shot the wingman off Glenn's tail, to score the final MiG kill of the Korean War.

Ralph Parr's tenth victory was perhaps the most controversial of the war. On June 27, 1953, leading a flight to escort a photo-reconnaissance mission to check on Communist cooperation with the terms of the pending ceasefire, Parr spotted a twin-engine transport north of the Yalu and watched it cross the Yalu. The photo pilot canceled his mission due to the cloudy weather, and Parr dove down on the unidentified airplane. Slowing 500 feet above it, he spotted North Korean markings. Parr checked his map to ensure he was south of the Yalu and attacked, setting first the left then the right engines afire; the right wing folded and the airplane crashed in a fiery explosion.

The Soviets protested that this was a civilian flight carrying a truce team, and that it had been shot down 60 miles north of the Yalu. Intelligence sources since have claimed the Il-12 "Crate" was carrying 17 general officers from Port Arthur to an intelligence conference at Vladivostok. Parr's Il-12 was the last airplane shot down in the Korean War.

CHAPTER 19

WHO WON?

The Korean War is thought of by those on the conservative side of the political aisle who support Douglas MacArthur and his "no substitute for victory" line in his famous "Old Soldiers Never Die" speech to Congress as "the first war the United States lost."

The past 65 years of US Air Force myth-making and propaganda has it that the Air Force was victorious in all areas of combat, most especially in that battle of the jet aces over MiG Alley, where the "fine American boys" defeated the forces of Communism by 10:1. While the other side's victory claim isn't as outlandish as the USAF victory ratio, their claims are also wildly out of line with actual losses.

The fighting over MiG Alley was the last "classic" aerial combat. While radar on both sides could guide their forces to the vicinity of the other, the pilots still found their opponents visually, with their "Mark I eyeball," in the same manner their forebears had done over the Western Front of World War I. The actual combat itself was only different from what Oswald Boelke had defined in 1916 in that the technology of the aircraft being flown would have been unimaginable to the father of fighter combat. It was still true that the man who saw the other first, and was able to maneuver to a favorable position to open fire, would be the likely winner of the fight.

This is also the explanation for why the claims of victory were so different from the records of losses, on both sides. Any pilot will admit that it is difficult to visually spot another airplane in the sky when the two aircraft are flying straight and level and there is no time to search the sky. From Boelcke's battles in 1916 on, every study of air combat has shown that victory claims made by individual pilots are more than double actual enemy losses. This is because when airplanes are maneuvering to get away from each other, and a pursuing pilot must divert his attention from following his prey to ensure he himself is not about to fall victim to another hunter, with everything happening quickly, it is almost impossible to know the ultimate outcome of such a brief encounter unless the target is immediately destroyed or the pilot bails out. Most victory claims are expressions more of hope than fact. This does not mean they are made in bad faith.

Both sides used gun camera film to support their claims. The Soviet gun cameras are well described by Russian historians Leonid Krylov and Yuriy Tepsurkaev:

> Soviet pilots were also hindered in their ability to gain confirmation for their claims by the unreliability of the gun camera fitted to the MiG-15. Operating at a rate of only eight frames per second, the cameras would stop immediately after the pilot released his gun trigger. A normal cannon burst lasted about a second, and when the target was engaged from a range of 400–600m (430–650 yards) the camera stopped working just as the first rounds reached the target! If a burst was shorter or the range was longer, the camera failed to register the target at the moment the shells hit home.

Given the rigid mount of the MiG's camera, photos were often blurry. The authors state that it was even difficult with some photos to recognize the aircraft type that was attacked. This is made more difficult by Soviet pilots lacking knowledge of Western types, leading to claims that mistake F-80s for F-84s or even F9Fs and vice versa. Since the battles were fought over territory controlled by the Communists, the Soviets did send teams into MiG Alley to find and identify aircraft claimed as shot down, which was something the USAF could not do.

For the USAF, the fact that MiG victories became the definition of combat command success for senior officers led to a "liberalization" of policy regarding confirmation of claims by gun camera film, a process started by Colonel Gabreski in the 51st Wing in 1952 out of his desire to compete with the 4th Wing for victory honors. This policy was expanded in 1953, since by then the air battles in MiG Alley were the only event attracting any correspondents, and the air battle was the one place where America was "winning" against the Communists. The "MiG kill" became for the US Air Force in Korea what the "body count" would be for Army and Marine ground units in Vietnam: the standard by which an officer was judged fit for promotion. This resulted in "grade inflation" in both wars.

With the Air Force high command demanding the production of "aces" for domestic publicity purposes, it was inevitable that the claims would become "malleable." This went back to the first ace, James Jabara, who was credited with six victories, but may only have scored three to a maximum of four confirmed by enemy losses. Even Dick Becker managed to be credited with a "probable" that was an actual "victory" and a "victory" that was a "damaged." With Air Force chief of staff General Vandenberg leaning heavily on FEAF commander Weyland to produce a "hero," it was no surprise that Jabara was only sent on missions where enemy opposition was likely, and that he would be held in the combat zone when his squadron completed its tour in order to achieve the goal. The official creation of "heroes" is important in military politics, to convince those back home that the struggle is worth the sacrifice.

The PLAAF claimed that, during the Korean War, Chinese pilots shot down 330 aircraft and damaged another 95 in air-to-air combat, for a loss of only 231 aircraft shot down and 151 damaged, for a victory ratio of 1.1:1 in the PLAAF's favor.

The Soviets admit a loss of 345 MiGs. If this admitted loss is added to the Chinese admitted loss of 231, the 576 total losses are approximately 50 percent of US claims. Considering the record through world wars I and II that victories claimed by either side are about double actual losses, these figures may be accurate. Again, there is a question about actual Soviet combat losses, since aircraft that were able to return so shot up that they were written off might not have been recorded as a "combat loss," in a way similar to the American practice of limiting combat loss claims.

The US Air Force claims 976 enemy aircraft destroyed in air-to-air combat, with total losses of 1,986 aircraft, 1,041 destroyed by "hostile action," which is mostly due to antiaircraft fire, while losing only 147 in air-to-air combat. Given that the US Air Force recorded any aircraft that managed to return to its base, no matter how badly damaged or its ultimate fate, or any aircraft returning from a combat mission that crashed over friendly territory, as an "operational accident," the American combat loss figures are not reliable. Former PLAAF commander Wang Hai, who flew in the Korean War, wrote in his autobiography regarding the claim of only 147 UN aircraft lost in air-to-air combat, "This is a lie as big as the heavens."

While the USAF produced gun camera film to support its claims, and the Chinese did not have such an accountability system, researchers who have compared USAF victory claims based on gun camera film with admitted Soviet losses have been able to demonstrate that MiGs claimed shot down by gun camera evidence did in fact return to base damaged. By 1952, gun camera film of aircraft not seen to go down, explode, disintegrate, or where the pilot ejected, was accepted as evidence of a "kill" regardless.

Recent studies of the battle for air superiority in the Korean War now regard the year 1951, remembered by Air Force pilots who were there as the "Year of the Honcho," as one of near equality between US and Soviet air units in terms of achievement. The victory/loss ratio was likely 1:1. As Dick Becker said, "It was a wash."

Air Force victory claims for 1952 and 1953 are subject to the "grade inflation" that happened as the high command searched for anything resembling "victory." While the majority of MiG pilots who opposed the Sabres were less-experienced Chinese, a victory/loss ratio of 10:1 as claimed after the war by the US Air Force, which was uncontradicted by information from the other side for 40 years, is not realistic. Researchers believe the actual figure was somewhere between 1.1:1–1.3:1 in favor of the Sabres.

If individual victory claims are inherently unreliable, how then is one to determine the answer to the question "who won?" The easy answer is, "who prevailed?" However, in the air battles over Korea, the two sides defined "victory" differently. And each can, by their definition of the term, claim they were victorious.

The Soviets sent their units to Manchuria for air defense, and their goal was to deny to the enemy the ability to bomb at will throughout North Korea, as had been the situation for the first nine months of the war. In this, they were successful. Following the Namsi raid in October 1951, the B-29 bombers did not venture over North Korea by daylight for the rest of the war, and they suffered losses at night that frequently stopped operations. As Lt Gen Charles Cleveland pointed out, this was the victory the German Luftwaffe had been unable to achieve over Germany against the USAAF.

Additionally, by the fall of 1952, Soviet and Chinese air strength was sufficient to significantly reduce US fighter-bomber sorties north of the Chongchon River. The MiG formations were able to overfly the Sabre patrols along the Yalu due to their high-altitude performance advantage and patrol as far south as Pyongyang. A report of MiGs over North Korea was oftentimes sufficient to see fighter-bomber missions aborted. Forcing the enemy to drop his bombs before he gets to his target is as effective in result as shooting down the bombers.

The PLAAF's wish to deploy frontline attack bombers in North Korea to provide support to the People's Volunteer Army was never achieved, due to the success of the airfield interdiction campaign that was just able to keep airfields in North Korea unable to operate aircraft despite the losses of the fighter-bombers. At the same time, the PLAAF fighter divisions were able to reinforce the Soviet units in denying air supremacy over North Korea to the US Air Force. The US Air Force based its claim of Korean War victory on air interdiction having kept the enemy from battlefield victory. The 1954 FEAF Report on the Korean War states: "It is beyond question that the FEAF interdiction effort in the Korean War had a major effect on the general success of our arms, and upon the ultimate Communist decision to end their attempt to bring all of Korea into the Communist sphere."

In 1966, the US Army Center for Military History commissioned a study, "The Effectiveness of Air Interdiction During The Korean War." The study compared US Air Force claims for success in Korea with battlefield results.

As regards the validity of pilot claims for aerial victories and bombing success, the Army report concluded:

In 1952, for example, the Fifth Air Force in Korea noted that the experience of World War II had proved the validity of halving pilot claims, and that the need for a similar reduction of claims was being born out by the Korean experience. The USN, in a study of close air support in Korea, went even farther, concluding that pilot claims were of such questionable reliability as an index of performance that they should be omitted from consideration altogether.

In his preface for the official Far East Air Forces Report on the Korean War prepared in 1954, General Weyland, who had commanded FEAF for much of the war, declared that "air power was the decisive force in the Korean War. Seizing the initiative as soon as authorized to do so, it blunted the first sharp thrusts of Communist aggression and prevented the expulsion of our forces from the peninsula."

Lt Gen Walton H. Walker, commander of the Eighth Army during the first six months of the war, stated to a US Air Force Evaluation Group in November, 1950, that, "I will gladly lay my cards right on the table and state that if it had not been for the air support that we received from the Fifth Air Force we would not have been able to stay in Korea."

The official Army history gives air operations during that period similar credit as that given by General Walker, but presents a more nuanced evaluation of the degree of effectiveness than that claimed by FEAF:

> By early July 1950, UN air attacks on North Korean armor, transport, and foot columns had become sufficiently effective so that the enemy no longer placed his tanks, trucks, and long columns of marching men on the main roads in broad daylight. Afterward the enemy generally remained quiet and camouflaged in orchards and buildings during the daytime and moved at night. The North Koreans also used back roads and trails more than in the first two weeks of the invasion, and already by day were storing equipment and supplies in tunnels.

Most important, the Army study concluded:

> Overall, the North Korean People's Army had shown a remarkable ability to maintain transport to its front lines over long lines of communications despite heavy and constant air attacks. This accomplishment is one of the outstanding feats of the North Korean war effort in the Pusan Perimeter period. The United Nations air effort failed to halt military rail transport. Ammunition and motor fuel, which took precedence over all other types of supply, continued to arrive at the front, though in diminished quantity. There was still a considerable resupply of heavy weapons, such as tanks, artillery, and

mortars, at the front in early September, although a steady decline
in artillery can be traced from the middle of August. There was a
sufficient supply of small-arms ammunition, but a shortage of small
arms themselves became apparent by mid-August and continued
to worsen with each passing week. Rear areas were able to fill only
about one third of the requisitions from the front for small arms
in mid-August and resupply ceased entirely about the middle of
September. New trucks were almost impossible to obtain. There was
no resupply of clothing. At best there were rations for only one or
two meals a day.

Regarding the period immediately following the Chinese intervention
in November 1950, FEAF claimed that air support to UN ground
forces was decisive in allowing a retreat out of North Korea and later
stabilization of the front. In fact, the retreat out of North Korea was a
rout in almost all instances, remembered by those who experienced it
as "The Big Bug-Out," with the only bright spot being the withdrawal
of the First Marine Division from the Chosin Reservoir; Operation
Strangle was ultimately admitted by the Air Force to be a failure. The
Army study states:

During the withdrawal of the UN forces from North Korea in
late 1950, the primary attention of the Far East Air Force, which
included Navy and Marine units, had been directed towards the
close support of the ground forces. As the situation stabilized
early in January 1951, FEAF directed that emphasis be shifted to
the interdiction of the enemy's rearward lines of communication
and supply. By June 1951, it was apparent that in spite of the
destructive and widespread attacks of aircraft, the battlefield had
not been interdicted. The enemy had been able to mount two
large-scale offensives within a month, and it was obvious that
sufficient supplies, troops, and equipment were getting through
from China to the front lines in North Korea. The Chinese placed
more dependence on night-truck traffic to offset the rail damage.
The vehicle count of enemy trucks jumped from 7,300 in January
1951 to 54,000 in May 1951. Practically everything traveled at
night. The skillful and highly-organized repair efforts of the enemy
generally matched the rate of destruction.

By September 1951, both the Air Force and Navy agreed that Operation *Strangle* had failed. The reasons for the failure were simple: on a dirt road, a bomb crater couldn't stop a truck, since the hole (or holes) could be quickly filled in. A damaged highway bridge provided no blockage since a simple bypass could be built, or a ford created to allow trucks to cross the summer-dry streams. FEAF's final assessment was that "Operation *Strangle* was not successful due to the flexibility of the Communist logistic system."

Regarding the result of interdiction efforts during the final two years of the war, the postwar FEAF report claimed:

> Airpower, by denying enemy reconstitution of forward units, supplies, and airbases in North Korea, proved to the Communists that seizure of Korea by force could never occur. Concurrently, the full impact of war in North Korea by our air offensive created the havoc and confusion that brought enemy accession to an armistice.

The Army report reached an opposite conclusion:

> American logistics officers never ceased to be amazed at the staying power of the Communist armies opposing them in Korea. Here was a force operating on a peninsula without the benefit either of naval or air superiority. United Nations warships ranged its coasts continuously, and American and Allied aircraft attacked its supply lines almost daily. Yet this force was able not only to maintain itself logistically, but actually to build up its strength.
>
> Notwithstanding the heavy damage inflicted by UN air power, the overall air interdiction campaign in Korea had only partial success. The destruction did not succeed in significantly restricting the flow of the enemy's supplies to the front lines, or in achieving interdiction of the battlefield. The attrition caused the enemy to triple and re-triple his efforts to supply the front lines; it laid a costly burden upon his supply organization; it caused him widespread damage and loss. Yet no vital or decisive effect could be observed at the fighting front. Throughout the campaign, the enemy seemed to have ample strength to launch an attack if he wished. His frequent and heavy artillery barrages were evidence that he did not suffer

from a shortage of ammunition. Captured prisoners said they had plenty of food, clothing, medical supplies, and ammunition for their small arms.

General Mark Clark, who was Commander-in-Chief of the United Nations Command during the final year of the Korean War, judged the air interdiction campaign as follows:

> The Air Force and the Navy carriers may have kept us from losing the war, but they were denied the opportunity of influencing the outcome decisively in our favor. They gained complete mastery of the skies, gave magnificent support to the infantry, destroyed every worthwhile target in North Korea, and took a costly toll of enemy personnel and supplies. But as in Italy, where we learned the same bitter lesson in the same kind of rugged country, our air power could not keep a steady stream of enemy suppliers and reinforcements from reaching the battle line. Air could not isolate the front.

There is in fact a strong case to be made that Operation *Bingo*, also known as "The Battle of the Brenner Pass," an air campaign fought against the rail transportation system from Germany to Italy through the Brenner Pass, which was fought with high losses from November 1944 to the end of March 1945, did in fact isolate the German Army's Gothic Line in Northern Italy, which had withstood Allied attacks from July–October 1944, yet surrendered unconditionally ten days after the commencement of the Allied spring offensive in 1945 due to its supplies being reduced 80 percent by the bombing. However, in Korea, there was no single system of targets like the Brenner railroad that could be attacked.

Indeed, the only time the Air Force was able to directly affect a Communist ground offensive came in the final weeks of the war, when the 18th Fighter-Bomber Group discovered the Chinese ammunition trains north of the battlefield and destroyed them, which stopped the offensive and led directly to Communist acceptance of the armistice. Unfortunately, since the operation managed to violate all the Air Force command and control of air operations policy and procedure, and was not officially approved by Fifth Air Force, no credit could be taken for the success. This singular operational success disappeared from the official historical record and has only been rediscovered in the past ten years.

Captains Malcolm W. Cagle and Fred Munson, writing the official US Navy history of the Korean war, stated:

> It must be grudgingly admitted that one of the key reasons why isolation of the battlefield could not be achieved in Korea was the surprising tenacity, determination, and ingenuity displayed by the Communists to keep their rail and highway networks in operation. In spite of incessant daylight attacks and night-time harassment, despite the necessity of working at night, of using old equipment, of having long, exposed, and vulnerable supply lines, the Chinese were able to maintain and even increase the flow of supplies to the battlefront.
>
> Thus, even during the period of heaviest attack upon the North Korean rail network by the several UN air forces, the Reds – by the regimentation of mass labor to repair bridges and breaks, by shuttling trains between breaks, and by use of the system only at night or in inclement weather – could still transport between 1,000 and 2,000 tons over the entire east and west rail systems every day. In other words, despite an all-out UN air effort by the US Navy, the US Air Force, and the US Marines, and by various UN air units, the Communists could supply approximately half their needs by rail alone.
>
> At no time during the course of the war did either the UN's surface or air interdiction efforts succeed in stopping the flow of enemy supplies from Manchuria to the front to a decisive degree. By every index, in fact, the Communists were able to steadily increase their flow of supplies to the front lines. The enemy was never kept from supplying his needed requirements. At no time, except locally and temporarily, did the enemy limit his combat effort because of supply considerations.

Vice Admiral J. J. Clark, Commander of the Seventh Fleet during the final year of the war, made the following assessment:

> The interdiction program was a failure. It did *not* interdict. The Communists got the supplies through; and for the kind of a war they

were fighting, they not only kept their battle line supplied, but they had enough surplus to spare so that by the end of the war they could even launch an offensive.

Surprisingly, the conclusion of the official FEAF largely agrees with the Army and Navy assessments:

Of the three classical missions of tactical air power, interdiction had the most checkered history in the Korean War. We got off to a slow start in interdiction due to the urgency of the ground situation, our limited air power, and the preoccupation of the Far East Command with direct support of ground fighting. During the first year of the war, when the ground fighting was conducive to an intensive interdiction campaign, the majority of our airpower was concentrated on battlefield support. Later, the ground fighting slackened, and FEAF could devote a major portion of its efforts to interdiction. By this time, however, the enemy's logistic requirements were low enough so that he could satisfy them even with his limited transportation. By not pressing the ground war the UN permitted the enemy to hoard his supplies, and thus nullify much of the value of interdiction.

We learned that our developed tactics, our weapons, and the capabilities of our aircraft, limited our ability to interdict a ground logistic system, particularly at night or under bad weather conditions. The enemy's superb use of passive defense measures, and route management techniques, and his adroit employment of antiaircraft protection indicates the kind of obstacles which our tactical commanders in a future war must be prepared to overcome. In spite of our limitations in equipment and weapons, the enemy's countermeasures, and the low logistic requirements of the Communist forces in the last two years of the war, intensive air interdiction campaigns made the war very costly to the enemy.

In 1959, the North Korean government published what was called the official North Korean history of the war, which included the following summary of the UN air interdiction effort:

The American imperialist aerial insurgents' mad bombardments neither destroyed our front line transportation capability nor did they weaken it. Our military transportation personnel, locomotive and vehicle drivers, under the constant threat of continuous enemy bombardment and strafing, made a great historical war record in transporting supplies to the front under the cover of darkness and complete blackout.

Thus, due to the heroic struggle of the Korean people, the American imperialist "air power" had come to nothing.

The various assessments support the following conclusions:

1. The air interdiction campaign made a worthwhile contribution to UN accomplishments during the war, and was particularly effective during the early months of the war in supporting the ground forces to overcome the North Korean Army. It was a costly harassment to the operation of enemy forces throughout the war.

2. However, because it could not inflict sufficient damage on enemy lines of communication and transportation to block the flow of enemy personnel and materiel to the front or even to reduce the flow below minimum requirements, the air interdiction campaign was not a decisive factor in shaping the ultimate course of the war. The principal reasons for the lack of success were the flexibility of the enemy logistical system and the magnitude of the organized effort to keep the lines of communication open.

Since the end of the Korean War, it has become an article of faith in China that the nation in fact won the war, and it is seen as the most successful war in Chinese history. This position is based on the argument that the Chinese intervention in 1950 stopped the Western powers from invading and occupying North Korea. Given Chinese inability to block Western military humiliation in the hundred years prior to the Korean War, the achievement of fighting the Americans to a draw by 1953 is seen as a victory that restored China's position and forced the West to take the country seriously again.

In the end, both sides may be correct in their assessment of who won. The Sabres did keep the Soviet and Chinese air forces from operating aircraft in North Korea to provide direct air support to their armies and attack UN forces, and they protected UN fighter-bombers that would not have been able to operate over the battlefield in the face of direct opposition by MiG-15s, while the Communist air forces did deny the West a conclusive victory.

One thing is certain: while virtually no one in the West has any detailed understanding of the three-year UN bombing in North Korea, there is no North Korean alive who is unaware of the suffering of their parents, grandparents or great-grandparents as a result of that bombing campaign. Every American bomb dropped on North Korea unremembered in the United States is remembered by the North Korean people, and that is why the government of North Korea has been able to maintain its opposition to the United States over the past 65 years.

BIBLIOGRAPHY

Allmon, William B., "Captain James Jabara: Ace of the Korean War," *Aviation History*, March 1995.

Beagle, T. W., "Effects of Based Targeting: Another Empty Promise," *Air University Press*, December 2001.

Bergin, Bob, "The Growth of China's Air Defenses: Responding to Covert Overflights, 1949–1974," *Studies in Intelligence*, Vol. 57, No. 2, June 2013.

Blackburn, Al, *Aces Wild: The Race for Mach 1* (Scholarly Resources Inc., 1998).

Buckland, Ross, "Shooter's Odds," *Sabrejet Classics*, Vol. 5, No. 1, Spring 1997.

Burrows, William E., "Thunderjet," *Air & Space Magazine*, August 2013.

Buttelman, Hank, "Interview," *Sabrejet Classics*, Vol. 5, No. 2, Summer 1997.

Cagle, Malcolm W. and Frank A. Manson, *The Sea War In Korea* (US Naval Institute Press, 2000).

Chen, Jian, *China's Road to the Korean War: The Making of Sino-American Confrontation* (Columbia University Press, 1996).

Crane, Conrad C., "Raiding the Beggars Pantry: The Search for Airpower Strategy in the Korean War," *The Journal of Military History*, October 1999.

Dildy, Douglas C. and Warren E. Thompson, *F-86 Sabre vs MiG-15: Korea 1950–53* (Osprey Publishing, 2013).

Dorr, Robert F., *B-29 Superfortress Units of the Korean War* (Osprey Publishing, 2003).

Dorr, Robert F., Jon Lake and Warren Thompson, *Korean War Aces* (Osprey Publishing, 1994).

Ebersole, Howard R., "The 18th Fighter-Bomber Group's F-86F Conversion in Korea," *Sabrejet Classics*, Vol. 2, No. 1, Spring 1993.

Foster, Cecil G., "Nine Was Enough!" *Sabrejet Classics*, Vol. 2, No. 4, Winter 1993.

Futrell, Robert F., *The United States Air Force in Korea 1950-53* (Air Force History & Museums Program; Revised edition, June 1983).

Harper, Flamm D., "My Favorite Fighter-Bomber Sabre Story," *Sabrejet Classics*, Vol. 2, No. 4, Winter 1993.

Henderson, John, "My Favorite Sabre Story," *Sabrejet Classics*, Vol. 2, No. 1, Spring 1993.

Hinton, Bruce, "The First Sabre Versus MiG-15 Combat," *Sabrejet Classics*, Vol. 1, No. 2, Spring 1992.

Hinton, Bruce, "Casey Jones and the Eagle," *Sabrejet Classics*, Vol. 3, No. 2, Spring 1995.

Jackson, Robert, *Air War Over Korea* (Charles Scribner's Sons, 1973).

Joiner, Stephen, "The Jet That Shocked the West," *Smithsonian Air & Space Magazine*, December 2013.

Jones, George, "Test Flight," *Sabrejet Classics*, Vol. 6, No. 1, Spring 1998.

Kalow, Norm, "The Sabre Jet in Korea: A Crew Chief's Recollection," *Sabrejet Classics*, Vol. 2, No. 1, Spring 1993.

Krylov, Leonid and Yuriy Tepsurkaev, *Soviet MiG-15 Aces of the Korean War* (Osprey Publishing, 2008).

McLellan, David S., "Dean Acheson and the Korean War," *Political Science Quarterly*, Vol. 83, No. 1, March 1968: 16-39.

Meilinger, Phillip, "Trenchard and Morale Bombing," *The Journal of Military History*, Vol. 60, No. 2, April 1996: 250.

Mossman, Billy C., *The Effectiveness of Air Interdiction During The Korean War* (US Army Center of Military History, Department of the Army, 1966).

Parr, Ralph, "My First Victories," *Sabrejet Classics*, Vol. 5, No. 2, Spring 1997.

Rawlings, Robert, "My Favorite F-86F Story," *Sabrejet Classics*, Vol. 1, No. 4, Winter 1992.

Sears, David, "Showdowns in MiG Alley," *Aviation History*, March 2017.

Shiner, Linda, "The Mach 1 Whodunit," *Smithsonian Air & Space Magazine*, September 2014.

Simha, Rakesh Krishnan, "Korean War: How the MiG-15 Put an End to American Mastery over the Skies," *Russia Beyond*, April 27, 2017.

Spinetta, Lawrence, "MiG Madness: The Air War Over Korea," *Aviation History*, March 2008.

Spurr, Russell, *Enter the Dragon: China's Undeclared War Against the U.S. in Korea, 1950-51* (Newmarket Press, 1988).

Thompson, Warren, *F-86 Sabre Aces of the 4th Fighter Wing* (Osprey Publishing, 2006).

Thompson, Warren, *F-86 Sabre Aces of the 51st Fighter Wing* (Osprey Publishing, 2006).

Werrell, Kenneth P., *Sabres Over MiG Alley* (Naval Institute Press, 2005).

Wetterhahn, Ralph, "To Snatch a Sabre," *Air & Space Magazine*, July 2003.

Wilson, David, *Lion over Korea : 77 Fighter Squadron, RAAF, 1950-53* (Banner Books, 1994).

Winnefeld, James A. and Dana J. Johnson, *Command and Control of Joint Air Operations* (RAND Corporation, 1991).

Zhang, Xiaoming, *Red Wings over the Yalu: China, the Soviet Union, and the Air War in Korea* (Texas A&M University Press, 2002).

INDEX